Paris FOR DUMMIES®

6TH EDITION

by Joseph Alexiou

WILEY

Wiley Publishing, Inc.

Paris For Dummies®, 6th Edition

Published by
Wiley Publishing, Inc.
111 River St.
Hoboken, NJ 07030-5774
www.wiley.com

WILEY

About the Author

Joseph Alexiou works as a freelance journalist and has contributed to *France For Dummies* and *Europe For Dummies*. His work has appeared in the *New York Press*, the *New York Observer*, *Newsday*, and *Paper Magazine*. He is currently pursuing an MS at the Columbia University Graduate School of Journalism; he lives in Brooklyn.

Dedication

To my grandmother, the all-loving Esther Braun Sparberg; and in the memory of her father, Abraham Braun.

Author's Acknowledgments

Many thanks to Jennifer Polland and Andrea Kahn; a huge thank you to Emilie Abrams for her expert foodie knowledge, insight, wit, and talent. To my parents, my brother and sister-in-law, and my family for their constant love and support. A giant merci beaucoup to Anne de Turenne, Sara Dalziel, Caitlin Polus, Eglantine Graf, Samuel Ronfard, Jean-Marie Hupiel and Bryan Pirolli for their uniquely Parisian expertise and tips. Special thanks to Ariane Mavroidis, Diane Joly, Julie Cunat, Donatien Dufour, Florent Gaudet, Michael Lopes, Vincent Sieli — *mes Équatoriens* — and their lovely friends, for their warmth and uninhibited introduction to yet another side of Paris. Finally, to you, dear reader: May your trip to Paris fulfill and far exceed your dreams.

Publisher's Acknowledgments

We're proud of this book; please send us your comments through our Dummies online registration form located at www.dummies.com/register/.

Some of the people who helped bring this book to market include the following:

Editorial

Editors: Jennifer Polland & William Travis, Development Editors; Michael Brumitt, Production Editor

Copy Editor: Elizabeth Kuball

Cartographer: Liz Puhl

Editorial Assistant: Andrea Kahn

Senior Photo Editor: Richard Fox

Cover Photos: Front: ©Gavin Hellier / Alamy Images. Description: View of the Eiffel Tower from Pont Alexandre III along the river Seine, Paris, France. Back: ©Blaine Harrington III Photography. Description: Waiters serving coffee at Cafe La Closeries des Lilas, Boulevard Montparnasse, Paris, France.

Cartoons: Rich Tennant (www.the5thwave.com)

Composition Services

Project Coordinator: Sheree Montgomery

Layout and Graphics: Carrie A. Cesavice, Heather Pope, Lavonne Roberts

Proofreaders: The Well-Chosen Word, Jessica Kramer

Indexer: Slivoskey Indexing Services

Publishing and Editorial for Consumer Dummies

Diane Graves Steele, Vice President and Publisher, Consumer Dummies

Kristin Ferguson-Wagstaffe, Product Development Director, Consumer Dummies

Kelly Regan, Editorial Director, Travel

Publishing for Technology Dummies

Andy Cummings, Vice President and Publisher, Dummies Technology/ General User

Composition Services

Debbie Stailey, Director of Composition Services

Contents at a Glance

Introduction.. 1

Part 1: Introducing Paris.. 7
Chapter 1: Discovering the Best of Paris.................................9
Chapter 2: Digging Deeper into Paris.................................17
Chapter 3: Deciding When to Go 32

Part 11: Planning Your Trip to Paris 41
Chapter 4: Managing Your Money..................................43
Chapter 5: Getting to Paris...51
Chapter 6: Catering to Special Travel Needs or Interests..........59
Chapter 7: Taking Care of the Remaining Details....................67

Part 111: Settling into Paris 77
Chapter 8: Arriving and Getting Oriented 79
Chapter 9: Checking in at Paris's Best Hotels.........................101
Chapter 10: Dining and Snacking in Paris 134

Part 1V: Exploring Paris 187
Chapter 11: Discovering Paris's Best Attractions 189
Chapter 12: Shopping the Local Stores 246
Chapter 13: Following an Itinerary...................................280
Chapter 14: Going Beyond Paris: Five Day Trips 287

Part V: Living 1t Up After Dark:
Paris Nightlife 307
Chapter 15: Applauding the Cultural Scene...........................309
Chapter 16: Hitting the Clubs and Bars 318

Part V1: The Part of Tens 329
Chapter 17: Ten (or So) Hidden Corners of Paris 331
Chapter 18: Ten Great Places for a Picnic............................334

Appendix A: Quick Concierge 338

Appendix B: A Glossary of French Words
and Phrases.. 348

Index.. 354

Maps at a Glance

Paris at a Glance 10
Paris Neighborhoods 82
Hotels in the Heart of the Right Bank (1–4, 8–12, and 16–18) 108
Hotels in the Heart of the Left Bank (5–7 and 13–14) 112
Restaurants on the Right Bank 142
Restaurants on the Left Bank...146
Light Meals in the Heart of the Right Bank 164
Light Meals in the Heart of the Left Bank..166
Paris's Top Attractions...190
Notre-Dame de Paris 195
The Louvre 205
Père-Lachaise Cemetery 210
More Fun Things to Do in Paris 214
Paris Shopping..248
Day Trips from Paris 289
Versailles 291
Fontainebleau..295
Notre-Dame de Chartres 299

Table of Contents

Introduction 1
   About This Book 1
   Conventions Used in This Book 2
   Foolish Assumptions 3
   How This Book Is Organized 3
       Part I: Introducing Paris 3
       Part II: Planning Your Trip to Paris 3
       Part III: Settling into Paris 4
       Part IV: Exploring Paris 4
       Part V: Living It Up After Dark: Paris Nightlife 4
       Part VI: The Part of Tens..4
       Appendixes 5
   Icons Used in This Book..5
   Where to Go from Here 6

Part 1: Introducing Paris 7

Chapter 1: Discovering the Best of Paris 9
   The Best Accommodations...12
   The Best Food..12
   The Best Sights..13
   The Best Parks and Gardens 14
   The Best Shopping 15
   The Best of Culture..16
   The Best Clubs 16

Chapter 2: Digging Deeper into Paris 17
   History 101: The Main Events 17
       The ancient times 17
       Revolutionary Paris 18
       The era of Napoléons 18
       Modern Paris 19
   Building Blocks: Local Architecture 20
   A Taste of Paris: The Local Cuisine 23
       A glossary good enough to eat...23
       Salivating over French cooking.......................................26
   Words to the Wise: The Local Language............................28
   Background Check: Books and Movies 29
       Books..29
       Movies 30

Chapter 3: Deciding When to Go 32

Revealing the Secret of the Seasons....................32
    Paris in the springtime.................................33
    Paris is a beach 33
    Fabulous festive fall....................................33
    Winter wonderland......................................34
A Paris Calendar...34
    January...34
    February...35
    March 35
    April...36
    May 36
    June 37
    July and August..38
    September..39
    October 39
    November 40
    December...40

Part II: Planning Your Trip to Paris 41

Chapter 4: Managing Your Money...................43

Planning Your Budget.......................................43
Cutting Costs 45
    Accommodations..45
    Transportation..46
    Restaurants..46
    Attractions, shopping, and nightlife.........47
Handling Money 48
    Converting to euros....................................48
    Pulling out your plastic: Using credit cards...........49
    Going the way of the dinosaur: The
       extinction of traveler's checks.................49
Dealing with a Lost or Stolen Wallet.................49

Chapter 5: Getting to Paris 51

Flying to Paris...51
    Getting the best deal on your airfare 53
    Booking your ticket online 54
Arriving by Other Means....................................54
Joining an Escorted Tour....................................56
Choosing a Package Tour....................................57

Chapter 6: Catering to Special Travel Needs or
   Interests **59**
   Taking the Family Along..59
   Making Age Work for You: Tips for Seniors.......................62
   Accessing Paris: Advice for Travelers with Disabilities.....62
   Following the Rainbow: Resources for
      Gay and Lesbian Travelers 65
Chapter 7: Taking Care of the Remaining Details 67
   Getting a Passport...67
      Applying for a U.S. passport.......................................67
      Applying for other passports 69
   Why Not to Rent a Car in Paris...69
   Playing It Safe with Travel and Medical Insurance...........71
   Staying Healthy when You Travel.......................................72
   Staying Connected by Cellphone or E-mail........................73
   Accessing the Internet Away from Home............................74
   Keeping Up with Airline Security Measures 75

Part III: Settling into Paris **77**
Chapter 8: Arriving and Getting Oriented.....................79
   Navigating Your Way through Passport
      Control and Customs..79
   Making Your Way to Your Hotel 80
      If you fly into Charles de Gaulle................................80
      If you fly into Orly..85
   Figuring Out the Neighborhoods 86
      On the Right Bank...87
      On the Left Bank 90
   Finding Information after You Arrive 91
   Getting around Paris...92
      By Métro 92
      By bus..96
      By taxi...97
      By car 98
      By bicycle 99
      Paris à pied (on foot) 99
Chapter 9: Checking in at Paris's Best Hotels 101
   Getting to Know Your Options 102
   Finding the Best Room at the Best Rate...........................103
      Finding the best rate 104
      Surfing the Web for hotel deals 105
   Arriving without a Reservation 106

Paris's Best Hotels 107
Index of Accommodations by Neighborhood 131
Index of Accommodations by Price................................132

Chapter 10: Dining and Snacking in Paris 134

Getting the Dish on the Local Scene................................135
    Making reservations for dinner................................135
    Dressing to dine..136
    Knowing the difference between a cafe
        and a bistro..136
    Understanding the order of a meal 139
Trimming the Fat from Your Budget 140
Paris's Best Restaurants 141
Dining and Snacking on the Go 163
    Partaking of Paris street food................................168
    Assembling a picnic, Parisian style 168
    Watching the world go by at a cafe........................172
    Steeping and sipping at a tea salon
        (salons de thé) 176
    A heady mix of wine bars................................177
    Getting the scoop on Paris ice cream 179
Index of Establishments by Neighborhood 180
Index of Establishments by Cuisine................................181
Index of Establishments by Price................................183

Part IV: Exploring Paris 187

Chapter 11: Discovering Paris's Best Attractions 189

Paris's Top Sights 189
More Fun Things to See and Do 213
    Especially for kids..213
    Especially for teens 219
    Especially for history buffs................................220
    Especially for art lovers 225
    Especially for the literary 231
    Especially for nature lovers................................234
    Houses of the holy..237
Paris's Bridges..240
Paris by Guided Tour 240
    Embarking on a bus..241
    Touring by boat 242
    Horsing around: A guided tour at
        2 horsepower..243
    Walking your way across Paris 243
    Paris en vélo (by bike) 244

Chapter 12: Shopping the Local Stores 246

Surveying the Scene..246
    Getting the VAT back 250
    Getting your goodies through Customs.................252
Checking Out the Big Names 253
Taking It to the Street (Markets)......................................256
Scoring Bargains in Paris 257
Hitting the Great Shopping Neighborhoods 259
    The cost of high fashion: The 8e...........................259
    Classically hip: The 3e and 4e 260
    Smart and sophisticated: The 6e 261
    Young and edgy: The 2e..263
Shopping in Paris from A(ntiques) to W(ine).................264
    Antiques..265
    Bookstores...265
    Ceramics, china, and glass 267
    Clothing for children 268
    Clothing for men 269
    Clothing for teens and the young-at-heart.............270
    Clothing for women 271
    Crafts 272
    Food..272
    Gifts and jewelry 275
    Home and housewares..277
    Toys...278
    Wine..279

Chapter 13: Following an Itinerary 280

Making the Most of Paris in Three Days 280
Planning a Five-Day Visit..282
A Walking Tour through the Marais 282
Take a Stroll through a Parisian Village...........................284

Chapter 14: Going Beyond Paris: Five Day Trips 287

The Château de Versailles 287
    Getting there..288
    Exploring Versailles...290
    Dining options 293
The Palais de Fontainebleau...294
    Getting there..294
    Exploring Fontainebleau 295
    Dining options 296
The Cathedral at Chartres 297
    Getting there..297
    Exploring the cathedral 297
    Dining options 300

Disneyland Paris 301
    Getting there..302
    Exploring the park 302
    Staying at Disneyland..303
Monet's Gardens at Giverny 303
    Getting there..304
    Exploring the gardens 304
    Dining options 305

Part V: Living It Up After Dark: Paris Nightlife 307

Chapter 15: Applauding the Cultural Scene 309

Getting the Inside Scoop 309
Finding Out What's Playing and Getting Tickets............311
Raising the Curtain on the Performing Arts 312
    Attending the theater 312
    Seeking English-language theater 314
    Listening to classical music and the symphony...315
    Enjoying opera and ballet.................................316

Chapter 16: Hitting the Clubs and Bars.......................318

Hot Spots for Cool Jazz 318
Rockin' Out to Live Music.......................................319
Glam and Glitz in the Club and Lounge Scene.................321
Nightlife in Gay Paree 323
Kicking Back with Classy Cocktails 326
Spending an Evening at a French Cabaret 327

Part VI: The Part of Tens................................. 329

Chapter 17: Ten (or So) Hidden Corners of Paris 331

Beauty in an Ugly Place...331
Jardin de la Vallée Suisse.......................................332
La Maison Normande..332
La Pagode...332
Le Jardin Alpin...332
Les Arènes de Lutèce 333
Les Villas du Danube 333
Odd Sculpture at the Place Marcel-Aymé 333
Saint-Denis Holds His Head......................................333

Chapter 18: Ten Great Places for a Picnic.................334

Bois de Boulogne 334
Bois de Vincennes...334
Jardin du Luxembourg 335

Les Champs de Mars 335
Parc de Belleville...335
Parc de la Villette...336
Parc des Buttes-Chaumont 336
Parc Monceau..336
Pont des Arts 337
Square du Vert Galant 337

Appendix A: Quick Concierge 338
Fast Facts 338
Toll-Free Numbers and Web Sites....................................345
Where to Get More Information 345
    Tourist offices 345
    Surfing the Web..346

Appendix B: A Glossary of French Words and Phrases.. 348

Index.. 354
General Index...354
Accommodations Index 367
Restaurant Index...368

Introduction

● ●

*P*aris has been coveted since the Romans wrested away this settlement from a tribe of peaceful fishermen called the Parisii and
named it Lutetia Parisiorum. A fascination with the city grew over nearly
2,000 years. It's not just the culture — although you can visit a different
museum every day for a year and still not hit all the exhibits. Nor is it
Paris's breathtaking beauty — from the curved Beaux Arts apartment
buildings to the graceful bridges arching over the Seine to the eye-
pleasing formal gardens balanced by natural parks to exquisite store
windows and unexpected vistas.

If this is your first visit or if you haven't been to Paris in a decade or
more, you may just find your heart stolen by this legendary city.

You're also in for some changes. Parisians are trying mightily to over-
come the stereotype that they're collectively a rude bunch. Service at
stores and in restaurants can actually be downright warm, especially
when foreigners take the time to acknowledge storekeepers and waiters
with a pleasant smile and a simple *bonjour* (hello).

I hope, during your visit, you'll find, as I do, that Paris is an eternal
source of discovery. Even what looks to be a familiar walk will yield
surprises — a passage that veers off the main road into a park, an
unusual building, a cluster of houses containing some half-forgotten
history from centuries past. Or maybe you'll discover the Parisian way
of life, where relaxing in a cafe and watching the world go by is a natural
part of every day. It can be quite addictive!

Paris is more than a city; it's an encounter. Every visitor here experiences Paris's glory in an individual and unique way, and as always, I
hope the city grabs a hold of your heart so that, when your time here is
finished, you'll itch to return.

About This Book

Consider this a textbook of sorts that you don't have to read from front
to back, with your visit to Paris your test (there are no failing grades,
however!). Basically *Paris For Dummies* presents you with to-the-point
information on Paris that's fun and easy to access. I provide very basic
information about the city for readers who have never visited and discuss points of interest for the seasoned traveler.

Please be advised that travel information is subject to change at any
time — and this is especially true of prices. Always write or call ahead

for confirmation when making your travel plans. The author, editors, and publisher cannot be held responsible for the experiences of readers while traveling. Your safety is important to us, however, so we encourage you to stay alert and be aware of your surroundings. Keep a close eye on cameras, purses, and wallets, all favorite targets of thieves and pickpockets.

Conventions Used in This Book

Paris For Dummies is a reference book, meaning you may read the chapters in any order you want. We use some standard listings for hotels, restaurants, and sights. These listings enable you to open the book to any chapter and access the information you need quickly and easily.

In this book, I include lists of hotels, restaurants, and attractions. As I describe each, I often include abbreviations for commonly accepted credit cards. Take a look at the following list for an explanation of each:

AE: American Express

DC: Diners Club

MC: MasterCard

V: Visa

I also include some general pricing information to help you as you decide where to unpack your bags or dine on the local cuisine. I use a system of dollar signs to show a range of costs for one night in a hotel (the price refers to a double-occupancy room) or a meal at a restaurant (included in the cost of each meal is soup or salad, an entree, dessert, and a nonalcoholic drink). Check out the following table to decipher the dollar signs:

Cost	Hotel	Restaurant
$	100€ or less	20€ or less
$$	101€–150€	21€–50€
$$$	151€–300€	51€–100€
$$$$	301€ or more	101€ or more

Included with each address is the Paris *arrondissement* (administrative district), to give you a better idea of where each place is located. Paris is divided into 20 *arrondissements,* which spiral out like a snail shell from the 1st *arrondissement* in the very center of Paris (abbreviated 1er), to the 20th *arrondissement* on the outer edges of the city (abbreviated 20e). The *arrondissement* number appears after the street address in each citation in this book. For example, "55 bd. St-Michel, 5e," indicates the building numbered 55 on the boulevard St-Michel is in the fifth *arrondissement.* To get an idea of where each *arrondissement* is located, consult the "Paris at a Glance" map in Chapter 1. Street abbreviations used throughout the book include not only *bd.* (boulevard), but also *rue* (street), *av.* (avenue), *place* (square), *bis* (an odd term generally meaning an address between two buildings), *ter* (terrace), or *quai* (quay or riverbank).

To help you orient yourself, we also give the nearest Métro (subway) stop for all destinations (for example, "Métro: Pont Marie").

Foolish Assumptions

As I wrote this book, I made some assumptions about you and your needs as a traveler:

✔ You may be an experienced traveler who hasn't had much time to explore Paris and wants expert advice when you finally do get a chance to enjoy a particular locale.

✔ You may be an inexperienced traveler looking for guidance when determining whether to take a trip to Paris and how to plan for it.

✔ You're not looking for a book that provides all the information available about Paris or that lists every hotel, restaurant, or attraction available to you. Instead, you're looking for a book that focuses on the places that give you the best or most unique experience in Paris.

If you fit any of these criteria, *Paris For Dummies* gives you the information you're looking for!

How This Book Is Organized

Paris For Dummies is divided into six parts, with two appendixes. Here's what each part covers.

Part I: Introducing Paris

This part includes a "best-of" overview of the city, offers some basic history and architecture, and covers the variety of events Paris offers at different times of the year.

Part II: Planning Your Trip to Paris

Should you use a travel agent or go it alone? Is travel insurance a good idea? These chapters touch on everything you need to consider before planning a trip, including hints on developing a realistic budget and what options are available to travelers with special needs or interests.

Part III: Settling into Paris

Here are tips on everything from navigating your way through Customs to getting to your hotel from the airport to discovering Paris neighborhood by neighborhood. You find out how to use the city's terrific transportation system, why you shouldn't rent a car here, and what to know when you hail a cab. I introduce the euro and tell you where to turn if your wallet gets stolen.

I list some of the city's best moderately priced hotels (with a few superbudget and some deluxe resorts thrown in for good measure) and offer advice on how to tie up those frustrating last-minute details that can unnerve even the most seasoned of travelers. You'll learn in no time what kind of accommodations to choose in Paris and why you don't have to pay full price at hotel chains.

Paris is known for its fine food, and Chapter 10 helps you choose some of the best restaurants for your taste and budget. Everything from moderately priced restaurants to haute cuisine is listed here, so you can discover that a fine meal is truly an art in itself. I also provide street food and light-fare options for those occasions when you don't have the time, or the desire, for a full-course meal.

Part IV: Exploring Paris

This part's chapters on how to get to Paris's top sights, how much they cost, and how much time to devote to them make Paris's most famous attractions (and some not so famous but just as good) easier to find. I fill you in on kid- and teen-specific sights, and give you information on tours, a shopper's guide to Paris, three recommended itineraries, and five great day trips if you'd like to explore outside the city.

Part V: Living It Up After Dark: Paris Nightlife

Part V gives you all the information you need about seeing plays, opera, ballet, and live music as well as which nightclubs and bars are the most fun. I'm honest about whether the spectacles for which Paris has come to be known — the cabarets — are truly worth it. I tell you what's going on and where you can get reduced-rate tickets.

Nothing is more beautiful than Paris at night, when the city's monuments are lit up like a stage. Anything can happen!

Part VI: The Part of Tens

What *For Dummies* book would be complete without a Part of Tens? In this book, you find such fun tidbits as hidden corners of Paris and the best places for a picnic — a quintessential Parisian pastime!

Appendixes

Appendix A is your Quick Concierge, containing lots of handy information you may need when traveling in Paris: phone numbers and addresses of emergency personnel, area hospitals, and pharmacies; lists of local newspapers and magazines; protocol for sending mail and finding taxis; and more. Check out this appendix when searching for answers to lots of little questions that may come up as you travel. You can find the Quick Concierge easily because it's printed on yellow paper.

Appendix B is a glossary of English-to-French translations of basic vocabulary as well as health, travel, and (of course) shopping terms.

Icons Used in This Book

The following icons are scattered throughout the margins of this book and are meant to draw your attention to especially useful text.

 Keep an eye out for the Bargain Alert icon as you seek out money-saving tips and/or great deals.

 The Best of the Best icon highlights the best Paris has to offer in all categories — hotels, restaurants, attractions, activities, shopping, and nightlife.

 When you need to be aware of a rip-off, an overrated sight, a dubious deal, or any other trap set for unsuspecting travelers, this icon alerts you to that fact. I also use this icon when I offer the lowdown on the quirks, etiquette, and unwritten rules of the area so you can avoid looking like a tourist and, instead, be treated more like a local.

 This icon is a catchall for any special hint, tip, or bit of insider's advice that can help make your trip run more smoothly. Really, the point of a travel guide is to serve as one gigantic tip, but this icon singles out those nuggets of knowledge you may not have run across before or that you can use right away.

 This icon, in addition to flagging tips and resources of special interest to families, points out the most child-friendly hotels, restaurants, and attractions. If you need a baby sitter at your hotel, a welcoming relaxed atmosphere at a restaurant, or a dazzling site that delights your child, look for this icon. Information is included regarding larger, family-sized rooms at hotels and restaurants that serve meals that go easy on your little ones' tummies.

Sometimes a great hotel, restaurant, or attraction may be a bit out of the center or require a bit of effort to get to. This icon alerts you to these secret finds and you can rest assured no spots are included that aren't truly worth the energy. This icon also signifies any resource that's particularly useful and worth the time to seek out.

Where to Go from Here

Where else? To Paris! *Paris For Dummies* shows you just how accessible this city can be. Included is a selective list of some of the best hotel, dining, and touring options along with insider info to help you make informed decisions. Follow the advice laid out here, and you'll want to return to Paris again and again.

Part I
Introducing Paris

"I know it's a wedding present from your niece, I just don't know why you had to wear it to the Louvre."

In this part . . .

Are you a stranger to Paris? Or has it been a long time since you last visited? Then (re)introduce yourself to the city and whet your appetite to find out more about it. In Chapter 1, you get an overview of Paris and learn about the best the city has to offer. Chapter 2 gives you a crash course in Paris's history and architecture, briefly introduces you to French cuisine, soothes any worries you may have about the language, and recommends some great books and movies to enhance your understanding of the city. In Chapter 3, the pros and cons of the seasons as well as a Paris calendar of events help you decide the perfect time for your visit.

Chapter 1

Discovering the Best of Paris

In This Chapter
- ▶ Paris's best sights
- ▶ Paris's best accommodations for every price range
- ▶ Food, glorious food, the best bars, a shopping nirvana, and the best culture, parks, and gardens

*T*here are a million and one reasons why people from all over the globe love to visit Paris. This city boasts some of the most beautiful monuments in the world, the best dining that one could hope to sample, and unique charm and romantic appeal on practically every street corner. For those who love to shop, the window displays alone will get your heart racing. There is no end to the activities and sights to see here — you can spend all day wandering through museums viewing some of the best art the world has to offer or you can simply meander through the city's streets and have an equally fulfilling experience.

So, go ahead and visit one of the world's most beautiful and celebrated cities, which boasts the most appealing lifestyle — one in which relaxing in a cafe and watching the world go by are expected parts of the day. Give yourself an itinerary that includes lingering and getting lost — these are some of the best ways to enjoy this wonderful city. Discovering a tiny shop instead of a subway station or a pretty park around a bend can be more fun than a planned trip to a famous monument. And as for those famous monuments and museums: Yes, you'll discover that the **Louvre** is as incredible as its reputation, but did you know that the **Musée de l'Orangerie** is only steps away from the famous glass pyramid and is home to some of the best Impressionist paintings in the world? You'll find that taking a **motorboat tour of the Seine** is one of the best ways to see Paris, but why not rent a rowboat in the **Bois de Boulogne** and the **Bois de Vincennes,** two big, beautiful parks on each side of Paris that are a haven from the city's bustle? Whatever you do, you'll quickly discover that Paris (see the "Paris at a Glance" map in this chapter) is more of an experience than merely a city, and each visitor has an entirely individual encounter. Imagine that Paris is your newest friend, and I'm introducing you.

Paris at a Glance

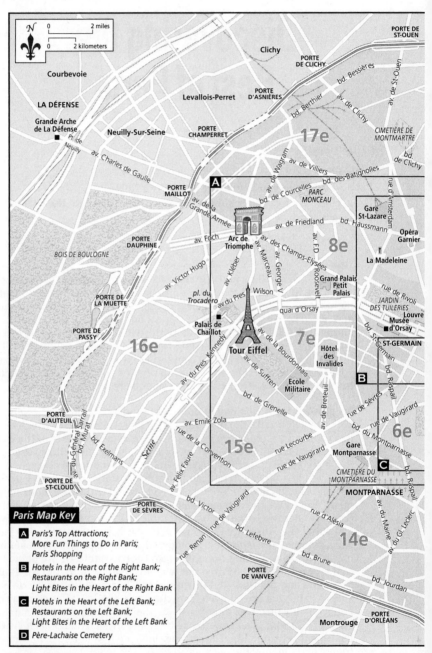

Paris Map Key

A Paris's Top Attractions;
More Fun Things to Do in Paris;
Paris Shopping

B Hotels in the Heart of the Right Bank;
Restaurants on the Right Bank;
Light Bites in the Heart of the Right Bank

C Hotels in the Heart of the Left Bank;
Restaurants on the Left Bank;
Light Bites in the Heart of the Left Bank

D Père-Lachaise Cemetery

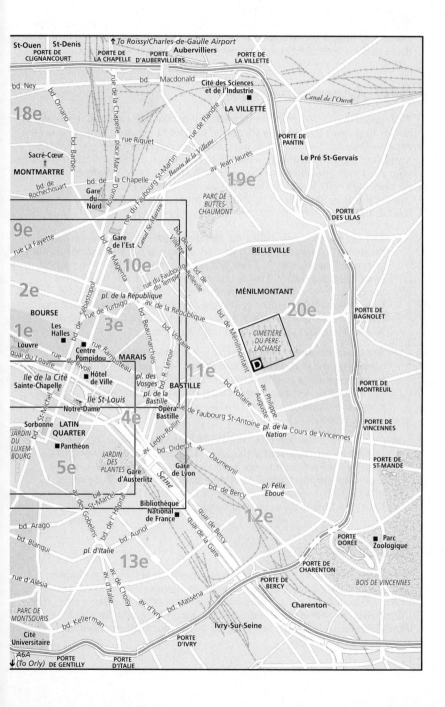

This chapter is an at-a-glance reference to the absolute best — the best of the best, in my opinion — that Paris has to offer. Each of these experiences and places is discussed in detail later in the book; you can find them in their indicated chapters, marked with a Best of the Best icon.

The Best Accommodations

With more than 1,500 chain hotels, deluxe palace-like accommodations, hotels that cater to business travelers, budget hotels, and mom-and-pop establishments, it's difficult to narrow things down to just a few. But the hotels here are the hotels that, in my opinion, you'll want to return to on your next visit (because no one can see Paris just once!). *Note:* In this section, I list only hotels in the first nine *arrondissements,* the most central locations in Paris. See Chapter 9 for more information on the accommodations listed here.

- The impressive, airy **Hôtel du Jeu de Paume** (4e) on the exclusive île Saint-Louis was once a 17th-century *jeu de paume* (the precursor to tennis) court, and you can still see the wooden skeleton rising from the open lobby. This is one of Paris's more unusual hotels, successfully combining sumptuous ancient and modern décor. Guests have their choice of staying in rooms or, for more than five days, private apartments. It's located right down the street from Notre-Dame and Left and Right Bank bridges.

- Seasoned budget travelers in the know make reservations well ahead of time in the **Hôtel Esmeralda** (5e), and not just because of its ideal location or charming and quirky interior. Indeed, the floral printed fabric wallpaper and sunny views of Latin Quarter rooftops speak for themselves, but its impossibly low prices somehow translate to comfort.

- Once part of the palace of the Reine Margot and then the seedy flophouse where Oscar Wilde died, **L'Hôtel** (6e) is a velvet-and-marble-clad gem of a hotel. Sprinkled with antique furniture and a unique spiral staircase, this well-maintained property exudes classy calm — plus, it's mere steps away from Saint-Germain-des-Prés, the Musée d'Orsay, and the Seine.

The Best Food

No matter where you decide to dine or what kind of food you choose, you can count on having some of the most memorable meals of your life in Paris! The following list contains some of my favorite restaurants (the information in parentheses indicates the arrondissement in which each establishment is located). See Chapter 10 for more information on the restaurants listed here.

✔ **Au Bascou** (3e): Basque food, which comes from the southwestern Gascogne region of France, is some of the best and most interesting dishes to come out of the country. Atypical for French food, it includes the use of spicy peppers, the *espelette*. Although everything is good here, there's something truly divine about a simple dessert: tangy sheep's milk cheese paired with blackberry jam. Divine!

✔ **Le Cinq** (8e): Ah, to be able to dine here daily! This multi-Michelin-starred restaurant in the Four Seasons Hotel George V Paris is truly extraordinary, from its exquisite pull-out-all-the-stops food to its award-winning sommelier and fantastic wine cellar. If you want a once-in-a-lifetime dining experience, you won't be disappointed.

✔ **Les Bouquinistes** (4e): This baby bistro of world-renowned chef Guy Savoy is the place to get a tasting menu. With the freshest ingredients, prepared in ingenious ways that only an artist could assemble so beautifully, a meal here is unforgettable.

The Best Sights

What's a visit to Paris without seeing the view from the Eiffel Tower (even though some of the best views *include* the Eiffel Tower)? For most people, the real reason for visiting Paris is to see the quintessentially French attractions for which the city is known. Are the sights really as great as returning travelers say? *Mais oui!* Here are just a few of the best. See Chapter 11 for more information on the sights listed here.

✔ The **Arc de Triomphe** (8e) was commissioned by Napoléon to honor his army and its 128 victorious battles, but the real reason people visit is for the view — one that takes in the Eiffel Tower. From the top, 49m (162 ft.) up, you can see in a straight line the Champs-Elysées, the obelisk in the place de la Concorde, the Louvre, and the Grande Arche de la Défense in St-Denis, a giant open cube built to be the modern equivalent to this arch.

✔ Your first glimpse of the nearly 900-year-old **Cathédrale Notre-Dame de Paris** (4e) just may take your breath away. Flying buttresses lend a graceful air to what would otherwise be an imposing structure. Play Quasimodo and climb to the top of the bell tower (get there early — the lines grow huge from late morning through closing, especially in summer) or marvel at the gorgeous rose windows.

✔ You can't miss the city's most famous landmark, the **Eiffel Tower** (7e), which graces the city skyline with its lacy presence. At night, for ten minutes each hour until it closes, the tower bursts into glittering light from 30,000 bulbs. Mail your postcards and letters from the tower's very own post office located the first level up; they'll get a special Eiffel Tower postmark.

✔ The **Musée de Cluny** (5e) is one of the jewels of Paris museums and is home to the famous tapestry series *The Lady and the Unicorn*. It houses ancient Roman hot and cold baths, the original statues pulled off Notre-Dame in 1790 by furious revolutionaries, and so much more. It has a terrific gift shop to boot.

✔ The **Musée d'Orsay** (7e), a former train station, has an unsurpassed collection of Impressionist masterpieces and beautiful displays of Art Nouveau furnishings. More manageable and less crowded than the Louvre (and well located near the Seine and Eiffel Tower), this museum should make everyone's top five!

✔ The **Musée Rodin** (7e) is one of Paris's more relaxing museums. There are only 16 medium-size rooms here, and after taking in the sensual sculptures, you can stroll through the gardens to see more of the legendary artist's masterpieces, such as *The Thinker* and *The Gates of Hell.*

The Best Parks and Gardens

Paris has parks for every taste and interest offering flowers, rare plants, and views of the city as well as puppet shows, pony rides, and museums. Here are some of its best. Chapter 11 has more information.

✔ The **Jardin des Tuileries** (1er) is Paris's most-visited park, where visitors to the Louvre next door like to revive in the fresh air and rest their feet on conveniently placed wrought-iron chairs surrounding the garden's fountains. In keeping with the French style of parks, trees are planted according to an orderly design and the sandy paths are arrow straight. During the summer, a carnival features an enormous Ferris wheel (with great views of the city) and some other thrill rides, a fun house, arcade-style games, and snacks.

✔ The **Jardin du Luxembourg** (6e) in the Latin Quarter is Parisians' most-beloved park. Children love it for its playground, pony rides, and puppet theater, as well as for the Fontaine de Médicis, where they can sail their toy boats. Make use of the tennis and boules courts (*boules* is a French game, also known as *pétanque,* with the same origins as lawn bowling and Italian bocce in which players try to be the first to roll their balls closest to the small object ball, called the *cochonnet*), or appreciate the art exhibited on the wrought-iron fence at the garden's northwestern entrance near boulevard St-Michel and rue de Médicis. Classical music concerts are held during the warm seasons and the park's orchard grows apples and pears that end up on the plates of staff at the French Senate, which is housed in the garden's Palais du Luxembourg.

- **Parc de la Villette** (19e) is a decidedly modern park with a series of themed gardens, including an exotic bamboo garden and one featuring steam and water jets. Scattered throughout are playgrounds and other attractions — this is a must-visit if you've spent time at the huge children's science complex, Cité des Sciences et l'Industrie.

- **Parc des Buttes Chaumont** (19e) has some of the best views in Paris, featuring bucolic cliffs, a suspension bridge, waterfalls, a lake, and a cave topped by a temple. The waterfall cave is musty but romantic — it's listed in *Où S'Embrasser à Paris (Where to Kiss in Paris)* as one of the top hidden make-out spots in the city. Commissioned by Napoléon III, it is made to resemble the English gardens he grew to love during his exile in England.

The Best Shopping

Though the city has a well-deserved reputation as a bastion of over-the-top luxury (to understand why, head for the eighth *arrondissement*), discount, resale, and overstock stores also abound. The best shopping is really in the boutiques and covered passageways, but I always end up spending time in the following stores. See Chapter 12 for more information on the stores listed here.

- **BHV** (4e), or the Bazaar de l'Hôtel de Ville, is a massive department store selling everything you could possibly need: Cosmetics from Clinique to Chanel, men's and women's garments from underwear to fancy apparel, kitchen accessories that you didn't know you desperately needed, and so much more. The bottom-level hardware smorgasbord has electronics (need a power converter? Look no further) and even the typical Parisian signage from house numbers to no parking signs. If you need gifts in a hurry and on a budget, this multilevel shopping festival is no secret, but it's generally overlooked compared to other pricier places.

- **Lafayette Gourmet** (9e) is a luxurious grocery store and *traiteur* (creator of high-quality prepared foods) in the Galleries Lafayette department store near the Opéra. Although the Bon Marché's Grand Epicerie was the first of its kind to exist, Lafayette Gourmet has all the olive oil, homemade chocolate, wine, cheese, and everything else you need for a picnic or gift basket at much more reasonable prices.

- **Le Bon Marché** (6e) is elegant, but small enough to be manageable. It's the Left Bank's only department store. You can find the top designers here, and the basement toy store has great gift selections. The third floor is particularly renowned for its large shoe selection and lingerie department (where dressing rooms have phones to summon a salesperson).

The Best of Culture

Getting "cultured" is not a problem in Paris. There are more than 100 theaters, competing opera houses, and ballet and chamber music concerts in many churches. Even if your French is rusty or not up to par, many avant-garde productions and English-language theaters serve as alternatives to French-language plays. In this section, I list some of the best places to see theater, watch a ballet, or hear a symphony. See Chapter 15 for more information.

✔ Whatever your choice of the classic arts — opera, ballet, concerts, recitals — you'll find it performed at the **Châtelet, Théâtre Musical de Paris** (1er) by local and international performers of the highest caliber.

✔ A good mix of modern and classic tragedies and comedies comes alive in wonderful performances in the **Salle Richelieu** of the **Comédie-Française** (1er).

✔ You can see dazzling performances by the national opera and ballet troupes that perform at both the radiant **Palais Garnier** (9e) and the ultramodern **Opéra Bastille** (12e). The Palais Garnier conducts more ballet performances, and the Opéra Bastille puts on more opera.

✔ More than a dozen Parisian churches regularly schedule relatively inexpensive organ recitals and concerts. The most glorious, where the music is nearly outdone by the glorious stained-glass windows, is **Sainte-Chapelle** (1er) on île de la Cité, right near Notre-Dame.

✔ For popular, contemporary plays, the **Théâtre National de Chaillot** (16e) is your place.

The Best Clubs

Each neighborhood makes a different contribution to Paris's vibrant nightlife scene. Listed here are some of the best places to dance the night away. See Chapter 16 for more information.

✔ **Elysée Montmartre** (18e) is a venerable music hall that has hosted many bands, and continues to throw fantastic shows and club nights.

✔ **L'Alimentation Générale** (11e) is part of the new generation of Paris' nightlife scene and keeps the new- and indie-music-heads on their toes (and in the air).

✔ **Le Truskel** (2e) is an atypical rock club that boasts famous clientele. A fantastic place to end up at midnight (and return home whenever).

Chapter 2

Digging Deeper into Paris

* *

In This Chapter

▶ Discovering the rich history of Paris

▶ Admiring the city's architecture

▶ Enjoying the local cuisine

▶ Getting to know the local language

▶ Previewing the city in books and movies

* *

*P*aris is a key to all of French history and culture, and this chapter will give you insights to help you understand the city's history, the basics of French architecture, and the art of the meal. With some key French phrases to help you get around and a glossary of food to order once you get there, you'll be ready to take on Paris in no time.

History 101: The Main Events

This section outlines the most important periods of Parisian history, from the pre-Roman period to the French Revolution to the Napoléonic era and up to today. In the "Modern Paris" section, you'll read about some of the political events that have taken place in the last decade — this will bring you up to speed on some of the most current political, social, and economic issues.

The ancient times

The Celtic-speaking Parisii tribe settled Paris in the third century B.C. on the **Ile de la Cité** (one of two islands in the Seine around Central Paris — these days, Notre-Dame sits on Ile de la Cité). The Parisii were peaceful fishermen who traded with other tribes along the river and with travelers on the main north–south trading road that connected the Mediterranean with northern Europe. Unfortunately, the road made attacking the Parisii all too convenient for invaders. The first and most successful were the Romans, led by Julius Caesar in 52 B.C. During the Romans' 500-year stay, the settlement became known as Lutetia Parisiorum (*Lutèce* in French). You can still see the Roman public baths at the **Musée National du Moyen Age/Cluny Museum** in the **Latin Quarter,** and the remains of the Roman arena **Les Arènes de Lutèce** in the nearby sixth *arrondissement.*

Years of barbarian invasions eventually weakened Rome's hold over the territory. Around A.D. 450, Attila the Hun, on his way to sack Paris, changed course at the last minute, purportedly due to the prayers of a young girl named **Geneviève,** who became the patron saint of Paris. In the late 480s, Frankish king Clovis I successfully wrested control away from the Romans and, in 508, established Paris as his capital. The city was all but abandoned 250 years later, only to regain the status of capital in 987, when Hugh Capet was proclaimed king of France. Celebrating the city's importance, two Gothic masterpieces — the cathedrals of **Notre-Dame** and **Sainte-Chapelle** — were built on the Ile de la Cité. Across the river, on the **Left Bank,** the **University of Paris** was founded in the mid–12th century, although now it's referred to as **La Sorbonne,** named after the **Collège de Sorbonne,** founded in 1257.

Revolutionary Paris

Under Louis XIV, who ruled for 72 years, the monarchy's power reached its height, supported by heavy taxes. Although he added monuments and splendor to the city, the Sun King moved his court to Versailles, alienating the citizenry and paving the way for the French Revolution.

On July 14, 1789, a mob stormed the **Bastille** prison, which held many who were out of favor with French royalty. To most French citizens at the time, the Bastille was a symbol of much that was wrong with the monarchy, and the attack came to represent the end of the monarchy. Three days later, at the Hôtel de Ville, **Louis XVI** was forced to kiss the new French tricolor. On July 14, 1790, the Festival of the Federation was celebrated on the Champs de Mars, and an estimated 300,000 attended a Mass at which the king swore an oath of loyalty to the constitution. Still, radical factions grew. On August 10, 1792, revolutionary troops joined a Parisian mob storming the **Tuileries Palace,** where the king lived, and took him prisoner. In 1793, the king and **Queen Marie Antoinette** were beheaded in the place de la Concorde. At this time, **Maximilien Robespierre** was elected leader of the Committee of Public Safety, which conducted witch hunts for those it deemed counterrevolutionaries; this became known as the Reign of Terror. Between September 1793 and February 1794, 238 men and 31 women were tried and executed for crimes against the state. Nearly 5,500 more awaited trial in prisons until Robespierre's arrest in July 1794. He was executed the same month.

The era of Napoléons

During the last stage of the French Revolution, a directory of five men was ushered in to govern France. After four years, in 1799, Napoléon staged a coup, turning the country into a dictatorship. Five years later, in 1804, at Notre-Dame, Napoléon crowned himself emperor and his wife, Joséphine, empress. After applying the Code Napoléon over all French territory, the Corsican general embarked on a series of military campaigns until his defeat at Waterloo in 1815. During his reign, he gave Paris many of its most grandiose monuments, notably the **Arc de Triomphe** and the **Bourse,** but his greatest gift was starting the **Louvre.**

After the fall of Napoléon, the monarchy was restored through the **Bourbon Restoration,** placing **Charles X** on the throne. In 1830, the **July Monarchy** replaced Charles with **King Louis Philippe,** of the House of Orléans. His government lasted until the **Revolution of 1848,** which brought about the **Second Republic** and the 1851 election of **Louis Napoléon,** nephew of the original emperor. The first president of the French Republic, Louis was also known as **Napoléon III** after he established the **Second French Empire** (1852–1870) and therefore also holds the distinction of being France's last monarch.

During the 19th century, France experienced the intellectual and artistic developments that define it as a nation today. In Paris, the Second French Empire was a time of architectural and urban evolution through the plans of **Baron Georges-Eugène Haussmann.** Commissioned by Napoléon III to modernize the twisty medieval city, it was Haussmann who created the wide boulevards and the wrought-iron balconies that so clearly define the Paris of today.

Modern Paris

The **Eiffel Tower** (La Tour Eiffel), built only as a temporary structure for the 1889 World's Fair, was at one time the tallest structure in the world. Paris opened its first Métro line in 1900, and by the turn of the 20th century, had thousands of restaurants and 27,000 cafes.

In the years that followed, Paris witnessed two world wars with more than ten million military casualties, nearly one million Jews losing their lives, and four years of German occupation. Tens of thousands of soldiers died fighting the end of French colonial rule around the world.

In 1968, students took to the streets of Paris, rebelling against France's antiquated educational system among a host of other issues, including the rights of workers; this period of time is known in France as *Mai 1968.* **Charles De Gaulle**'s government tried to quash the strikes with police action but only made the situation worse. Young people hurled paving stones at police in street battles, and ten million French workers throughout the country went on strike. This nearly led to the collapse of the government, and De Gaulle called for new elections. Almost as quickly as the student and worker revolution started, it was over; in June 1968, voters elected an even stronger De Gaulle administration. De Gaulle, himself, resigned in 1969. The government flirted unsuccessfully with socialism in the 1980s and ended the decade with a great celebration of democracy — the bicentennial of the French Revolution and the centennial of the Eiffel Tower.

Former Paris Mayor **Jacques Chirac** was elected president in 1995 on his promise to jump-start the economy, but growth remained stagnant, and the president was forced to share power with Prime Minister Lionel Jospin. In 2004, Chirac signed a controversial law making it illegal for headscarves, part of the dress code for Muslim women, to be worn in public. This ruling included minors attending public schools, making religious headscarves in public schools illegal (a decision that continues to receive criticism from France's Muslim community to this day). In 2010, the French legislature voted to ban the wearing of *burqas* (garments worn by Muslim women that cover the entire face), which was supported by a vast majority of the French population.

In 2005, as a result of the accidental electrocution of two teenagers of African and North African descent, riots broke out in Paris resulting in the burning of thousands of cars and trucks in the île-de-France region. The anger and violence turned into a months-long series of riots that spread throughout urban areas of France. The year 2006 saw continual clashes between the citizenry and the French government, when over a million people took part in student strikes opposing proposed changes to the basic layout of workers' rights in France, specifically changes that would allow employers to fire workers under the age of 26 without giving an officially stated reason.

In a very heated and publicly debated election, in 2007 **Nicolas Sarkozy** became the president of France. His presidency has proven to be controversial for a number of reasons: The French have been totally put off by his personality; supposedly he's often tactless and impulsive. The media frenzy covering his marriage to former model and singer-songwriter Carla Bruni and the subsequent tabloid coverage of their life together are regarded as unnecessary and distasteful. Politically and economically, Sarkozy's promise to totally revamp the nation's economy to a more American model (including a stronger work ethic) was met with equal parts welcome and disdain from various sectors of society. Implementing his proposed changes has proven to be less fruitful than many hoped (or feared), but since Sarkozy's election, France no longer has a maximum 35-hour workweek and some taxes have been reduced.

The effects of the recent crisis and subsequent recession in the United States was felt worldwide, and the French economy suffered for four quarters before continuing to grow again, performing better, on average, than many other countries. However, in an effort to slow down a rapidly growing public deficit, in 2010, President Sarkozy announced a national budget with the greatest spending cuts in the last two decades — this was met with much public anger for the semi-socialist republic.

Another cultural and political shift in France that may surprise return voyagers is the February 2007 legislation making it illegal to smoke in public places; this includes cafes, bars, restaurants, and other venues. The public has responded with polarized opinions about the ban but now ultimately respects the new laws.

Building Blocks: Local Architecture

First-time visitors to Paris are struck by the graceful curves and balconies of the city's gorgeous apartment buildings, many of which were built during the reign of Napoléon III (mid-1800s) under Baron

Haussmann, the appointed urban planner by the emperor (see "The era of Napoléons," earlier in this chapter). In addition to the mixture of styles associated with the 19th and 20th centuries, different architectural eras are represented in Paris, among them the Ancient Roman, Romanesque, Gothic, Renaissance, classical (classicism), and rococo periods. You can see artifacts from Paris's founding in the third century B.C. by a tribe of fishermen, as well as such modern-day projects as the guts-on-the-outside Centre Georges Pompidou and I. M. Pei's glass pyramid at the Louvre.

Paris's important architectural periods are outlined here:

- **Ancient Roman (125 B.C.–A.D. 450):** After Julius Caesar conquered the island of Lutetia, his legions began using bricks and concrete in building and introduced the load-bearing arch, which led to the construction of stronger bridges and doorways. You can see examples of excavated Roman ruins at the **Crypte Archéologique** (see Chapter 11), about 60m (200 ft.) directly in front of the entrance of Notre-Dame. Possibly the most important ancient ruins are the Roman baths in the cellar of the **Musée de Cluny** (also in Chapter 11), a former private residence that was built around and on top of the ruins, and the Arènes de Lutèce, an amphitheater from the 1st century A.D. Unearthed during the construction of rue Monge in the 1860s, the public gathering place held gladiator competitions and could house up to 15,000 people.

- **Romanesque (800–1100):** This style is characterized by arches and curves, thick walls with small windows, huge piers to hold up the roof, simple geometric arrangements, and painting in decorative hues. The architects during this period built large churches. None survive intact in Paris; all were improved upon with different architectural styles or rebuilt. **Saint-Germain-des-Prés** (see Chapter 11) is a Romanesque building with a Gothic interior. **Saint-Julien le Pauvre** (also in Chapter 11) was originally a Romanesque church, but later Gothic additions obscure the original details.

- **Gothic (1100–1500):** Known for its slender vertical piers and counterbalancing buttresses and for vaulting and pointed arches that allow for taller and thinner structures, the interiors of these buildings force the eyes upward. Windows with stained glass were constructed so that most of the illiterate population could understand the stories told in each pane. *Gargoyles* (drain spouts), spires, flying buttresses, rose windows, and choir screens were all features of the Gothic church. The best examples are **Notre-Dame** (see Chapter 11) and the **Cathédrale de Notre-Dame de Chartres** (see Chapter 14).

- **Renaissance (1500–1630):** This architectural style is characterized by harmonious form, mathematical proportion, and a unit of measurement based on the human scale. Roofs became steeply pitched, and dormer windows were built taller, using stone. The mansions surrounding the **place des Vosges** (see Chapter 11) are all Renaissance, as is the **Hôtel Carnavalet,** home to the **Musée Carnavalet** (also in Chapter 11).

✔ **Classicism (1630–1800):** In this school, the emphasis was on form, simplicity, proportion, and restraint, influenced by the architecture of ancient Greece and Rome. Exteriors in the classical style may feature Doric, Corinthian, and Ionic columns; low and simple dormer windows; mansard roofs (having two slopes on all sides with the lower slope steeper than the upper, invented by François Mansard); and simple proportions. The interiors of classical buildings went over the top; this interior style is known as **rococo,** derived from the words *rocaille* (rock) and *coquille* (shell), delicate decorative motifs that appeared along with scrolls, branches of leaves, flowers, and bamboo stems. The best example of classicism and rococo is **Versailles** (see Chapter 14). The **Louvre** (see Chapter 11) is also a classical tour de force.

✔ **Nineteenth century (1800–1889):** This style began with *neoclassicism,* a return to the majesty of past civilizations, and an adoption of classical forms and styles. Examples include the **Arc de Triomphe** and **La Madeleine** (both in Chapter 11). The **Second French Empire** brought wide boulevards lined with six-story apartment buildings with balconies and mansard roofs with dormer windows. The **Third Republic**'s industrial age produced glass and steel structures; the most famous from this time is the **Eiffel Tower** (see Chapter 11). The other well-known (but by no means steel) monument completed at this time is the curiously neo-Byzantine **Sacré-Coeur** (also in Chapter 11).

✔ **Art Nouveau (1890–1914):** This period saw the end of the 19th century and continued into the 20th with beautiful renderings of plants and flowers in wrought iron **(Abbesses Métro station entrance),** stained glass, wood, tile, and hand-painted wallpapers. For a wonderful introduction to Art Nouveau, visit the middle floor of the **Musée d'Orsay** (see Chapter 11).

✔ **Twentieth to twenty-first century (1900–):** Twentieth-century style may be defined by late President François Mitterrand's *grands projets* (grand projects), most of which were controversial when completed. Richard Rogers and Renzo Piano's **Centre Georges Pompidou** (see Chapter 11), with its "guts on the outside" architecture, horrified Parisians, as did I. M. Pei's glass pyramids at the Louvre, but residents have slowly come to accept them. The four looming towers shaped like open books that comprise Mitterrand's last project, the Bibliothèque Nationale de France, are another story; the building, which is still suffering from the occasional technological glitch, has gotten little respect since its opening in the late 1990s.

The Grande Arche de la Défense in nearby Saint-Denis was designed to be a modern-day equivalent to the Arc de Triomphe.

Mitterrand commissioned the Danish architect Johann Otto von Spreckelsen to build the Arche, which also completes the *axe historique* (a line of historic buildings and monuments extending west from its origin in the center of Paris and including the Arc de Triomphe and the obelisk in place de la Concorde). The Grande Arche looks like a floating square when seen from afar.

Paris's "starchitect" Jean Nouvel, who used glass to great effect in the Fondation Cartier and Institut du Monde Arabe late in the 20th century, has given Paris the Musée du Quai Branly in the 21st century, again making use of glass but also promoting a more ecological theme: a wall bursting with 15,000 live plants. The result was beautiful, although some locals complain that the plants suffer due to drainage problems. Finished in 2000, the Promenade Plantée, a 4.5km (2¾-mile) elevated park constructed on an abandoned railway line, was regarded as an ingenious reclamation of unused space. It inspired the construction of New York City's High Line park in the Meatpacking District and Chelsea.

A long-term development plan to expand Paris's population of skyscrapers has been around since the late 2000s, as the need for space has increased greatly. Although plans for a new Jean Nouvel building in La Défense, known as the Signal Tower, was recently scrapped due to financing issues, plans for the construction of up to ten others in the area are still underway, to be completed by 2016. The expansion is greatly welcomed; however, the main opposition to it is part of the Parisian Green movement, which sees the buildings as a waste of resources.

A Taste of Paris: The Local Cuisine

Parisians have such wonderful meals from which to choose — regional French, three-star haute cuisine, North African *couscouseries,* tasty crêpes sold from street vendors, and more. During the last decade, the city witnessed the rise of *baby bistros* (restaurants opened by celebrity chefs and their talented young apprentices, offering simpler and less-expensive meals than those served at their deluxe establishments). Also in vogue is a back-to-*Grandmère*'s-kitchen approach featuring chefs turning out homey meals such as *blanquette de veau* (veal stew in white sauce), *cassoulet* (meat-and-vegetable casserole), and *confit de canard* (duck preserved and cooked in its own fat until it's so tender it falls off the bone). Asian influences are also in vogue; witness the success of L'Atelier de Joël Robuchon and Ze Kitchen Galerie. I talk in more depth about dining in Paris in Chapter 10.

A glossary good enough to eat

Use this helpful guide when you're trying to decide what to order and how you want it cooked.

General Terms

compris (comb-*pree;* included)
déjeuner (*day*-zhu-nay; lunch)
dîner (*dee*-nay; dinner)
ménu dégustation (may-*noo* day-goo-*stah*-sion; sampler, or tasting, menu)
petit déjeuner (pet-*tee day*-zhu-nay; breakfast)
prix fixe (pree feeks; set price)
supplément (sup-play-*mahn;* extra charge)

Les Entrées (layz ahn-trays; appetizers)

charcuterie (shar-koot-*ree;* assorted cold cuts)
crudités (kroo-dee-*tay;* assorted raw vegetables)
foie gras (fwah grah; goose liver pâté)
salade composée (sa-*lad* com-poh-zay; mixed salad)
salade de chèvre chaud (sa-*lad* duh-shev-rah-*sho;* salad with warm goat cheese on croutons)
salade gésiers (sa-*lad* jeh-*zyay;* salad with sautéed chicken gizzards)
salade landaise (sa-*lad* lahn-*dehs;* salad containing duck breast, duck liver, and duck gizzards)
salade niçoise (sa-*lad* nee-*shwahz;* salad with tuna, corn, anchovies, and potato)
saumon fumé (soh-*moh foo*-may; smoked salmon)
soupe à l'oignon (soop ah lowh-*yon;* onion soup)
velouté (vay-loo-*tay;* light, cream-based soup)
vichyssoise (vee-shee-*swahz;* cold leek and potato soup)

Boeuf (bewf; beef)

bavette (bah-*vet;* flank steak)
chateaubriand (cha-tow-bree-*ahn;* porterhouse)
contre-filet (*kahn*-trah-fee-lay; filet steak)
côte de boeuf (cote dah bewf; T-bone)
entrecôte (ahn-trah-*cote;* rib-eye)

faux-filet (foe-fee-*lay;* sirloin)
filet mignon (fee-*lay* mee-*nyahn;* tenderloin)
langue de boeuf (lahng dah bewf; tongue)
onglet (ahn-*glay;* hanger steak)
pavé (pah-*vay;* thick steak; literally: paving stone)
queue de boeuf (keuh duh beuf; oxtail)
rôti de boeuf (*roe*-tee duh beuf; roast beef)
steak haché (stake *ah*-shay; minced meat or hamburger)
steak tartare (stake tar-*tar;* a lean cut of beef minced and served raw — a high-quality dish prepared by experts, people rarely get sick from eating this)
tournedos (*tor*-nah-doh; small tender filet usually grilled or sautéed)

Other Meats

agneau (ah-*nyoh;* lamb)
gigot (*gee*-go; leg — usually of lamb)
jambon (zhahm-*bon;* ham)
médaillon (may-dye-*on;* medallions — beef, veal, lamb)
merguez (mare-*gez;* spicy lamb sausage)
porc (por; pork)
saucisses (soh-*sees;* sausage)
saucisson (soh-see-*sohn;* little sausage)
veau (voh; veal)

Volailles (voe-lie; fowl)

blanc de volaille (blahn duh voh-*lai;* chicken breast)
caille (kai; quail)
canard (kah-*nahr;* duck)
dinde (dand; turkey)
magret de canard (mah-*gret* duh kah-*nahr;* duck breast)
oie (wah; goose)
pigéon (pee-*zhohn;* game pigeon)
pintade (pan-*tahd;* guinea fowl)
poulet (*poo*-lay; chicken)

Fruits de Mer (free duh mair; seafood)

bar (bar; bass)
cabillaud (ka-bee-*oh;* cod)
coquilles Saint-Jacques (*koh*-kee san-*jahk;* scallops)
crevettes (kreh-*vet;* shrimp)
daurade (doh-*rahd;* sea bream)
homard (oh-*mahr;* lobster)
huîtres (wee-*tra;* oysters)
langoustine (lang-oo-*steen;* crayfish)
morue (moh-*roo;* cod)
moules (mool; mussels)
poisson (pwah-*son;* fish)
raie (reh; skate)
rascasse (ras-*kass;* scorpion fish)
rouget (roo-*zhay;* red mullet)
saumon (soh-*monh;* salmon)
thon (tohn; tuna)
truite (trweet; trout)

Les Légumes (lay lay-goom; vegetables)

artichault (ar-tee-*show;* artichoke)
asperge (as-*perzh;* asparagus)
aubergine (oh-bare-*zheen;* eggplant)
cèpe (sep; mushroom)
champignon (sham-peen-*nyonh;* mushroom)
choucroute (shoo-*kroot;* sauerkraut)
choux (shoo; cabbage)
choux de bruxelles (shoo dah broo-*sells;* brussels sprouts)
courgette (kor-*zhette;* zucchini)
épinard (ay-pee-*nahr;* spinach)
girolle (*gee*-roll; mushroom)
haricots (ah-ree-*koh;* beans)
haricots verts (*ah*-ree-koh vare; string beans)
oignons (oh-*nyonh;* onions)
petits pois (*puh*-tee pwah; peas)
poireaux (pwah-*roh;* leeks)
poivron rouge (pwah-vrohn *roozh;* red pepper)
poivron vert (pwah-vrohn *vare;* green pepper)
pomme de terre (pom duh *tare;* potato)
pommes frites (*pom* freet; french fries)

riz (*ree;* rice)
tomate (toh-*maht;* tomato)
truffe (troof; mushroom)

Les Fruits (lay free; fruit)

abricot (*ah*-bree-koh; apricot)
ananas (a-*na*-nas; pineapple)
banane (bah-*nan;* banana)
cerise (sare-*ees;* cherry)
citron (see-*tronh;* lemon)
citron vert (see-tronh *vare;* lime)
fraise (frehz; strawberry)
framboise (frahm-*bwahz;* raspberry)
myrtille (meer-*teel;* blueberry)
pamplemousse (pahmp-luh-*moos;* grapefruit)
pêche (pehsh; peach)
poire (pwahr; pear)
pomme (pom; apple)
prune (proon; plum)
pruneau (proo-*noh;* prune)
raisin (rah-*sahn;* grape)
raisin sec (rah-sahn *sek;* raisin)

Les Desserts (lay day-sare; desserts)

baba au rhum (bah-bah oh rhoom; spongecake soaked in rum)
charlotte (shar-*lote;* molded cream ringed with a biscuit)
clafoutis (clah-foo-*tee;* thick batter filled with fruit and fried)
crème brûlée (krem broo-*lay;* creamy custard with caramelized surface)
fondant aux chocolat (fohn-*don* oh sho-ko-*lah;* small chocolate cake with molten chocolate interior)
fromage blanc (froe-*mahzh* blahn; smooth yogurt-like cheese)
gâteau (gah-*toh;* cake)
glace (glahs; ice cream)
mille-feuille (meel-*foye;* a puff pastry, usually filled with custard)
moelleux au chocolat (mwah-luh oh sho-ko-*lah;* small chocolate cake with molten chocolate interior)
mousse au chocolat (moos oh sho-ko-*lah;* chocolate mousse)
profiterole (pro-fee-tay-*rol;* variety of cream puff served cold)

tarte (tart; pie)
Tarte Tatin (tart ta-*ta;* caramelized upside-down apple pie)

Preparation Methods

aioli (ay-oh-lee; sauce made of garlic, olive oil and herbs)
à l'ail (ah lye; with garlic)
à point (ah pwahn; medium)
au four (oh fore; baked)
béarnaise (bare-*nayse;* hollandaise sauce with tarragon, vinegar, and shallots)
béchamel (beh-sha-*mel;* white sauce made with onions and nutmeg)
beurre blanc (bur blahn; white sauce made with butter, white wine, and shallots)
bien cuit (byen kwee; well done)
bleu (bluh; very rare; literally: blue)
bordelaise (bore-duh-*lez;* brown meat stock made with red wine, mushrooms, shallots, and beef marrow)
bouilli (bwee-*ee;* boiled)
bourguignon (bore-gee-*nyonh;* brown meat stock flavored with red wine, mushrooms, and onions)
confit (kahn-*fee;* meat — usually duck or goose — cooked in its own fat)
consommé (kahn-soh-*may;* clear broth)
coulis (koo-*lee;* any nonflour sauce, purée, or juice)
cru (kroo; raw)

diable (dee-*ah*-bluh; brown sauce flavored with cayenne pepper, white wine, and shallots)
en croûte (ahn *kroot;* in a pastry crust)
en papillote (ahn pah-pee-*oat;* cooked in parchment and opened at the table — usually fish)
estouffade (ay-too-*fahd;* meat that has been marinated, fried, and braised)
farçi (fahr-*see;* stuffed)
feuilleté (foy-eh-*tay;* in puff pastry)
fumé (*foo*-may; smoked)
gratiné (*grah*-tee-nay; topped with browned bread crumbs or cheese)
grillé (*gree*-ay; grilled)
hollandaise (oh-lan-*dez;* white sauce with butter, egg yolks, and lemon juice)
lyonnais (lee-ohn-*nay;* with onions)
marinière (mar-ee-*nyair;* steamed in garlicky wine stock)
meunière (moo-*nyur;* fish rolled in flour and sautéed)
parmentier (pahr-men-tee-*ay;* with potato)
Provençal (pro-vahn-*sal;* tomato-based sauce, with garlic, olives, and onions)
rôti (*roe*-tee; roasted)
saignant (sen-*yahn;* rare)
terrine (tuh-*reen;* cooked in an earthenware dish)

Salivating over French cooking

Even with English translations, confronting a French menu can be a daunting experience. Dishes that have been familiar to French people since childhood are often unknown to outsiders. The following list is a user's guide to typical French dishes that you're likely to encounter.

✔ **Andouillette** (ahn-dwee-*et*): A sausage of pork organs encased in intestines. *Andouillette* has a strong flavor with a distinct aftertaste and is usually grilled and served with mustard and french fries. Look for the A.A.A.A.A. label — the Association Amicale des Authentiques Amateurs d'Andouillettes (Association of Real *Andouillette* Lovers) stamps it on the best *andouillettes*.

✔ **Blanquette de veau** (blahn-*ket* duh voe): Veal cooked in a white stew that includes eggs and cream.

✔ **Boeuf bourguignon** (bewf bor-gee-*nyon*): Beef cooked with red burgundy wine, mushrooms, and onions.

✔ **Boudin** (boo-*dan*): A rich sausage made from pig's blood, usually combined with crème fraîche, onions, and eggs. More elaborate versions may feature a touch of garlic or chestnuts. The dish is often served with sautéed apples or mashed potatoes, which enhance the slightly sweet taste of the sausage.

✔ **Boudin blanc** (boo-*dan* blahn): A white sausage made from veal, chicken, or pork.

✔ **Bouillabaisse** (*bwee*-ah-bess): A fish stew from the Mediterranean that includes assorted shellfish and white fish accompanied by croutons, grated cheese, and *rouille* (a mayonnaise made with garlic).

✔ **Brandade** (brahn-*dahd*): *Morue* (salt cod) soaked in cold water, shredded, and cooked with garlic, olive oil, milk, and potato. It has the look and consistency of mashed potatoes but tastes like a very garlicky salted fish. Take it easy after this one.

✔ **Cassoulet** (cass-oo-*lay*): A rich stew made of white beans, dry sausage, onion, duck, prosciutto, herbs, carrots, and tomatoes. It's cooked slowly and usually served in a ceramic bowl or pot. Absolutely delicious, but heavy; don't plan any serious physical exertions after eating — digestion will be enough.

✔ **Cervelles** (suhr-vel): Pork or sheep brains.

✔ **Cheval** (sheh-vahl): Horse meat.

✔ **Choucroute** (shoo-*kroot*): Sauerkraut cooked with juniper berries and wine, served with an assortment of pork cuts, usually including brisket, pork shoulder, ham, frankfurters, or spicy sausage.

✔ **Confit de canard** (con-*fee* duh kah-*nahr*): A duck leg cooked and preserved in its own fat. The fatty skin is usually salty, but the meat underneath is tender and juicy.

✔ **Coq au vin** (coke oh vahn): Braised chicken cooked for several hours in red wine, garlic, and mushrooms.

✔ **Cuisses des grenouilles** (kwees day gran-*wee*): Frogs' legs.

✔ **Escalope** (es-kah-lope): Cutlets of veal, pork, steak, or chicken, pounded to a thin, tender strip.

✔ **Escargots** (es-car-*go*): Snails.

✔ **Foie** (fwah): Liver.

✔ **Foie gras:** (fwah *grah*): Goose liver pâté; a delicacy.

✔ **Gésiers** (jeh-*zyay*): Poultry gizzards; very good in salads.

- **Lapin à la moutarde** (la-*pan* ah la moo-*tard*): Rabbit cooked with mustard, crème fraîche, and sometimes white wine. The mustard perks up the rabbit meat, which has a mild flavor.

- **Lièvre** (lee-*yevr*): Hare.

- **Magret de canard** (mah-*greh* duh kah-nahr): The sliced breast of a fattened duck, sautéed and sometimes served with a green peppercorn sauce. The result more closely resembles red meat than poultry. As with any meat, specify how you want it cooked.

- **Pieds de cochon** (pyay duh coh-*shon*): Pig's feet.

- **Plateau de fruits de mer** (plah-*toe* duh free duh mair): A variety of raw and cooked seafood served on ice, usually in brasseries. You usually find two kinds of oysters — flat, round *belon,* and larger, crinkly *creuse.* In addition to various kinds of shrimp, clams, and mussels, you also see *bulots* (periwinkles, edible marine snails).

- **Pot-au-feu** (*pot*-oh-fuh): A hearty dish of boiled vegetables and beef that sometimes includes the marrow bone. Scrape out the marrow, spread it on toast, and sprinkle it with salt. Sometimes the broth is served first, followed by the vegetables and beef. Mustard is the preferred condiment.

- **Ratatouille** (rah-tah-*too*-ie): A Provencal vegetable stew, with tomatoes, zucchini and eggplant as key ingredients, as well as garlic, onions, bell peppers, and plenty of locally grown herbs.

- **Ris de veau** (ree duh voe): The thymus gland of a calf (a white meat) sautéed in a butter and cream sauce. It has a delicate, pleasant taste but is high in cholesterol.

- **Rognons** (*ron*-yawn): Kidneys.

- **Soufflé** (soo-*flay*): A light and puffy cake made of egg whites and yolks beaten, combined with other ingredients, and baked. Can be sweet or savory.

- **Tête de veau** (tet duh voe): Calf's head; the meat includes brains, cheeks, and tongue.

Words to the Wise: The Local Language

Parisians *do* speak English and, yes, they're willing to speak it — especially with visitors who do them the courtesy of trying to speak a few phrases of French. You often find that you can't even complete a sentence in French before you're answered in English. Don't be afraid to say that you don't understand French — *Je ne comprends pas* (juh nuh cohm-*pren* pah). You'll save yourself, and the person with whom you're conversing, a lot of time and get help that much faster.

Phrases to remember are the essential *Parlez-vous anglais* (par-*lay*-voo ahn-*glay;* do you speak English?); the common courtesy (and obligatory) phrase of *Bonjour madame/monsieur* (bohn-*joor* mad-*am*/mis-*yoo;* hello, madam/sir) when you enter a store or place of business, or speak to anyone in general; and *au revoir madame/monsieur* (oh-*vwah* mad-*am*/ mis-*yoo;* goodbye, madam/sir) when you leave. This book, too, has an extensive glossary of words and phrases that anticipate nearly every situation (see Appendix B).

Background Check: Books and Movies

Compiled here are lists of books and movies to help prepare you for your trip to Paris.

Books

Numerous books have been written about the experiences of travelers who fell under the city's spell, or the doings of a particular French person, or the efforts of those who try to figure out just what it is that makes France such a peculiar culture but such a wonderful place to visit. The following list provides just a sample:

- ✔ *C'est la Vie: An American Conquers the City of Light, Begins a New Life, and Becomes — Zut Alors! — Almost French,* by Suzy Gershman (Viking): Frommer's *Born to Shop* author Gershman had long planned to retire in France with her husband. But when he died of an unexpected illness, she moved to Paris alone to try to work through her grief. A deliciously chatty chronicle of her first year in Paris.

- ✔ *The Flâneur: A Stroll through the Paradoxes of Paris,* by Edmund White (Bloomsbury): Edmund White, who lived in Paris for 16 years, wanders through the streets and avenues and along the quays, taking readers into parts of Paris virtually unknown to visitors — and to many Parisians.

- ✔ *A Moveable Feast,* by Ernest Hemingway (Scribner): This is the memoir of this Lost Generation writer's life in Paris during the '20s and '30s. Beautifully written, the book is full of anecdotes about life in the city during the period and, of course, the expatriate writing community that thrived.

- ✔ *Paris Tales,* a collection of classic literature translated by Helen Constantine (Oxford University Press): This book contains 22 stories on the sights and sounds of the City of Light by famous French writers such as Nerval, Maupassant, and Colette. Readers see through the eyes of Parisian characters from all walks of life and time periods from the 19th century to the present.

- ✔ *Paris to the Moon,* by Adam Gopnik (Random House): This is the often humorous and tender account of the five years that *New Yorker* writer Gopnik spent in Paris with his wife and young son.

✔ *Savoir Flair: 211 Tips for Enjoying France and the French,* by Polly Platt (Culture Crossings Ltd.): This book details cultural do's and don'ts by an American who has lived in Paris since 1967. This guide is simply essential!

✔ *Seven Ages of Paris,* by Alistair Horne (Vintage): This is a colorful narrative history of Paris and, due to its designation as the center of the French world, the history of France, as well. Interesting and informative, it's a great, unintimidating introduction to a city with a whole lot of history.

✔ *Sixty Million Frenchmen Can't Be Wrong: Why We Love France but Not the French,* by Jean-Benoit Nadeau and Julie Barlow (Sourcebooks): Two Canadian journalists who move to France on a two-year fellowship deconstruct French ideas about land, food, privacy, and language.

✔ *A Year in the Merde* and *Talk to the Snail: Ten Commandments for Understanding the French,* both by Stephen Clarke (Bloomsbury USA): In the first book, Clarke describes how he, an Englishman, arrives in Paris to set up some English tearooms in Paris, giving a laugh-out-loud account of the pleasures and perils of being a Brit in France. In his follow-up, Clarke gives us his hilarious 11 commandments for understanding the French, with a great section on the typical tourist experience.

Movies

It's difficult to cull this down into a small list because there are so many terrific films about France. Most of the movies here take place in Paris, and their shots of this beautiful city will only increase your anticipation of visiting.

✔ *À Bout de Souffle (Breathless):* In this classic by Jean-Luc Godard, a small-time gangster kills a cop and then flees to Paris to get enough money together to leave the country with his girlfriend. Wonderful shots of Paris in the late 1950s.

✔ *Before Sunset:* In this sequel to the 1995 film *Before Sunrise,* the two main characters, who had met in Vienna and spent a memorable night together, reunite after one gives a reading from his new book at Shakespeare and Company.

✔ *Gigi:* This 1958 Lerner and Loewe musical set in Paris at the turn of the 20th century follows a young girl as she is groomed into a would-be courtesan (based on a story by the French author Colette).

✔ *Jules et Jim:* In this François Truffaut classic, two best friends fall in love with the same woman in 1912 Paris. Breathtaking!

✔ *Le Fabuleux Destin d'Amélie Poulain (Amélie):* It's hard to tell who the star is in this movie about a young woman trying to do good, actress Audrey Tautou or the city of Paris.

- *La Vie en Rose:* In 2007, Marion Cotillard won an Oscar and a César (the French equivalent of the Oscar) for best actress for her portrayal of Édith Piaf in this biographical film of the singer's tumultuous life.

- *Paris:* Starring Romain Duris and Juliette Binoche, this 2008 comedy prominently features some of the best sights of Paris in its background. Described by *New York Times* film critic Stephen Holden as "a surrogate for a first-time visitor to the City of Light."

- *Paris, Je T'Aime:* This 2006 collaboration of 18 short films, all named after different Parisian neighborhoods, is a beautiful collection of humorous, dramatic, and heart-wrenching oeuvres. It gives some great insight to the diversity of Parisian life while featuring the architecture and character in the City of Light.

- *Ratatouille:* Watching this 2007 Pixar film with your kids is a perfect way to get them (and you!) excited about a trip to Paris. Remy, a French rat with keen olfactory senses, dreams of being a chef and, after a near-death experience, gets his chance at a high-class Parisian bistro.

- *Zazie Dans le Métro:* In Louis Malle's very funny 1962 film, a young girl is foisted on her unwilling transvestite uncle, and they have a series of madcap adventures in Paris.

Chapter 3

Deciding When to Go

● ●

In This Chapter
▶ Choosing the best season to visit
▶ Checking out a calendar of events

● ●

*T*his chapter lists the pros and cons of each season to help you
decide when you can make the most of your visit to Paris. I also
compile a calendar of the most memorable events in Paris; you may
want to consider planning your trip to coincide with one of the festivals,
sporting events, or celebrations.

 For further research on seasonal events and festivals in Paris, check out
the "Practical Paris" and "What's On" sections of the official English-
language tourist and visitor Web site (http://en.parisinfo.com).

Revealing the Secret of the Seasons

Residents and visitors alike find Paris ideal in spring and autumn, when
weather is kind, crowds are reasonable, and Parisian life runs at a steady
hum. Winter can be gray and bone-chillingly damp, but there are plenty
of things to do inside: You can fill an entire trip with visits just to the
Louvre, and January has its own joy: *les soldes* (twice yearly government-
mandated sales, lasting two or three weeks each). In summer, you can
bask in daylight that lasts until 10 p.m.

Table 3-1 presents Paris's average daytime temperatures by month to
help you plan your trip. (In Paris, temperatures are reported in Celsius.)

Table 3-1	Average Daytime Temperatures for Paris											
	Jan	*Feb*	*Mar*	*Apr*	*May*	*June*	*July*	*Aug*	*Sep*	*Oct*	*Nov*	*Dec*
Fahrenheit (F)	38°	39°	46°	51°	58°	64°	74°	76°	61°	53°	45°	40°
Celsius (C)	3°	4°	8°	11°	14°	18°	28°	29°	16°	12°	7°	6°

Paris in the springtime

In 2010, France and much of Europe saw some unseasonable heat that picked up around mid-April and continued through the rest of the spring and summer at record highs. Spring generally arrives in Paris at this time and brings some beautifully clear, fresh days. The parks and gardens of Paris — and those at Versailles, Fontainebleau, and Giverny (see Chapter 14) — burst with colorful, fragrant blooms. Crowds of visitors don't kick in until July summer vacation (except during the spring fashion shows in Mar), so lines are relatively short at the top attractions, and airfares have yet to reach their summertime highs.

 But keep in mind that April in Paris is *not* as temperate as Cole Porter would have you believe. In fact, Paris weather can be very similar to that in London: It's fickle. Pack for warm, cold, wet, dry, and every other eventuality; in other words, bring layers and an umbrella. Also, nearly every Monday in May is a holiday in France — stores and many museums are closed, the Métro runs on a holiday schedule, and other venues are affected.

Paris is a beach

Long and sultry days — 6 a.m. sunrises and 10 p.m. sunsets — make visiting Paris in summer ideal; you're afforded additional hours to wander and discover. You can find discounts of 30 percent to 50 percent in most stores during July, one of the two big months for shopping sales (the other is Jan). Be sure to stop by Paris Plages, an artificial beachfront set up along the highways next to the Seine during the summer months. Sand, palm trees, and beach umbrellas are brought in, and residents are encouraged to stroll and take some sun (but don't jump into the river!).

 But remember that an influx of tourists during the summer means long lines at museums and other sites. The weather also is capricious: You may have a week of rain and mid-50s temperatures, followed by days of cloudless skies and (as of recently) very high temperatures. Also, much of the city is without air-conditioning, including most trains and buses.

Because most Parisians take their vacations in August, the city is wonderfully tranquil in some places and devoid of life in others. Although the entire city doesn't exactly shut down in August, some shops and restaurants close for the entire month. The city's cultural calendar slows down, too, and you may have to walk an extra block or two to find an open shop or newsstand. And if you go to Paris in August with thoughts of practicing your French, think again — French may be the language you're least likely to hear.

Fabulous festive fall

The fall is one of my favorite times to visit Paris. The city bursts into life starting the first week of September, a time typically known as *la rentrée* (the return). Important art exhibitions open along with trendy new restaurants, shops, and cafes, and students repopulate the many universities. By the middle of September, airfares drop from summertime highs. And with daytime temperatures in the 60s and 70s and nights in the 50s, the weather is especially pleasant.

Keep in mind, however, that finding a hotel at the last minute in the fall can be difficult due to the number of business conventions and trade shows that take place in the city, including the October fashion shows. Be sure to book ahead.

Transportation strikes of varying intensities traditionally occur during the fall. Some go virtually unnoticed by the average traveler, but others can be giant hassles.

Winter wonderland

You can find great airfare deals during the winter; airlines and tour operators often offer unbeatable prices on flights and package tours. Lines at museums and other sights are mercifully short. You can ice-skate in front of the Hôtel de Ville (City Hall). And, if shopping is your bag, you can save up to 50 percent during the sales in January.

But remember that although Paris winters may appear mild on paper, in reality, residents know that they're gray (sometimes the sun doesn't shine for weeks), dreary, and bone-chillingly damp (there's a reason French women wear scarves!). And look out for those winds that lash up and down the city's grand boulevards. Bring a warm, preferably waterproof, coat and umbrella. *Remember:* All this weather is an excellent excuse to go shopping!

A Paris Calendar

When you arrive, check with the **Paris Convention and Visitors Bureau** (☎ **08-92-68-30-00** at a charge of 0.35€ per minute; http://en.paris info.com) and pick up a *Pariscope* (www.pariscope.fr) and a *L'Officiel des Spectacles* (www.offi.fr) for dates, places, and other up-to-date information. Or, if you pass by an English-language bookstore or bar, pick up a copy of the English-language free publications, *Paris Voice* (www.parisvoice.com) and *FUSAC* (www.fusac.fr).

In the following sections are Paris's month-by-month attractions.

January

A big, noisy parade on New Year's Day makes Paris more Rose Bowl than City of Light. **La Grande Parade de Montmartre** is fun and flashy with majorettes, high school bands, and elaborate floats that traverse the city streets. The parade begins at 2 p.m. (so you *can* sleep in) in the place Pigalle, 18e (the 18th arrondissement, or neighborhood), and ends at the place Jules-Joffrin (18e). January 1.

The **Fête des Rois,** the celebration of the Feast of the Three Kings, is a holiday that kids love; custom dictates the wearing of gold paper crowns to celebrate. The main object of celebration is a flaky, almond-paste-filled pie that conceals a ceramic charm (so watch your teeth). According to custom, whoever finds the charm becomes king or queen for the day, is entitled to wear the crown, and has free reign, as it were, in his or her choice of a consort. The pie with the charm is available at all *patisseries* (dessert shops). January 6.

Residents go all out for the **Chinese New Year Festival** and celebratory events take place in Chinatown (13e), although pockets of celebration unfold in the smaller Chinese neighborhoods in the Marais (3e) and in Belleville (11e and 20e). A parade features dragons, dancers, and fireworks. Plan on grabbing a bite to eat in one of the many excellent Chinese restaurants in the area. Between January 21 and February 19, depending on the Chinese calendar.

Twice a year, in January and September, more than 40,000 buyers make their way to the **Ready-to-Wear Fashion Shows** in the Salon International de Prêt-à-Porter at the Parc des Expositions, Porte de Versailles (15e; Métro: Balard or Porte de Versailles). The exposition hall hosts shows of the new clothing lines from some 1,200 designers. Admission for non-trade visitors can range from 20€ to 65€. Invitation-only fashion shows are also held at the major design houses. End of January.

February

Hundreds of farmers display animals and produce and win prizes for the biggest and best at **Salon International de l'Agriculture,** a country fair in the heart of the city. Regional food stands offer tastes from all parts of France, and the atmosphere is friendly and quintessentially French at the Parc des Expositions de Paris, Porte de Versailles (15e). For more information, call the Parc des Expositions information line at ☎ 01-43-95-37-00 or check out www.salon-agriculture.com. Admission is 12€ adults; 6€ students and kids. Last week of February.

March

Professional actors and residents of the neighborhood perform in **La Passion à Ménilmontant,** the Passion play (the events leading up to and including the Crucifixion of Christ), for a month around Easter. The play is staged at the Théâtre de Ménilmontant (20e). The event is a local tradition that's been observed since 1932. Admission is around 9€ to 20€. Call ☎ 01-46-36-98-60 or 01-46-36-03-43 for the schedule. Mid-March to mid-April.

The **French Fashion Week** exhibits the following year's read-to-wear fall and winter collections. Check www.modeaparis.com for more information. Early March.

When the **Foire du Trône** (www.foiredutrone.com), a tacky and fun annual carnival, comes to town, spring is just around the corner. Take a trip up on the Ferris wheel and other rides, try your hand at games, buy hokey souvenirs, and sample fairground food. The fair is located at the Pelouse de Reuilly in the Bois de Vincennes (12e; Métro: Porte Dorée, Porte de Charenton, or Liberté). Late March to end of May.

April

Follow Paris's archbishop as he performs **Le Chemin de la Croix (The Stations of the Cross)** from the square Willette in Montmartre up the steps to the basilica of Sacré-Coeur (18e) where he leads prayers to commemorate the Passion and Crucifixion of Jesus Christ. Good Friday, 12:30 p.m. March or April.

One of the most popular athletic events of the year, the **Marathon de Paris** (www.parismarathon.com) has runners sprinting past a variety of the city's most beautiful monuments. The 42km (26-mile) event attracts enthusiastic crowds. Early April.

The huge annual fair **Foire de Paris** (www.foiredeparis.fr) is a great place to bargain-hunt and people-watch, and signals the start of spring with hundreds of stands selling good-priced food and wine and a variety of clothing and household goods. The fair takes place at the Parc des Expositions, Porte de Versailles (15e). Late April to early May.

The **Grandes Eaux Musicales** and the **Fêtes de Nuit de Versailles** bring the sounds of classical music to life at the magnificent fountains in the gardens of the Château de Versailles every Sunday from mid-April to mid-October, and every Saturday and national holiday from June through August. Even better are the **Grandes Fêtes,** spectacular sound-and-light shows with fireworks that take place one Saturday in June, three Saturdays in July, one Saturday in August, and two Saturdays in September. These events are held at the Château de Versailles. Log on to www.chateauversailles.fr for more information. (See Chapter 14 for tour companies that go to Versailles.)

May

May is a month of one holiday after the next in France. Banks, post offices, and most museums are closed for **May Day,** the French version of Labor Day, but you can watch a workers' parade that traditionally ends at the place de la Bastille. May 1.

Museums around the country stay open late with special exhibits and entertainment during **La Nuit des Musées.** Mid-May.

The weather is usually beautiful during **Les Cinq Jours Extraordinaire (The Five Extraordinary Days),** when the shops in the rue du Bac, de Lille, de Beaune, des Saints-Pères, and de l'Université, and on the quai Voltaire, feature a free open house focusing on a special object chosen according to the annual theme. The whole quarter takes on a festive ambience, red carpets line the streets, and plants and flowers decorate storefronts. Third week of May.

If you're lucky enough to procure hard-to-find tickets to the **French Open,** Paris's biggest tennis event, you'll find yourself watching the red-clay matches in the Stade Roland Garros, 2 av. Gordon Bennett, in the Bois de Boulogne (16e), on the western edge of the city. Unsold tickets — those not reserved for corporate sponsors — go on sale two weeks before the competition starts. Call the French Federation of Tennis at the stadium for more information (☎ **01-47-43-48-00**) or visit the Web site at www. frenchopen.com. Last week in May and first week in June.

June

Paris's other *orangerie* (an architecturally beautiful greenhouse where citrus fruits were grown), in the beautiful Bagatelle gardens on the edge of the Bois de Boulogne (16e; Métro: Porte Maillot, then take bus no. 244), is the backdrop for the **Festival Chopin à Paris,** a much-loved annual series of daily piano recitals. Mid-June to mid-July.

The celebration of the summer solstice has never been louder! The entire country becomes a concert venue in celebration of the first day of summer, and this musical day is called the **Fête de la Musique.** You can hear everything from classical to hip-hop for free in squares and streets around Paris. A big rock concert usually happens in the place de la République, and a fine classical concert generally takes place in the gardens of the Palais-Royal. June.

World-renowned jazz acts play weekends in the Bois de Vincennes' lovely Parc Floral (12e) during the **Paris Jazz Festival,** now a fixture on the international jazz circuit. Check out www.parisjazzfestival.fr for more information. Middle of June until the beginning of August.

Being a musical month, June is the time of the **Solidays,** an annual concert festival that raises money for HIV and AIDS research and education. Well-known international and French music acts play during the three-day festival, during which over 100,000 young Euro hippie types descend upon the Hippodrome de Longchamp in the Bois de Bologne (16e). End of June.

One of the most distinguished aviation events in the world is the **Paris Air Show,** which takes place in odd-numbered years at Le Bourget Airport, just outside Paris. Visitors can check out the latest aeronautic technology on display. Contact the Paris Convention and Visitors Bureau (☎ **08-92-68-30-00** at a charge of 0.35€ per minute; http:// en.parisinfo.com) for more information.

Art exhibits, concerts, and a fantastic parade are staged in the Marais, the boulevard Saint-Michel, eventually finishing up in a massive dance party at place de la Bastille to celebrate **Gay Pride** (known as the Marche des Fiertés). Call the Centre Gai et Lesbien (☎ **01-43-57-21-47**) for dates, or check out www.gaypride.fr. Mid- to late June.

July and August

French independence day, **Bastille Day,** is July 14, but the festivities actually begin the night before, with free *bals* (dances) open to everyone at fire stations all over the city. (Some of the best *bals* are in the fire stations on the rue du Vieux-Colombier near the place Saint-Sulpice [6e]; the rue de Sévigné [4e]; and the rue Blanche, near place Pigalle [9e].) Although the *bals* are free, drinks cost. On July 14, be sure to get to the Champs-Elysées *way* before the 10 a.m. start of the Bastille Day military parade if you hope to see anything. Later that night, a sound-and-light show with terrific fireworks can be seen at the Trocadéro. Rather than face the crowds, many people watch the fireworks from the Champs de Mars across the river, from bridges along the Seine (I recommend the usually ignored pont de Bir-Hakeim), from hotel rooms with views, or even from the hill on rue Soufflot, in front of the Panthéon. July 13 and 14.

The **Paris, Quartier d'Été (Paris, Summer Neighborhood)** celebration has contemporary music, dance, and film as the bills of fare at outside venues around the city. The outdoor movies shown on a giant screen at Parc de la Villette (19e; Métro: Porte de la Villette) are particularly popular. Mid-July to mid-August.

If you plan to be in Paris in July, bring your beach clothes! **Paris Plages,** a month-long festival, turns a bit of the Right Bank into the Riviera. From mid-July to mid-August, the city closes off 3.5km (2 miles) of its quays between the Pont Henri IV and the quai des Tuileries so that people can enjoy the same activities they would at the beach — all but swimming in the swift and dangerous Seine (a pool was added between pont Marie and pont Sully in 2004). There are three "beaches" made from sand, grass, or wooden planks; palm trees and wooden lounge chairs; snack bars and cafes; a climbing wall; trampolines; an area to play boules; and even old-time dance halls known as *guinguettes.* Concerts are organized by the electronics store Fnac, and there are dance and comedy performances as well. Mid-July to mid-August.

On the final day of the three-week-long **Tour de France,** the winner is crowned at the Champs-Elysées (8e). If you plan to attend the celebration, be sure to arrive very early because the crowds are tremendous. You need a special invitation for a seat in the stands near place de la Concorde, but you can see the cyclists farther up the Champs-Elysées and, depending on the route (which changes each year), elsewhere in the city, too. Check the newspapers the day before or log on to www. letour.com. Third Sunday of July.

Since 2003, the **Rock en Seine** (www.rockenseine.com) has been held at the Domaine National de Saint-Cloud, a park just outside of Paris on the Seine. The three-day festival welcomes world-class rock acts from Björk and Beck to Oasis, who famously split up during the 2009 festival (but not a reason to miss it!). Three-day passes generally cost around 100€. End of August.

The **Fête de l'Assomption** celebrates the journey of Mary, Jesus' mother, to heaven after her death. Church services at Notre-Dame are the most popular and colorful on this important French holiday (many stores are closed, and transportation runs on a holiday schedule), and banners are draped over the church's towers to celebrate the day. August 15.

September

One of the largest and most prestigious antiques shows in the world, the **Biennale des Antiquaires** (www.bdafrance.eu), opens to the public in even-numbered years in the Cour Carrée du Louvre (1er), the underground exhibition space connected to the museum. For more information, contact the Paris Convention and Visitors Bureau (☎ **08-92-68-30-00** at a charge of 0.35€ per minute; http://en.parisinfo.com). Early September.

Planning your trip to Paris around September 15? Then be sure to visit the off-limits palaces, churches, and other official buildings that throw open their doors to the public for two days during **Les Journées de Patrimoine (Heritage Days).** Get a list and a map of all the open buildings from the Paris Convention and Visitors Bureau. Weekend closest to September 15.

The annual arts festival, the **Festival d'Automne** (www.festival-automne.com), is recognized throughout Europe for its innovative programming and the high quality of its artists and performers. It's an exciting beginning of the year, so to speak, as it's the first major event after *la rentrée,* when unhappy schoolchildren and equally unhappy parents return to Paris after their frolicking, month-long summer vacations.

The second of two annual **Ready-to-Wear Fashion Shows** takes place in September (see the previous entry under "January").

Since 1998, the growing street party–cum–parade, **Techno Parade** (www.technoparade.fr), brings in over 300,000 viewers to turn out to listen to over 150 DJs celebrate musical freedom with a conscience.

October

More than a half million people visit museums, libraries, swimming pools, churches, and bars and restaurants during **Nuit Blanche** (http://nuitblanche.paris.fr), the French expression for an all-nighter. Open very late or all night for one night, parts of the city become a nighttime art installation with impromptu concerts. Early October.

The wine might not taste that great, but it's all about the celebration of the harvest at Montmartre's one remaining vineyard, Clos Montmartre. Watch as the wine is auctioned off at high prices to benefit local charities during the **Fêtes des Vendanges de Montmartre** (18e; www.fetedesvendangesdemontmartre.com). Locals dress in period costumes, and the streets come alive with music. First or second Saturday of October.

As interesting for browsing as for buying is the **Foire Internationale d'Art Contemporain** (FIAC; www.fiac.com), one of the largest contemporary art fairs in the world. With stands from more than 150 galleries, half of them foreign, the fair takes place at the Parc des Expositions, Porte de Versailles (15e; Métro: Balard or Porte de Versailles). Admission is 28€. Mid- to late October.

November

The **Paris International Photo Fair,** also known simply as Paris Photo (www.parisphoto.fr) is held every year in the Carrousel du Louvre (1er), with more than 100 galleries and publishers exhibiting important works from the 19th century to the present. This also coincides with **Mois de la Photo,** the biennial national photography month, where many museums and galleries have special shows throughout the month. Check listings in the weekly guide *Pariscope* or at http://en.paris info.com.

The French commemorate those who died fighting in both world wars with a wreath-laying ceremony at the Arc de Triomphe (8e; the location of the Tomb of the Unknown Soldier), and veterans sell poppy corsages in memory of **Armistice Day.** November 11.

November in Paris can be awfully gray and chilly, but you'll warm up quickly just after midnight for the annual celebration of the public release of **Beaujolais Nouveau,** a lightweight red wine that is bottled after the fall harvest and meant for immediate consumption as it has a short shelf life. Wine bars and cafes are packed just for the event. Third Thursday of November.

The annual **Lancement des Illuminations des Champs-Elysées,** the lighting of the avenue's Christmas lights, makes for a festive evening, with jazz concerts and an international star to push the button that lights up the avenue. Trees all the way from the Arc de Triomphe (8e) to the Tuileries (1er) are brightly lit through New Year's. Late November.

December

Aside from the light-drenched Champs-Elysées, **the lights and holiday-themed window displays** in the Grands Magasins (Galeries Lafayette and Printemps) are a destination for Parisians and tourists alike, eager to see the sights as they elbow through the crowds to complete their yearly shopping. December.

A very serious event for the French, **Le Grand Tasting** (www.grand tasting.com) is a huge annual wine festival held at the Carrousel du Louvre (1er), where over 100 of the best French wines (as chosen by wine gurus Michel Bettane and Thierry Desseauve) are sampled by some of Paris's top food enthusiasts.

Each year, a different foreign city installs a life-size Christmas manger scene **(La Crèche sur le Parvis)** in the plaza in front of the Hôtel de Ville (City Hall). The crèche is open daily from 10 a.m. to 8 p.m. December 1 to January 3.

Part II
Planning Your Trip to Paris

The 5th Wave   By Rich Tennant

" And how shall I book your flight to Paris -First Class, Coach, or Medieval?"

In this part . . .

*L*ook no further than these chapters to help you plan everything for your trip — from where to stay and how much to spend on traveling successfully with kids to what to do if your wallet has been stolen. Chapter 4 tells you what to expect in each price category so you can plan a workable budget. Chapter 5 gets you to Paris, whether it be by plane, train, automobile, or hovercraft, and discusses the pros and cons of package tours. Chapter 6 takes into account special interests and gives advice to families, seniors, people with disabilities, and gays and lesbians. And in Chapter 7, you get some advice about those last-minute details that can frustrate even the most experienced of travelers.

Chapter 4

Managing Your Money

•••

In This Chapter

▶ Developing a workable budget

▶ Cutting costs — but not the fun

▶ Handling your money

▶ Dealing with a lost or stolen wallet

•••

A good way to budget your trip to Paris is to mentally walk through the journey, from the moment you leave to the minute you get back home, and don't forget to figure in your transportation to and from the airport. Then add in the flight cost (see Chapter 5 on how to fly to Paris for less), the price of getting from the Charles de Gaulle or Orly airport to your hotel, your hotel rate per day, meals, transportation costs, admission prices to museums and the theater, and other entertainment expenses. Add another 25 percent to the total for good measure. You never know when you might stumble across a cute boutique or a *brocante* (a flea market with one-of-a-kind items).

Planning Your Budget

Cities rarely are cheap or expensive across the board; Paris tends to be pricey for dining but more reasonable for accommodations, so booking a good hotel shouldn't be a problem. The following list offers guidelines for what you're likely to spend while in Paris.

✔ **Accommodations:** Before you start shelling out money for lodging, think about how much time you'll actually spend in your room. For between 80€ and 100€ per night, you can rent a clean, functionally furnished hotel room with a private bathroom and cable TV and Wi-Fi. This type of budget room is comfortable and has the basic furnishings and décor; the drawbacks are thin yet serviceable towels and thin bars of packaged soap. (**Hint:** You can buy better soaps in the grocery store or at the chain store Monoprix for just a few euros.)

If you're feeling extravagant and willing to spend 180€ or more, luxury, upper-tier hotels offer more services, such as room service, air-conditioning, and toiletries.

✔ **Transportation:** The Paris Métro, the model for subways around the world since its inauguration in 1900, is one of the best transit systems around in terms of price and efficiency. Getting across town in less than half an hour is no problem, and the cost is lower when you purchase one of several available discount tickets or a *carnet* (booklet) of ten tickets. (See Chapter 8 for options and prices.)

If navigating a maze of narrow and twisted one-way streets, dodging angry taxis drivers in chaotic traffic circles, and never being able to find a parking space appeal to you, then by all means rent a car in Paris. Otherwise, I strongly suggest relying on taxis and the city transit. Even many Parisians refuse to drive in their own city! If you want to rent a car to see other parts of France or make a day trip outside of Paris, rent on your way out of the city. (See Chapter 7 for addresses and phone numbers of car-rental agencies in Paris.)

✔ **Restaurants:** The French consider dining out one of the finer joys in life, and they pay for it. You can expect to do the same. An average Parisian dining experience — a three-course dinner in a popular upscale restaurant — runs about 50€ to 80€ per person.

You can find establishments serving satisfying two-course meals for as little as 12€ and ethnic eateries and sandwich shops that are as tasty as they are economical. Dining reasonably in Paris isn't impossible when you know where to look. Chapter 10 helps you discover just that.

✔ **Attractions:** Entry fees to museums and other sights can add up quickly; find money-saving advice in Chapter 11, after which making a list of must-dos will give you a feel for how much money to set aside.

✔ **Shopping:** Paris is one of the world's best places to shop. Store owners arrange their wares in such enticing window displays (with prices) that you'll find plenty to buy in no time. You can find some great deals during *les soldes* (the semiannual sales in January and July), but remember that a steep 19.6 percent value-added tax (VAT or TVA) is added to most goods. If you live outside the European Union, you're entitled to get back part of the tax if you meet certain requirements (see Chapter 12 for more information).

✔ **Nightlife:** Don't forgo the spectacles at the Lido or Moulin Rouge if you've always wanted to see them — just know beforehand that you'll be charged a small fortune for entry and alcoholic beverages. Plan on seeing the show without dinner, and exit with a wallet that isn't quite as light as it otherwise would be. Budget big, too, especially when you plan to visit clubs and other nightspots; nightclubs usually have covers (though the first drink is generally included) and bars are rarely cheap. You can save money for ballet, opera, and plays at the national theaters by buying half-price or same-day tickets. (See Chapters 15 and 16 for more information.)

Table 4-1 gives you approximate prices for some common expenses.

Table 4-1	What Things Cost in Paris
Item	*Euro*
Taxi from Charles de Gaulle Airport to the city center (depending on traffic)	50€
Taxi from Orly Airport to the city center	40€
Public transportation for an average trip on the Métro within the city (from a Métro *carnet* of ten)	1.20€
Glass of wine	6€
Coca-Cola (at a cafe)	3.50€
Cup of coffee (espresso)	2€
Admission to the Louvre	9.50€
Movie ticket	9€
Concert ticket (at the Palais Garnier)	5€–150€

Cutting Costs

One of the primary ways to save money is to book a package tour. For many destinations, you can book airfare, hotel, ground transportation, and even some sightseeing just by making one call to a travel agent or searching the Internet, for a lot less than if you tried to put the trip together yourself. (See Chapter 5 for specific companies to call.)

I can't repeat it enough: Always ask for discount rates. Membership in AAA, AARP, frequent-flyer plans, trade unions, or other groups may qualify you for savings on car rentals, plane tickets, hotel rooms, even meals. Ask about everything — you may be pleasantly surprised.

The following sections offer additional cost-cutting strategies for various expenses.

Accommodations

- **Book your hotel room early.** Rooms at the best prices fill up quickly, especially in the fall.

- **Negotiate the room price, especially in the low season.** It never hurts to ask for discounts either: Ask for a discount if you're 60 or over or a student. Ask for a discount when you're staying three days or more (even if you're not a senior or a student).

- **Check the Web for specials.** Most Parisian hotels have their own Web sites and offer promotions, especially for stays of three days or longer.

✔ **Reserve a room with a kitchen.** It may not seem like much of a vacation if you cook your own meals and wash your own dishes, but you can save a lot of money by not eating in restaurants three times a day. Even if you make only breakfast and pack an occasional bag lunch, you can save a little extra cash for souvenirs and gifts for your family and friends back home. Shopping the open-air markets and grocery stores offers a fun peek into the French way of life.

✔ **Rent an apartment instead of staying in a hotel.** Renting a Paris apartment can be surprisingly cheap, and apartment-rental services flourish online. You save money by eating more meals in the apartment, and you experience a little of what it's like to live like a resident of Paris. (See Chapter 9 for specific rental agencies.)

✔ **Consider a housing swap.** If you have a house in a desirable locale for French tourists (in a big city or near a national park), you may just be able to arrange a mutually beneficial arrangement — for free. (See Chapter 9 for details.)

Transportation

✔ **Fly during the week rather than on weekends.** Many airlines charge slightly less if you fly on weekdays.

✔ **Travel during the *off season* (also called the *low season*), (the period from approximately October to April).**

✔ **Pack light so that you can take the cheapest way into the city from the airport and won't have to worry about lugging around heavy bags.** You can save around 38€ by taking a train or bus instead of a cab from Charles de Gaulle Airport and about 32€ from Orly.

✔ **While in Paris, use the bus or Métro or walk.**

✔ **Buy a *carnet* of ten Métro tickets at a time.** A single ticket costs 1.70€, but if you plan on staying a few days, a *carnet* (pack of ten) costs only 12€. Better yet, if you know you're going to be in Paris one or two days, buy a **Paris Visite** pass, which is good for unlimited subway and bus travel; at 9€ for one day or 15€ for two days (kids 4–11 are half-price; kids 3 and under ride free), it's a good deal. If you'll be in Paris three or more days, your best bet is the **Navigo** weekly pass. It costs 18€ for zones 1 and 2 (Paris and some of the suburbs) and 24€ for zones 1 through 3 (Paris and suburbs, including Disneyland). You'll need to provide a passport-size photo (or snap one at one of the photo booths in major train and Métro stations for 5€). (See Chapter 8 for more details.)

Restaurants

✔ **Make lunch your main meal.** Many restaurants offer great deals on a *prix fixe* (fixed price) lunch or offer a *formule* (daily special) of appetizer, main course, and dessert that can often be cheaper than ordering off the regular menu. After two or three courses at midday, you won't want a big dinner.

✔ **Eat outside the box.** Look for restaurants away from touristy areas, like in the ninth and tenth *arrondissements,* where the good chow isn't priced at a premium. Sandwiches from *boulangeries* and crêpes provide an excellent and filling meal.

✔ **Try the ethnic neighborhoods.** You can get terrific Chinese and Vietnamese foods in the 13th *arrondissement* between the place d'Italie and the Porte de Choisy; the 10e, 18e, and 20e have restaurants with North African, Turkish, Vietnamese, and Thai menus. Couscous is on the menu at many restaurants and usually is an inexpensive offering, and falafel stands abound in the Marais (3e and 4e).

✔ **Keep in mind that the *plat du jour* (daily entree special) usually is the cheapest main dish at a budget restaurant.**

✔ **Remember that wine is cheaper than soda.** Some mineral waters, likewise, are less expensive than others. Ask for *une carafe d'eau* (oon kar-*ahf* doh; tap water), which is free.

✔ **If you're just having drinks or coffee, do it standing at the bar.** You pay twice as much when you're seated at a table.

✔ **Know the tipping rules.** Most restaurants include the gratuity in the bill. Look for *service compris* on your bill, which means 15 percent has been added already. It's customary to leave an extra 5 percent if the service was good.

Attractions, shopping, and nightlife

✔ **If you plan to visit two or three museums a day for multiple days, buy the Paris Museum Pass.** It's offered in three versions: a two-consecutive-day pass (32€), a four-consecutive-day pass (48€), and a six-consecutive-day pass (64€). It's a great deal if you plan to visit many museums; plus, it allows you to skip long lines. (See Chapter 11 for more information.)

✔ **Take advantage of the reduced admission fees at museums.** The reduced prices usually apply after 3 p.m. (at the Louvre, it's after 6 p.m.) and all day Sunday. Remember that on the first Sunday of every month, admission to national museums is free.

✔ **For discounts on fashion, try the rue Saint-Placide in the 6th *arrondissement* and rue d'Alésia in the 14th.** You find plenty of overstock and *dégriffe* (clothes with labels removed) items on this street near Le Bon Marché department store (where clothes are decidedly *not* cheap). You can also find stylish but inexpensive clothing at Monoprix stores located all over the city.

✔ **Buy half-price theater and other performance tickets.** You can find same-day half-price tickets at one of the kiosks by La Madeleine or at the Gare Montparnasse. The kiosks are little huts with panels indicating if the performance is sold out (symbolized by a little red man) or if tickets are still available (a little green man). (See "Saving money on tickets," in Chapter 15 for more information.)

✔ **Avoid going to clubs on weekends.** Some clubs are cheaper than others, and some are cheaper during the week. Many allow women in free until a certain time (usually 11 p.m.).

Handling Money

The euro, the single European currency for much of the European Union, became the official currency of France and 11 other participating countries on January 1, 1999, but it didn't go into general circulation until January 1, 2002. The old currency, the French franc, disappeared into history on March 1, 2002. Exchange rates of participating countries are locked into a common currency fluctuated against the dollar.

Converting to euros

Frommer's lists exact prices in the local currency. The currency conversions quoted in Table 4-2, above, were correct at press time. However, rates fluctuate, so before departing consult a currency exchange website such as www.oanda.com/currency/converter to check up-to-the-minute rates.

Table 4-2 The Value of the Euro vs. Other Popular Currencies

Euro (€)	Aus$	Can$	NZ$	UK £	US$
€1	A$1.35	C$1.35	NZ$1.75	£0.85	$1.34

You can withdraw euros at any ATM in Paris, and ATMs are everywhere and open 24 hours. Find them — they're outside nearly every bank, in major department stores, airports, and train stations. MasterCard and/or Cirrus cards can be used at any ATM that displays the MasterCard and/or Cirrus marks. Visa and/or PLUS can also be used at ATMs displaying Visa and PLUS signs.

You won't be able to check your balance or transfer funds between accounts, so keep track of your withdrawals while you travel.

Remember that every time you withdraw cash from an ATM, your bank hits you with a fee, sometimes as much as $5. (Check how much your bank charges before leaving home.) On top of this fee, the bank from which you withdraw cash may also include its own fee. For this reason, taking out larger amounts of money every two to three days makes more sense than more frequent withdrawals of smaller amounts. Likewise, remember that banks place limits on the amount of money you can take out per day, usually between 300€ and 500€. This number may be adjustable; call your bank to find out.

Some U.S. banks have relationships or agreements with French banks, allowing their customers to withdraw euros from French ATMs without any transaction fees. Bank of America, for example, allows unlimited free withdrawal from BNP Paribas ATMs and may allow you to withdraw up to 1,000€. HSBC has its own machines dotted throughout Paris that can be used free of charge (and even be used to check your balance). Before leaving call your bank's customer service department to find out what kind of international services they offer.

Pulling out your plastic: Using credit cards

MasterCard and Visa are accepted at nearly any establishment that takes credit cards in Paris. But American Express and Diners Club aren't widely accepted at small restaurants, shops, or budget hotels in Paris or the rest of the country.

Refer to your card by the name of the company (Visa, American Express, and so on), rather than as a *carte de credit* because the term *credit card* doesn't translate into French correctly.

Remember that you pay interest on cash advances on your credit card from the moment you receive the cash. And, many credit card companies now tack on additional fees for foreign-currency transactions — sometimes up to 4 percent, on top of the 1 percent service charge that MasterCard and Visa charge. If you don't know how much your credit card charges for currency conversion, contact a company representative.

Going the way of the dinosaur: The extinction of traveler's checks

These days, there's no need to waste valuable time standing in long lines at the American Express office or in search of *bureaux de change* to cash traveler's checks. Simply use your ATM card to withdraw the money you need. Relatively few banks in Paris exchange currency or cash traveler's checks; they prefer to send visitors to *bureaux de change* in touristy areas that charge a hefty fee.

You can cash traveler's checks at **American Express,** 11 rue Scribe, 9e (☎ 01-53-30-99-00; Métro: Auber or Opéra); **Travelex,** 45 av Opéra, 2e (☎ 01-42-96-18-17; Métro: Tuileries); or **Global Change,** 240 rue de Rivoli, 1er (☎ 01-42-36-14-82).

Dealing with a Lost or Stolen Wallet

Every credit card company has an emergency international number that you can call if your wallet or purse is stolen. In the unlikely event that this happens, be sure to block charges against your credit card account immediately. Your credit card company may be able to wire you a cash advance off your credit card immediately and, in many places, can deliver an emergency credit card in a day or two. Call ☎ **0-800-90-11-79** if you've lost or had your **Visa** card stolen. **American Express** card and traveler's check holders in France can call collect to the United States at ☎ **336-393-1111** for money and lost card emergencies. For **MasterCard,** call ☎ **0-800-90-13-87.**

If your traveler's checks are lost or stolen, you need to be able to report exactly which checks are gone in order to get them replaced. The check issuer can tell you where to pick up the new checks.

Here's what to do if your pocket has been picked: First, make a police report as soon as possible. There are three or four *commissariats* (police stations) in each *arrondissement;* the train stations also have small police stations. Go to the station closest to where the crime took place. If you were robbed in the subway, however, you can go to any police station. You will receive a *Récépissé de Déclaration de Perte ou de Vol* (Receipt for Declaration of Loss or Theft). If you've lost your passport, identification documents, and/or valuables, you'll be given separate receipts — one for your papers *(pièces d'identité)* and one for your valuables. The police receipts are sometimes necessary in applying for the replacement of airline tickets, **Eurail** passes (formerly known as the Europass), passports, and traveler's checks or for supporting insurance claims.

The report must be made in person and most police stations have English-speaking personnel. Call the **U.S. Embassy** (☎ **01-43-12-22-22**) for assistance in interpreting if you have difficulty being understood.

Though it's unlikely that the police will recover your lost or stolen items, contact the police and file a report anyway — you may need it for credit card or insurance purposes later.

Finally, you can visit the lost-and-found office, run by the French police, to verify whether your belongings were returned: **Centre des Objets trouvés de la Prefecture de Police de Paris,** 36 rue des Morillons, 75015 (☎ **08-21-00-25-25** at a charge of 0.10€ per minute; Métro: Convention), open Monday through Thursday 8:30 a.m. to 5 p.m., Friday 8:30 a.m. to 4:30 p.m.

Chapter 5

Getting to Paris

- -

In This Chapter

▶ Identifying which airlines fly to Paris
▶ Finding the best fare
▶ Arriving by train or ferry
▶ Choosing a package tour

- -

*T*hough the Internet has drastically changed travel planning, you still need to decide what kind of travel best suits you. This chapter will make you an expert in no time and well able to get yourself to Paris simply and easily.

Flying to Paris

Though Paris has two major airports — **Charles de Gaulle** and **Orly** — most non-European visitors land at the larger, busier, and more modern Charles de Gaulle. Its international airport code is CDG, and it's sometimes referred to as Roissy–Charles de Gaulle. Charles de Gaulle is located 23km (15 miles) northeast of downtown Paris in a town called Roissy. Orly Airport is located 14km (8½ miles) south of the city; its airport code is ORY. Web sites and phone numbers for the major airlines serving Paris are in the list that follows. The Web sites offer schedules, flight bookings, and package tours. Most allow you to sign up for e-mail alerts that list weekend deals and other late-breaking bargains.

The following airlines fly to Paris from the United States and Canada:

✔ **Aer Lingus** (☎ 800-474-7424; www.aerlingus.com) often has below-market fares and flies from Boston, Chicago, and New York to Paris, with a stopover in Dublin.

✔ **Air Canada** (☎ 888-247-2262; www.aircanada.ca) flies direct to Paris from Chicago, Montréal, Quebec City, Toronto, and Washington, D.C.

✔ **Air France** (☎ 800-237-2747; www.airfrance.com) flies direct from Atlanta, Boston, Chicago, Cincinnati, Detroit, Houston, Los Angeles, Miami, Minneapolis, Newark, New York, Philadelphia, Pittsburgh, Salt Lake City, San Francisco, Seattle, and Washington, D.C.

- ✔ **Air Tahiti Nui** (☎ 877-824-4846; www.airtahitinui-usa.com) flies from Los Angeles.

- ✔ **American Airlines** (☎ 800-433-7300; www.aa.com) flies direct from Boston, Chicago, Dallas, Miami, and New York.

- ✔ **British Airways** (☎ 800-247-9297; www.britishairways.com) flies to Paris directly from Newark, New York, and Washington, D.C. With a layover in London, it flies from Atlanta, Baltimore, Boston, Chicago, Dallas, Denver, Houston, Las Vegas, Los Angeles, Miami, Montreal, Orlando, Philadelphia, Phoenix, San Francisco, Seattle, and Toronto.

- ✔ **Continental Airlines** (☎ 800-523-3273; www.continental.com) flies direct to Paris from Houston and Newark.

- ✔ **Delta Air Lines** (☎ 800-221-1212; www.delta.com) flies direct from Atlanta, Cincinnati, Minneapolis, New York, and Salt Lake City. It shares flights with Air France from Boston, Chicago, Cincinnati, Detroit, Houston, Los Angeles, Philadelphia, San Francisco, Seattle, and Washington, D.C.

- ✔ **Icelandair** (☎ 800-223-5500; www.icelandair.com) flies to Paris with a layover in Reykjavik from Boston, Minneapolis, New York, Orlando, Seattle, and Toronto.

- ✔ **United Airlines** (☎ 800-864-8331; www.united.com) flies direct from Charlotte, Chicago, Philadelphia, and Washington, D.C.

- ✔ **US Airways** (☎ 800-428-4322; www.usairways.com) flies direct from Charlotte, Los Angeles, Miami, and Philadelphia.

The following airlines fly to Paris from the United Kingdom:

- ✔ **Air France** (☎ 0870-142-4-343; www.airfrance.co.uk) flies from numerous cities, including Aberdeen, Birmingham, Bristol, Cardiff, Edinburgh, Glasgow, Leeds, London, and Manchester.

- ✔ **British Airways** (☎ 0870-850-9-850; www.britishairways.com) flies direct to Paris from London and with a layover in London from Edinburgh, Glasgow, and Manchester.

- ✔ **easyJet** (☎ 0871-244-2366; www.easyjet.com) flies from Belfast, Bristol, Glasgow, Edinburgh, Liverpool, London, Luton, and New Castle.

The following airlines fly to Paris from Australia and New Zealand:

- ✔ **Qantas** (☎ 13-13-13 in Australia; www.qantas.com.au) flies from Sydney.

- ✔ **Singapore Airlines** (☎ 13-10-11 in Australia, ☎ 0800-808-909 in New Zealand; www.singaporeairlines.com) flies from Auckland and Sydney.

Getting the best deal on your airfare

Though every airline offers virtually the same product, prices can vary by hundreds of dollars. Competition among the major U.S. airlines is unlike that of any other industry.

Business travelers who need the flexibility to buy their tickets at the last minute and change their itineraries at a moment's notice — and who want to get home before the weekend — pay the premium rate, known as the *full fare.* If you're lucky enough to fly to Paris this way, more power to you. It certainly isn't cheap! But if you can book your ticket far in advance, stay over Saturday night, and are willing to travel midweek (Tues–Thurs), you can qualify for the least-expensive price — usually a fraction of the full fare. On most flights, even the shortest hops within the United States, the full fare is close to $1,000 or more, but a 7- or 14-day advance-purchase ticket may cost a good bit less. Obviously, planning ahead pays.

The airlines also periodically hold sales, in which they lower the prices on their most popular routes. These fares have advance-purchase requirements and date-of-travel restrictions and may be nonrefundable, but you can't beat the prices. As you plan your vacation, keep your eyes open for these sales, which tend to take place in seasons of low travel volume (Nov, Jan–Apr). You almost never see a sale around the peak summer vacation months of July and August, or around Thanksgiving or Christmas, when many people fly, regardless of the fare they have to pay.

Consolidators, also known as *bucket shops,* negotiate bulk quantities of airline tickets and sell them at a discount. They're great sources for international tickets, although they usually can't beat the Internet on fares within North America (some say that early consolidator Web sites paved the way for the numerous current travel Web sites available today). Start by looking in Sunday newspaper travel sections; their ads are usually formatted to look like classified ads. U.S. travelers should focus on *The New York Times,* the *Los Angeles Times,* and *The Miami Herald.*

Several reliable consolidators are worldwide and available on the Web. **STA Travel** (☎ **800-781-4040;** www.statravel.com), the world's leader in student travel, offers good fares for travelers no matter your age. **StudentUniverse.com** (☎ **800-272-9676**) also offers discounts to students and faculty. **Flights.com** (☎ **201-541-3826** for air travel originating in the U.S. and Canada) started in Europe and has excellent fares worldwide, particularly to Europe. **OneTravel.com** (☎ **866-794-6049**) is a lesser-known source of especially cheap consolidator prices, and the site **Lowestfare.com** (☎ **800-FLY-CHEAP**) is owned by Priceline.com. Montreal-based **AirTicketsDirect.com** (☎ **888-858-8884**) has been operating since 1991.

Booking your ticket online

Booking tickets online is an ever-changing art. The most popular online travel agencies are **Expedia** (www.expedia.com), **Orbitz** (www.orbitz.com), and **Travelocity** (www.travelocity.com). (Canadian travelers should try www.expedia.ca and www.travelocity.ca; U.K. residents can go for www.expedia.co.uk and www.opodo.co.uk.) Other sites include **Cheapflights.com, CheapTickets.com,** and **Opodo** (www.opodo.com), which is a European travel Web site. I suggest using **Kayak** (www.kayak.com) or **SideStep** (www.sidestep.com) to book tickets; these sites consolidate and search all the flights and deals from the major travel sites as well as the booking sites of the actual airlines. Each of the big sites has business deals with the airlines and may offer different fares on the same flights, so shopping around is wise. Expedia, Kayak, Orbitz, and Travelocity will also send you an **e-mail notification** when a cheap fare becomes available to your favorite destination.

If you're willing to give up some control over your flight details, use **Priceline's** (www.priceline.com) *opaque* fare service. I say "opaque" because it offers rock-bottom prices in exchange for travel on a mystery airline at a mysterious time of day, often with a mysterious change of planes en route (sometimes more than one change of planes). The mystery airlines are all major, well-known carriers, but your chances of getting a 6 a.m. or 11 p.m. flight are pretty high. Priceline also has nonopaque service; you can pick exact flights, times, and airlines from a list of offers.

Great **last-minute deals** are also available directly from the airlines themselves. Each week, the airline sends you a list of discounted flights, usually leaving the upcoming Friday or Saturday and returning the following Monday or Tuesday. Sign up for weekly e-mail alerts at airline Web sites or check megasites that compile comprehensive lists of last-minute specials, such as **Smarter Travel** (www.smartertravel.com). For last-minute trips, **lastminute.com** often has better deals than the major-label sites.

Arriving by Other Means

If you're arriving in Paris by **train** from Belgium, northern Germany, or London, you disembark in the **Gare du Nord** (10e). Trains from Normandy come into the **Gare Saint-Lazare** (8e), in northwestern Paris near Galeries Lafayette and Opéra Garnier. Trains from western France (Bordeaux, Brittany, Chartres, Versailles) head to the **Gare de Montparnasse** (14e); those from the southwest (the Loire Valley, Pyrenees, Spain) arrive at the **Gare d'Austerlitz** (13e), near the Jardin des Plantes. Those from the south and southeast (Geneva, Italy, Lyon, the Riviera) pull in at the **Gare de Lyon** (12e). Trains coming from Alsace and eastern France, Luxembourg, southern Germany, and Zurich arrive at the **Gare de l'Est** (10e). All train stations connect to Métro stations with the same name. All Paris train stations are located within the first 15 *arrondissements* and are easily accessible.

Buses connect Paris to most major European cities and the most well-known of the companies are **Eurolines.** There are no U.S. offices, so you should make bus transportation arrangements after arriving in Europe. From outside France, contact **Eurolines** (☎ **08-92-89-90-91,** 0.35€ per minute; www.eurolines.com); from Paris, call the local number (☎ **01-41-86-24-24**) or visit the offices in the Latin Quarter, place de Clichy, or at the **Gare Routière Internationale (International Bus Terminal)** in the suburb of Bagnolet, where all the international buses pull in. The station is located just across the *périphérique* (ring road) from the Gallieni Métro station. To get into Paris proper, take line no. 3 and change buses according to your final destination.

If you're arriving in Paris from the United Kingdom, about a dozen companies run **hydrofoil, ferry,** and **hovercraft** across the English Channel, or *La Manche* (pronounced la mahnsh; literally: the sleeve), as the French say. Services operate daily and most carry cars. Hovercraft and hydrofoils make the trip across the channel in about 40 minutes; the shortest ferry route between Dover and Calais is about 1½ hours. The major routes are between Dover and Calais and Folkestone and Boulogne (about 12 trips per day). Depending on weather conditions, prices and timetables can vary. You can check schedules and reserve space on ferries on **Ferrybooker.com** (www.ferrybooker.com). Special fares at press time included Dover to Calais for 42€ per car with up to five passengers.

This is not the best way to get to Paris from the United Kingdom; the entire trip from London to Dover by train, then from Dover to Calais by ferry, and Calais to Paris by train takes about 11 hours. If you still want to go this way, be sure to make reservations — the ferries are crowded.

The **Channel Tunnel** (known as the Chunnel) opened in 1994, and the popularity of its Eurostar train service has had the happy effect of driving down prices on all cross-channel transport. This remarkable engineering feat means that if you hop aboard the Eurostar in Britain, you can be eating a meal in France two to four hours later. You can purchase tickets in advance or at the station. Eurostar tickets start around 45€ one-way off-season if you book at least seven days in advance; however, expect to pay at least twice as much for last-minute purchases, or from April through late July, when prices rise. Eurostar transports passengers only (no vehicles) between Ashford (in Kent) or London and Brussels, Calais, Lille, Paris, and beyond. For more information on Eurostar, including online booking, go to www.eurostar.com. For special package information in the United States, visit Rail Europe (www.raileurope.com).

A separate company known as **Eurotunnel** (☎ **08-705-35-35-35** in the U.K., ☎ **08-10-63-03-04** in France; www.eurotunnel.com) transports passengers with their cars between Folkestone in the United Kingdom and Calais in France in under an hour. Car prices start at £44 for a round-trip day trip and rise to £199 for a round-trip journey longer than five days. One-way prices start at £53.

Joining an Escorted Tour

On escorted tours, the tour company takes care of all the details, and tells you what to expect at each leg of your journey. You know your costs upfront, and you don't get many surprises. Escorted tours can take you to the maximum number of sights in the minimum amount of time with the least amount of hassle.

It's the least independent way to travel, but some travelers find escorted tours liberating — no hassles with public transportation, no deciphering maps, and the comfort of knowing what you're getting. Others fervently despise escorted group tours, because they feel as if they're being herded from one sight to the next, missing the element of surprise and individuality that independent travel affords.

If you decide to go with an escorted tour, I *strongly* recommend purchasing travel insurance, especially if the tour operator requires payment upfront. But don't buy insurance from the tour operator! If the tour operator doesn't fulfill its obligation to provide you with the vacation you paid for, there's no reason to think that it'll fulfill its insurance obligations either. Get travel insurance through an independent agency. (For more about the ins and outs of travel insurance, see Chapter 7.)

When choosing an escorted tour, along with finding out whether you have to put down a deposit and when final payment is due, ask a few simple questions before you buy:

- ✔ **What is the cancellation policy?** Will the tour operator cancel the trip if it doesn't get enough people? How late can you cancel if you're unable to go? Do you get a refund if you cancel? If the tour operator cancels?

- ✔ **How jam-packed is the schedule?** Does the tour schedule try to fit 25 hours into a 24-hour day, or does it give you ample time to relax by the pool or shop? If getting up at 7 a.m. every day and not returning to your hotel until 6 or 7 p.m. sounds like a grind, certain escorted tours may not be for you.

- ✔ **How large is the group?** The smaller the group, the less time you spend waiting for people to get on and off the bus. Tour operators may be evasive about this, because they may not know the exact size of the group until everybody has made reservations, but they should be able to give you a rough estimate.

- ✔ **Is there a minimum group size?** Some tours have a minimum group size, and the tour operator may cancel the tour if it doesn't book enough people. If a quota exists, find out what it is and how close they are to reaching it. Again, tour operators may be evasive in their answers, but the information may help you select a tour that's sure to happen.

✔ **What exactly is included?** Don't assume anything. You may have to pay to get yourself to and from the airport. A box lunch may be included in an excursion, but drinks may be extra. Beer may be included but not wine. Find out how much flexibility you have: Can you opt out of certain activities, or does the bus leave once a day, with no exceptions? Are all your meals planned in advance? Can you choose your entree at dinner, or does everybody get the same chicken cutlet?

Depending on your recreational passions, I recommend one of the following tour companies:

✔ **French Experience (☎ 800-283-7262;** www.frenchexperience. com) has been around since 1983 and offers several fly/drive programs through different regions of France (the quoted price includes airfare and a rental car). You can specify the type and price level of hotels you want. The agency arranges the car rental in advance, and the rest is up to you.

✔ Perhaps the most instantly recognizable tour operator in the world, **American Express Vacations (☎ 800-335-3342;** www.american expressvacations.com) has more-comprehensive offerings than those of other companies and includes package tours and independent stays.

Choosing a Package Tour

For lots of destinations, package tours can be a smart way to go. In many cases, a package tour that includes airfare, hotel, and transportation to and from the airport costs less than the hotel alone on a tour you book yourself. That's because packages are sold in bulk to tour operators who then resell them to the public. It's a bit like buying your vacation at a Costco or Sam's Club — except the tour operator is the one who buys the 1,000-count box of garbage bags and resells them ten at a time.

Package tours can vary as much as those garbage bags, too. Some offer a better class of hotels than others; others provide the same hotels for lower prices, while others exclude children. Some book flights on scheduled airlines; others sell charters. In some packages, your choice of accommodations and travel days may be limited. Some let you choose between escorted vacations and independent vacations; others allow you to add on just a few excursions or escorted day trips (also at discounted prices) without booking an entirely escorted tour.

To find package tours, check out the travel section of your local Sunday newspaper or the ads in the back of national travel magazines such as *Travel + Leisure, National Geographic Traveler,* and *Condé Nast Traveler.*

Air France Holidays (☎ 800-2-FRANCE; www.airfranceholidays.
com) has France-specific package tours; their six-night Paris vacation
starts at around $1,000 per person and includes airfare, hotel, breakfast,
and a Seine River cruise. Options such as a private guided tour are
available for additional prices. **Liberty Travel** (☎ 888-271-1584; www.
libertytravel.com) is one of the biggest packagers in the Northeast
and usually boasts a full-page ad in Sunday papers.

Another good source of package deals is the airlines themselves. Most
major airlines offer air/land packages, including **American Airlines
Vacations** (☎ 800-321-2121; www.aavacations.com), **Continental
Airlines Vacations** (☎ 800-301-3800; www.covacations.com), **Delta
Vacations** (☎ 800-654-6559; www.deltavacations.com), and **United
Vacations** (☎ 888-854-3899; www.unitedvacations.com). Several
big **online travel agencies** — Expedia, lastminute.com, Orbitz, and
Travelocity — also do a brisk business in packages. If you're unsure
about the pedigree of a smaller packager, check with the Better Business
Bureau in the city where the company is based, or go to www.bbb.org.
If a packager won't tell you where it's based, don't fly with them.

Chapter 6

Catering to Special Travel Needs or Interests

- -

In This Chapter

▶ Taking the family along

▶ Getting discounts for seniors

▶ Locating wheelchair-accessible attractions and accommodations

▶ Identifying resources for gay and lesbian travelers

- -

*I*t seems unimaginable that there once was a time when people dressed up for a trip through the air and walked onto a plane unhindered. Pleasant flight attendants brought free and copious drinks and snacks, though rampant cigarette smoke made breathing a challenge. These days, no one finds traveling a piece of cake, but for some people it poses more challenges. If you're bringing your family to Paris, or you have a disability and are wondering how to pilot yourself down cobblestone streets and winding Métro corridors, if you're a senior citizen, or you want to see the gay side of Paris, this is the chapter for you.

Taking the Family Along

Luckily for grownups, Paris is one of the best places in the world to travel with kids. There are parks and playgrounds throughout the city, as well as kid-catering sights and museums, puppet shows, boat rides, bike tours, and lots of delicious sweets and foods that they'll undoubtedly love (if you don't allow chocolate for breakfast at home, Paris is a great place to make an exception). Best of all, the French are especially welcoming to children. It doesn't hurt that you're less than an hour away from Disneyland Paris in the suburb of Marne-la-Vallée, easily accessible by train or bus. Paris is just as safe as, if not safer than, most big American cities. Though taking your children thousands of miles away may seem at times like an insurmountable challenge, it can be immensely rewarding, giving you new ways of seeing the world through younger eyes.

Look for good family-oriented vacation advice on the Internet from sites like **Family Travel Forum** (www.familytravelforum.com), a comprehensive site with customized trip planning and discussion boards; the award-winning **Family Travel Network** (www.familytravelnetwork.com), which offers travel features, deals, and tips; **TravelWithYourKids** (www.travelwithyourkids.com), which was started by parents whose daughters were born abroad and is a clearinghouse for information on traveling (and even moving) abroad with your children from those who have been there; and **Family Travel Files** (www.thefamily travelfiles.com), which provides an online magazine and a directory of off-the-beaten-path tours and tour operators for families.

If you plan your trip well in advance, your kids may get a kick out of learning the language from one of the many French-language instructional DVDs on the market.

Such books as Ludwig Bemelmans's *Madeline* series, Albert Lamorisse's *The Red Balloon,* and Kay Thompson's *Eloise in Paris* are great for kids 8 and under. Older teens may appreciate Ernest Hemingway's *A Moveable Feast* (Scribner paperback reissue), Victor Hugo's *Les Misérables,* Mark Twain's *Innocents Abroad,* Rose Tremain's *The Way I Found Her* (Washington Square Press paperback reprint), and Dan Brown's *The Da Vinci Code* (Anchor). All kids will probably like the popular French comic-book series *The Adventures of Asterix,* by René Goscinny and Albert Uderzo (translated into English and available at bookstores), or *The Adventures of Tintin,* who is, admittedly, Belgian but still great fun and dear to the French.

Children 17 and under are admitted free to France's national museums (although not necessarily to Paris's city museums), and some attractions offer a lower rate for families of four or more. When purchasing tickets, ask if there is a *carte famille nombreuses* (kart fam-*ee* nohm-*brooz;* family rate).

The following bargains will require some skill in the French language. If you don't understand French, you may want to recruit someone who does because these are terrific bargains. Kids 11 and under traveling by rail through France can use the **Carte Enfant Plus,** a children's rail pass. It's available at any SNCF (French National Railroads) station or, for non-Americans, online at www.tgv-europe.com/en. If you can read French, the direct site can be found at www.enfantplus-sncf.com.) You can purchase these cards in France at any French train station. The pass offers up to a 50 percent discount for the child and one to four adult travel companions on non-TGV (Train Grand Vitesse, France's high-speed train) mainline trains in off-peak periods, and 25 percent off on TGV trains (except overnight trains) and mainline trains during peak travel times. The pass costs 70€, and you can reserve it online right before you leave and pick it up at any Paris train station within the time limit (usually two days). Similarly, a discount travel card is available for those ages 12 to 25 called **Carte 12-25** (www.12-25-sncf.com). For 49€, a cardholder is entitled to up to 60 percent discounts on all TGV and non-TGV rail services and couchette (sleeping car) berths. A guaranteed 25 percent reduction is available on all TGV rail services and couchette berths on non-TGV mainline services at all times where no seats are available at the 50 percent reduction rate. A passport photo must be presented when applying for these cards. *Note:* To find out where to buy or pick up these passes in any of Paris's major train stations, go to their *Acceuil* (Welcome) information kiosk and have an English-speaking representative direct you.

When traveling with a baby, you can arrange ahead of time for such necessities as a crib and bottle warmer at your hotel and, if you're driving, a car seat (small children are prohibited from riding in the front seat). Find out whether your hotel stocks baby food; if it doesn't, take some with you for your first day, but then plan to buy some. Plenty of choices are available, from Nestlé to Naturalia.

Transportation in Paris isn't as stroller-friendly as in the United States. Be prepared to lift your child out of the stroller when boarding buses, climbing up and down stairs, and/or walking long distances in some Métro subway stations. The upside of all this is that once you get to your destination, you and your child can stroll and play in some of the world's prettiest parks and gardens.

And when you need some kid-free time, consider visiting the basement bulletin board of the **American Church,** 65 quai d'Orsay, 7e (☎ **01-45-62-05-00;** Métro: Invalides), where English-speaking (often American) students post notices offering baby-sitting services. Or try one of the following agencies, which employ some English-speaking baby sitters: **Allô Maman Dépannage** (☎ **01-34-05-00-47**) or **Kid Services** (☎ **08-20-00-02-30** at a charge of 0.10€ per minute); specify when calling that you need a sitter who speaks English.

The following books are full of good, general advice that can apply to travel anywhere: *Travels with Baby: The Ultimate Guide for Planning Trips with Babies, Toddlers, and Preschool-Age Children,* by Shelly Rivoli (Travels with Baby Books); *How to Take Great Trips with Your Kids* by Sanford Portnoy (The Harvard Common Press); *Trouble-Free Travel With Children: Over 700 Helpful Hints for Parents on the Go,* by Vicki Lansky (Book Peddlers); and *Adventuring with Children: An Inspirational Guide to World Travel and the Outdoors,* by Nan Jeffrey (Avalon House).

Finally, a word of advice: Although French people love kids and welcome them just about anywhere, they expect them to be well mannered. Proper behavior is expected everywhere, but especially in restaurants and museums — this means no loud or disturbing yelling, good table manners, and saying *s'il vous plait* and *merci beaucoup.* French children are taught at an early age to behave appropriately in these settings, and French adults expect the same from your kids.

Making Age Work for You: Tips for Seniors

Mention that you're a senior citizen when you first make your travel reservations; you may be entitled to some discounts before you even get to Paris. When you arrive in Paris, don't be shy about asking for senior discounts (in French, a senior is *une personne âgée, une personne du troisième âge,* or simply *un senior*), and always carry a form of identification that shows your date of birth.

People over the age of 60 qualify for reduced admission to theaters, museums, and other attractions and for other travel bargains like the **Carte Senior** (www.senior-sncf.com), which entitles holders to up to 50 percent discounts on TGV rail services and couchette berths on non-TGV mainline services, subject to seating availabilities. There is 25 percent off all TGV rail services and couchette berths on non-TGV mainline services at all times, where no seats are available at the 50 percent reduction. The Carte Senior also triggers some discounts on admissions to museums and historic sites. It's valid for one year and costs 50€; you can buy it at any SNCF (train) station. You have to present a passport photo when applying for the card. *Note:* To find out where to buy the card within the train station, go to the *Acceuil* (Welcome) information kiosk, where an English-speaking representative will direct you.

Membership in certain organizations can qualify you for some discounts. Be sure to bring whatever membership card the organization issues. If you're 50 or older, consider joining **AARP** (☎ 888-687-2277; www.aarp.org) for discounts on hotels, airfares, and car rentals. As a member, you're eligible for a wide range of special benefits, including *AARP The Magazine.*

Hundreds of travel agencies specialize in senior travel, and although many of the vacations are of the tour-bus variety, which may cramp the style of an independent senior, one bonus is that free trips are often thrown in for organizers of groups of 20 or more.

Recommended publications offering travel resources and discounts for seniors include the quarterly magazine **Travel 50 & Beyond** (www.travel50andbeyond.com); *101 Tips,* available from Grand Circle Travel (☎ 800-959-0405; www.gct.com); and *Unbelievably Good Deals and Great Adventures That You Absolutely Can't Get Unless You're Over 50* (McGraw-Hill), by Joan Rattner Heilman.

Accessing Paris: Advice for Travelers with Disabilities

Unfortunately, those features that make Paris so beautiful — uneven cobblestone streets, quaint buildings with high doorsills from the Middle Ages, and twisting lanes too narrow and traffic-clogged to simultaneously admit pedestrians and autos — also make using a walker or a wheelchair a nightmare. According to French law, newer hotels with three stars or more are required to have at least one wheelchair-accessible guest room. Most of the city's older budget hotels, which are exempt from the law, occupy buildings with winding staircases or elevators smaller than phone booths, and generally aren't good choices for travelers with disabilities.

Slowly, but surely, however, Paris is becoming more accessible. There is now space for wheelchairs in the first class cars of France's high-speed trains (le Train Grand Vitesse or TGV) — for the price of a second-class ticket. For more information in English about traveling through France by train go to www.voyages-sncf.fr.

Few Métro stations have elevators, most feature long tunnels, and some have wheelchair-unfriendly moving sidewalks and staircases. Escalators often lead to flights of stairs, and many times when you climb a flight of stairs, you're faced with another set of stairs leading down. However, line no. 14 of the Métro is wheelchair accessible, as are the stations at Auber, Barbès-Rochechouart, Charles de Gaulle–Étoile, Châtelet–Les Halles, Cité Université, Denfert-Rochereau, Nation, Madeleine, Gare de Lyon, Pyramides, Saint-Lazare, and Saint-Michel–Notre-Dame, to name a few. Certain stops on the RER's lines A and B are also wheelchair accessible.

Luckily, wheelchair lifts or kneeling stairs are standard equipment on all the city buses (with the exception of the Balabus, the Montmartrebus, and the Roissybus). Many high-speed and intercity trains are equipped for wheelchair access, and a special space is available in first class (at the price of a second-class ticket) for wheelchairs, although you must reserve well in advance.

Don't let inconveniences change your mind about visiting Paris. Before your trip, go to the **Paris Convention and Visitor's Bureau** Web site (http://en.parisinfo.com/guide-paris/disabled-people-access-services), which provides an overview of facilities for people with disabilities in the French transportation system and at monuments and museums in Paris and the provinces. This site covers everything from tour guides to accessible parks to organizations for people with disabilities to specialized transport.

L'Association des Paralysés de France (The Association of the Paralyzed of France), 17 bd. Auguste-Blanqui (☎ **01-40-78-69-00;** Web site in French: www.apf.asso.fr), publishes (in French only, unfortunately) *Le Guide Vacances (The Vacation Guide),* which lists accessible hotels as well as cultural and sporting activities taking place all over France.

Go to www.ratp.info/informer/reseau_ferre.php and scroll down for a list of Métro and RER stops that offer elevator access to the platforms, either with the assistance of an attendant *(avec agent)* or free service *(service libre).*

If you speak French, contact the **Groupement pour l'Insertion des Personnes Handicapées Physiques (Help for the Physically Handicapped),** Paris Office, 10 rue de Georges de Porto Riche (☎ 01-43-95-66-36; www.gihpnational.org), and **Les Compagnons du Voyage** of the **RATP** (☎ **01-58-76-08-33;** Web site in French: www.ratp.fr), Paris public transportation, for an actual trained "companion" to help you navigate the city's public-transportation system.

An excellent English-language resource is the U.K. organization RADAR: The Disability Network (www.radar.org.uk). A new version of their thoroughly researched guidebook for people with disabilities, *Access in Paris,* hit presses in 2008 and includes such information as maps of all the curbs in Paris and good public toilet facilities. You can access the guide for free (a small donation is suggested) at www.accessinparis.org.

Check out www.miusa.org, the Web site of **Mobility International USA** (☎ **541-343-1284** voice and TTY), which promotes international exchange. Another place to try is **Access-Able Travel Source** (www.access-able.com), a comprehensive database of travel agents who specialize in travel for people with disabilities and a clearinghouse for information about accessible destinations around the world.

Many travel agencies offer customized tours and itineraries for travelers with disabilities. **Flying Wheels Travel** (☎ **877-451-5006;** www.flyingwheelstravel.com) is a full-service travel agency for people with disabilities and offers escorted tours and cruises and private tours in minivans with lifts. **Accessible Journeys** (☎ **800-846-4537** or 610-521-0339; www.disabilitytravel.com) addresses the needs of wheelchair travelers and slow walkers and their families and friends.

Organizations that offer assistance to travelers with disabilities include **MossRehab** (www.mossresourcenet.org), with a library of accessible-travel resources online, and the **American Foundation for the Blind** (☎ **800-232-5463;** www.afb.org), a referral resource for the blind or visually impaired that includes information on traveling with guide dogs. Also check out the **Society for Accessible Travel & Hospitality** (☎ **212-447-7284;** www.sath.org; annual membership fees are $49 adults, $29 seniors and students), an educational nonprofit membership organization whose mission is to raise awareness of the needs of all travelers with disabilities, remove physical and attitudinal barriers to free access, and expand travel opportunities in the United States and abroad. SATH has travel resources for all types of disabilities and informed recommendations on destinations, access guides, travel agents, tour operators, vehicle rentals, and companion services.

For more information specifically targeted to travelers with disabilities, check out the quarterly online magazine *Emerging Horizons* ($16.95 for 5 issues, $33.90 for ten; www.emerginghorizons.com).

Following the Rainbow: Resources for Gay and Lesbian Travelers

France is one of the world's most tolerant countries toward gays, transgender, bisexual, and lesbians. It has no discriminatory laws. A casual indifference to non-heterosexual lifestyles — the French have long considered sexuality to be a truly private manner that has no bearing on how individuals should be treated in public life — has led many to settle here: Oscar Wilde and James Baldwin lived in Paris, as did Gertrude Stein and Alice B. Toklas. Technically, sexual relations are legal for consenting partners ages 16 and older.

The biggest concentration of gay bookstores, cafes, bars, and clothing boutiques is in the Marais, which stretches from the Hôtel de Ville to the Bastille. The best source of information on Parisian gay and lesbian life is the **Centre LGBT,** 63 rue Beaubourg, 3e (☎ **01-43-57-21-47;** www. centrelgbtparis.org; Métro: Rambuteau), open Monday 6 to 8 p.m.; Tuesday 4 to 8 p.m.; Wednesday, Friday, and Saturday 12:30 to 8 p.m.; Thursday 3 to 8 p.m.; Sunday 4 to 7 p.m. The center is a source of information, and members of its staff coordinate the activities and meetings of gay people around the world. Another helpful source is **Maison des Femmes de Paris,** 163 rue Charenton, 12e (☎ **01-43-43-41-13;** maison desfemmes.free.fr; Métro: Reuilly-Diderot), which has a cafe and a feminist library for lesbians and bisexual women. Meetings about everything from sexism to working rights and informal dinners and get-togethers all take place here. The areas adjacent to the Marais, such as Beaubourg and Bastille, are considered extensions of the "gayborhood," but other pockets of the city, such as Oberkampf in the 11th *arrondissement,* Montmartre, and the area south of Pigalle in the 9th *arrondissement,* have played host to gay populations throughout recent history.

Gay magazines that focus on parties and cultural events include *Illico* (www.e-llico.com), *2x* (www.2xparis.com; free in gay bars), and *Têtu* (www.tetu.com), France's national gay magazine available at almost all newspaper stands. *Têtu* is similar to the U.S. publications *Out* and *The Advocate,* and each issue has a separate pullout section with cultural and nightlife events in Paris and every major city in France. *Lesbia* is available for women. You can find these and other magazines at Paris's largest and best-stocked gay bookstore, **Les Mots à la Bouche,** 6 rue Ste-Croix-la-Bretonnerie, 4e (☎ **01-42-78-88-30;** www.motsbouche. com; Métro: Hôtel de Ville). Open Monday through Saturday 11 a.m. to 11 p.m., Sunday 1 to 9 p.m.

Other Web sites, like www.paris-gay.com and www.parismarais. com, offer English-language guides to the day and nighttime activities and places for gay and lesbian travelers to go. **Paris Gay Village** (www. parisgayvillage.com) is a tour company that leads gay-themed historical tours of different areas of Paris that have enjoyed a gay presence (unfortunately, most, if not all, of these tours are in French only).

The **International Gay & Lesbian Travel Association (IGLTA; ☎ 800-448-8550** or 954-776-2626; www.iglta.org) is the trade association for the gay and lesbian travel industry. It offers an online directory of gay- and lesbian-friendly travel businesses.

Many agencies offer tours and travel itineraries specifically for gay and lesbian travelers. **Now, Voyager** (☎ **800-255-6951;** www.nowvoyager.com) is a well-known San Francisco–based gay-owned and -operated travel service. Canada's **Gaytraveler** (www.gaytraveler.ca) is a Web site dedicated to travel for the gay, lesbian, bisexual, and transgendered communities. The site has discussion boards and a free monthly newsletter in addition to lists of all-gay cruises, tours, packages, and other holiday events.

The following travel guides are available at most bookstores: *Passport* (www.passportmagazine.com), a gay travel magazine with a Web site full of useful tips for LGBT travelers; *Spartacus International Gay Guide* (Bruno Gmünder Verlag; www.spartacusworld.com/gayguide), a good, annual English-language guidebook focused on gay men; and the *Damron* guides (www.damron.com), with separate annual books for gays and lesbians. Also check out *Out Traveler* (www.outtraveler.com), a Web site packed with solid information on the global gay and lesbian travel scene.

Chapter 7

Taking Care of the Remaining Details

In This Chapter

▶ Obtaining a passport

▶ Renting a car — or not — in Paris

▶ Understanding travel and medical insurance

▶ Guarding your health while traveling

▶ Keeping in touch via cellphone and e-mail

▶ Navigating airline security

*P*lanning a trip to Paris can be half the fun. This chapter helps you organize those inevitable last-minute loose ends and details.

Getting a Passport

A valid passport is the only legal form of identification accepted around the world. You can't cross an international border without it. Getting a passport is easy, but the process takes some time.

Although the U.S. government offers the Passport Card, these wallet-size cards are not valid identification for traveling to Europe and most international destinations.

Applying for a U.S. passport

If you're applying for a first-time passport, follow these steps. Also check out the **U.S. Department of State** Web site (http://travel.state. gov/passport) for application requirements.

1. Complete a **passport application** in person at a U.S. passport office; a federal, state, or probate court; or a major post office. To find your regional passport office, see the Web site listed above or call the **National Passport Information Center** (☎ 877-487-2778) for automated information.

2. Present a **certified birth certificate** as proof of citizenship. Also bring along your **driver's license or city, state, federal, or military ID** as a valid identification card is required, along with appropriate photocopies. If you're a naturalized citizen of the United States, you'll have to provide your Naturalization Certificate or Certificate of Citizenship as proof.

3. Submit **two identical color passport-size photos,** measuring 2 x 2 inches in size. You often find businesses that take these photos near passport offices. *Note:* You can't use a strip from a photo-vending machine because the pictures aren't identical.

4. Pay a **fee.** For people 17 and over, a passport is valid for ten years and costs $135, or $165 for both a passport and passport card. (A passport card can be used to enter the U.S. from Canada, Mexico, and the Caribbean at land border crossings or sea ports of entry.) For those 16 and under, a passport is valid for five years and costs $105, or $115 for a passport and passport card.

Allow plenty of time before your trip to apply for a passport; processing normally takes four to six weeks and perhaps longer during busy periods, such as spring. Expedited delivery costs an addition $60; see the above Web site for additional instructions.

If you have a passport in your current name that was issued within the past 15 years (and you were 17 or over when it was issued), you can renew the passport by mail. Renewal fees are now the same as fees for first-time applicants.

If you're a U.S. citizen and you lose or have your passport stolen in Paris, go immediately to the **Office of American Services,** Embassy of the United States, 4 av. Gabriel, 8e (☎ **01-43-12-22-22;** http://france. usembassy.gov/pass-lost.html; Métro: Concorde), Monday through Friday from 9 a.m. to noon. If you're a Canadian and your passport is lost or stolen, visit the **Consulate of the Canadian Embassy,** 35 av. Montaigne, 8e (☎ **01-44-43-29-00;** http://france.gc.ca; Métro: Franklin D. Roosevelt or Alma Marceau). Australians must go to the **Australian Embassy** at 4 rue Jean Rey, 15e (☎ **01-40-59-33-00;** www. france.embassy.gov.au; Métro: Bir-Hakeim). New Zealanders need to visit the **New Zealand Embassy,** 7ter rue Léonard de Vinci, 16e (☎ **01-45-01-43-43;** www.nzembassy.com/france; Métro: Victor Hugo).

Always keep a photocopy of the inside page of your passport with your picture packed separately from your wallet or purse. If your passport is lost or stolen, the photocopy can help speed up the replacement process. When traveling in a group, never let one person carry all the passports. If the passports are stolen, obtaining new ones can be much more difficult, because at least one person in a group needs to be able to prove his or her identity to identify the others.

Applying for other passports

The following list offers more information for citizens of Australia, Canada, New Zealand, and the United Kingdom.

- ✔ **Australians** can visit a local post office or passport office, call the **Australia Passport Information Service** (☎ **131-232** for the cost of a local call within Australia), or log on to www.passports.gov.au for details on how and where to apply. The fee for Australian passports is AU$208 for adults, and AU$104 for children and seniors.

- ✔ **Canadians** can pick up applications at passport offices and post offices throughout Canada (☎ **800-567-6868**; www.ppt.gc.ca). Applications must be accompanied by two identical passport-size photographs and proof of Canadian citizenship. Processing takes 10 to 18 days if you apply in person, about three weeks by mail. The cost is C$87 for adults, C$37 for children.

- ✔ **New Zealanders** can pick up a passport application at any New Zealand Passports Office or download it from its Web site. For information, contact the **Passports Office** at ☎ **0800-225-050** in New Zealand or go to www.passports.govt.nz. The cost for a passport is NZ$150 for adults, NZ$80 for children. Processing takes ten business days.

- ✔ **United Kingdom** residents can pick up applications for a standard ten-year passport (five-year passport for children 15 and under) at passport offices and Check & Send post offices. For information, contact the **United Kingdom Passport Service** (☎ **0300-222-0000**; www.passport.gov.uk). Passports cost £78 for adults, £49 for children.

Why Not to Rent a Car in Paris

Even compared to the inflated prices the United States has experienced in the last few years, gas in Europe is much more expensive. This should be reason enough to make use of France's excellent national train system. However if you're an aficionado of death-defying extreme sports, driving in Paris is for you. Parisian drivers are ruthlessly aggressive. Traffic is dense. Roundabouts pop up everywhere, and cars seem to hurtle at you from the left — no better example than the Étoile circle that surrounds the Arc de Triomphe, where cars enter and exit from *12 different locations* at high speeds. Additionally, unlike most traffic circles in France, the drivers *entering* at Étoile have right of way — flying into the dense circle at taxi-driver speeds feels like a near-death experience. Parking is difficult, both in terms of finding a space and the size of the spaces available (Parisians with cars shamelessly bump the surrounding vehicles). Most hotels, except luxury ones, don't have garages. And if you drive to Paris from somewhere else and get on the limited-access roadway called the *périphérique* that circles the city, you'll find that its exits aren't numbered. Because the Paris Métro is one of the world's best urban transportation systems, having a car in Paris is highly unnecessary. Even the day trips described in Chapter 14 are easily accessible by public transportation.

If you must drive in Paris, make sure that you have a copilot helping you navigate the streets. By law, children are required to sit in the backseat, and all passengers must wear seat belts. *Remember:* The majority of rentals available in France (and, indeed, most of Europe) have manual (stick-shift) transmissions. In fact, if you request an automatic transmission, you'll probably end up paying more for the car, if a car is even available.

When you rent a car, try doing so for three days or more because the cost usually works out to be less per day than renting for one day, and unlimited mileage is thrown in. Reserve before you leave home (make sure to print out your reservation!), and keep in mind that government taxes are calculated at about 21 percent of the total contract, collision-damage insurance tacks on 15€ to 20€ per day, gas is very expensive, and a surcharge of about 15€ is assessed if you pick up the car at the airport.

Car-rental agencies in Paris include the following:

- ✔ **Avis,** Gare d'Austerlitz, arrivals gate, 13e (☎ **01-45-84-22-10;** www. avis.com): A compact car, such as a Renault Twingo, that seats four runs about 65€ per day with unlimited mileage before tax.

- ✔ **Europcar,** across from 8 avenue Foch, 8e (☎ **08-25-82-55-13;** www. europcar.fr): A two-door compact car with air-conditioning, such as the Volkswagen Golf, costs 62€ per day with unlimited mileage before tax.

- ✔ **Hertz France,** Gare Saint-Lazare, 92 rue Saint-Lazare, 9e (☎ **01-42-80-35-45;** www.hertz.com): A compact car, such as a Peugeot 107, costs about 73€ per day (before tax) with limited mileage.

- ✔ **National,** Gare de Montparnasse, 15e (☎ **01-42-79-06-11;** www. nationalcar.com): A five-door compact car that seats four, such as a Citroën Picasso, costs around 56€ per day with unlimited mileage before tax.

The major highways *(autoroutes)* to Paris are the **A1** from the north (the United Kingdom and Belgium); the **A13** from Normandy and other points in northwest France; the **A109** from Spain and the southwest; the **A7** from the Alps, the Riviera, and Italy; and the **A4** from eastern France. At the beginning and end of long weekends, school breaks, and August summer vacations, these roads become parking lots.

Playing It Safe with Travel and Medical Insurance

Three kinds of travel insurance are available: trip-cancellation insurance, medical insurance, and lost-luggage insurance. The cost of travel insurance varies widely, depending on the cost and length of your trip, your age and health, and the type of trip you're taking, but expect to pay between 5 percent and 8 percent of the vacation itself.

- **Trip-cancellation insurance** helps you get your money back if you have to back out of a trip, if you have to go home early, or if your travel supplier goes bankrupt. Allowed reasons for cancellation can range from sickness to natural disasters to the Department of State declaring your destination unsafe for travel. Protect yourself by paying for the insurance with a credit card — by law, consumers can get their money back on goods and services not received if they report the loss within 60 days after the charge is listed on their credit card statement.

  Note: Many tour operators, particularly those offering trips to remote or high-risk areas, include insurance in the cost of the trip or can arrange insurance policies through a partnering provider, a convenient and often cost-effective way for the traveler to obtain insurance. Make sure the tour company is a reputable one, however: Some experts suggest you avoid buying insurance from the tour or cruise company you're traveling with, saying it's better to buy from a third-party insurer than to put all your money in one place.

- Most health plans (including Medicare and Medicaid) don't provide **medical insurance** coverage for travel overseas, and the ones that do often require you to pay for services upfront and reimburse you only after you return home. Even if your plan does cover overseas medical treatment, most out-of-country hospitals make you pay your bills upfront and send you a refund only after you return home and file the necessary paperwork with your insurance company. As a safety net, you may want to buy travel medical insurance, particularly if you're traveling to a remote or high-risk area where emergency evacuation is a possible scenario. If you require additional medical insurance, try **MEDEX Global Solutions** (☎ **800-537-2029;** www.medexassist.com) or **Travel Assistance International** (☎ **800-821-2828;** www.travelassistance.com).

- **Lost-luggage insurance** is not necessary for most travelers. On international flights (including U.S. portions of international trips), baggage coverage is limited to approximately $9 per pound, up to approximately $635 per checked bag. If you plan to check items more valuable than the standard liability, see if your valuables are covered by your homeowner's policy, or get baggage insurance as part of your comprehensive travel-insurance package. **Travel**

Guard International's travel insurance packages (☎ 800-826-1300; www.travelguard.com) include additional baggage insurance among various other kinds of insurance products, including health, rental cars, and last-minute cancellations. Don't buy insurance at the airport, as it's usually overpriced. Be sure to take any valuables or irreplaceable items with you in your carry-on luggage, because many valuables (including books, money, and electronics) aren't covered by airline policies.

If your luggage is lost, immediately file a lost-luggage claim at the airport, detailing the luggage contents. For most airlines, you must report delayed, damaged, or lost baggage within four hours of arrival. The airlines are required to deliver luggage, once found, directly to your house or destination free of charge.

For more information on travel insurance, contact one of the following recommended insurers: **Access America** (☎ 800-284-8300; www.accessamerica.com); **Travel Insured International** (☎ 800-243-3174; www.travelinsured.com); **Travelex Insurance Services** (☎ 800-228-9792; Mon–Fri 8 a.m.–7 p.m. Central time; www.travelex-insurance.com); and **IGT Worldwide** (☎ 877-598-8646; http://itgworldwide.com), which also specializes in international health insurance.

Staying Healthy when You Travel

Of course, you're not going to get sick on this vacation, so feel free to skip over this section! But then again, with seasonal allergies, airplane-related head colds, or the occasional "runny tummy" that comes with traveling abroad, I'll leave the important information just in case.

The French government pays 70 percent of the cost of doctor visits, and its national health insurance covers 99 percent of France's population. Visitors needing medical care in France find that same-day appointments are easily made, and patient fees are relatively inexpensive. Patients almost always have to pay upfront, unless they're citizens of European Union countries with reciprocal medical arrangements. Some U.S. health-insurance companies reimburse you for the cost of treating illnesses in foreign countries; make sure to keep all your receipts. In the unlikely event of having to buy medication, you'll be pleasantly surprised to find that, compared to what Americans pay out-of-pocket, the French equivalents cost next to nothing.

French pharmacies, with their ubiquitous green crosses above the entrances, are not like the big U.S. chains where you can buy anything from beer to bath salts. Instead, they deal only with products specifically for health and hygiene and are run by trained medical professionals who give free consultations and can diagnose minor ailments. Additionally, pharmacists can supply medications that would otherwise require a doctor's prescription back home. For aches and pains, stomach bugs, colds, and any discomforts that would require antibiotics, visit a pharmacist before heading to a doctor — most speak English and will be able to help you for unbelievably low costs.

If you do get sick enough that the pharmacies are not sufficient, ask the concierge at your hotel to recommend a local doctor — even his or her own doctor, if necessary. You can also call **SOS Médecins** (☎ **01-47-07-77-77**), a 24-hour service; ask for an English-speaking doctor. The **Centre Médical Europe,** 44 rue d'Amsterdam, 9e (☎ **01-42-81-93-33;** www. centre-medical-europe.com), is another good and efficient option. It has a host of specialists, and foreigners pay around 35€ for a consultation. If you're in urgent need of a dentist, try **SOS Urgences Stomatologiques et Dentaires,** 87 bd. Port-Royal (☎ **01-43-36-36-00**).

Talk to your doctor before leaving on a trip if you have a serious and/or chronic illness. For conditions such as epilepsy, diabetes, or heart problems, wear a **MedicAlert identification tag** (☎ **888-633-4298;** www. medicalert.org), which immediately alerts doctors to your condition and gives them access to your records through MedicAlert's 24-hour hot line. Contact the **International Association for Medical Assistance to Travelers** (IAMAT; ☎ **716-754-4883;** www.iamat.org) for tips on travel and health concerns in the countries you're visiting, and lists of local, English-speaking doctors. The **U.S. Centers for Disease Control and Prevention** (☎ **800-232-4636;** www.cdc.gov) provides up-to-date information on health hazards by region or country and offers tips on food safety.

Staying Connected by Cellphone or E-mail

Since the speed at which communication technology advances seems so immeasurable, I'll reiterate that everything written here is accurate at press time, but anything from prices to the very modes of communication may have changed by the time you read these words.

That said, take comfort in the fact that if you so desire, cellphone technology has advanced to the point that if you wish to be reachable or have access to a cell phone *(un mobile),* it's relatively easy.

Certain U.S. cellphones will work in Europe because the service provider or carrier uses a tri-band or quadra-band system, generally known as a **GSM** (Global System for Mobiles) network — the kind used in Europe and most of the world. At press time, **T-Mobile** and **AT&T** Wireless offer phones that use this system. If your phone has a SIM card (a small chip usually near or around the battery), then chances are, it's GSM-capable. If you're a BlackBerry user, regardless of your cellphone carrier, your phone is GSM capable.

If this is the case and you want to use your U.S. cellphone number to be roaming while traveling in Paris, get in touch with your cellphone provider to inquire about the possibility of using your phone internationally. Be warned: You may be charged a huge international-roaming fee for receiving and sending calls and texts, as well as for data transfer such as e-mail. Each provider is different, so I strongly suggest you check with yours before using your phone liberally while traveling abroad.

Most GSM phones are sold locked, meaning that you can only use a SIM card from the provider that sold you the phone. However, if your phone is unlocked, then you can easily buy a prepaid SIM card from a French provider for relatively cheap (around 6€), and you can purchase minutes to be used while traveling. Check with your cellphone company; they may allow you to unlock your phone so that you can use a local provider while you're traveling. The other two possibilities for having cellphone access are purchasing a cheap cellphone and using prepaid minutes while traveling in France, or renting a phone; I strongly recommend the former.

Buying a cheap phone is easy because there are mobile stores all over the place in Paris. The biggest providers are **SFR,** with a branch at 125 rue de Rennes, 6e (Métro: Saint-Placide); **France Télécom,** the national phone company, with a central location at 46 bis rue de Louvre, 1e (Métro: Les Halles); and **Bouygues Telecom,** 33 rue de Rivoli, 4e (Métro: Hôtel de Ville). The first two companies provide better-quality service and fewer blackout periods, while Bouygues Telecom is generally cheaper.

In most stores, you can find pay-as-you-go phones for as cheap as 20€, which usually come with 5€ of credit free. You can buy more credit (known as *rechargement,* or a recharge) at the respective boutiques or in most tobacconists *(tabacs)* — look for carte orange for France Télécom and sfr la carte for SFR. When your phone is working, you can call or text to anywhere in the world, even back home.

Unlike in the United States, receiving a phone call or text message (known as an SMS or *un texte*) on a French mobile is free and will not reduce your minutes. In the other direction, calling a landline from a cellphone in France is relatively inexpensive.

Although renting a cellphone has been a possible choice for travelers for years, I would advise against it because rental services are quite expensive and no more convenient than buying your own phone.

Accessing the Internet Away from Home

Travelers have any number of ways to check their e-mail and access the Internet on the road. Of course, using your own laptop or handheld device is the most flexible way of doing it. Most hotels have free Wi-Fi, and more and more cafes, especially in the hip areas, are beginning to offer free Wi-Fi as well. But even if you don't have a computer, you can still access your e-mail and even your office computer from cybercafes.

It's hard nowadays to find a city that *doesn't* have a few cybercafes. Although there's no definitive directory for cybercafes — they are independent businesses, after all — two places to start looking are at **www. cybercaptive.com** and **www.cybercafe.com.**

Aside from formal cybercafes, most hotels and **youth hostels** nowadays have at least one computer you can use to get on the Internet. And most **public libraries** across the world offer Internet access free or for a small charge. You can always find a cybercafe near a college; in France the Latin Quarter abounds with them around rue des Écoles and boulevard Saint-Michel. Try **Luxembourg Micro,** 81 bd. Saint-Michel, 5e (☎ **01-46-33-27-98;** Métro: Saint-Michel).

Avoid **hotel business centers** unless you're willing to pay exorbitant rates.

If you plan to take a laptop to Paris, check to see if your hotel has Wi-Fi access. **T-Mobile Hotspot** (www.t-mobile.com/hotspot) serves up wireless connections at more than 1,000 Starbucks coffee shops nationwide and at the Starbucks locations in Paris. **Boingo** (www.boingo.com) has networks in airports and high-class hotel lobbies. **iPass** (http://ipass.com/hotspot) providers also give you access to a few hundred wireless hotel-lobby setups, in such Parisian hotels as Le Méridien Montparnasse and the Plaza Athénée. The companies' pricing policies can be complicated, but they also provide directories of Wi-Fi hotspots in major cities, including Paris. Check out the Web sites for more information.

If Wi-Fi is not available at your destination (what is this, the Moyen Age?), most business-class hotels throughout the world offer dataports and Ethernet network cables. **Call your hotel in advance** to see what your options are.

Keeping Up with Airline Security Measures

Today, security procedures at airports around the world mean longer waits in lines and getting to the airport earlier, especially for international flights. Generally, you'll be fine if you arrive at the airport 1½ **hours** before a domestic flight and **3 hours** before an international flight.

Bring a **current, government-issued photo ID** such as a driver's license or passport (of course, you'll need your passport if you're traveling to France). Keep your ID at the ready to show at check-in, the security checkpoint, and sometimes even the gate. (Children 17 and under don't need government-issued photo IDs for domestic flights, but they need passports for international flights.)

Speed up security by not wearing metal objects such as big belt buckles, and make sure to check your airline's guidelines for bringing liquids in carry-on bags — in many cases, you'll have to put everything (including makeup, toothpaste, and other toiletries) in your checked baggage; however, some airlines, such as Air France, allow 100ml of cosmetics and related liquid items, sealed in an appropriately sized plastic bag (such as an 8-x-8-inch freezer bag). If you have metallic body parts, a note from your doctor can prevent a long chat with the security screeners. Keep in mind that only ticketed passengers are allowed past security, except for folks escorting passengers with disabilities or children.

The Transportation Security Administration (TSA) has stabilized **what you can carry on** and **what you can't.** The general rule for carry-on luggage is that sharp things and combustibles are out. Any liquids or gels must be in 3.4-ounce (100ml) or smaller containers, and placed in a see-through resealable 1-quart plastic bag, which is put separately through the scanner. (After you've passed through security, you can buy bottled water and bring it on the plane.) Travelers in the United States are allowed one carry-on bag, plus a "personal item" such as a purse, briefcase, or laptop bag. For the most up-to-date regulations, visit www. tsa.gov/travelers for a current list of restricted items.

Part III
Settling into Paris

The 5th Wave   By Rich Tennant

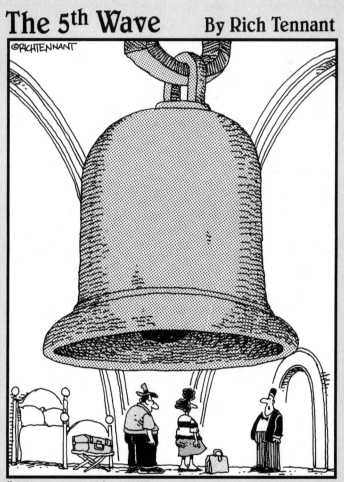

"Welcome to the Hotel de Notre-Dame. If there's anything else I can do for you, please don't hesitate to ring."

In this part . . .

This section helps you get from point A to point B without wasting time and money. Better yet, it suggests great places to stay and tells you all you want to know about eating French-style and then directs you to some memorable eateries. Chapter 8 guides you from the airport to your hotel, describes the most popular neighborhoods, and tells you where to go for information once you're in Paris. Read Chapter 9 for reviews of the best accommodations in Paris — for all budgets. Chapter 10 proves that Paris is indeed a feast. It offers an overview of the local dining scene, advice on how to trim the fat from your food budget, and recommendations for some of the best restaurants, brasseries, cafes, wine bars, tea salons, and sandwich places in the city. Handy indexes cross-reference all of the hotel accommodations and the dining establishments by neighborhood, price, and type.

Chapter 8

Arriving and Getting Oriented

. . . .

In This Chapter

▶ Passing through passport control and Customs

▶ Securing transportation to your hotel

▶ Discovering Paris by neighborhood

▶ Getting information on Paris in Paris

▶ Navigating the city

. . . .

*T*he Paris experience begins for most people on the plane, where announcements are made in English and French. For others it begins at the airport — with bi- and trilingual signs directing you to passport control and baggage claim. The airports are now completely nonsmoking. Luggage carts are free! Depending on when you travel, you may experience long lines at passport control. People dress a little more formally than at home. It all may seem a little astonishing. But the important thing is, you've arrived! Now you can move on to the first item of the day — getting from the airport to your hotel.

Navigating Your Way through Passport Control and Customs

Most visitors to Paris land at **Charles de Gaulle Airport.** It's known as CDG and sometimes called Roissy–Charles de Gaulle (Roissy is the town closest to the airport). Nearly all direct flights from North America land at Charles de Gaulle. Over the next five years, all the major terminals of the airport are set for multi-million-dollar renovations, beginning with Terminal 2B, but including terminals 2A through C. Terminal 2D will be closed temporarily, and a new building is under construction to replace the missing space during renovations. Terminal 1, also set for renovations, has already begun exterior work.

A free shuttle bus *(navette)* connects terminals 1 and 2. Signs in French and English in both terminals direct you to Customs, baggage claim, and transportation to the city. Staff at information desks are also on hand to answer questions.

Two lines are set up for passport control, one for European Union nationals and the other for everyone else. These lines can move quite quickly or horrendously slowly; it usually depends on the clerk checking your passport.

When passing through Customs, keep in mind that restrictions are different for citizens of the European Union than they are for citizens of non-EU countries. As a non-EU national, you can bring in 200 cigarettes or 100 cigarillos or 50 cigars or 250 grams of smoking tobacco duty-free. You can also bring in 2 liters of wine and 1 liter of alcohol of more than 80 proof. In addition, you can bring in 50 grams of perfume, and 0.25 liter of eau de toilette. Travelers can also bring in 175€ in other goods. (See Chapter 12 for what you're allowed to bring home.) Because you probably aren't going to need to make a claim, you should be waved through by an officer pretty quickly. Customs officers do, however, pull random travelers over to check luggage. Whenever that happens to you, don't be offended; be polite and as helpful as you can, and if you don't speak French, let them know by saying, *"Je ne parle pas français"* (zhe ne *parl* pah frahn-*say*).

 Regardless of the terminal, you need euros to get from the airport into Paris. You can find ATMs in the arrival areas of the airports along with *bureaux de change,* where you can exchange dollars for euros, but you're better off buying and bringing around 300€ from your bank at home. Airport ATMs are notorious for being broken when you need them most, and the airport *bureaux de change* are just as notorious for their bad rates of exchange.

Making Your Way to Your Hotel

You can travel to and from the airports by several different means, and the amount of text here notwithstanding, they're all easy!

If you fly into Charles de Gaulle

Charles de Gaulle Airport (CDG) is located 23km (15 miles) northeast of downtown Paris. Transportation into the city is plentiful.

Taking a taxi

Probably the easiest, but certainly not the cheapest, mode of transportation to your hotel from the airport is by **taxi.** A cab into town from Charles de Gaulle can take from 30 to 50 minutes, depending on traffic. The initial fare for up to three passengers is 2.20€ and rises 0.90€ for each kilometer (⅔ mile) between 10 a.m. and 5 p.m. (known as *Tarif A*). Between 5 p.m. and 10 a.m., the standing charge remains the same, but the per-kilometer charge rises to 1.15€ *(Tarif B)* and on Sunday mornings (from midnight to 7 a.m.) the charge is 1.40€ per kilometer *(Tarif C).*

Tarif C, the highest fare, is enacted when driving outside metropolitan Paris, while *Tarif B* is enacted in suburban areas regardless of the time of day. Charles de Gaulle Airport is located outside the metropolitan area.

An additional fee of 1€ is imposed for luggage weighing more than 5kg (11 pounds) or for an extra bag, and a 2.95€ surcharge is added for a fourth passenger. If your French is poor or nonexistent, write down the name and full address of your hotel. The five-digit postal code is the most important morsel of information, because it tells the driver the *arrondissement* where you need to go. Look up the code and check the meter before you pay — rip-offs of arriving tourists are not uncommon. Whenever you strongly think that you may have been overcharged, demand a receipt (*un réçu,* uh ray-soo), which drivers are obligated to provide, and contact the **Paris Préfecture of Police** (☎ 01-53-71-53-71).

The taxi stands at Charles de Gaulle are located at:

- ✔ **CDG Terminal 1:** Exit 20, arrivals level

- ✔ **CDG terminals 2A and 2C:** Exit 6

- ✔ **CDG terminals 2B and 2D:** Exit 7

- ✔ **CDG terminal 2E and 2F:** Exit 1

- ✔ **CDG Terminal 3:** Arrivals level

Taking a shuttle

If you don't want to schlep your bags through Paris's streets and Métro stations, taking a private airport shuttle is definitely the way to go. Although more expensive than airport buses and trains, shuttles are much cheaper and roomier than taxis. And you can reserve a seat in advance and pay by credit card. **World Shuttle,** 13 rue Voltaire, 94400 Vitry-sur-Seine (☎ 01-46-80-14-67; www.world-shuttles.com), costs 26€ for one person, 17€ per person for two or more people, from Charles de Gaulle and Orly. Between midnight and 5:30 a.m., the price per van is 60€ for one to three people, 70€ for four to five people, and 90€ for six to eight people.

Parishuttle (☎ 01-53-39-18-18; www.parishuttle.com) offers a similar service. You're picked up in a minivan (shared with other passengers) at Orly or Charles de Gaulle and taken to your hotel for 20€ for one person, 18€ per person for groups of two, 17€ per person for groups of three, and so on. The cost for children 10 and under is 10€.

Riding the rails

A good option when you're not overloaded with baggage and you want to keep your expenses down is to take the suburban commuter train to the Métro. **RER** (Réseau Express Régional) **Line B** stops near terminals 1 and 2. Easy, cheap, and convenient, you can ride both to and from the

Paris Neighborhoods

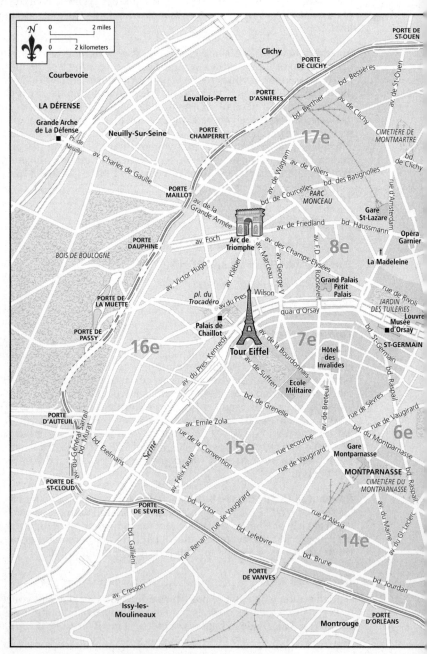

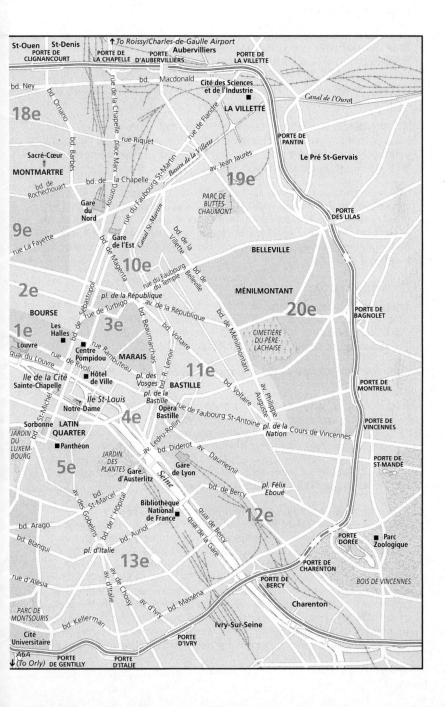

airport Monday through Friday from 5 a.m. to midnight, Saturday and Sunday from 7 a.m. to 9 p.m.

Free shuttle buses (the **CDGVAL**) connect CDG Terminal 1 to the RER train station. You can pick up the free shuttle bus in CDG Terminal 1 by following the RER B logos (with a picture of a bus alongside) to the exit on the arrivals level. CDG Terminal 2 has direct access to the RER station; follow the round RER B logos.

Buy the **RER** ticket, which costs 8.50€ at the RER ticket counter, and hang onto it in case of ticket inspection. (You can be fined if you can't produce your ticket for an inspector.) You need your ticket later to get off the RER system and onto the Métro.

Depending where your hotel is located, you exit either on the Right or the Left Bank. From the airport station, trains depart about every 15 minutes for the 40- to 50-minute trip into town and stop on the **Right Bank** at Gare du Nord and Châtelet–Les Halles, and on the **Left Bank** at Saint-Michel, Luxembourg, Port-Royal, and Denfert-Rochereau, before heading south out of the city.

Boarding the bus

There are two national airport shuttles: Roissybus, run by the **RATP** (the Paris metropolitan transit authority) and **Les Cars Air France** (☎ **08-92-35-08-20** at a charge of 0.35€ per minute), run by Air France. These buses are better than the RER if

✔ You're heading into Paris during off-peak driving hours, and you're not in a hurry.

✔ Your hotel is located near one of the drop-off points. *Note:* The bus is most convenient for the hotels I recommend in the second and eighth *arrondissements.* If you're staying outside these *arrondissements,* you can take a taxi from the shuttle drop-off point or board the closest subway if you aren't loaded down with luggage. If a bus isn't convenient, check out the door-to-door airport shuttle services in the "Taking a shuttle" section, earlier.

If your hotel is located on the **Right Bank** in the 8e, 16e, or 17e *arrondissements,* take Les Cars Air France **Line 2,** which stops at the Palais des Congrès on rue Gouvion-Saint-Cyr at Porte Maillot before ending up at 1 av. Carnot at place Charles de Gaulle–Étoile, the name for the huge traffic roundabout at the Arc de Triomphe. The bus costs 15€ one-way and runs every 15 minutes from 5:45 a.m. to 11 p.m. You don't have to be a passenger on an Air France flight to use the service, and tickets are available in a small office next to the bus or from the bus driver. The trip from the airport into the city and vice versa takes about 40 minutes in light traffic, such as on weekend mornings. During weekday morning rush hour, however, the same trip can take twice as long.

If your hotel is located on the **Right Bank** near the **Bastille** (11e or 12e) or on the **Left Bank** in **Montparnasse** (14e), take the **Air France Line 4** coach, which stops at boulevard Diderot in front of the Gare de Lyon before ending up on rue du Commandant Mouchotte near the back of the Gare de Montparnasse. The bus costs 17€ one-way and runs every 30 minutes from 5:55 a.m. to 10:55 p.m. both to and from the airport. It takes about 50 minutes to get from the airport into the city in light traffic. Catch these coaches from:

- **CDG Terminal 1:** Exit 34, arrivals level

- **CDG Terminals 2A and 2C:** Gate B1

- **CDG Terminals 2B and 2D:** Gate C2

- **CDG Terminals 2E and 2F:** Exit 3, arrivals level

Take the **Roissybus** if your hotel is on the **Right Bank** near the **Opéra** (2e or 9e). It costs 9.40€ and leaves every 15 minutes from the airport between 5:45 a.m. and 7 p.m. and every 20 minutes between 7 p.m. and 11 p.m. The drop-off point is on rue Scribe, a block from the **Opéra Garnier** near American Express. You can get to your destination in 45 to 60 minutes in regular traffic. Buy your tickets in the small office next to where the bus is parked or on the bus. Pick up this coach from:

- **CDG Terminal 1:** Gate 30, arrivals level

- **CDG Terminals 2A and 2C:** Gate 9 from Terminal 2A

- **CDG Terminals 2B and 2D:** Gate 11

- **CDG Terminals 2E and 2F:** Arrivals level

If you fly into Orly

Orly Airport, 14km (8½ miles) south of the city, has two terminals — **Ouest** (West) and **Sud** (South) — and English speakers find the terminals easy to navigate. French domestic flights land at Orly Ouest, and intra-European and intercontinental flights land at Orly Sud. Shuttle buses connect these terminals, and other shuttles connect them to Charles de Gaulle every 30 minutes or so. A tourist-information desk is conveniently located on the arrivals level of both terminals.

Like Charles de Gaulle Airport, two lines are set up for passport control, one for European Union nationals, and one for visitors carrying passports from all other countries, and you should be waved through Customs. (See the earlier section "Navigating Your Way through Passport Control and Customs" for information about what you can bring into France.)

Taking a taxi

A cab from Orly into Paris costs about 40€, depending on traffic, and takes anywhere from 25 minutes to an hour. The taxi stand at Orly Sud is just outside Exit M; at Orly Ouest it's at Exit I. The same advice as when taking a taxi from Charles de Gaulle holds true here: Write down the full name and address of your hotel for the driver. And remember that cabs charge 1€ for each piece of luggage put in the trunk.

Busing is best — sometimes

Take Les Cars Air France **Line 1** if your hotel is located on the **Left Bank** near **Gare Montparnasse (15e), Les Invalides (7e), Duroc (7e),** or on the **Right Bank** near the **Champs-Elysées (8e).** Buses leave Orly Sud at Gate L and Orly Ouest at Gate B–C, arrivals level, every 20 minutes from 6 a.m. to 11:40 p.m. The trip takes about 30 minutes and costs 12€ for adults and 5.50€ for children.

The **Orlybus** takes passengers from the airport directly to the entrance to the **Denfert-Rochereau station (14e)** with a brief stop at la Porte de Gentilly at the edge of the city. Buses run from 5:35 a.m. to 11:22 p.m. from Denfert-Rochereau and from 6 a.m. to 11:50 p.m. from Orly Sud; a one-way trip costs 6.30€. You can pick up the bus in front of Gate H at Orly Sud and at the Gate D arrivals level at Orly Ouest.

Taking the train

If you're staying on the **Left Bank,** take the **RER C line** by catching a shuttle bus (called *Paris par le train* and costing 2.50€) from Gate F at Orly Sud or Gate G at Orly Ouest arrivals level to the **Rungis** station, where RER C trains leave every 15 minutes for **Gare d'Austerlitz** (13e), Saint-Michel–Notre-Dame (6e) or Les Invalides (7e). A one-way fare for the train is 6€ for adults, 4.25€ for children. The trip into the city takes about 30 minutes, making the various stops along the Seine on the **Left Bank.**

If you're staying on the **Right Bank,** you can take the **Orlyval/RER B line** to **Antony** Métro station (from Gate K in Orly South; from Gate A, arrivals level, in Orly West). You connect at the **Antony** RER station where you board the RER B train to Paris. Hold on to the ticket purchased at the airport because you will need it to get into the Métro/RER system. A trip to the Châtelet station on the Right Bank takes about 30 minutes and costs 10€ for adults, 5.10€ for children 4 to 11. Once in Paris, the train stops at **Denfert-Rochereau, Port-Royal, Luxembourg,** and **Saint-Michel** on the Left Bank, and then crosses to the Right Bank for stops at **Châtelet** and **Gare du Nord.**

Figuring Out the Neighborhoods

You arrive at your hotel, check in, and maybe unpack a little. But taking a nap prolongs your jet lag. So, go out and act like a Parisian by having a cup of coffee at a cafe before getting ready to explore.

The Seine River divides Paris into two halves: the **Right Bank** *(Rive Droite)* on the north side of the river and the **Left Bank** *(Rive Gauche)* on the south side of the river. The larger Right Bank is where you find the city's business sector, stately monuments, and high-fashion industry. The Left Bank has the publishing houses, universities, and a reputation as bohemian because students, philosophers, and creative types have been congregating here for centuries. Two of the city's tallest monuments are on the Left Bank — the **Tour Montparnasse** (that lonely, tall, black building hovering on the edge of the city) and the **Eiffel Tower.**

The city is divided into 20 numbered *arrondissements* (municipal districts). The layout of these districts follows a distinct pattern. The first (abbreviated 1er for *premier*) *arrondissement* is the dead center of Paris, comprising an area around Notre-Dame and the Louvre. From there, the rest of the districts spiral outward, clockwise, in ascending order. The lower the *arrondissement* number, the more central the location. To get a better idea, consult the "Paris Neighborhoods" map.

Arrondissement numbers are key to locating an address in Paris, and this book lists addresses the way they appear in Paris, with the *arrondissement* number following the specific street address (for instance, 29 rue de Rivoli, 4e, is in the fourth *arrondissement*). *Arrondissement* numbers are noted on street signs and are indicated by the last two digits of the postal code. An address with a postal code of 75007 is located in the seventh *arrondissement.* Once you know the *arrondissement* in which an address is located, finding that spot is much easier. Numbers on buildings running parallel to the Seine usually follow the course of the river east to west. On north–south streets, numbering begins at the river.

Neighborhoods in the following sections are listed first by *arrondissement,* and then by neighborhood name. Only the better-known *arrondissements* — meaning the ones that you're most likely to stay in or visit — are mentioned here.

On the Right Bank

The following are the neighborhoods you're likely to visit on the Right Bank.

1er: Musée du Louvre/Palais-Royal/Les Halles/Île de la Cité

Traditionally, people consider the Right Bank to be more upscale, with Paris's main boulevards such as **Champs-Elysées** and museums such as the **Louvre.** One of the world's greatest art museums (some say *the* greatest), the **Louvre** still lures visitors to Paris to the first *arrondissement.* You can see the contrast between many of the city's elegant addresses along the rue de Rivoli and arched arcades under which all kinds of touristy junk is sold. Walk through the **Jardin des Tuileries,** the most formal garden of Paris, and take in the classic beauty, opulence, and wealth of the **place Vendôme,** which is home to the Ritz Hotel. Browse the arcaded shops and view the striped columns and seasonal art on display in the garden of the **Palais Royal,** once the home to Cardinal Richelieu. The somewhat seedy **Forum des Halles,** an above- and below-ground shopping and entertainment center, is also here.

This *arrondissement* tends to be crowded, and hotel prices are higher during Paris's high tourist season (in early fall) because the area is so convenient. Aristocratic town houses, courtyards, antiques shops, flower markets, the **Palais de Justice, Notre-Dame Cathedral,** and **Sainte-Chapelle** (the chapel built in 1243 for St. Louis, famous for its gorgeous stained-glass windows) are also part of the 1er on Ile de la Cité, an island in the Seine and the site of the original pre-Roman settlement that became Paris. This is one of the city's prettiest and most crowded neighborhoods, as is its sister island, Ile Saint-Louis (see "4e: Le Marais/Ile Saint-Louis/Beaubourg," later).

2e: La Bourse

Often overlooked by tourists, the 2e houses the **Bourse** (stock exchange), and some of the pretty 19th-century covered shopping passageways. The district, lying between the Grands Boulevards and the rue Etienne Marcel, is also home to the shopping **Sentier** area, where the garment trade is located, and wholesale fashion outlets abound. Sex shops and prostitutes line parts of the rue Saint-Denis, but the nearby area known as Montorgueil has lined former seedy streets with upscale and trendy cafes and boutiques, as well as upscale groceries, *boulangeries,* and other purveyors of fine edibles. The once-seedy area has thus long been transformed into a desirable location and a nice tourist destination.

3e: Le Marais

Le Marais (translated as "the swamp") is one of Paris's hippest neighborhoods. One of the city's most popular attractions, the **Musée Picasso,** and one of the more interesting museums, **Musée Carnavalet,** are located here. Paris's old Jewish neighborhood is located around the rue des Rosiers, and the rue Vieille-du-Temple is home to numerous gay bars and boutiques. Sadly, the hip boutiques that can pay the area's extremely high rents are beginning to crowd out the old stalwarts. Jo Goldenberg, the venerable Jewish deli, closed its doors in 2007.

4e: Le Marais/Ile Saint-Louis/Beaubourg

Aristocratic town houses, courtyards, and antiques shops, the **Brasserie Ile-Saint-Louis** (a historic brasserie with literary associations), **Berthillon** (reputed to be Paris's best ice cream), the **Centre Georges Pompidou museum,** and the **place des Vosges** make up the 4e *arrondissement,* which is located partly on the Ile Saint-Louis and partly in the Marais district. The area around the Centre Pompidou (known as Beaubourg) is one of Paris's more eclectic; you see everyone from pierced and Goth-style art students to chic Parisians walking their children to school to tourists buying football shirts from one of the many souvenir stores.

8e: Champs-Elysées/Madeleine

The 8e is the heart of the Right Bank, and its showcase is the **Champs-Elysées.** The Champs stretches from the **Arc de Triomphe** to the city's oldest monument, the Egyptian obelisk on **place de la Concorde.** The **place de la Madeleine** features a Roman Catholic church, built in the late 18th century in the style of a Greek temple. The fashion houses, the most elegant hotels, expensive restaurants and shops, and the most fashionably attired Parisians are here.

9e: Opéra Garnier/Pigalle

Everything from the **Quartier de l'Opéra** (the neighborhood around the Opéra Garnier) to the strip joints of **Pigalle** falls within the 9e, which was radically altered by Baron Haussmann's 19th-century redevelopment projects; his Grands Boulevards radiate through the district. You'll probably pay a visit to the 9e to shop at its famous department stores, **Au Printemps** and **Galeries Lafayette.** Try to visit the **Opéra Garnier** (Paris Opera House), if only to see the gorgeous ceiling by Marc Chagall.

10e: Gare du Nord/Gare de l'Est

In the movie *Amélie,* the young heroine likes to skip stones on the Canal Saint-Martin in the hip neighborhood of the same name with a burgeoning night scene, located here. The canal's **quai de Valmy** and **quai de Jemmapes** are scenic, tree-lined promenades. The classic movie *Hôtel du Nord* was also filmed here. Although the areas around **Gare du Nord** and **Gare de l'Est** are as dreary as can be expected near major train stations, the southern part of the 10e west of the canal is a diverse area brimming with hip kids and musicians, as well as African and Middle Eastern immigrants.

11e: Opéra Bastille

The 11e has few landmarks (though its Bastille monument is one of France's most well-known) or famous museums, but the area has long been a mecca for hordes of young Parisians looking for nightlife more casual and less pretentious than the center of the city. Always crowded on weekends and in summer, the overflow retires to the steps of the **Opéra Bastille,** where inline skaters and skateboarders skate and teens flirt. A market on the weekends on boulevard Richard Lenoir across from the Bastille monument features the creations of more than 200 artists.

16e: Trocadéro/Bois de Boulogne

This area of Paris is where the moneyed live. Highlights include the **Bois de Boulogne** (the huge wooded park on Paris's western edge), the **Jardin du Trocadéro** (known for its famous fountains bordering the Eiffel Tower), the **Musée de Balzac,** the **Musée Guimet** (famous for its Asian collections), and the **Cimetière de Passy** (final resting place of

Manet, Talleyrand, Giraudoux, and Debussy). One of the largest *arrondissements,* the 16e is known today for its exclusivity, its BCBG residents (*Bon Chic Bon Genre,* or yuppie), its upscale rents, and some rather posh (and, according to its critics, rather smug) residential boulevards. The *arrondissement* includes what some visitors consider the best place in Paris from which to view the Eiffel Tower, the **place du Trocadéro.**

18e: Montmartre

The **Moulin Rouge,** the **Basilique du Sacré-Coeur** (the white domed structure on a hill overlooking Paris), and the **place du Tertre** (the square filled with restaurants behind it) are only some of the attractions in this outer *arrondissement.* Take a walk through the winding old streets here, and you feel transported into a small village from another era. The **Bateau-Lavoir,** Picasso's first studio in Paris, is also here. The city's most famous flea market, **Marché aux Puces de la Porte de Saint-Ouen,** is nearby in the 20e.

On the Left Bank

The following are neighborhoods you're likely to visit on the Left Bank.

5e: Latin Quarter

Bookstores, schools, churches, nightclubs, student dives, Roman ruins, publishing houses, and expensive boutiques characterize this district, which is called *Latin* because students and professors at the Sorbonne, located here, once spoke Latin exclusively. Stroll along **quai de Montebello,** inspecting the inventories of the *bouquinistes* (booksellers), and wander the shops in the old streets of rue de la Huchette and rue de la Harpe (but don't eat here — you can find much better places). The 5e also stretches down to the **Panthéon** and to the steep cobblestone rue Mouffetard behind it, where you can visit one of the city's best produce markets, eat at a variety of ethnic restaurants, or stroll past the hip cafes to find the charming **Place Monge** at the southern border of this neighborhood.

6e: Saint-Germain and the Luxembourg Gardens

The art school that turned away Rodin, the **École des Beaux-Arts,** is here, and so are some of the chicest designers and specialty boutiques around. But the secret of the district lies in discovering its narrow streets and hidden squares. Everywhere you turn here, you encounter famous historical and literary associations. For instance, the restaurant **Brasserie Lipp** is where Hemingway lovingly recalls eating potato salad in *A Moveable Feast,* and the **Café les Deux Magots** is depicted in the movie adaptation of Hemingway's *The Sun Also Rises.* The 6e takes in the **rue de Fleurus** where Gertrude Stein lived with Alice B. Toklas, and down the street is the wonderful **Luxembourg Gardens,** probably local residents' most loved park. (Try to find the Statue of Liberty in the garden.)

7e: Near the Eiffel Tower and Musée d'Orsay

The city's most famous symbol, the **Eiffel Tower,** dominates the 7e, and the western edge of the **Saint-Germain** neighborhood is here, too. The **Hôtel des Invalides,** which contains **Napoléon's Tomb** and the **Musée de l'Armée,** are in the 7e, in addition to the **Musée Rodin** and the **Musée d'Orsay,** the world's premier showcase of 19th-century French art and culture. The Left Bank's only department store, **Le Bon Marché,** is also located here, and so is a warren of streets along which beautiful shoes, clothing, and household objects are sold.

13e: Butte-aux-Cailles and Chinatown

Although high-rises dominate much of the 13e, a nightlife scene emerged around 2000 on barges along the **quai Tolbiac** (where the **Bibliothèque François Mitterrand** sits) and in the cozy network of winding streets that make up the **Butte-aux-Cailles** (literally "hill of pebbles") neighborhood. The 13e is a lively hub for Paris's Asian community with Vietnamese and Chinese restaurants along **avenue d'Ivry** and **avenue de Choisy** next to stores selling all kinds of items from France's former colonies in Southeast Asia. The Chinese New Year Parade takes place here in late January or February.

14e: Montparnasse

Montparnasse is the former stomping ground of the Lost Generation — writers Gertrude Stein, Ernest Hemingway, Edna St. Vincent Millay, Ford Madox Ford, and other American expatriates gathered here in the 1920s. After World War II, it ceased to be the center of intellectual life in Paris, but the memories linger. Some of the world's most famous literary cafes, including **La Rotonde, Le Select, Le Dôme,** and **La Coupole,** are in the northern end of this large *arrondissement,* near the Rodin statue of Balzac at the junction of boulevard Montparnasse and boulevard Raspail. Some of those same literary giants (most notably Jean-Paul Sartre and Simone de Beauvoir) are buried nearby, in the Cimetière du Montparnasse. At its southern end, the *arrondissement* contains pleasant residential neighborhoods filled with typically Parisian apartment buildings, many built between 1910 and 1940.

Finding Information after You Arrive

The Office de Tourisme et des Congrès de Paris (http://en.paris info.com) provides maps, brochures, and advice in English about any of the innumerable activities Paris has to offer. Branches can be found throughout the city at the following locations:

> ✔ The **main welcome center** at 25 rue des Pyramides, 1er, is open daily from 9 a.m. to 7 p.m. June through October, and daily 10 a.m. to 6 p.m. November through May (Métro: Pyramides).

✔ **The Gare du Nord** welcome center beneath the glass-roofed terminal can be found at 18 rue Dunkerque, 10e. It's open seven days a week from 8 a.m. to 6 p.m. (Métro and RER: Gare du Nord).

✔ **The Gare de Lyon** welcome center, 20 bd. Diderot, 12e, is open Monday to Saturday 8 a.m. to 6 p.m. (Métro and RER: Gare de Lyon).

✔ The **Anvers** bureau at **72 bd. Rochechouart,** Montmartre, 18e, is open daily 10 a.m. to 6 p.m. (Métro: Anvers).

The following seasonal welcome kiosks, (called Welcome Ambassadors) are open during the summers from June 3 through October 29 (closed July 14–15):

✔ The **Champs-Elysées Clemenceau** kiosk is on the north side of the Champs-Elysées and Avenue de Marigny, 8e; it's open daily from 9 a.m. to 7 p.m. (Métro: Champs-Elysées Clemenceau).

✔ The **Bastille** kiosk, 4 place de la Bastille, 12e, is open daily from 11 a.m. to 7 p.m. (Métro and RER: Gare de Lyon).

✔ The **Notre-Dame** kiosk is located in the square in front of the cathedral next to the Hôtel Dieu, 4e; it's open daily from 10 a.m. to 7 p.m. (Métro: Cité).

Getting around Paris

Probably your best introduction to Paris, and to the way the city is laid out, is from the north tower at Notre-Dame. You can see the magnificent cathedral from many parts of the city, and a visit helps you get oriented.

By Métro

The best way to get around Paris is to walk, but for longer distances, the Métro, or subway, rules. The **Métropolitain** is fast, safe, and easy to navigate. Open from 5:45 a.m. to 12:45 a.m. on weekdays and until 2 a.m. Friday and Saturday nights, it's an efficient and cheap way to get around. You may want to avoid the Métro during rush hour, between 7 and 10 a.m. and 6 and 8 p.m. Operated by the Régie Autonome des Transports Parisiens (RATP), the Métro has a total of 16 lines and 300 stations, making it likely that one is near your destination. The Métro is connected to the suburban commuter train, the **Réseau Express Régional (RER),** which connects downtown Paris with its airports and suburbs.

You can recognize a Métro station either by an elegant Art Nouveau gateway reading métropolitain (some only say métro) or by a big yellow *M* sign. Unless otherwise marked, all Métro stations have ticket booths, where a single ticket costs 1.70€ or a group of ten tickets, called a *carnet* (kar-*nay*), is 12€. You can buy tickets from an attendant or, in most stations, from a machine using cash or credit cards. Every Métro stop has maps of the system; you can get portable maps by asking at a ticket booth for *un plan du Métro* (uh plahn doo may-troh). Near the exits, you can find a *plan du quartier,* a very detailed pictorial map of the streets and buildings surrounding the station, with all exits marked. A good idea is to consult the *plan du quartier* before you exit the system, especially at very large stations. You may want to use a different exit to reach the other side of a busy street or wind up closer to your destination.

Navigating the Métro is easy, and you'll be a pro in no time. Here's what you do:

1. **Use the Métro map on the inside front cover of this book to figure out which station is closest to you.**

   For example, if you want to go to the Louvre and are in your hotel in the Latin Quarter (say, the Familia), check this book's hotel listing for your hotel's nearest Métro station. That station, or your starting point, is Jussieu. Look at the Métro map on the inside front cover of this book for the line containing the Jussieu station. (Each end of the lines on the Métro map is marked with the number of the line.) The Jussieu station is on Line 7.

2. **Look for your destination station.**

   In this case, it's the Louvre. You see that the Louvre has two stops: the Palais Royal–Musée du Louvre station on lines 7 and 1 and the Louvre-Rivoli station on Line 1. Choose the Palais Royal–Musée du Louvre station, and you won't have to change trains.

3. **Enter the Métro system through a turnstile with two ticket slots.**

   With the magnetic strip facing down, insert your ticket into the nearer slot. Your ticket pops out of the second slot. Remove it, and either walk through a set of rubberized doors that briskly open on each side or push through a turnstile.

   Keep your ticket with you until you exit the station. At any point while you're in the Métro, an inspector may ask to see your ticket again. If you fail to produce it, you may have to pay a steep fine. When you ride the RER, or suburban rail, you must keep your ticket because you have to insert it into a turnstile when you exit the station.

4. **Make sure you're going in the right direction.**

   When you're past the entrance, look at your subway map and trace the line past your destination to its end. The station's name at the end of the line is the name of the subway train on which you'll be traveling; in the case of Line 7, the train is La Courneuve. To get back to your hotel from the Louvre, you take the train going in the opposite direction, marked villejuif louis aragon, and exit at the Jussieu station.

5. **Enter the train and exit at the station you want.**

   Blue signs reading sortie mark all exits.

Although the names and lines may seem daunting at first, after a few tries the whole thing will become intuitive. Suppose, however, that the Métro line nearest to you doesn't directly go to your destination. For example, you want to go to the Arc de Triomphe from Jussieu, and the stop is Charles de Gaulle–Étoile. Find the Charles de Gaulle–Étoile stop on the Métro map. You see that you can reach Charles de Gaulle–Étoile on Line 6 or Line 1. But you're on Line 7. You have to change trains. Changing trains is called a *correspondance,* or transfer.

To make a **transfer** *(correspondance),* follow these steps:

1. **Figure out which transfer station you need.**

   On your map, blank white circles indicate where a number of lines intersect. These circles denote *transfer stations,* where you can change subway trains.

   To figure out where you need to change from the 7 train to Line 1 or Line 6 (to get from Jussieu to the Arc de Triomphe), use the map to see where Line 7 intersects with Line 1 and with Line 6. Line 7 and Line 6 intersect at Stalingrad, opposite from where you want to go. But Line 7 and Line 1 intersect at Concorde, very close to Charles de Gaulle–Étoile. This is the train you want to take. To make sure you go in the right direction on Line 1, look on your map for the name of the station at the very end past Charles de Gaulle–Étoile. It's called Grande Arche de la Défense, and this is the name of the train you want to ride.

2. **Look for a bright orange correspondance sign above the platform at the transfer station.**

   Beneath it is a white sign that has the number of the line you can transfer to in a circle (in the example, Line 1).

3. **Follow the direction the sign indicates for the line you want.**

   You eventually come to two stairwells leading to the platforms. Navy blue signs mark this area, indicating the train's direction and listing all the stops the train makes. Make sure you choose the stairwell leading to the train going in the direction you want — in the example, you want the train to Grande Arche de la Défense, so that you can exit at Charles de Gaulle–Étoile.

The distances between platforms at the *correspondance* stations can be very long. You may climb stairs, walk a short distance, only to descend stairs to walk some more. Châtelet is particularly long, as is Saint-Lazare. Some lines are connected by moving sidewalks that seem to do nothing but make a very long walk a little less long. Those with limited mobility should take the bus or a cab.

The Métro connects with the suburban commuter train, the RER, in several stations in the city. The RER operates on a zone fare system, but Métro tickets are valid on it in the city. You probably won't go past the first two zones, unless you visit Disneyland on the A4 or Versailles on the C5. When you ride the RER, keep your ticket because you need to insert it into a turnstile to leave the station.

The doors on most Métro cars don't open automatically. You must lift a door handle or press a button to get on and off.

Anyone who has ever been crushed on a Paris subway at rush hour can attest that commuters don't easily give up their places. If you step out of the train to let someone off, you may just be giving others on the platform the chance to squeeze in before you. Be polite, but stand your ground.

After the subway shuts down around 1 a.m., the RATP operates the **Noctilien,** 47 different lines of night buses that run from 12:30 a.m. to 5:30 a.m. The network uses the areas around Châtelet, Montparnasse, Gare de l'Est, Gare Saint-Lazare, and Gare de Lyon as the transfer stations, covering most areas of the city (but not all — some walking may be required). A blue-and-white *N* symbol identifies bus stops during the evening hours. All Métro tickets, Navigo passes, Paris Visite cards, and Mobilis passes are accepted on the Noctilien.

A ten-ticket *carnet* for the metro and buses is a great idea, as it will save you a healthy 5€ extra over individual tickets — a good deal because it provides a small price reduction per ticket. You can purchase a *carnet* at all Métro stations as well as *tabacs* (cafes and kiosks that sell tobacco products).

How long do you plan to be in Paris? If you plan to use public transportation frequently, consider buying a **Navigo,** the system that replaced the venerable **Carte Orange.** This system allows passengers to quickly get through the turnstiles by waving the pass over a magnetic sensor. Only residents of île-de-France have a right to a free Navigo pass, but that doesn't mean you can't get the same savings a Parisian can; you just have to ask for the Navigo *découverte,* which, for an additional 5€ fee, is open to any transit customer.

The passes must be accompanied by a passport-size identity photo affixed (snap one at photo booths in major train and Métro stations, usually 4€ for four photos). Make sure you get the Navigo *semaine* (week) pass, which costs 17€.

Word has it that some station agents are misleading tourists to believe that they have to be a resident of Ile-de-France to get a Navigo, but be firm and persistent. By law, anyone *(tout le monde)* can purchase one. The Navigo should be purchased by the Monday of the week you want to use it for the most value — so don't buy the pass on Wednesday, the last day it's on sale for the week in which it's valid, because you won't get your money's worth. Passes purchased later on in the week won't be activated until the following Monday, so make sure you have a trusty *carnet* to get you through the weekend until then.

The heavily publicized **Paris Visite** card offers free or reduced entry to some minor attractions and free souvenirs from others in addition to unlimited travel on Métro and buses, but make sure the attractions that interest you are included on the list (ask for it at the ticket window first). Buy the **Paris Visite** (the regular pass covers zones 1–3, which include all of central Paris and many of its suburbs) if you're in Paris for only a day or two. At 9€ for one day or 15€ for two days (kids 4–11 pay half-price; kids 3 and under ride free), it's a good deal. The most comprehensive pass covers zones 1 through 6 (all the suburbs and Disneyland Paris). However, the three-day 20€ and the five-day 29€ Paris Visites are a waste of money. Instead, consider the **Navigo** (see earlier in this section).

If you're planning to mostly walk around and are only planning to use the Métro heavily on certain days of the week, consider the **Mobilis,** a one-day pass that gives you unlimited travel in zones 1 and 2 (within the city limits) for 6.10€. These passes are also useful for traveling to day trips outside of Paris, like **Versailles** (in zone 4, 10€), which will allow you to take the RER and use the buses in the area.

For more information on the city's public transportation, call the **RATP's** English information line (☎ **08-92-69-32-46** from outside France, or ☎ **32-46** within France at a charge of 0.35€ per minute; www.ratp.fr).

By bus

The bus system is convenient and can be an inexpensive way to sightsee without wearing out your feet. Most Parisian buses run from 6:30 a.m. to 8:30 p.m.; a few run until 12:30 a.m. Each bus shelter has a route map, which you want to check carefully. Because of the number of one-way streets, the bus is likely to make different stops depending on its direction. Main stops are written on the sides of the buses with the endpoint shown on the front above the driver. Furthermore, the back of every bus shelter has posted large bus maps, with smaller maps inside the shelter, showing the specific bus route. Métro tickets are valid for bus travel; although you can buy single tickets from the conductor, you can't buy ticket packages *(carnets)* on the bus.

Board at the front of the bus. If you have a single-trip ticket, insert it into the slot in the small machine right behind the driver. The machine punches your ticket and pops it back out. If you have a pass, show it to the driver. To get off at the next stop, press one of the red buttons on the safety poles; the arrêt demandé (stop requested) sign above the driver lights up.

Since 2009, bus passengers can now use their single tickets to transfer to any bus within 90 minutes of a ticket's original use. This makes quick errands en route to a destination very simple — on your way to a picnic in a park, for example, you can get off to do your food shopping at any destination and get back on the same line using only one ticket. Super!

Keeping the picks out of your pockets

Although Paris is as a safe as any other major world city, anywhere you find a high concentration of tourists, you also find pickpockets. These include in the Métro, hovering around the lines outside the Eiffel Tower, Sacré-Coeur and Notre-Dame, and in the church and its bell tower. Keep an eye out for little bands of scruffy children, who often surround you, distract you, and make off with your belongings. Also, don't accept handwritten note cards from disheveled-looking people — they often give a short, sad, hard-luck story in several languages, and taking one suggests that you'll give them money in return.

Your best bet is to use common sense. Be aware of the people around you at all times. Get a money belt. Women wear purses diagonally across the body with the flap facing the body. Make sure zipper purses are closed at all times. (In fact, zippered purses aren't recommended.) See Chapter 4 for what to do if you get pickpocketed.

The downside of taking the bus is that it often gets mired in heavy Parisian traffic, so I don't recommend it if you're in a hurry. And, like the Métro, avoid the bus during rush hours when it seems *le monde* (the world) is sharing the bus with you (and most likely, without air-conditioning).

Bus routes great for sightseeing include

- ✔ **Bus 69:** Eiffel Tower, Invalides, Louvre, Hôtel de Ville, place des Vosges, Bastille, Père-Lachaise Cemetery

- ✔ **Bus 80:** Department stores on boulevard Haussmann, Champs-Elysées, avenue Montaigne haute couture shopping, Eiffel Tower

- ✔ **Bus 96:** Saint-Germain-des-Prés, Musée de Cluny, Hôtel de Ville, place des Vosges

By taxi

You have three ways to get a taxi in Paris, and I rank them in order of how successful they are:

- ✔ The best way to find a cab is by phoning **Alpha Taxis** (☎ 01-53-60-63-50) or **Taxis G7** (☎ 01-47-39-47-39). Keep in mind, however, that phoning ahead is more expensive because the meter starts running as soon as the driver commences the journey to get you.

- ✔ You can also **wait at a taxi stand** *(station de taxis)* marked by a blue taxi sign. Depending on the time of day, however, you may wait in a long line of people, or a very limited number of cabs stop.

✔ Finally, you can **hail a cab,** as long as you're not within 60m (200 ft.) of a taxi stand. Look for a taxi with its taxi parisien sign illuminated, which means the cab is available. If one of the three small lights on the bottom of the sign (which are white, orange, or blue) is lit, it means that the cab is occupied or unavailable.

 Taxi service in Paris is notoriously bad — even current president Nicolas Sarkozy was quoted as saying, "Paris is the only city in the world where you just cannot find a taxi." Although it isn't always the case (and is against the rules), some chauffeurs will flat-out refuse to go to a destination if they think it's inconvenient. It's possible you'll have no issues at all, but in this case, it's best to prepare for the worst.

Be prepared, as well, for the selective vision of drivers, especially when you hail a cab. Don't be surprised to see a free taxi or two pass you by.

The initial fare for up to three passengers is 2.20€; between 10 a.m. and 5 p.m., the fare rises 0.90€ for each kilometer (⅔ mile). Between 5 p.m. and 10 a.m., the standing charge remains the same, but the per-kilometer charge rises to 1.15€. An additional fee of 1€ is imposed for luggage weighing more than 5kg (11 pounds) or for an extra bag. A fourth passenger incurs a 2.95€ charge. Common practice is to tip your driver 10 percent to 15 percent on longer journeys when the fare exceeds 15€; otherwise, round up the charge to the nearest euro and give it to the driver.

By car

Streets are narrow, parking is next to impossible, and nerve, skill, ruthlessness, and a knowledgeable copilot are required if you insist on driving in Paris. I *strongly* recommend that you don't. (If you must drive in Paris, do it in Aug when residents are away on vacation, and traffic is lighter.)

A few tips: Get an excellent street map at a bookstore, Monoprix, or the Fnac, and ride with another person; traffic moves so lightning fast you don't have time to think at intersections. You must pay to park Monday through Saturday from 9 a.m. to 7 p.m. Parking is free on Sundays and public holidays; Saturdays and during August certain streets offer free parking (look for yellow stickers on the parking meters). Street parking is limited to two hours and fees start at 1.20€ an hour on Paris's outskirts, 2.40€ in most of central Paris, and 3.60€ in the neighborhoods surrounding the Champs-Elysées. Note that meters don't accept coins and take only a Paris Carte card, available in *tabacs* for 15€ to 40€. After you insert the Paris Carte, the meter issues a ticket to be placed on the windshield.

Drivers and all passengers must wear seat belts. Children 11 and under must ride in the backseat. Drivers are supposed to yield to the car on the right, except where signs indicate otherwise, as at traffic circles.

Watch for the *gendarmes* (police officers), who lack patience and who consistently contradict the traffic lights. Horn blowing is frowned upon except in emergencies. Flash your headlights instead.

By bicycle

 In 2007, Mayor Bertrand Delanoë launched the Velib' bicycle rental program, bringing 10,000 bikes into the city, placing them in specially built bike racks in high-pedestrian destinations. Three years later, with over 20,000 bicycles and over 1,200 stations, the program is quite successful (though it has its detractors, most of all overly excited car enthusiasts). You can spot regular Velib' users riding around the city at all hours of the day and night.

After you purchase your short-term subscription card (see the next paragraph) any Velib' can be used for free as long as it's returned to any of the stations before a 30-minute interval. Afterward, you'll be charged 1€ for the next 30 minutes, then 2€ for the next 30 minutes, and then afterwards an additional 4€.

Buy a one-day (1€) or seven-day (5€) short-term ticket *(abonnement courte durée)* at any Velib' station or *tabac.* You'll need a valid credit card (in order to charge a temporary security deposit). Only bank cards with a microchip will work at the automated Velib' stations (at the time of writing, American Express Blue credit cards and some Chase debit cards have a chip).

The banks of the Seine are closed to cars and open to pedestrians and cyclists March through November Sunday from 10 a.m. to 5 p.m. Certain streets are also blocked off as pedestrian-only, and since 2009 the city has continually added bike lanes and pictographic signage indicating the right of bicyclists to travel along certain one-way streets in both directions, among other "green" transportation initiatives.

Paris à pied (on foot)

Paris is one of the prettiest cities in the world for strolling, and if you don't spend at least half your trip wandering the city, you've done the wrong thing. After all, getting around on foot is probably the best way to really appreciate the city's character. The best walking neighborhoods are **Saint-Germain-des-Prés** on the Left Bank and the **Marais** on the Right Bank, both of which are filled with romantic little courtyards, wonderful boutiques, and congenial cafes and watering holes. The **quays of the Seine,** as well as its bridges, are also lovely, especially at sunset when the sun fills the sky with a pink glow that's reflected on the water. **Montmartre,** with its twisted (and sometime) steep streets, is worth the workout, with a more-than-equal payout in charm. And try not to miss the pretty **Canal Saint-Martin** with its arched bridges and locks in the 10e, featured in the movies *Amélie* and *Hôtel du Nord.*

Take special care when crossing streets, even when you have the right of way. The number-one rule of the road in France is that whoever is coming from the right side has the right of way. Drivers often make right turns without looking, even when faced with pedestrians at crosswalks. And don't ever attempt to cross a traffic circle if you're not on a crosswalk. The larger roundabouts, such as the one at the Arc de Triomphe, have pedestrian tunnels.

Chapter 9

Checking in at Paris's Best Hotels

In This Chapter

▶ Getting the best room at the best rate
▶ Finding a place to stay without a reservation
▶ Reviewing Paris's favorite accommodations
▶ Locating hotels by neighborhood and price

*I*f this is your first trip to Paris, your expectations about what a hotel room should look like may be based on what you have seen in your own country. For those visiting from North America, one important thing to know is that rooms in Paris tend to be on the smaller side, even in expensive places (unless you opt for a modern chain hotel, which can lack charm, or ultra-deluxe lodgings). Parisian doubles are almost never big enough to hold two queen-size beds, and the space around the bed usually isn't big enough for more than a desk and perhaps a chest of drawers. The story is the same in London, Berlin, Rome, and most other Continental capitals where buildings date back two, three, four, or more centuries, when everything was smaller.

Parisian hotels also vary widely in their plumbing arrangements. The cheapest units come equipped with only a sink; others may also have a toilet and either a shower or tub. Private bathrooms with tubs often have handheld shower devices (known in North America as "European" showers), and some shower stalls don't have curtains (the water often drains into a grate in the floor). Even some baths with a showerhead won't have a curtain — try not to spray the water everywhere. The trend is toward renovating small hotels by installing a small shower, toilet, and sink in each room, but don't count on having *all* these amenities in your room unless you're in a hotel of a certain price.

Acoustics tend to be unpredictable in old Parisian hotels. Your quarreling neighbors may compete with street noise for the prize of most annoying, so bring earplugs for the neighbors, or ask for a room in the rear of the hotel or with a courtyard view. Another point to remember: Most budget hotels in Paris don't have air-conditioning, so consider this if you're visiting in July or August.

Getting to Know Your Options

More than 1,500 hotels are located in Paris — chain hotels, deluxe palace-like accommodations, hotels that cater to business travelers, budget hotels, and mom-and-pop establishments.

The French government grades hotels with a star system, ranging from one star for a simple motel or inn to four stars for a deluxe hotel. Moderately priced hotels usually get two or three stars. This system is based on a complex formula of room sizes, facilities, plumbing, elevators, dining options, renovations, and so on.

To find the hotel that's right for you, you need to weigh five variables: price, location, room size, amenities, and — the least tangible, but perhaps most desired of them all — a charming Parisian ambience. If the first variable, price, poses no problem, then you can have it all: great location, huge room, super perks, and sumptuous surroundings. Most travelers, however, need to make some compromises.

Before committing to a hotel, keep in mind that Paris offers alternative options for lodging — renting an apartment, for example. Nothing beats living in Paris as a Parisian. In your own **apartment,** you can cook with fresh and unusual ingredients from the local green markets, taste fine wines that would be too expensive in a restaurant, and entertain new friends. Although the daily rate can be higher than a budget hotel, the room will be larger, you can save money on meals, and in the end, you may end up paying the same rate you would for room and board at a hotel — or less.

The most practical way to rent an apartment is through an agency. Most agencies require a seven-day minimum stay and offer discounts for longer stays. Parisian apartments come in all shapes, sizes, and locations, with varying amenities. At the bottom end — for about 60€ per day — you'll find yourself in either a small, centrally located studio or a larger studio in a neighborhood a bit far from the center of Paris. Studio apartments usually feature a convertible couch; an armchair or two; a bathroom with a tub or shower; and a tiny kitchenette with a refrigerator, stove, coffeemaker, and maybe a microwave. Dishes, cutlery, pots and pans, telephone, TV, iron, vacuum cleaner, linens, and sometimes a washing machine are also provided. Pay a bit more — around 150€ per day — and you get a more centrally located one-bedroom apartment. As with anything else, higher prices pay for larger, more luxurious spaces, often with really appealing décor.

You can find many rental agencies online and comparison-shop among them. Companies offering attractive apartments at reasonable prices are **Apartment Living in Paris** (www.apartment-living.com), which, at press time, advertised a 40-sq-m (450-sq.-ft.) two-room, one-bedroom rental in the Latin Quarter for 135€ per night, and **Lodgis** (www.lodgis. com), which also rents apartments in New York, the French Riviera, and Marrakech, and, at press time, advertised a chic one-bedroom with exposed wooden beams in the trendy **Marais** area for 650€ per week. **Rentals in Paris** (www.rentals-paris.com) is an agency that deals in short-term rental of upscale apartments at very good prices (a good-size one bedroom near the Louvre was renting for 900€ a week at press time). A little more expensive is **New York Habitat** (www.newyork habitat.com), a New York real-estate brokerage that rents flats in Paris and elsewhere as a sideline (a duplex one-bedroom near the Louvre and Opéra was going for 540€ per week at press time). Check out **Bonjour Paris** (www.bonjourparis.com) for reviews and information about apartment rental agencies.

Keep in mind that this is a short-term apartment rental with a signed contract. Take into account the agency fees and a security deposit, which may not be refunded if you damage the apartment in any way.

If the agency offers optional gift baskets or transportation to and from the airport, refuse them. The gift basket usually contains items you can buy more cheaply at the grocery store, and the transportation is usually twice as much as a cab.

If you bring the kids with you to Paris, your best option may be the *aparthotel,* a hybrid between an apartment and a hotel where you can have the autonomy of an apartment with some of the amenities of a hotel. You book an aparthotel just like you do any other hotel, through its Web site or phone number. And, like hotels, they have 24-hour reception desks, satellite TVs, housekeeping services, kitchenettes, and laundry. For a family of four, a one-bedroom apartment is a good-value alternative to two double rooms in a cheap hotel. And if you use your kitchenette to prepare even half your own meals in Paris, you can reap huge savings on your dining bill.

If you don't mind opening your house or apartment to others during your vacation, you might find that an **apartment swap** is your best bet. Several agencies will work with you for a small fee to advertise your residence and find a place for you to stay abroad. Check out **Home Xchange Vacation** (www.homexchangevacation.com) or **Home Base Holidays** (www.homebase-hols.com). It's almost always better to do an apartment swap through an agency, which screens members so that you're protected from problems.

Finding the Best Room at the Best Rate

The *rack rate* is the maximum rate a hotel charges for a room. It's the rate you get if you walk in off the street and ask for a room for the night.

But you often don't have to pay it! This section gives tips on finding the best rooms in Paris at the best rate.

Finding the best rate

At chain hotels (especially the American ones) and other luxury hotels, you can often get a good deal simply by asking for a discounted rate. Your odds of getting a reduced rate improve drastically if you're staying for more than a few nights.

Keep in mind that bartering for a cheaper room isn't the norm at Paris's budget hotels. Small and privately owned, owners post their rates in the reception area and are not willing to negotiate. To be fair, they may not be able to afford to let rooms go for less.

Room rates change with the seasons as occupancy rates rise and fall. In Paris, late summer is the off season. Yes, you're reading that correctly: Room rates tend to be lower toward the end of July and August, which is typically when the French flee the big cities for the beaches and the mountains. November and December are also an off season, but early fall is high season, with October, in particular, heavy with convention-eers, which may make it difficult to find a room. If a hotel is close to full, it's less likely to extend discount rates.

Prices for the hotels recommended here are designated with dollar signs; Table 9-1 explains how this works. In a nutshell, the more dollar signs you see, the more expensive the hotel. The number of dollar signs corresponds to the hotel's rack rates (full rate), from the cheapest double room in the off season to the most expensive in high season. The most notice-able difference between budget hotels and the most expensive hotels is better amenities and services, followed by a more luxurious décor. None of the recommended hotels listed in this chapter is a dump; the places are decent and reputable. Naturally, the level of luxury in a 1,000€ room is substantially higher than in a 100€ one.

Table 9-1		Key to Hotel Prices
Dollar Sign(s)	Price Range	What to Expect
$	100€ or less	These accommodations are relatively simple and inex-pensive. Rooms are likely to be small, with limited toilet-ries and thin towels. Televisions are not necessarily provided. Parking is not provided but is rather catch-as-you-can on the street.
$$	101€–150€	A bit classier, these midrange accommodations offer more room, more extras (such as irons, hair dryers, a trouser press, cable or satellite TV, and Wi-Fi), and a more convenient location than the preceding category.

Dollar Sign(s)	Price Range	What to Expect
$$$	151€–300€	Higher class still, these accommodations are on the plush side with chocolates on your pillow, a classy restaurant, room service, good-quality toiletries, and maybe a view of the Eiffel Tower or another landmark.
$$$$	301€ or more	These top-rated accommodations come with luxury amenities such as on-premise spas, deluxe toiletries, stereo and DVD players, multistar gourmet restaurants with room service, views, robes — frankly nearly every luxury you can imagine but not without adding some points to your credit card.

Room prices are subject to change without notice, so the rates quoted in this book may be different from the actual rate you receive when you make your reservation. Be sure to mention membership in AAA, AARP, frequent-flier programs, and any other corporate rewards programs you belong to when making your reservation at a chain hotel. You never know when it may be worth a few dollars off your room rate. Family-run establishments rarely have arrangements with large organizations.

Keep this advice in mind when you're trying to save money on a room.

- ✔ A **travel agent** may be able to negotiate a better price at top hotels than you can get yourself. (The hotel gives the agent a discount for steering business its way.)

- ✔ Always ask if the hotel offers any **weekend specials,** which typically require you to stay two nights (either Fri–Sat or Sat–Sun). In Paris, you can find this kind of deal from September through March at almost all price levels.

- ✔ A *forfait* (*fohr*-feh) is a discount that requires you to stay a certain number of nights — perhaps a minimum of three or five. Sometimes something else is thrown in (like a bottle of champagne) to sweeten the deal. If you're going to be in Paris for more than three days, always ask if there's a *forfait,* and then pick the hotel with the best deal.

- ✔ Don't forget about **package deals** (see Chapter 5) that include airfare, hotel, and transportation to and from the airport.

- ✔ Always look first on the **Internet** for deals (see below).

Surfing the Web for hotel deals

Although the major travel booking sites (such as Cheap Tickets, Expedia, Orbitz, and Travelocity; see Chapter 5 for details) offer hotel booking, using a site devoted primarily to lodging can be best because you may find properties that aren't listed on more general online travel agencies. The **Paris Convention and Visitors Bureau** (http://en. parisinfo.com) gives detailed information on hotels and other lodging they sanction and provides links to accommodations reservation centers (but the Web site doesn't tell you about special rates). Some lodging sites specialize in a particular type of lodging, such as bed-and-breakfast accommodations, which you won't find on the more mainstream booking services. Others offer weekend deals on major chain properties that cater to business travelers and have more empty rooms on weekends. And finally, some individual hotels offer an "Internet bonus" for a reservation made on their personal Web site. Therefore, checking out some of the online lodging sites, many of which offer discounts, is in your best interest.

Hotel Discounts (www.hoteldiscounts.com) offers bargain room rates at hotels in more than two dozen U.S. and international cities. The service prebooks blocks of rooms in advance, so sometimes it has rooms — at discount rates — at hotels that otherwise are considered sold out. **France Hotels Online** (www.france-hotel-online.com) offers detailed listings of independent hotels, apartments, and bed-and-breakfasts according to budget and neighborhood. **AllHotels** (www.all hotels.com) lists 140,000 lodgings throughout the world; the hotels on this site pay a fee to be listed. **PlacesToStay** (www.placestostay.com) lists inns, B&Bs, resorts, hotels, and properties you may not find anywhere else. **Hostelworld** (www.hostelworld.com) lists youth hostels and cheap hotel deals in Paris and major cities around the world and offers ratings written by former clients of the various accommodations; budget travelers can find excellent deals here.

Arriving without a Reservation

If you arrive in Paris without a reservation, you have two choices. You can pick up a phone and start dialing (after you purchase a phone card for public phones at the nearest *tabac,* a cafe or kiosk that sells tobacco products). Or you can walk into one of the branches of the **Paris Convention and Visitors Bureau** (http://en.parisinfo.com) and let the multilingual staff make you a reservation. The main switchboard for any branch is ☎ **08-92-68-30-00** (.35€ per minute). (*Note:* These centers are closed on May 1, and the switchboard is closed Sun and public holidays, which includes Dec 25.)

- ✔ The **Anvers** welcome center, on the median strip facing 72 bd. Rochechouart, 9e, is open daily 10 a.m. to 6 p.m. (Métro: Anvers)

- ✔ The welcome kiosk beneath the modern glass-roofed terminal of the **Gare du Nord,** 18 rue Dunkerque, 10e, is open daily 8 a.m. to 6 p.m. (Métro and RER: Gare du Nord)

- ✔ The main welcome center at **Pyramides** (near the Louvre), 25 rue des Pyramides, 1e, is open Monday through Saturday 10 a.m. to 7 p.m., Sunday 11 a.m. to 7 p.m. (Métro: Pyramides)

Hotels with unsold rooms offer them through the Paris Convention and Visitors Bureau at rock-bottom prices, so you may get a three-star hotel at a two-star price. The staff will make a reservation for you on the same day that you want a room, free of charge, but it must be on a credit card or debit card (which will act as a credit card while you're in a foreign country).

Note that during the summer season, you'll have to wait in a long line, and you aren't guaranteed a room.

Paris's Best Hotels

The thousands of hotels in Paris range from small alcove singles in historic buildings to the historic and palatial that anticipate a traveler's every need. But only around 50 are described in this chapter. The reason? You don't need an overwhelming, encyclopedic list of all the hotels — just ones that are right for you, and an equally right backup in case your first choice is booked solid. In compiling this list, my first step was to consider the typical traveler's wish list. And for most people, the main priority is location. Thus, the first criterion, though ruthless, was simple: **If a hotel isn't located in the first nine *arrondissements,* it isn't recommended in this book.** The second concern was price. The most expensive category listed here, $$$$, contains hotels that cost more than 300€ a night, which is expensive by nearly anyone's standards. Only a few hotels described here fall into the $$$$ category because most travelers are on a budget. (For a complete rundown on the $ system, see Table 9-1.) Three-quarters of the hotels in this chapter rent doubles for less than 150€ a night but nevertheless give you comfort, some nice amenities, and a taste of Parisian character for which the city's hotels are known. None of the hotels listed here is a dive. Finally, a variety of neighborhoods between the first and ninth *arrondissements* are represented here, with a nice range of styles from conservative to trendy. The aim? I want to make sure that everyone is accounted for, regardless of budget, taste, or style of travel.

In this chapter, two maps pinpoint the locations of the hotels: "Hotels in the Heart of the Right Bank" and "Hotels in the Heart of the Left Bank." Reviews are arranged alphabetically for easy reference. Hotels that are especially good for families are designated with the Kid Friendly icon. Listed immediately beneath the name of the hotel is the neighborhood in which it's located and the number of dollar signs corresponding to the hotel's rack rates, from the cheapest double room in the off season to the most expensive in high season. At the end of the chapter are indexes of accommodations by price and neighborhood for easy reference.

Almost all hotels serve breakfast in some form. Note that a normal *petit déjeuner* (breakfast), also referred to as *continental,* will usually include coffee or tea, juice, a croissant, *pain au chocolat* (a croissant with a thin

Hotels in the Heart of the Right Bank (1–4, 8–12, and 16–18)

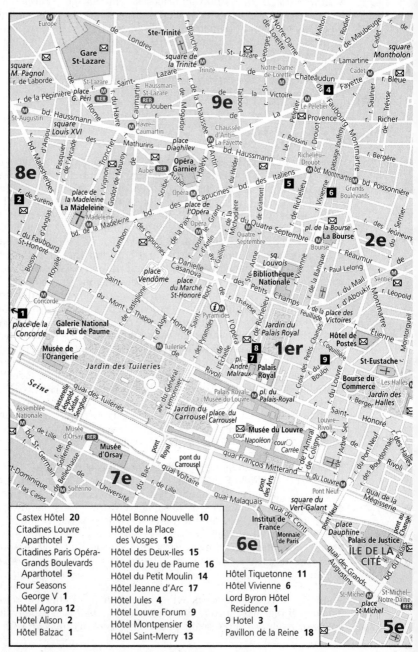

Castex Hôtel **20**	Hôtel Bonne Nouvelle **10**	
Citadines Louvre Aparthotel **7**	Hôtel de la Place des Vosges **19**	
Citadines Paris Opéra-Grands Boulevards Aparthotel **5**	Hôtel des Deux-Iles **15**	
	Hôtel du Jeu de Paume **16**	
Four Seasons George V **1**	Hôtel du Petit Moulin **14**	Hôtel Tiquetonne **11**
Hôtel Agora **12**	Hôtel Jeanne d'Arc **17**	Hôtel Vivienne **6**
Hôtel Alison **2**	Hôtel Jules **4**	Lord Byron Hôtel Residence **1**
Hôtel Balzac **1**	Hôtel Louvre Forum **9**	9 Hotel **3**
	Hôtel Montpensier **8**	Pavillon de la Reine **18**
	Hôtel Saint-Merry **13**	

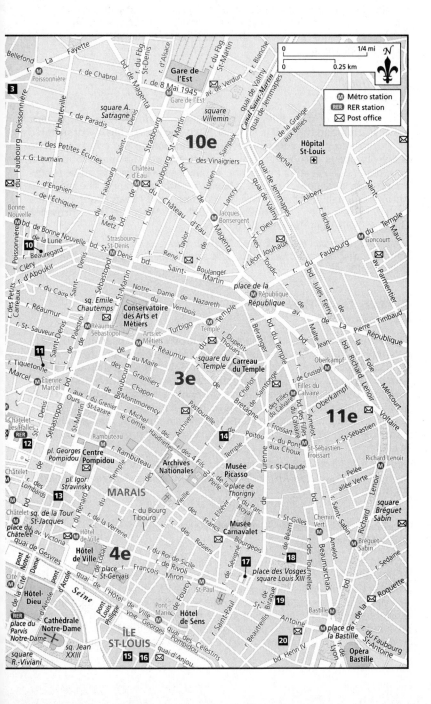

thread of chocolate filling) or similar pastry, and toast with various *confitures* (jams). If a hotel also offers *un petit déjeuner Américain* (an American breakfast), it means the hotel offers a buffet with eggs and meats — but you'll pay for it.

Castex Hotel
$$ Le Marais (4e)

The Castex is a popular budget classic, near *everything* in the eastern part of the Marais, and the staff is friendly. Each large room has a writing table or a desk and chair; some have views overlooking the courtyard. The entryway opens onto a wide and comfortable wood-beamed lobby with newspapers and seating for guests. Rooms have televisions; some rooms are also wood-beamed. Reserve at least a month in advance. The rue Saint-Antoine is a half-block away and offers some good cheap shopping and a variety of places to eat. Booking through the Web site often provides cheaper deals than the rates listed here.

See map p. 108. 5 rue Castex. ☎ **01-42-72-31-52.** *www.castexhotel.com. Métro: Bastille or Sully-Morland. Rack rates: 125€ single, 155€ double or twin, 220€ triple. Breakfast 12€. AE, MC, V.*

Citadines Louvre Paris
$$$ Louvre (1er)

This seven-story aparthotel is in a terrific location in an upscale and pretty neighborhood just opposite the Comédie-Française and next to the Jardin du Palais-Royal. Once a students' residence, it has several studios (each with a double pullout sofa) and apartments equipped for travelers with disabilities. Studios and one-bedrooms (a separate bedroom with two single beds and pullout double sofa) have fully equipped kitchenettes, and services include a 24-hour reception desk, satellite TV, air-conditioning, housekeeping, baby-equipment rental, and laundry facilities. Book well in advance.

See map p. 108. 8 rue de Richelieu (one block north of the Louvre). ☎ **01-55-35-28-00.** *www.citadines.com. Métro: Palais-Royal or Pyramides. Rack rates: 188€–300€. AE, MC, V.*

Citadines Opéra–Grands Boulevards Paris
$$$–$$$$ Opéra (2e)

Around the corner from the Opéra Comique, the Musée Jacquemart-André, and the Comédie-Française and near the Grands Boulevards, this five-story aparthotel is the most central in the Citadines chain. It's located in a peaceful passage, and rooms come with fully equipped kitchenettes; available services include a 24-hour reception desk, satellite TV, Internet, air-conditioning, baby-equipment rental, dry cleaning, laundry facilities, housekeeping, bar, billiard table, and fitness center. A one-bedroom apartment here (two single beds in the bedroom, a double pullout couch) can be a good alternative to renting two rooms in a cheap hotel because cooking in the kitchenette saves on your dining costs.

See map p. 108. 18 rue Favart. ☎ **01-40-15-14-00.** www.citadines.com. *Métro: Richelieu-Drouot. Rack rates: 178€–225€ two-person studio, 298€–345€ three-person duplex (one-bedroom) apartment, 295€–345€ four-person (one-bedroom) apartment. AE, MC, V.*

Familia Hotel
$–$$ Latin Quarter (5e)

This hotel has many repeat visitors and no wonder — the rooms have been painstakingly restored with either provincial-inspired wallpaper or sepia frescoes painted by students from l'École des Beaux-Arts (Paris's best art school). The cozy lobby exudes the atmosphere of a tiny castle with rich tapestries, a winding staircase, and frescoed walls. Some rooms (nos. 22, 23, 52, 53, 61, 62, and 65) have balconies with furniture and boast captivating views of the Latin Quarter. From the fifth and sixth floors, you can see Notre-Dame. Bathrooms are small but modern and tiled. All rooms have satellite TV, stocked minibar and fridge, and hair dryers. There is Wi-Fi but it isn't free; access costs 6€. The staff provides kid-friendly services (such as bottle heating) and larger rooms for the weary traveler who requests ahead. Take note that most rooms in the hotel are on the small side, and the least-expensive doubles in the corners are tiny. No air-conditioning is provided — remember that it can get hot in Paris heat waves.

See map p. 113. 11 rue des Écoles. ☎ **01-43-54-55-27.** *Fax: 01-43-29-61-77.* www.familiahotel.com. *Métro: Cardinal Lemoine or Jussieu. Rack rates: 86€–97€ single, 97€–127€ double, 149€ triple, 176€ quad. Breakfast 6€. AE, DC, MC, V.*

Four Seasons Hotel George V Paris
$$$$ Champs-Elysées (8e)

This is one of Paris's truly legendary palace hotels, combining the old (Murano chandeliers and Louis XIV tapestries) with a sleek, light-wood-and-marble lobby opening onto an outside marble courtyard decorated with bright blue awnings and umbrellas. A team of concierges greets guests staying in 245 large rooms, separated from the public corridors by their own hallways for more peace and quiet. Louis XVI–style furniture, marble bathrooms with Bulgari toiletries, stereo systems with iPod docking stations, DVD players, and wireless Internet access are the norm. The Honeymoon Suite has three terraces; other suites offer a stone's-throw view of the Eiffel Tower — some from their bathtubs. Amenities include the signature Four Seasons mattresses (930 coils instead of the industry-standard 800); a spa (with its own elevator) offering 24-hour massage services and a huge pool, sauna, and hot tub; an American bar; and multistar

Hotels in the Heart of the Left Bank (5–7 and 13–14)

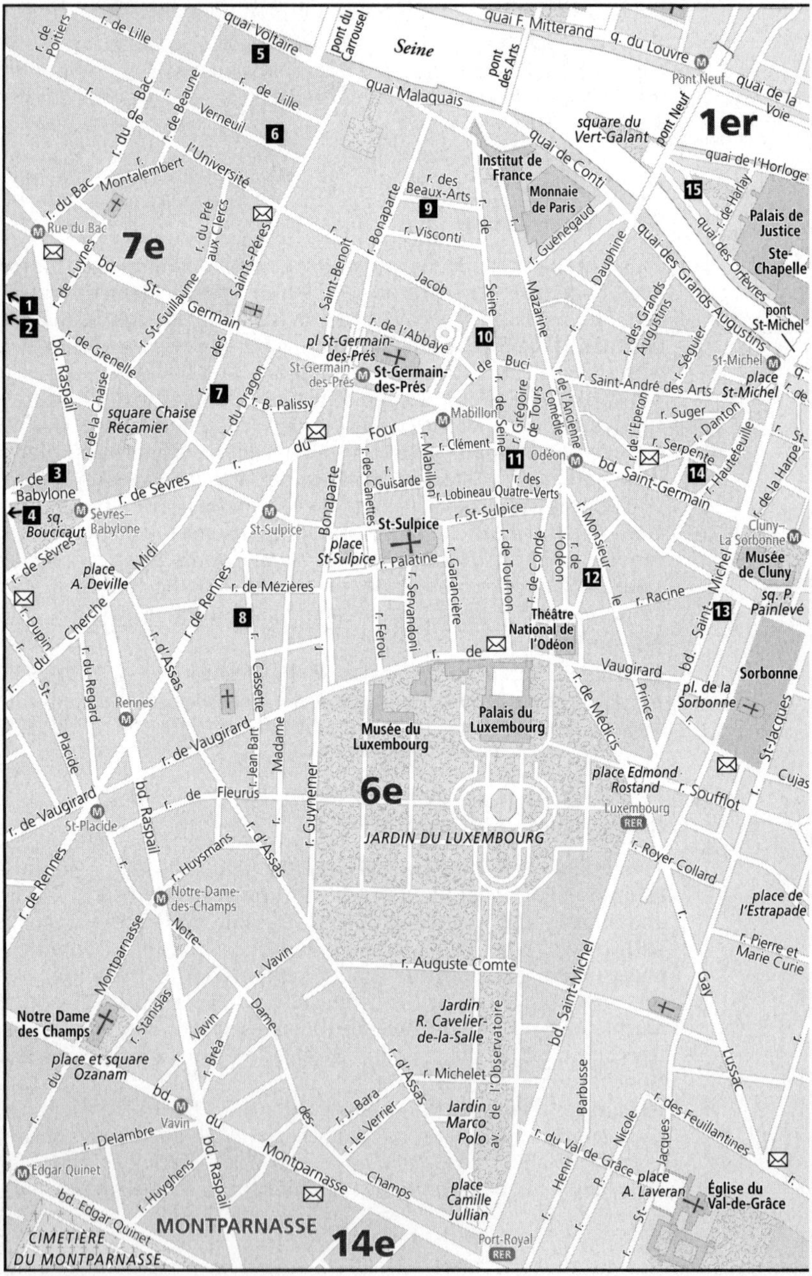

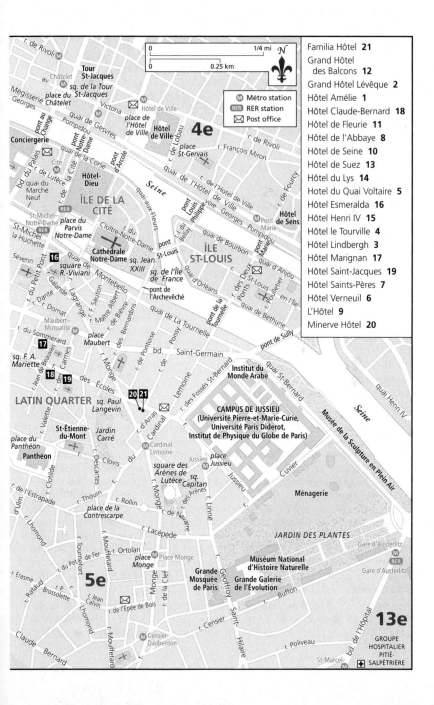

Familia Hôtel **21**
Grand Hôtel des Balcons **12**
Grand Hôtel Lévêque **2**
Hôtel Amélie **1**
Hôtel Claude-Bernard **18**
Hôtel de Fleurie **11**
Hôtel de l'Abbaye **8**
Hôtel de Seine **10**
Hôtel de Suez **13**
Hôtel du Lys **14**
Hotel du Quai Voltaire **5**
Hôtel Esmeralda **16**
Hôtel Henri IV **15**
Hôtel le Tourville **4**
Hôtel Lindbergh **3**
Hôtel Marignan **17**
Hôtel Saint-Jacques **19**
Hôtel Saints-Pères **7**
Hôtel Verneuil **6**
L'Hôtel **9**
Minerve Hôtel **20**

restaurant, Le Cinq (see Chapter 10). Check online for package deals; some of the rates are up to 50 percent off.

See map p. 108. 31 av. George V (1½ blocks from the Champs-Elysées). ☎ **01-49-52-70-00**. *Fax: 01-49-52-70-10.* www.fourseasons.com/paris. *Métro: George V. Rack rates: 750€–1,095€ double, 1,795€–13,000€ suite. Continental breakfast at Le Cinq 40€, American breakfast 50€. AE, DC, MC, V.*

Grand Hotel des Balcons
$$–$$$ Saint-Germain-des-Prés   (6e)

Steps from Théâtre de l'Odéon is this gracious and comfortable hotel with balconied rooms, modern light oak furnishings, bright fabrics, 19th-century stained-glass windows, and Art Nouveau lobby furnishings (look for the voluptuous statue of Venus in the breakfast room). Although most rooms and their wrought-iron balconies are small and basic, clever use of space allows for full-length mirrors and some rooms have closets on the larger side. Bathrooms are small to minuscule but well designed. The higher-priced doubles, triples, and quads are bigger and luxurious; some have double-sink bathrooms. All rooms have satellite television, hairdryers, and Wi-Fi access. If you opt to have breakfast here, it's a sumptuous and filling breakfast buffet. The Jardin du Luxembourg is a five-minute walk south.

See map p. 113. 3 rue Casimir Delavigne. ☎ **01-46-34-78-50**. *Fax: 01-46-34-06-27.* www.balcons.com. *Métro: Odéon. RER: Luxembourg. Rack rates: 80€–90€ single, 113€–125€ double, 198€–220€ triple or quad. Buffet breakfast 10€. AE, DC, MC, V.*

Grand Hôtel Lévêque
$ Invalides/Eiffel Tower (7e)

This 1930s-era hotel is just three blocks from the Eiffel Tower on a colorful pedestrian street bustling with the rue Cler market, bakeries, restaurants, a terrific crêpe stand, wine shops, and florists. The lobby has a comfortable lounge area with a bar and fireplace and a new breakfast chamber. The snug rooms have chic décor (think contemporary touches like black leather headboards against red wallpaper with Rorschach-like flower designs), flat-screen satellite TV, hair dryer, Wi-Fi, and air-conditioning. The bathrooms are small but have modern fixtures and sleek design. Staff members are very friendly and helpful, and if you ask, they may be able to give you a higher-priced room on the fifth floor with a balcony and partial view of the Eiffel Tower. This hotel fills up fast, so book well in advance. Street-side rooms (which have good views) cost a little more than interior rooms; as always, check online for deals — the Web site lets you choose exactly which room you want to stay in.

See map p. 113. 29 rue Cler (where rue Cler meets rue de Grenelle). ☎ **01-47-05-49-15**. *Fax: 01-45-50-49-36.* www.hotel-leveque.com. *Métro: École-Militaire or Latour-Maubourg. Rack rates: 62€–85€ single room with bathroom in corridor,*

95€–130€ double or twin beds with bathroom, 132€–150€ triple with bathroom. Breakfast 9€. AE, MC, V.

Hôtel Agora
$–$$ Louvre (1er)

This is a very good find on a busy pedestrian street near Les Halles and has a traditional French air once you mount a curved staircase (after the initial climb, an elevator leads from reception to upper floors) to its eclectic reception area. Rooms have antique furniture, marble mantelpieces, floral prints, and old-fashioned wallpapers (and the occasional leopard-print upholstered chair). If you want a room on the larger side, ask for no. 1, 2, or 6. The windows are double-glazed, thankfully, which helps muffle the outside noise. The bathrooms are decently sized; some have bathtubs and even bidets, an often confusing French charm, which is rarely offered at hotels with such reasonable prices. Satellite TV and Wi-Fi are also included. Fifth-floor rooms have balconies with views of the impressive Saint-Eustache Church.

See map p. 108. 7 rue de la Cossonnerie. ☎ **01-42-33-46-02.** *Fax: 01-42-33-80-99.* www.hotel-paris-agora.com. *Métro: Châtelet. Rack rates: 86€–111€ single, 111€–169€ double, 189€ triple. Breakfast 9.50€. AE, MC, V.*

Hotel Alison
$$ Madeleine (8e)

This hotel has a retro 1970s ambience that somehow manages to be perfectly in tune with the classy neighborhood. The large, well-appointed rooms are furnished in modern style, with black furniture and light walls, and have plenty of storage space, a safe, a minibar, a trouser press, satellite TV, Wi-Fi, and double-glazed windows. Hair dryers and upscale toiletries grace gleaming, tiled bathrooms with wall-mounted showers. You can relax on low, orange-leather couches in the plush lobby or enjoy a drink in the vaulted brick lounge. Breakfast is served under a vaulted stone ceiling. The hotel is located between the Madeleine and the Elysée Palace and near the Champs-Elysées and rue Faubourg Saint-Honoré.

See map p. 108. 21 rue de Surène. ☎ **01-42-65-54-00.** *Fax: 01-42-65-08-17.* www.hotel-alison.com. *Métro: Madeleine or Concorde. Rack rates: 86€–98€ single, 120€–174€ double, 174€–194€ triple, 218€–308€ for two adjoining rooms. Breakfast 10€. AE, DC, MC, V.*

Hôtel Amélie
$ Invalides/Eiffel Tower (7e)

This is a modest 16-room hotel bedecked with overflowing flower pots at each window. The rooms are small and basic with tiny closets, writing desks, telephone, minibars, and a downscale décor, but the tiled bathrooms offer hair dryers and good-quality toiletries. The location is excellent for seeing such seventh *arrondissement* sights as the Eiffel Tower and Napoléon's Tomb, yet the atmosphere is peaceful, almost serene. Stroll down nearby rue Cler for some great fruit and veggie markets or for an expert crêpe made by a lovely Greek *vendeur* who has been there for years. There is no elevator. The owners often have seasonal promotions; check online for specials.

See map p. 113. 5 rue Amélie. ☎ **01-45-51-74-75.** *Fax: 01-45-56-93-55.* www. hotelamelie-paris.com. *Métro: Latour-Maubourg. Rack rates: 90€–120€ single, 110€–130€ double or twin. Breakfast 9€. AE, DC, MC, V.*

Hôtel Balzac
$$$$ Champs-Elysées (8e)

Just one quiet street from the Arc de Triomphe is this gorgeous jewel box of a hotel. Luxuriously renovated for 11€ million in 2007, this is the place to stay if you want all the amenities of a palace hotel in a more intimate setting. Enjoy butler service; a bar, lounge, and tearoom; 24-hour room service; oak flooring; in-room entertainment systems that include a wall-mounted plasma TV and DVD player; free Wi-Fi; minibar; thick high-quality duvets and high-thread-count linens. The 90-sq.-m (968-sq.-ft.) Suite Royale (2,500€) is the hotel's best, with its own 25m (269-ft.) terrace where you can dine with a beautiful view of the Eiffel Tower and soak in a Jacuzzi bath after a busy day of sightseeing.

See map p. 108. 6 rue Balzac. ☎ **01-44-35-18-00.** *Fax: 01-44-35-18-05.* www.hotel balzac.com. *Métro: Charles de Gaulle–Étoile. Rack rates: 420€ standard single, 470€ superior double, 520€ deluxe double, 990€ deluxe and superior rooms, 790€ junior suite, 950€ corner suite, 2,000€ Presidential Suite. Breakfast 30€. AE, MC, V.*

Hôtel Bonne Nouvelle
$–$$ Montorgueil (2e)

For those who prefer good location to large rooms, this hotel is perfect. Lovingly renovated from a divey property into one that is personable and charming, Hotel Bonne Nouvelle is truly a central location in the 2nd *arrondissement*. The hotel, with its welcoming service and friendly staff, has six floors (a truly minuscule elevator services the first four; you have to climb the stairs to the top two) and 20 rooms, most of which have high ceilings and big windows looking out onto the Parisian rooftops. The sixth-floor rooms boast panoramic views of the city (and the secret to the owner's devotion to the hotel). The hotel is decorated with simple and nice touches like red cloth wallpaper, matching armoires, and countryside wooden bedside tables. Most of the bathrooms have bathtubs and marble tiles (some of upper-floor rooms have a separate-but-still-private bathroom across the hall, accessible with a key). A less than five-minute walk spills you onto the ultrahip and bustling rue Montorgueil, and ten minutes gets you to the Louvre or île de la Cité.

See map p. 108. 17 rue Beauregard. ☎ **01-45-08-42-42.** *Fax: 01-40-26-05-81.* www.hotel-bonne-nouvelle.com. *Métro: Bonne Nouvelle or Strasbourg–Saint-Denis. Rack rates: 60€–69€ single, 75€–145€ double (the most expensive double has a panoramic view of Paris), 95€ triple. Breakfast 7€, 9€ for in-room breakfast (served until 10 a.m.). MC, V.*

Hotel Claude Bernard
$$–$$$ **Latin Quarter (5e)**

This is one of the most highly recommended hotels because it keeps very high standards while keeping costs down. The inside features a lobby bar (but it's not manned by a regular bartender; you have to ask at reception if you want to be served), a lounge area with comfortable banquettes, and a two-person elevator. The decently sized rooms have warm and tasteful wallpaper, sleek bathrooms, minibars, Wi-Fi, satellite TV, decorative balconies with flowers, and often a well-preserved piece of antique furniture. Some particularly attractive suites come with couches and armchairs. A sauna is available for guests to use, and all rooms are air-conditioned. Nearby are the Panthéon, the Sorbonne, and the fantastic Musée de Cluny. The best prices are found in the online package deals, up to 50 percent off.

See map p. 113. 43 rue des Écoles. ☎ **01-43-26-32-52.** *Fax: 01-43-26-80-56.* www.hotelclaudebernardparis.com. *Métro: Maubert-Mutualité. Rack rates: 58€–178€ single, 188€ double, 228€ triple, 288€ quad. Buffet breakfast 10€.*

Hôtel de Fleurie
$$$–$$$$ **Saint-Germain-des-Prés (6e)**

Just off place Odéon, the pretty Fleurie has a unique facade with white statues flanking every level, which are beautifully lit at night (a nice touch to come home to after dinner and drinks in the neighborhood). The rooms boast every comfort, including air-conditioning, marble bathrooms with heated towel racks, quality toiletries, Oriental rugs, Wi-Fi, and satellite TV. Small but comfortable, the rooms are furnished in a modern or classic style with such touches as fresh flowers, pretty gingham curtains, and wood-paneled accents. Book at least six weeks in advance for one of the *chambres familiales* — two connecting rooms with two large beds in each room. Continental breakfast is served in the cozy vaulted stone cellar dining room; the homemade jams are sure to please. Located near the church of Saint-Germain-des-Prés, the historic Café de Flore, Les Deux Magots, and Brasserie Lipp, it's also a few blocks from the Seine and the Jardin du Luxembourg. Check the Web site for specials.

See map p. 113. 32-34 rue de Grégoire-de-Tours. ☎ **01-53-73-70-00.** *Fax: 01-53-73-70-20.* www.hotel-de-fleurie.com. *Métro: Odéon. Rack rates: 115€–205€ single, 135€–235€ double with queen-size bed, 175€–270€ deluxe rooms (large room with two twin beds or one king-size bed), 430€–465€ family suite. Breakfast 15€ for adults, 8€ for children 11 and under. AE, DC, MC, V.*

Hôtel de l'Abbaye
$$$–$$$$ **Saint-Germain-des-Prés (6e)**

This former convent on the Left Bank is a wonderful choice for travelers who aren't willing to spend deluxe hotel prices but still want elegance, tranquillity, and deluxe-quality service. Some of the 42 rooms and two- and four-bedroom suites have their original exposed oak ceiling beams, 19th-century-style furnishings, and damask upholstery; all are air-conditioned, with Wi-Fi and satellite TV. The rooms are a good size by Paris standards, and the suites are absolutely spacious. The style of décor depends on the room: Some are modern with funky bedspreads and framed drawings and prints of famous Andy Warhol creations, while others have more classic wallpapering and floral printed quilts and curtains. Some first-floor rooms open onto a vine-covered terrace. Rooftop suites also have terraces, and there is one fabulous duplex terrific for honeymooners. You can eat breakfast — included in the price of your room — in the flower-filled courtyard. Book online to get the best deals.

See map p. 113. 10 rue Cassette (four short blocks from the northwest corner of the Jardin du Luxembourg). ☎ **01-45-44-38-11.** *Fax: 01-45-48-07-86.* www.hotel abbayeparis.com. *Métro: Saint-Sulpice. Rack rates: 240€–260€ classic double, 352€–380€ deluxe double, 442€–477€ suite, 498€–538€ duplex apartment. Rates include breakfast. AE, MC, V.*

Hotel de la Place des Vosges
$$–$$$ **Le Marais (4e)**

The entrance to the place des Vosges is only steps away from this hotel, which used to be the stables of King Henri IV. Now the exposed stone walls, medieval tapestries, and beamed ceilings complement a somewhat dark and dusty, antiques-filled lobby. The hotel staff is personable and charming. The small rooms have beamed ceilings, satin-cotton-blend bed sheets with anti-allergen spreads, and tiled bathrooms. All rooms have satellite TVs (the entertainment centers in the most expensive rooms are of the vogue Danish audiovisual company Bang & Olufsen), and free Wi-Fi. The larger top-floor room (no. 10) has a pretty view over the Right Bank and a Jacuzzi, but the elevator stops a floor down, which is a consideration if you have a lot of luggage.

See map p. 108. 12 rue de Birague. ☎ **01-42-72-60-46.** *Fax: 01-42-72-02-64.* www. hotelplacedesvosges.com. *Métro: Bastille. Rack rates: 90€ single, double, or twin beds with shower or tub; 95€ room with large bed and massaging showerhead; 150€ top-floor room with loft, shower, and Jacuzzi. Breakfast 8€. MC, V.*

Hôtel des Deux-Îles
$$$ **Île Saint-Louis (4e)**

This appealing jewel box of a hotel is superbly located on the île Saint-Louis (practically in Notre-Dame's backyard). The owners are interior decorators, and it shows; the 17 rooms have exposed oak ceiling beams and provincial upholstery, and the lobby is a warm and cozy gem with fresh flowers and bamboo furniture. Off the lobby are a rock garden (which some of the rooms overlook) and a basement breakfast room with a fireplace. Although amenities include completely renovated bathrooms with cable TV, Wi-Fi, minibar, and air-conditioning, rooms are small, so if you have a large amount of luggage, you may want to look elsewhere. Paris's best ice cream shop, Berthillon (closed in Aug), is just around the corner, and you can find Berthillon ice cream in neighborhood brasseries and sold from stands around the area, too. So much is nearby — the Memorial de la Déportation; Sainte-Chapelle; the Conciergerie; and the bird and flower markets on île de la Cité, to name only a few — you may not know where to begin, so start early in the morning with Notre-Dame.

See map p. 108. 59 rue Saint-Louis-en-l'île. ☎ *01-43-26-13-35. Fax: 01-43-29-60-25. www.deuxiles-paris-hotel.com. Métro: Pont Marie. Rack rates: 159€ single with shower, 195€ double or twin beds with bath or shower. Breakfast 13€. AE, V.*

Hotel de Seine
$$$ Saint-Germain-des-Prés (6e)

The Hotel de Seine is truly charming. Centrally located on a street full of art galleries in Saint-Germain-des-Prés, between boulevard Saint-Germain and rue Jacob, it's a few blocks from the Seine and the pedestrian bridge Pont des Arts that leads to the Louvre. Each room is distinctly decorated with either French provincial furniture and flowered wallpaper or Provence-inspired jewel-toned paint and Louis XVI reproductions. Though they are small, the rooms are particularly cozy and inviting, with satellite TV, Wi-Fi, marble bathrooms, and hair dryers. For added comfort, the entire hotel is cooled by central air-conditioning during the warmer months. Check the Web site for specials and promotions.

See map p. 113. 52 rue de Seine. ☎ *01-46-34-22-80. Fax: 01-46-34-04-74. www. hoteldeseine.com. Métro: Saint-Germain-des-Prés, Mabillon. Rack rates: 175€–195€ single, 195€–205€ double or twin, 230€ triple. Breakfast 15€. AE, MC, V.*

Hotel de Suez
$–$$ Latin Quarter (5e)

Ask for rooms at the back of this hotel in a great Latin Quarter location; those that face boulevard Saint-Michel are quite loud late into the night on weekends (but proof of the quality of nearby nightlife). The rooms in this hotel are a good size, beds are firm, storage space is ample, and the modern bathrooms have hair dryers. Décor is typical modern hotel: a comfortable mirrored lobby furnished with couches and Art Nouveau lamps, rooms with striped or flowered bedspreads, and curtains with color-coordinated artwork and blond furniture. Each room has satellite TV with 30 channels and Wi-Fi is available throughout the building. The hotel is near Musée de Cluny, Jardin du Luxembourg, and the Panthéon. The Seine and Notre-Dame are a ten-minute walk away.

See map p. 113. 31 bd. Saint-Michel. ☎ **01-53-10-34-00.** *Fax: 01-40-51-79-44.* www. hoteldesuez.fr. *Métro: Saint-Michel. Rack rates: 80€–150€ single, 95€–165€ double, 130€–195€ triple, 200€ quad (for families with young children). Breakfast 5.95€ (served in-room at no additional cost). MC, V.*

Hôtel du Jeu de Paume
$$$$ île Saint-Louis (4e)

Madame Elyane Prache and her golden retriever, Scoop, will give you a friendly greeting at this impressive, airy hotel on the exclusive île Saint-Louis. The wooden skeleton of a 17th-century *jeu de paume* (precursor to tennis) court rises from the open lobby two stories above a stone and wood entry with a fireplace, couches, glassed-in elevator, and spiral staircases. Most accommodations are snug to medium, but the simple stylish décor under hewn beams keeps rooms from feeling cramped. Free Wi-Fi is available. Eat breakfast in the plant-filled garden or indoors in the inviting lobby. The three standard duplexes with spiral stairs are roomier (and don't cost any more than a double), but if you're staying five days or longer and want true bliss, check into the three-bedroom 900€ duplex apartment with a private terrace. A 620€ two-bedroom apartment is also available for stays of five days or longer.

See map p. 108. 54 rue Saint-Louis-en-L'île. ☎ **01-43-26-14-18.** *Fax: 01-40-46-02-76.* www.jeudepaumehotel.com. *Métro: Pont-Marie. Rack rates: 185€–255€ single, 285€–360€ double, 360€–450€ junior suite, 450€–560€ suite. Breakfast 18€. Pets 10€. AE, MC, V.*

Hotel du Lys
$$ Saint-Germain-des-Prés (6e)

Housed in a 17th-century mansion on a street that dates back to 1180, this hotel, with original tall casement windows and homey, intimate rooms decorated in floral wallpaper with exposed-beam high ceilings, is a haven from the bustling neighborhood. Rooms feature double glazing to keep out the noise, and room nos. 19 and 22 have balconies. People with disabilities need to heed the lack of an elevator, and the staircase, although historic, is narrow. The Lys is just a few blocks from the Seine and Notre-Dame in an area that gets quite crowded in summer. Breakfast is included.

See map p. 113. 23 rue Serpente. ☎ **01-43-26-97-57.** *Fax: 01-44-07-34-90.* www. hoteldulys.com. *Métro: Saint-Michel or Odéon. Rack rates: 100€ single, 105€–120€ double, 140€ triple. Rates include breakfast. MC, V.*

Hôtel du Petit Moulin
$$$–$$$$ Le Marais (3e)

You'll know you've arrived at this adorable boutique designer hotel because of colorful boulangerie sign mounted over the door, paying homage to the good taste of the previous tenant. The ultramodern interior includes four floors and 17 rooms, each uniquely decorated in colorful mismatched patterns and whimsical touches (look for zebra print alongside large-scale photorealistic flowers, or a polka-dot carpet matched with exotic birds). The rooms are comfortably large with exposed beams and furnished in a minimalist style to offset the intensity of the walls and upholstery. A minibar, flat-screen TV, and free Wi-Fi are included in the rooms, all of which have full tiled bathrooms, some with bathtubs. Rooms are rated by size and level of luxury (all are equipped with double beds and sleep up to two people). The downstairs bar (for hotel guests only) has more of a classic feel, with an oak-paneled bar matching the walls and mismatched pink and purple chairs. Conveniently located in a particularly artsy and hip corner of the 3e *arrondissement,* you're less than ten minutes to the Hôtel de Ville or Bastille from this polychromatic experience. Check Web site for promotions and deals.

See map p. 108. 29 rue de Poitou. ☎ *01-42-74-10-10. Fax: 01-42-74-10-97.* www. hotelpetitmoulinparis.com. *Métro: Saint-Sébastien–Froissart. Rack rates: 190€ comfort double, 250€ superior double, 290€ executive room, 350€ deluxe room. Breakfast: 15€. AE, MC, V.*

Hotel du Quai Voltaire
$$ Saint-Germain-des-Prés (6e)

Clean and brightly lit, the main reason that guests stay in this hotel is for the spectacular views of the Seine and île de la Cité: Few hotels can boast such a clear view of some of the iconic monuments of Paris. The location is also ideal — it puts you smack in the middle, making a walk to the Latin Quarter, Notre Dame, and the Louvre a piece of cake. Recent renovations transformed the previously shabby rooms to small but comfortable and clean, with the occasional replica antiques to spice up the otherwise basic decor. Most rooms lack televisions (the view is plenty to look at), but TVs are available for free upon request. Double-paned windows drown out only some of the traffic noise, so those seeking absolute quiet should consider other places. You can get reduced rates by booking online, so check the Web site ahead of time.

See map p. 113. 19 quai Voltaire. ☎ *01-42-61-50-91. Fax: 01-42-61-62-26.* www. quaivoltaire.fr. *Métro: Palais Royal–Musée du Louvre or Rue du Bac. Rack rates: 130€ single, 150€–160€ double or twin, 180€ triple. Breakfast 12€. AE, MC, V.*

Hôtel Esmeralda
$–$$ Latin Quarter (5e)

This offbeat and ramshackle hotel is a favorite with budget travelers, so you'll want to book at least three months in advance. Its creaky wood floors and cramped hallways (recently refinished, along with several rooms in 2009) pale in comparison to its superior location just steps away from the Seine and Notre-Dame. If you prefer hotels with such amenities as satellite TV, free toiletries, or space, then the Esmeralda is probably not for you. There is an old, winding wooden staircase (no elevator) and out-standing views of Notre-Dame and the Seine from the hotel's front rooms (make sure to specify these rooms when you reserve). East rooms over-look Saint-Julien-le-Pauvre and square Viviani. Repeat guests are happy to know that, despite the replacement of wallpaper and some furniture, there are still shabby-chic velvet coverings and antique furniture, creating homey warmth that almost makes up for the disappointingly dark rear rooms. The front rooms with a view have modern bathrooms with tubs, and some are exceptionally large for the location and relative size of this hotel, making them perfect for travelers with children. The hotel is just steps away from the landmark Shakespeare & Company bookstore.

See map p. 113. 4 rue Saint-Julien-le-Pauvre. ☎ *01-43-54-19-20. Fax: 01-40-51-00-68. Métro: Saint-Michel. Rack rates: 75€–110€ single, 90€–110€ double, 130€ triple, 140€ quad. Breakfast 7€. No credit cards.*

Hôtel Henri IV
$ Louvre (1er)

This hotel doesn't have an elevator and before its recent renovation, it had only two toilets. Although the super-budget Henri IV has more com-forts than it used to boast, it is still one of Europe's most famous budget hotels and nearly always is full. It occupies a dramatic location on place Dauphine — the northernmost tip of île de la Cité, across the river from Saint-Germain and the Louvre and a few steps from Pont Neuf. The 17th-century building, with its creaky stairs, houses cozy rooms that most folks will find romantic (cynical types may view the ones not yet renovated as rough around the edges). Each room has a sink and now most have pri-vate toilets, but those who opt for the cheaper route share the spotless WC (meaning "water closet," the standard European acronym for toilet) and showers on each of the five floors. The most expensive rooms boast either a huge bathtub or terrace. A few have beautiful views of place Dauphine. All in all, staying here is an adventure. Book far in advance.

See map p. 113. 25 place Dauphine. ☎ *01-43-54-44-53.* www.henri4hotel.fr. *Métro: Pont Neuf. Rack rates: 59€ single with shower, 69€–78€ single with shower and toilet, 74€–79€ double with shower and toilet, 81€ double with toilet and bathtub. Rates include breakfast. MC, V.*

Hôtel Jeanne d'Arc
$–$$ Le Marais (4e)

Reserve well in advance for this great budget hotel on a pretty little street just off the place Sainte-Catherine. The place is full of eccentric furniture and countryside touches, like soft tangerine-colored wallpaper decorating the halls of the ground floor and a plant-filled dining room. Reception is through a door on the right, which features the hotel's signature mosaic mirror, a tribute to French pride. Rooms are small to decent-size with large windows, Wi-Fi, card-key access, and large bathrooms, but storage space is a bit cramped. Other room features include direct-dial telephones, cable TV, and bedside tables. If a view is important, make sure you request a room at the top or facing the street because some rooms don't have one. The hotel is in the center of the Marais, and it can be a little noisy, but you're near the Musée Picasso and the Bastille, and the fabulous Au Bistro de la Place cafe is in the square next door.

See map p. 108. 3 rue de Jarente. ☎ **01-48-87-62-11.** *Fax: 01-48-87-37-31.* www. hoteljeannedarc.com. *Métro: Saint-Paul or Bastille. Rack rates: 64€ single, 79€–116€ double, 146€ triple, 160€ quad. Breakfast 7€. MC, V.*

Hotel Jules
$$$–$$$$ Grands Boulevards (9e)

One of several recently renovated boutique hotels popping up in the 9th *arrondissement,* the Hôtel Jules is just another sign that this quarter, beloved by Parisians for its less-touristy vibe, is becoming more of a spot for the hip design set. Self described as "casual-chic," this retro-leaning property is decorated in friendly tones of brown and cream. There are touches of 1970s "space age" furniture in the junior suites and 1950s leather suitcases make part of the display in the lobby (along with a very precariously stacked bookshelf). The especially friendly staff stands as proof that the French are beginning to understand the importance of customer service. Rooms are delightfully clean and simple, some of which are duplexes and suites. Some outrageously romantic touches include a huge set of plastic lips mounted on the wall above the bed, shamelessly lit by its own floodlight. Rooms include free Wi-Fi, flat-screen televisions, and a minibar. A superb location for those who don't mind not being in the center of the city's hubbub, the placement on rue Lafayette gives easy walking access to Montmartre (especially the celebrated rue des Martyrs) as well as the Opéra, and les Grands Magasins. Across the street a fantastically Art Nouveau–decorated brasserie/bistro, Le Générale Lafayette is the perfect introduction to the charm of dining with real Parisians at reasonable prices (and until 4 a.m. on weekends). Check Web site for details; paying in full upon reservation (with no refunds) may knock up to 100€ from the price.

See map p. 108. 49 rue La Fayette. ☎ **01-42-85-05-44.** *Fax: 01-49-95-06-60.* www. hoteljules.com. *Métro: Le Peletier or Cadet. Rack rates: 170€–230€ standard room, 230€–360€ superior room, 360€–432€ deluxe room, 488€–650€ suite. Breakfast 15€. AE, MC, V.*

Hôtel le Tourville
$$$ Invalides/Eiffel Tower (7e)

This splendid restored mansion, located just steps behind Les Invalides, boasts a four-star rating. You receive almost all the amenities of a pricier hotel — a lobby bar, with TV and newspapers, good-quality toiletries, hair dryers, air-conditioning, chic décor with antiques — for rates miraculously below four-star prices. Rooms are decorated in soft yellow, pink, or sand, with crisp white damask curtains, antique bureaus and lamps, fabulously mismatched old mirrors, marble bathrooms, Wi-Fi, and satellite TV. You may want to ask for one of the four rooms with vine-draped terraces or a junior suite with whirlpool bath. The executive suite is decorated in a more masculine, refined style with an especially luxurious bathroom. The staff is wonderfully helpful and polite. The best rates can be found on the hotel's Web site.

See map p. 113. 16 av. de Tourville. ☎ **01-47-05-62-62.** *Fax: 01-47-05-43-90.* www. hoteltourville.com. *Métro: École-Militaire. Rack rates: 210€ standard double, 270€ superior double, 300€ double with private terrace, 380€–470€ suites. Breakfast 18€. AE, MC, V.*

Hôtel Lindbergh
$$ **Invalides/Eiffel Tower (7e)**

This pretty aviation-themed hotel is in a terrific Saint-Germain-des-Prés location. Photos of the hotel's namesake, Charles Lindbergh, in his plane; standing with Louis Blériot, the first man to fly across the English Channel; and with Antoine de Saint-Exupéry, author of *The Little Prince,* add a nice touch to the taupe-colored lobby. The standard rooms are simple and modern with colorful bedspreads and matching bathrooms. Deluxe rooms have floor-length draperies, fabric headboards, and color-coordinated cushioned seating. In one of the city's most genteel districts, the hotel is right at the edge of the Saint-Germain-des-Prés shopping district, and Le Bon Marché department store, with its terrific L'Épicerie supermarket, is at the end of the block. The Musée Rodin is within walking distance. Those with energy can hoof the distance over to the Eiffel Tower; otherwise catch bus no. 69 from nearby rue du Bac to the Champ du Mars.

See map p. 113. 5 rue Chomel. ☎ **01-45-48-35-53.** *Fax: 01-45-49-31-48.* www.hotel lindbergh.com. *Métro: Sèvres-Babylone. Rack rates: 136€ smaller double with shower, 160€ double (or twin beds) with shower and tub, 180€ triple. Breakfast 10€. AE, MC, V.*

Hotel Louvre Forum
$ **Louvre (1er)**

If simple accommodations don't do it for you, you'll want to go elsewhere, but you'll miss out on a great deal. This is a truly central, reasonably priced hotel (with air-conditioning!) just steps from the Louvre. The brightly colored rooms have small tiled bathrooms, flat-screen TVs, Wi-Fi, minibars, writing tables with lamps, and somewhat uncomfortable chairs. Each room has a small armoire with hanging space and shelves; the rooms on the lower floors are a bit cramped. The lobby features a mural of the neighborhood, which is only a short walk from the elegant Palais Royal and the Louvre. The best rates can be found on the hotel Web site.

See map p. 108. 25 rue du Bouloi. ☎ **01-42-36-54-19.** *Fax: 01-42-36-66-31.* `www.paris-hotel-louvre-forum.com.` *Métro: Louvre-Rivoli. Rack rates: 119€–135€ single, 139€–180€ double or twin. Continental breakfast 10€. AE, MC, V.*

Hotel Marignan
$–$$ Latin Quarter (5e)

Paul Keniger is the third generation of his family to care for this very warm establishment that first opened in 1955. The Kenigers welcome families, don't mind if you bring your own food into the dining room, and even make the kitchen available during the off season. A washer/dryer and iron are at your disposal. Signs in English recommend neighborhoods to visit and tours to take, and you can always ask one of the Kenigers for recommendations. Rooms are modest but clean and cozy, especially for the prices offered. The hotel is very close to the Sorbonne — it's around the corner from the Panthéon, near the outdoor green market on rue Mouffetard — and its good rates attract students. Check out the very personable Web site for individual floor plans of each room, as well as the ever-present promotions. Rooms fill up quickly in July and August, so if you plan to travel then, book well in advance.

See map p. 113. 13 rue du Sommerard. ☎ **01-43-54-63-81.** *Fax: 01-43-25-16-69.* `www.hotel-marignan.com.` *Métro: Maubert-Mutualité or Saint-Michel. Rack rates: 52€ single with shared toilet, 62€ single with toilet, 68€ double with toilet in the hall, 80€ double with toilet, 95€ double with shower and toilet, 95€–135€ three to five people with toilet, 120€–160€ three to five people with shower and toilet. Rates include continental breakfast. MC, V.*

Hôtel Montpensier
$–$$ Louvre (1er)

Supposedly the former residence of Mademoiselle de Montpensier, cousin of Louis XIV, this hotel's high ceilings and windows, the stained-glass ceiling in its lounge, and its grand staircase all work together to create a sense of faded grandeur. Many rooms on the first two floors, which date from the 17th century, are serviceable with a budget-hotel décor, while rooms on the fifth floor (an elevator is available) have attractive slanted ceilings and good views over the rooftops. They're smaller than the first- and second-floor rooms, but all the sizes here are quite impressive given the rates. Most rooms are comfortably outfitted with easy chairs, ample closet space, and some have modern bathrooms with hair dryers. Reserve at least a month in advance for July. The prices are terrific for this location, just two blocks from the Jardin du Palais Royal and right down the street from the Louvre and the Jardin des Tuileries. Mind you, the venerable age of this hotel puts some of the showers and bathrooms outside the actual rooms. Check the Web site for special promotions.

See map p. 108. 12 rue Richelieu. ☎ **01-42-96-28-50.** *Fax: 01-42-86-02-70.* www. montpensierparis.com. *Métro: Palais Royal–Musée du Louvre. Rack rates: 71€–80€ single with shared toilet and shower down the hall, 80€–90€ double with shared toilet and shower, 105€–120€ double or twin with shower, 120€–130€ double or twin with bath, 152€–160€ triple, 165€–180€ quad. Breakfast 9€. AE, MC, V.*

Hôtel Saint-Jacques
$$–$$$ Latin Quarter (5e)

Not only was this hotel designed by Baron Haussmann (architect of Paris and its grand boulevards), but it also had a cameo in the Cary Grant–Audrey Hepburn film *Charade.* Several of its rooms have restored 19th-century ceiling murals, and most of the high ceilings have elaborate plasterwork, giving the décor an old-Paris feel that is accentuated with traditional furniture and fabric-covered walls. The owners have added their own touches in the hallways, with stenciling on the walls and *trompe l'oeil* painting. Modern comforts include generally spacious rooms, an elevator, tiled bathrooms with hair dryers and toiletries, double-glazed windows, ample closet space, fax and computer outlets, safes, and satellite TV. Although they aren't accessible by elevator (which stops a floor down), the rooms on the top floor are less expensive and have great views (be sure to ask for them specifically, as the doubles are classified as "standard," "superior," and "luxury" based on their size and comfort level with prices to match).

See map p. 113. 35 rue des Écoles (at rue des Carmes). ☎ **01-44-07-45-45.** *Fax: 01-43-25-65-50.* www.hotel-saintjacques.com. *Métro: Maubert-Mutualité. Rack rates: 125€–132€ single with bathroom, 145€–263€ double, 230€–263€ triple. Breakfast 13€. AE, DC, MC, V.*

Hôtel Saint-Merry
$$$ Le Marais (4e)

This unique hotel and its friendly staff can be found on a pedestrian-only street in the Marais and was formerly the presbytery of the Church of Saint-Merry next door. It was also once a brothel, but no matter what its history, it retains an almost spooky medieval atmosphere. In fact, the bed in room no. 9 has flying buttresses on either side (easy to bump your head on in the dark). The rooms have beamed ceilings, stone walls, wrought-iron chandeliers, and candelabras. Fabrics are sumptuous; bathrooms are fully tiled and equipped with hair dryers. Higher prices are for larger rooms with views. In keeping with its medieval feeling, you won't find an elevator in the building (***Note:*** 21 winding steps lead to the second-floor reception area). TVs are in suites only. The hotel is a few short blocks from the Seine and Hôtel de Ville. The Louvre is about a 15-minute walk away.

See map p. 108. 78 rue de la Verrerie. ☎ **01-42-78-14-15.** *Fax: 01-40-29-06-82.* www. hotelmarais.com *(for booking only). Métro: Hôtel de Ville or Châtelet. Rack rates: 160€–355€ double or twin, 335€–400€ suite. In-room breakfast 12€. AE, MC, V.*

Hôtel Saints-Pères
$$$ Saint-Germain-des-Prés (6e)

Travelers have made this romantic hotel one of the Left Bank's most popular. Designed in the 17th century, this was the residence of Daniel Gittard, royal architect of Louis XIV's, and the hotel looks the part, furnished with antiques, old paintings, tapestries, and gilt mirrors. The owners boast of a reputation for hosting famous artists, such as 20th-century figurative painter Francis Bacon. Many of its 39 rooms overlook an interior courtyard where breakfast and drinks are served. Rooms have modern amenities such as air-conditioning, flat-screen satellite TVs, and minibar. Each of the rooms has a unique portrait or work of art to set the tone, and the most requested is the magnificent *chambre à la fresque* where guests sleep beneath a 17th-century painted ceiling of a protective cherub. The hotel is a stone's throw from all the shopping in Saint-Germain as well as celebrated Brasserie Lipp, Café de Flore, and the Deux Magots. A baby-sitting service is available upon request. Check online for special offers.

See map p. 113. 65 rue des Saint-Pères. ☎ **01-45-44-50-00.** *Fax: 01-45-44-90-83.* www.paris-hotel-saints-peres.com. *Métro: Saint-Germain-des-Prés or Sèvres-Babylone. Rack rates: 140€ single, 160€–220€ double, 250€–320€ suite, 295€–315€ duplex suite, 295€–400€ chambre à la fresque. Buffet or in-room breakfast 14€. AE, MC, V.*

Hôtel Tiquetonne
$ Montorgueil (2e)

Though the happening neighborhood of Montorgueil is quickly losing its last vestiges of seediness, the somewhat shabby, though terrific bargain Tiquetonne still remains. If a view is more important than space, ask for one of the top rooms boasting views of the Eiffel Tower or Sacré-Coeur. Each room has the basics: a bed with a wall-mounted wooden headboard, table, and comfortable chairs and adequate storage space. Some rooms contain only a sink and bidet, while others have full showers. The shared showers in the hallways are surprisingly clean and spacious. Walls tend to be thin. The Tiquetonne is located just off the busy pedestrian street rue Montorgueil and is a stone's throw from the red-light district of rue Saint-Denis and a five-minute walk to the Marais and the Georges Pompidou center. Ask for rooms facing the quieter rue Tiquetonne. ***Note:*** The hotel is closed in August.

See map p. 108. 6 rue Tiquetonne. ☎ **01-42-36-94-58.** *Fax: 01-42-36-02-94. Métro: Etienne Marcel or Réamur-Sébastopol. Rack rates: 35€ single with toilet, 40€ single with shower, 55€ double with shower or tub. Shower 6€ per person. In-room breakfast 7€. V.*

Hôtel Verneuil
$$$ Invalides/Eiffel Tower (7e)

In a city where accommodations range from the ultraluxurious to the barely habitable, Hotel Verneuil offers the elegance of a small boutique hotel at a reasonable price. Located in the 7th *arrondissement* just a short walk from Saint-Germain-des-Prés, the Louvre, the Musée D'Orsay, and the Seine, Hotel Verneuil provides the location, quiet, and value that any visitor to Paris can appreciate. An added bonus is that no smoking is allowed in the hotel. The 17th-century building's sedate, classically decorated lobby complements the 26 rooms, which are small but decorated with a simple elegance (some even have original exposed wood beams). All the rooms have bathtubs (except the ground-floor room), cable TV, minibar, and free Wi-Fi. The continental buffet breakfast is served in a whitewashed cellar with vaulted ceilings. Art galleries, antique dealers, and more than a few good cafes, including the legendary Café de Flore and Les Deux Magots, line the streets around the hotel. It's an intimate, charming place that's nice to come home to after a day of sightseeing.

See map p. 113. 8 rue de Verneuil. ☎ *01-42-60-82-14. Fax: 01-42-61-40-38. Métro: Rue du Bac. Rack rates: 150€ single, 180€ double, 250€ deluxe double, 280€ triple. Extra bed 30€. Continental breakfast 13€. MC, V.*

Hôtel Vivienne
$–$$ Opéra (2e)

Hôtel Vivienne is well located between the Louvre and the Opéra and offers comfortable, simply decorated rooms with lots of light at a good price. They have the traditional molding found in classic Parisian apartments as well as soundproofing — something lacking in most Parisian lodgings. The bathrooms vary in size from adequate to huge, and all have hair dryers and wall-mounted showers in the tubs. Room nos. 14 and 15, as well as 3 and 4, have adjoining doors, perfect for families; others have small terraces. A few have views of the Eiffel Tower. Before venturing from the neighborhood, explore the Galeries Vivienne and Colbert, gorgeous historic covered passageways with pretty shops, intimate restaurants, and art galleries. Also of note, the French restaurant scene in the Diane Keaton–Jack Nicholson film, *Something's Gotta Give,* was filmed at Le Grand Colbert right down the street. Rates may vary based on season and size or level of comfort available.

See map p. 108. 40 rue Vivienne. ☎ *01-42-33-13-26. Fax: 01-40-41-98-19.* www. hotel-vivienne.com. *Métro: Bourse, Richelieu-Drouot, or Grands Boulevards. Rack rates: 77€–87€ single or double with shower or bath and shared toilet, 90€–116 double with shower or bath and toilet, 150€ for family-size room. Breakfast 10€. MC, V.*

L'Hôtel
$$$$ Saint-Germain-des-Prés (6e)

This beautiful hotel, originally part of the Reine Margot's palace, is no longer the flophouse where Oscar Wilde died in 1900. In fact, in 2007, *Harper's Bazaar* voted it the best urban hotel in the world. It's a funky velvet-and-marble monument, with 20 small but carefully decorated rooms with furnishings ranging from Louis XV and Empire styles to Art Nouveau. L'Hôtel's central spiraling staircase is a unique and charming bit of architecture that will give you the sensation of ascending a well-renovated medieval tower. Many of the upstairs rooms have splendid views over the rooftops of Saint-Germain and the surrounding area (the best is from the apartment-style suite), and the publicly accessible ground-floor restaurant is a find in its own. The rooms, classified with names like *Bijoux* and *Chic,* range from small and charmingly decorated to large and sumptuously ordained with antiques. The top-level apartment room is reputedly a favorite of many a visiting celebrity, but the staff would not confirm (or deny) the truth of this rumor. Booking online can save you a great deal on the rack rates.

See map p. 113. 13 rue des Beaux-Arts (between rue Bonaparte and rue de Seine, one block from the Quai Malaquais). ☎ **01-44-41-99-00.** *Fax: 01-43-25-64-81.* www. 1-hotel.com. *Métro: Saint-Germain-des-Prés or Odéon. Rack rates: 250€–345€ Mignon, 300€–370€ Bijoux, 490€–640€ Grand, 510€–640€ Chic, 590€–740€ Apartment. Breakfast 16€, AE, DC, MC, V.*

Lord Byron Hôtel Residence
$$$ Champs-Elysées (8e)

Located just off the Champs-Elysées on a narrow street lined with town houses, the Lord Byron is one of the best values in the neighborhood, which is calm and not subject to the bustle of France's widest avenue. Exuding a sense of luxury and peacefulness, draperies filter the sun in the Lord Byron's lobby, the reception desk is under an arch, and a pleasant little garden feels like it belongs in a far-flung suburb and not the center of everything. The rooms are furnished with antique reproductions, Provençal and classic French fabrics, and framed landscapes, and also feature minibars, satellite TVs, hair dryers, and full bathrooms. The staff is warm and friendly.

See map p. 108. 5 rue de Chateaubriand. ☎ **01-43-59-89-98.** *Fax: 42-89-46-04. Métro: George V, then walk down rue Washington for one block and turn left. Rack rates: 109€ single with bathroom, 135€–230€ double or twin, 198€–299€ apartment/suite. Breakfast 12€. AE, MC, V.*

Minerve Hotel
$$ Latin Quarter (5e)

Owners of the Familia Hotel (reviewed earlier in this chapter), Eric and Sylvie Gaucheron, also own this pretty and more upscale hotel next door. Rooms are large and romantic with wood-beamed ceilings, Provençal fabrics, exposed stone walls, and carved mahogany wood furnishings; expensive hand-painted sepia frescoes can be found in several of the rooms. All rooms have modern bathrooms with hair dryers, satellite TVs, Internet access via Wi-Fi (unfortunately not free, you'll have to pay 6€ to use it), and air-conditioning. The top two floors have views over the street, some of which include large balconies with tables and chairs. The Minerve is as welcoming to kids as the Familia is. If you're craving an American breakfast, head just a few blocks down to the delicious Breakfast in America, 73 rue des Écoles. Check online for special promotions.

See map p. 113. 13 rue des Écoles. ☎ *01-43-26-26-04. Fax: 01-44-07-01-96.* www. hotel-paris-minerve.com. *Métro: Cardinal Lemoine or Jussieu. Rack rates: 96€–142€ single, 126€–142€ double, 162€ triple, 182€ large double with balcony or patio, 295€ family suite. Breakfast 10€. AE, DC, MC, V.*

9 Hôtel
$$–$$$ Grands Boulevards (9e)

Run by the same company as Barcelona's Hotel Regina, this is another design-conscious boutique hotel that has popped up in the 9th *arrondissement.* The Andy Warhol quotes on the wall of the lobby are juxtaposed by angular minimalist furniture, matching the black, white, and wood tones that are used throughout the property. The neatness and simplicity of the décor extends to the rooms, giving the impression of quite a lot of space for the decent-size chambers. The bathrooms are especially comfortable — rooms either have bathtubs or spacious showers — and the staff is eager to cater to guests and show that this relatively new property is attentive to guests' needs. Fragonard toiletries, towel warmers, and comfy slippers are little touches you wouldn't normally get at these prices. At the time of writing, some renovations were not yet complete, such as the elevator and some of the corridors. However, the standards of boutique hotels mean that there's great air-conditioning, flat-screen satellite TVs, and free Wi-Fi in every room. The location, though not central, puts you near the Opéra in an interesting and true Parisian neighborhood, full of great restaurants and cafes while avoiding the annoyance of typical touristy settings. Check online for the best deals.

See map p. 108. 14 rue Papillon. ☎ *01-47-70-78-34.* www.le9hotel.com. *Métro: Cadet, and then walk up rue La Fayette in the direction of the traffic passing rue Riboutté, bearing right onto rue Papillon. Rack rates: 120€–210€ standard double, 140€–230€ superior double. Breakfast 10€. AE, DC, MC, V.*

Pavillon de la Reine
$$$$ Le Marais (3e)

Translated as "The Queen's Pavilion," this is more a French country house than a castle in the middle of Paris, just off the Place des Vosges. Enter through wrought-iron gates and pass through the pretty flowered court-yard and on into a cozy wood-beamed and flagstone-floored lobby where in winter, a fire burns in the marble fireplace in the antiques-filled lounge. The large standard rooms are decorated with such country touches as gingham wallpaper and Louis XIII–style furniture; the superior duplex rooms have modern beds (some decorated in velvets and taffeta) located in a loft above a cozy sitting room with ritzy but comfortable chairs and couches. The on-site Spa de la Reine includes two private spa rooms (massage and spa treatments are available for guest booking), a small workout room, a *hammam* (steam room), and a Jacuzzi. Rooms overlook the court-yard or a flowered patio and have all the amenities: air-conditioning, cable TV, Internet, room service, minibar, and laundry service. Breakfast is served in the vaulted cellar, amidst tapestries; pastries are made at the *boulangerie* next door. You'll definitely be treated like a queen (or king) here.

See map p. 108. 28 place des Vosges. ☎ *01-40-29-19-19. Fax: 01-40-29-19-20.* www. pavillon-de-la-reine.com. *Métro: Saint-Paul. Rack rates: 330€ standard room, 400€ superior room, 450€ deluxe room, 500€ duplex room, 550€–800 suite. Continental breakfast 25€, buffet breakfast 30€. AE, DC, MC, V.*

Index of Accommodations by Neighborhood

Louvre (1er)
Citadines Louvre Paris ($$$)
Hôtel Agora ($–$$)
Hôtel Henri IV ($)
Hotel Louvre Forum ($)
Hôtel Montpensier ($–$$)

Opéra/Montorgueil (2e)
Citadines Opéra–Grands Boulevards Paris ($$$–$$$$)
Hôtel Bonne Nouvelle ($–$$)
Hôtel Tiquetonne ($)
Hôtel Vivienne ($–$$)

Le Marais/île Saint-Louis (3e, 4e)
Castex Hotel ($$)
Hotel de la Place des Vosges ($$–$$$)
Hôtel des Deux-Iles ($$$)
Hôtel du Jeu de Paume ($$$$)
Hôtel du Petit Moulin ($$$–$$$$)
Hôtel Jeanne d'Arc ($–$$)
Hôtel Saint-Merry ($$$)
Pavillon de la Reine ($$$$)

Latin Quarter (5e)
Familia Hotel ($–$$)
Hotel Claude Bernard ($$–$$$)
Hotel de Suez ($–$$)
Hôtel Esmeralda ($–$$)
Hotel Marignan ($–$$)
Hôtel Saint-Jacques ($$–$$$)
Minerve Hotel ($$)

Saint-Germain-des-Prés (6e)
Grand Hotel des Balcons ($$–$$$)
Hôtel de Fleurie ($$$–$$$$)

Hôtel de l'Abbaye ($$$–$$$$)
Hotel de Seine ($$$)
Hotel du Lys ($$)
Hotel du Quai Voltaire ($$)
Hôtel Saints-Pères ($$$)
L'Hôtel ($$$$)

Invalides/Eiffel Tower (7e)
Grand Hôtel Lévêque ($)
Hôtel Amélie ($)
Hôtel le Tourville ($$$)
Hôtel Lindbergh ($$)
Hôtel Verneuil ($$$)

Champs-Elysées/Madeleine (8e)
Four Seasons Hotel George V Paris ($$$$)
Hotel Alison ($$)
Hôtel Balzac ($$$$)
Lord Byron Hôtel Residence ($$$)

Grands Boulevards (9e)
9 Hotel ($$–$$$)
Hotel Jules ($$$–$$$$)

Index of Accommodations by Price

$

Familia Hotel (5e)
Grand Hôtel Lévêque (7e)
Hôtel Agora (1er)
Hôtel Amélie (7e)
Hôtel Bonne Nouvelle (2e)
Hotel de Suez (5e)
Hôtel Esmeralda (5e)
Hôtel Henri IV (1er)
Hôtel Jeanne d'Arc (4e)
Hotel Louvre Forum (1er)
Hotel Marignan (5e)
Hôtel Montpensier (1er)
Hôtel Tiquetonne (2e)
Hôtel Vivienne (2e)

$$

Castex Hotel (4e)
Familia Hotel (5e)
Grand Hotel des Balcons (6e)
Hôtel Agora (1er)
Hotel Alison (8e)
Hôtel Bonne Nouvelle (2e)
Hotel Claude Bernard (5e)
Hotel de la Place des Vosges (4e)
Hotel de Suez (5e)
Hotel du Lys (6e)
Hôtel du Quai Voltaire (6e)
Hôtel Esmeralda (5e)

Hôtel Jeanne d'Arc (4e)
Hôtel Lindbergh (7e)
Hotel Marignan (5e)
Hôtel Montpensier (1er)
Hôtel Saint-Jacques (5e)
Hôtel Vivienne (2e)
Minerve Hotel (5e)
9 Hôtel (9e)

$$$

Citadines Louvre Paris (1er)
Citadines Opéra–Grands Boulevards Paris (2e)
Grand Hotel des Balcons (6e)
Hotel Claude Bernard (5e)
Hôtel de Fleurie (6e)
Hôtel de l'Abbaye (6e)
Hotel de la Place des Vosges (4e)
Hôtel des Deux-Iles (4e)
Hotel de Seine (6e)
Hôtel du Petit Moulin (3e)
Hotel Jules (9e)
Hôtel le Tourville (7e)
Hôtel Saint-Jacques (5e)
Hôtel Saint-Merry (4e)
Hôtel Saints-Pères (6e)
Hôtel Verneuil (7e)
Lord Byron Hôtel Residence (8e)
9 Hôtel (9e)

$$$$

Citadines Opéra–Grands Boulevards
  Paris (2e)
Four Seasons Hotel Georges V
  Paris (8e)
Hôtel Balzac (8e)
Hôtel de Fleurie (6e)

Hôtel de l'Abbaye (6e)
Hôtel du Jeu de Paume (4e)
Hôtel du Petit Moulin (3e)
Hotel Jules (9e)
L'Hôtel (6e)
Pavillon de la Reine (3e)

Chapter 10

Dining and Snacking
in Paris

In This Chapter

▶ Getting the inside scoop on Paris's dining scene

▶ Eating well without breaking the bank

▶ Grabbing something on the go

▶ Discovering the best bakeries, cafes, wine bars, and tea salons

▶ Finding a restaurant by location, cuisine, and price

*T*here's no question: Paris is a feast. Travelers may be surprised to find French dishes so familiar, because France's political history (and flair for excellent produce) has long influenced mainstream Western cuisine, especially in the big cities of the United States. Even the origin of the concept of restaurants, as we understand them, can be found in 18th-century France.

Traditional haute cuisine — a delicate balance of flavors, sauces, and ingredients blended with a studied technique — includes such classics as *blanquette de veau* (veal in an eggy cream sauce), *pot-au-feu* (an excellent stew of fatty beef and vegetables), *coq au vin* (chicken braised in red wine with onions and mushrooms), *bouillabaisse* (seafood soup), and that hearty staple *boeuf bourguignon* (beef stew with red wine).

But when people started thinking healthy a few decades back, buttery, creamy, saucy French cuisine quickly found itself on the outs. So the French invented *nouvelle cuisine,* popularized in the late '70s, which gave chefs an excuse to concoct new dishes — still French, mind you, but less fattening because they use fewer heavy creams and less butter and serve (much) smaller portions.

When the nouvelle trend lost steam (in part because of the minuscule portions), people began spinning off healthier and/or more-creative cooking styles with the traditional portions in mind. But inevitably, food enthusiasts are always looking for change: the latest establishment-rocking revolution was started by journalists Alexandre Cammas and Emmanuel Rubin in 1999. They created *Le Fooding,* a portmanteau of "food" and "feeling."

Naturally, it's hard to say what *Le Fooding* really is: Originally a guidebook with a philosophical view of both cooking and eating as full sensory experience, now it's a culinary movement with tasting parties and events all over Paris and the rest of France, and even other capitals across the Western Hemisphere. Essentially, it pushes French gastronomy to be even more inclusive of all cuisine, from fusion to street food and beyond. In a 2010 *New Yorker* article, Paris maven Adam Gopnik described the "ill defined" *Le Fooding* as a way to "Americanize French food without becoming American," that is to say, breaking down self-limiting traditions without sacrificing French character.

In fact, these people mean business: That American staple and butt of many French jokes — the hamburger — has finally become a hip menu item! Served in a variety of inventive and delicious ways, it's not what you'll find back home; despite the ever-present bun it's eaten with knife and fork! Leave it to the French. . . . Add to these styles the mix of French regional restaurants and the many ethnic dining rooms, and you'll never want for variety.

This chapter is designed to make you feel comfortable about dining in Parisian restaurants and have at least one experience of a true French meal that stretches over several incredible courses. Each restaurant listed has all the ingredients of an excellent dining spot — fantastic cooking, reasonable prices, and great atmosphere — and creates the kind of experience that lingers in your memory after the last dish is cleared away. Then, when you just can't sit down to another multiple-course meal, you can choose other options, from street and ethnic food, to cafeterias, tea salons, and cafes.

For detailed culinary information, see Chapter 2, where I give a brief rundown on French cuisine, a useful glossary of French culinary terms, and a user's guide to typical French dishes.

Getting the Dish on the Local Scene

This section discusses how to dine like a Parisian. You'll likely want to make a dinner reservation (a must for the more popular restaurants) and you'll need to know how to dress for that meal — we discuss all of that here. If you've ever wondered about the difference between a *bistro* and a *brasserie,* read below. Finally, this section summarizes the order of a traditional French meal — salad *after* the main course is usually the biggest surprise.

Making reservations for dinner

The vast majority of French restaurants are small establishments with limited seating, and tables are scrupulously saved for folks who book. Always try to make at least a same-day reservation, even for a modest neighborhood bistro. If you're concerned about your language skills, you can always visit the establishment before service starts to make a same-day or next-day reservation. Or ask the concierge in your hotel or the hotel's desk clerk to make a reservation for you. Some top restaurants require several weeks' notice. Remember to call if you're going to be more than 20 minutes late; showing up late is considered bad form.

If you're staying at a hotel with a staff concierge, call or e-mail ahead and ask the concierge to make a reservation if you'd like to eat at a sought-after restaurant. Make the call as early as possible, specifying your preferred date with a backup date or two. Don't forget to tip the concierge (slip 10€ into an envelope and discreetly present it when checking out).

Dressing to dine

Only the most expensive restaurants enforce dress codes (suit and tie), and in theory, you can dress up or down as you like. Parisians, however, are a pretty stylish lot (how do French women get their scarves to *do* that?), even when dressing informally in jeans. Relaxed dressing doesn't mean sloppy jeans and sneakers — *especially* not sneakers (and don't even think about cargo pants). The look to aim for is casual but upscale. You can't go wrong if you dress in neutrals — think black, beige, gray, cream, navy, and chocolate. If you wear jeans, pair them with a nice jacket, sweater, or shirt and good shoes and nice accessories. Go a notch dressier than what you'd wear at home.

Knowing the difference between a cafe and a bistro

Eateries go by various names in France, and in theory at least, these labels give you some clue as to how much a meal costs. From most expensive to least expensive, the lineup generally goes like this: restaurant, bistro, brasserie, cafe. The key word is *generally.* Never rely on the name of an establishment as the sole price indicator; some of the city's most expensive places call themselves cafes. Furthermore, the awnings above quintessential cafes often claim the labels of restaurant, cafe, brasserie, or some other combination. The only way to be sure of the price is to read the menu, which, by law, is posted outside.

The following is a list of the different types of establishments and what you should expect:

✔ **Restaurants** are where you go to savor French cuisine in all its glory. At their best, classic dishes are excellent, and new dishes are inventive. Dining is usually more formal than in bistros or brasseries, and service is slower. You may also have more than one server. Generally, restaurants serve lunch between noon and 2:30 p.m. and dinner between 7 and 10 p.m. You must be seated for lunch no later than 2 p.m., if you want a full meal.

Between 3 and 7 p.m., you may find it difficult to have a sit-down meal in a Paris restaurant or bistro. During this swing shift, your best bet is to head to a cafe, tearoom, or wine bar. Dining at 7 p.m. is considered very early for dinner in Paris; most Parisians wouldn't think about sitting down before 8 p.m. But starting too late — 10 p.m. is getting dangerous — can leave you without many options.

Restaurant critics are divided about the *menu dégustation* (meh-*noo* day-goo-*stah*-see-ohn; sampler, or tasting, menu), featured in many of the city's top restaurants. Made up of small portions of the chef's signature dishes, it offers tremendous value because you have the opportunity to try more dishes. Generally the experience is deeply satisfying and one-of-a-kind. But some say there are too many portions for a customer to get a sense of the chef's artistry, and the mixture of so many flavors just confuses, instead of enriches, the palate. Or, from a more practical point of view, they're often expensive and leave you feeling *very* full.

✔ The typical **bistro** used to be a mom-and-pop operation with a menu confined to such Parisian standbys as *boeuf bourguignon* (braised beef in red wine sauce) and *Tarte Tatin* (caramelized upside-down apple pie). Today, many bistros have expanded upon the old classics but retain the tradition of offering hearty, relatively inexpensive dishes in a convivial, intimate atmosphere. Think crush of elbows and the sounds of corks popping, glasses clinking, multitudes of conversations, and people having a good time. Bistros are where Parisians come to dine most often.

✔ Literally, the word **brasserie** means "brewery" and refers to the Alsatian menu specialties that include staples such as beer, Riesling wine, fish and other seafood, and *choucroute* (a sauerkraut-based dish, usually topped by cuts of ham). Most brasseries are large, cheerful, brightly lit places that open early and close late (some are open 24 hours a day), and have an immense selection of dishes on the menu, although many no longer specialize in Alsatian fare. At brasseries, you can usually get a meal any time of day, even in hours when restaurants and bistros are closed, and the food is relatively inexpensive.

Sadly, brasseries began to fall to corporate acquisition in the 1970s, and today most are part of one all-encompassing chain, the FLO Brasseries. Although this fact shouldn't stop you from visiting some of Paris's legendary eateries, look out for places that list mundane and repetitive food on their menus — they're more numerous than you think. Your best bet is to get a look at the menus of brasseries that interest you and compare costs, as well as listings. If *poulet rôti* (rotisserie chicken), *steak frites* (steak and fries), and omelets seem to be highlights (although tasty, these are quite unimaginative menu items), you may want to try eating somewhere else.

✔ **Cafes** are typically open from about 8 a.m. to 1 a.m. They serve drinks and food all day from a short menu that often includes salads, sandwiches, steak, mussels, and french fries. Prime locations or famous literary cafes carry higher price tags. Most cafes offer reasonably priced omelets, sandwiches, soups, or salads. Omelets come plain with just a sprinkling of herbs or filled with cheese, ham, or other hearty additions. *Soupe à l'oignon* (onion soup) is a traditional Parisian dish, and you may see *soupe de poisson* (fish soup) on the menu. Another cafe favorite is the *croque-monsieur,* a grilled ham sandwich covered with melted cheese (which often comes open-faced), or a *croque-madame,* the same dish topped with an egg. Or try a *salade niçoise* (a huge bowl filled with lettuce, boiled potatoes, tuna, hard-boiled eggs, capers, tomatoes, olives, and anchovies) or a *salade de chèvre chaud* (fresh greens topped with warm goat cheese on croutons). These dishes make a light, pleasant meal for 6€ to 12€.

Parisians use cafes the way the British use pubs — as extensions of their living rooms. They're places where you meet friends before heading to the movies or a party, read your newspaper, write in your journal, or just hang out and people-watch. Regardless of whether you order a cup of coffee or the most expensive cognac in the house, no one will ask you to leave before you're ready. Coffee, of course, is the chief drink, and when the French say *café,* they mean espresso. It comes black in a small cup, often with a thin wrapped square of dark chocolate, unless you order a *café crème* or *café au lait* (coffee with steamed milk, which Parisians usually have at breakfast). *Thé* (tay; tea) is also fairly popular but isn't always the highest quality (check on the menu for mentions of a specific brand — Thé Mariages Frères, for example, will be very good). *Chocolat chaud* (shock-o-*lah* shoh; hot chocolate), on the other hand, is absolutely superb and made from real ground chocolate. The result is a thick, rich, yet not too sweet taste of heaven.

✔ **Tearooms,** or *salons de thé,* usually open midmorning and close by early evening. Some serve light lunches, but most are at their best in the afternoon for desserts with coffee or tea.

✔ **Wine bars,** or *bars à vin,* operate from midmorning to late evening when you can order wine by the glass and munch on snacks such as *tartines* (open-faced sandwiches), olives, cured meats, and cheese. Some offer simple lunch menus, but like cafes and tearooms, they're generally better for light bites.

To tip or not to tip

In France, waiting tables is a profession with benefits and retirement security, and waiters are treated with respect (even though you may come across some who do not return the sensibility). When it comes to tipping them, you may have heard not to leave anything since a gratuity is already included in the bill. It's true that an 18 percent service charge, which appears on the bill as *service compris,* is added. But waiters never get the full 18 percent. Thus, it's customary to leave a few euro, or about 5 percent of the bill after a meal, unless the service was truly terrible.

Understanding the order of a meal

A proper meal consists of three, or sometimes four, courses, so portions are usually moderate. Be aware of the traditional way French restaurants serve food.

✔ An *aperitif* is a light drink that precedes the meal. The French don't like to start a meal by numbing the palate with strong liquor. They usually stick to such offerings as a *kir,* a mixture of white wine and *crème de cassis* (black currant liqueur), which is light and the most common premeal drink. France's other traditional *apéro* (the cutesy slang for aperitifs) is a glass of *pastis,* or anise-flavored liquor. The most well known brands are Ricard and Pernod, originally competing brands that became a big liquor conglomerate in the 1970s.

✔ You're always served bread with your meal, but you must request butter.

✔ Water isn't placed on the table automatically — you must ask for it. To get regular tap water (which is perfectly fine to drink), as opposed to the pricey equivalent in a bottle, simply ask for *une carafe d'eau* (oon kar-*aff* doh). Ice cubes, or *des glaçons* (des *glah*-son) are also not compulsory — just ask your waiter.

✔ Cheese comes after the main course and is usually accompanied by a red wine. And don't be surprised that the salad comes after the main course and before your cheese (to cleanse the palate!).

✔ Dessert comes after the cheese course, but dessert and cheese can be served at the same time at your request.

✔ Diners traditionally don't drink coffee during the meal. Black espresso is served after dessert in a demitasse cup with sugar cubes on the side. If you want milk with your coffee, you must ask for a *café au lait* (ka-*fay* oh lay), a *café crème* (ka-*fay* krem), or *du lait à côté* (doo lay ah koh-*tay*), or milk on the side.

✔ After the meal is finished, you can order a *digestif,* a small glass of liquor or fortified wine, thought to aid the digestion. Some classic *digestifs* are cognac, Calvados (an apple brandy from Normandy), sherry, and port.

✔ If you have food left on your plate, don't ask for a doggie bag. Restaurants are not accustomed to handling these types of requests.

The *menu du jour* (the fixed-price meal) at many establishments includes red or white wine. The standard measure is *un quart* (a quarter-liter carafe), sometimes served in *un pot* or *un pichet* (a pitcher). If wine isn't included, you can order *vin ordinaire* or *vin de table* (house wine) or a Beaujolais (a light, fruity red wine), a Côtes du Rhône (a dry red wine), or a Chardonnay (a light white wine), which are very reasonably priced. And you can always opt for soda, juice, or water instead (*l'eau plat* is still water; *l'eau gazeuse* is carbonated water). Cocktails are available but discouraged because they're thought to numb the palate. Note that soda is often more expensive than a glass of wine at many establishments.

In France, as anywhere, you should never underestimate the importance of good manners. Your meal will be much smoother if you remember essential but basic phrases such as *Bonjour, monsieur* (Hello, sir) and *Merci, madame* (Thank you, madam). Keep in mind, too, that French table manners require that all food, even fruit, be eaten with a knife and fork.

Contrary to what you may have seen in the movies, never, *ever* refer to the waiter as *garçon* (boy), and don't snap your fingers at him or her. Instead, say, *"Monsieur/Madame/Mademoiselle, s'il vous plaît!"* (Sir/Madam/Miss, if you please!). To put in your order if your waiter speaks no English, say, *"Pourrais-j'avoir . . ."* (pour-*ay* jha-vwar), which means "Could I have. . . ."

Trimming the Fat from Your Budget

If you're watching your pocketbook when it comes to dining out, following a few of these simple tips can go a long way toward making the bill as appealing as the food:

- ✔ **Order *prix fixe* (set-price) meals.** These set-price meals are up to 30 percent cheaper than ordering the same dishes a la carte. What's the tradeoff? Your options are more limited than if you order from the main menu. Review the *prix fixe* option carefully to determine what you're getting at that price. Does the meal come with wine, and if so, how much — a glass or a half-bottle? Is dessert or coffee included?

- ✔ **Make lunch your main meal.** Many restaurants offer great deals on a fixed-price lunch, some more than 50 percent cheaper than what you'd pay at night. You probably won't be hungry for a full meal at dinnertime after two or three courses at lunch.

- ✔ **Try the *crêperies*.** *Crêperies* (many are off the boulevard du Montparnasse around the square Délambre) offer a great value. Try savory meat, cheese or vegetable-filled crêpes, called *galettes,* with a bowl of cider for your main meal and honey, jam, *chantilly* (whipped cream), chocolate, or fruit-filled crêpes for dessert. Surroundings are usually Brittany-inspired with red-checked tablecloths, wooden beams, maritime souvenirs, and pictures of Bretagnons in native dress.

- ✔ **Try the falafel stands.** If your day's plans include a trip to the Marais (Musée Picasso, Place des Vosges, Maison de Victor Hugo, and shopping; see Chapters 11 and 13 for information on guided tours), have for lunch a delicious and cheap falafel or other Middle Eastern food from one of the storefronts on and around rue des Rosiers.

✔ **Hit up the *boulangeries* and *traiteurs* for lunch.** Every *boulangerie* sells a cheap *prix fixe* of a sandwich or quiche, drink, and pastry during lunch hours. That's how many hard-working Parisians take a quick lunch in parks near their businesses. *Traiteurs* often sell prepared salads, hot courses, and quiches.

✔ **Pay attention to the menu's details.** On most menus, the cheaper dishes are made of cheaper cuts of meat or the organs of animals, such as brains, tripe, and the like. Often appearing on menus are *cervelles* (pork or sheep brains), *tête de veau* (calf's head), and *rognons* (kidneys).

✔ **Don't eat breakfast at your hotel.** Doing so adds, at the very least, $5 more per person to your hotel bill. Grab a croissant or a *pain au chocolat* (chocolate-filled pastry) from a *boulangerie*.

✔ **Know the tipping rules.** Service is usually included at restaurants, but it's customary to leave about 5 percent extra for your server.

Paris's Best Restaurants

Restaurants are listed alphabetically for easy reference, followed by the price range, neighborhood, and type of cuisine for each. Price ranges reflect the cost of a three-course meal for one person ordered a la carte, featuring an appetizer, main dish, dessert, and coffee — alcohol is not included.

The number of dollar signs used to describe each restaurant gives you a general idea of how much a meal costs at dinner, but don't make price your only criteria for choosing a restaurant. Most establishments offer fixed-price menus (also called *formules* or *prix fixe*) that can bring the cost down one whole price category. Likewise, if you're dying to try a place that's beyond your budget, visit it at lunch when meals are cheaper. See Table 10-1 for a key to the restaurant prices.

Table 10-1	Key to Restaurant Prices
Dollar Sign(s)	*Price Range*
$	20€ or less
$$	21€–50€
$$$	51€–100€
$$$$	101€ or more

Restaurants on the Right Bank

MONTMARTRE

place de l'Europe
r. de Madrid
de Liège
Liège
de
r. de Clichy
Blanche
r. la Bruyère
St-Georges
de Lorette
Notre-Dame
r. des Martyrs
r. Milton
Cadet
de
r. de Maubeuge
square Montholon

Ste-Trinité
Londres
d'Amsterdam
Georges
r. Lamartine
de

Gare St-Lazare
square de la Trinité
Lazare
St- Lazare
Notre-Dame-de-Lorette
Chateâudun
Cadet
r. Bleue

square M. Pagnol
r. de Laborde
St-Lazare
Haussmann-St-Lazare
Trinité
Victoire
Fayette
r. Saulnier
Trévise

r. de la Pépinière
place G. Péri
r. Joubert
de
Le Peletier
Provence
r. Richer

St-Augustin
bd. Haussmann
square Louis XVI
des
Mogador
Caumartin
Chaussée
Chaussée d'Antin
La Fayette
Peletier
Drouot
Montmartre
r. Bergère

8e
r. d'Anjou
r. de l'Arcade
r. Pasquier
Tronchet
Mathurins
place Diaghilev
Rossini
Richelieu-Drouot
bd. Montmartre
bd. Poissonnière

Opéra Garnier
Auber
Halévy
bd. Haussmann
r. Vivienne
Grands Boulevards
r. des Jeûneurs
Sentier

place de la Madeleine
La Madeleine
Madeleine
Auber
Scribe
Opéra
Capucines
des Italiens
Richelieu
r. de Richelieu

r. de Surène
bd. de la Madeleine
place de l'Opéra
du Quatre Septembre
pl. de la Bourse
La Bourse
2e

r. du Faubourg St-Honoré
des Capucines
la Paix
Opéra
Grand
la Michodière
Quatre Septembre
Bourse
r. Réaumur
r. Léopold

Boissy
Royale
Saint-
r. Danielle Casanova
Louis
Gaillon
r. Paul Lelong
r. du Mail
d'Aboukir
Sentier

Concorde
place Vendôme
place du Marché St-Honoré
Ste Anne
Bibliothèque Nationale
de la Banque
de la place des Victoires
Étienne
Montorgueil

place de la Concorde
Galerie National du Jeu de Paume
du Mont Thabor
de Castiglione
Honoré
r. Thérèse
des Petits Champs
Feuillade
Hôtel des Postes
r. Coquillière

Musée de l'Orangerie
Tuileries
Pyramides
de l'Opéra
Jardin du Palais Royal
Croix des Petits Champs
St-Eustache

Jardin des Tuileries
Rivoli
pl. André Malraux
Palais Royal
du Bouloi
Bourse du Commerce
Les Halles
Jardin des Halles

Seine
quai des Tuileries
av. du Général Lemonnier
Palais-Royal
Musée du Louvre
pl. du Palais-Royal
Saint-
r. Berger
Honoré

Assemblée Nationale
r. de Lille
Musée d'Orsay
Jardin du Carrousel
place du Carrousel
Louvre-Rivoli
r. de l'Amiral de Coligny
r. de l'Arbre Sec
des Bourdonnais

passerelle Léopold-Sédar-Senghor
Musée d'Orsay
pont Royal
quai François Mitterrand
cour Napoléon
cour Carrée
du Louvre
Pont Neuf
quai de la Mégisserie

q. Malaquais
Institut de France
Monnaie de Paris
pont du Carrousel
quai Voltaire
pont des Arts
square du Vert-Galant
Pont Neuf
pont Neuf
place Dauphine
Palais de Justice
ÎLE DE LA CITÉ

6e
quai de Conti
quai des Grands Augustins
St-Michel
place St-Michel
St-Michel-Notre-Dame

N
0 — 1/4 mi
0 — 0.25 km

A l'Affiche **1**	La Poule au Pot **7**	
Au Bascou **12**	L'Aréa **18**	
Au Pied de Cochon **6**	Le Cinq **4**	
Bofinger **19**	Le 404 **14**	
Chateaubriand **11**	Le Kokolion **3**	
Chez Casimir **9**	Le Potager du Marais **16**	
Chez Michel **8**	Le Square **2**	
Chez Omar **15**	Maison Chardenoux **20**	
Frenchie **13**	Restaurant du Palais-Royal **5**	
La Fidélité **10**	Restaurant Plaza Athénée **4**	
L'Ambroisie **17**		

Ⓜ Métro station
RER RER station
✉ Post office

9e   **1er**   **6e**

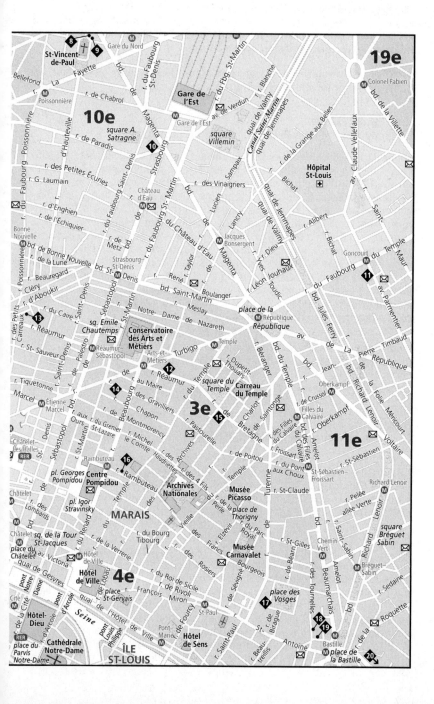

The restaurants listed here range from moderately priced establishments to homey neighborhood favorites to chic "in" spots. Also included are some bargain eateries and a few of the city's most sumptuous restaurants where haute cuisine is an art form.

See the "Restaurants on the Right Bank" and "Restaurants on the Left Bank" maps for locations of restaurants in this section.

A La Petite Chaise
$$ Saint-Germain-des-Prés (7e)   CLASSIC BISTRO

Founded in 1680, this small gem is alleged to be the oldest restaurant in Paris, and its roster of historic diners is quite impressive: Heir to the throne Philip d'Orléans and his priest, Cardinal Dubois, George Sand, Toulouse-Lautrec, Colette, and François Mitterrand, are just a few. The entryway, adorned with a smoky antique mirror from the early 18th century, leads to a softly illuminated, cozy dining room reminiscent of an old country inn, which it once was. Start with *aile de raie et pommes charlottes servies tièdes avec vinaigrette balsamique* (skate wing on a bed of potatoes served warm with a balsamic vinaigrette). Main courses may include a *filet de bar grille à la marinade de cerfeuil* (grilled fillet of sea bass in a chervil marinade) or grilled pork tenderloin with a blue cheese sauce. The house special dessert is *gateau au chocolat* — a rich chocolate cake topped with *crème anglaise* (a custard cream sauce).

See map p. 147. 36 rue de Grenelle. ☎ *01-42-22-13-35. Métro: Sèvres-Babylone. (Exit the station on boulevard Raspail and walk 1 block north to rue de la Chaise. Follow the street to the end, where it intersects rue de Grenelle.) Prix fixe lunch menu (including glass of wine and a café): 20€ or 26€; prix fixe dinner menu (main course with appetizer and dessert): 31€. AE, MC, V. Open: Daily noon to 2 p.m. and 7–11 p.m.*

A.O.C.
$$ Latin Quarter (5e)   CLASSIC BISTRO

Tucked away on a quiet street across from the Institut du Monde Arabe, this brasserie-style restaurant sounds the call for those who truly love meat — the owner is the scion of three generations of traditional French butchers. A.O.C. (which stands for *appellation d'origine contrôlée*, the official guarantee of the regional origin of food products by the French government) delivers high-quality meats in traditional dishes. The wooden floors, distressed bistro mirrors, and leather chairs create an air of intimacy, while a pleasant staff is knowledgeable about and happy to explain the diverse menu choices. Aside from the classic items like steak tartare, there are other more adventurous possibilities like the roasted bone marrow with *fleur de sel* served with garlic-rubbed Poujauran bread (Jean-Luc Poujauran is a celebrity baker in Paris), or there's a whole-roasted suckling pig, or even grilled veal kidney in a port wine sauce. The homemade terrines served with a succulent onion jam will have you requesting additional baskets of bread. After fulfilling your primal desire for meat, enjoy the Basque sheep's cheese served with traditional black cherry jam. You can lazily walk off your experience along the Seine afterwards.

See map p. 147. 14 rue des Fosses–Saint-Bernard. ☎ **01-43-54-22-52.** www. restoaoc.com. *Métro: Cardinale Lemoine. (Follow rue du Cardinale Lemoine towards the Seine to rue des Fosses–Saint-Bernard.) Three-course lunch menu: 29€; dinner main courses: 28€–46€. MC, V. Open: Tues–Sat noon to 2:30 p.m. and 7:30–11:30 p.m.*

Au Bascou
$$ Le Marais (3e)   BASQUE/SOUTHWEST

Located in a simple and softly lit rustic interior, some of the best Basque dishes in Paris can be found here. (The Basque region is the corner of southwestern France resting along the Spanish border and is known for its distinct language and the excellent culinary skills of its citizens.) Consider starting with a *pipérade basquaise* (a light terrine of eggs, tomatoes, and spices) before moving to on Chipiron calamari sautéed with Espelette peppers or guinea fowl supreme *à la bayonnaise* (served with a garnish of tomatoes, peppers, and onions). A bottle of Irouléguy, a smooth red Basque wine, makes a nice accompaniment to meals, and the service, though distant at times, is efficient and gracious.

See map p. 142. 38 rue Réaumur. ☎ **01-42-72-69-25.** www.au-bascou.fr. *Métro: Arts et Métiers. (Look for the corner of rue Réaumur and rue Volta.) Prix fixe two-course lunch menu (not including wine): 19€; dinner main courses: 16€–20€. AE, MC, V. Open: Mon–Fri noon to 2 p.m. and 8–10:30 p.m.*

Auberge Le Pot de Terre
$ Latin Quarter (5e)   CLASSIC BISTRO

Parisians looking for a fresh meal at dirt-cheap prices relish in the open secret of this restaurant just off of lively rue Mouffetard. Served in a rustic dining room with stone walls and exposed wooden ceiling beams, the classic market fare served by charming waitstaff includes such starters as a fantastic onion soup, mussels cooked in white wine with onions, and escargots served with a garlicky butter sauce. Main courses could be duck confit with parsleyed potatoes, roast leg of lamb with garlic, sautéed salmon with sorrel. You couldn't say that the food is terribly unique for a French restaurant, but it is well prepared and, at 17€ for a three-course menu, worth a visit.

See map p. 147. 22 rue du Pot de Fer. ☎ **01-43-31-15-51.** www.lepotdeterre. com. *Métro: Place Monge. (Exit the station and walk up the place to Rue Ortolan. Cross rue Mouffetard and continue on rue du Pot de Terre, just before rue Tournefort.) Main courses: 9.50€–16€; prix fixe lunch: 11€; prix fixe dinner: 17€. MC, V. Open: Daily noon to 11:30 p.m.*

Au Bon Accueil
$$ Eiffel Tower (7e)   MODERN BISTRO

A stone's throw from the Eiffel Tower, the elegant and Michelin-rated Au Bon Accueil's daily-changing, green market-based menu is simple and delicious. Tables are set with chewy grainy bread and a small plate of

Restaurants on the Left Bank

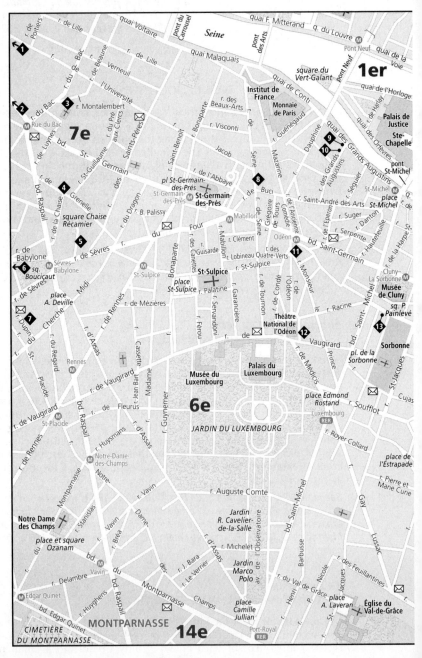

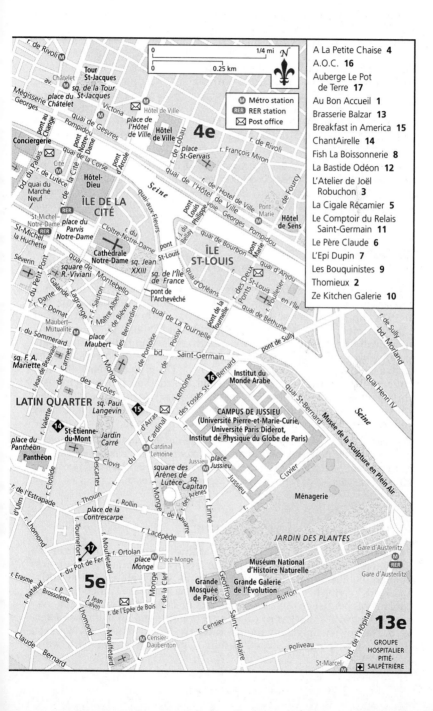

A La Petite Chaise **4**
A.O.C. **16**
Auberge Le Pot de Terre **17**
Au Bon Accueil **1**
Brasserie Balzar **13**
Breakfast in America **15**
ChantAirelle **14**
Fish La Boissonnerie **8**
La Bastide Odéon **12**
L'Atelier de Joël Robuchon **3**
La Cigale Récamier **5**
Le Comptoir du Relais Saint-Germain **11**
Le Père Claude **6**
L'Epi Dupin **7**
Les Bouquinistes **9**
Thomieux **2**
Ze Kitchen Galerie **10**

saucisson (thinly sliced sausage) in an unpretentious dining room with sand and wood colors and slate floors. If you're ordering from the *prix fixe* menu, you may start with a light cream soup of white asparagus with Morcon sausage, followed by a lightly seared swordfish served with a mini-ratatouille and basil sauce, finishing off with a *mille-feuille* (puff pastry) of mango and pineapple with a Szechwan pepper and vanilla sorbet on the side. Main dishes are divine and can include Bresse chicken preserved in its own fat, served with foie gras and a spicy puree of mushrooms and breadcrumbs, or more simple pan-fried Brittany scallops served with watercress and an oyster tartare. The dining room only seats 25, so reserve in advance.

See map p. 147. 14 rue de Monttessuy. ☎ **01-47-05-46-11.** *Reservations strongly recommended. Métro: Alma Marceau. (Exit the station, cross the Pont l'Alma and the quai Branly, and turn onto avenue Rapp. Follow avenue Rapp 2 blocks to rue de Monttessuy, and turn right.) Main courses: 19€–36€; three-course prix fixe menu: 27€. MC, V. Open: Mon–Fri noon to 2:30 p.m. and 7:30–10:30 p.m.*

Au Pied de Cochon
$$ Les Halles (1er) CLASSIC BISTRO

With marble, murals, elaborate sconces, chandeliers, an excess of tourists and some of the most patient waiters around, Au Pied de Cochon opened in 1946 and has played a vibrant part in the history of this old market neighborhood. Specialties here are platters of fish and, of course, pork, specifically *andouillette A.A.A.A.A.* (a strong-tasting regional tripe sausage), which you can get grilled with béarnaise sauce. There's also the namesake dish, *pied de cochon* (pigs' feet). Or, if you're daring — and hungry — have the *plateau rouge* (half a Canadian lobster, crayfish, shrimp, crabs, and other red fish served on a towering pile of shaved ice). Finish with melt-in-your-mouth *profiteroles* (cream puffs). Unlike many Parisian restaurants, this place never seems to close.

See map p. 142. 6 rue Coquillière (between rue du Jour and rue Jean-Jacques Rousseau on the northwest side of the garden of the Forum des Halles shopping center). www.pieddecochon.com. ☎ **01-40-13-77-00.** *Métro: Châtelet-Les Halles. Main courses: 17€–30€. AE, DC, V. Open: Daily 24 hours.*

Bofinger
$$ Bastille (4e) ALSATIAN/BRASSERIE

Parisians like to joke that the clientele at this famous restaurant near the Bastille is made up of tourists and the elderly. But Bofinger, which first opened in 1864, continues to pack them in, with waiters in long white aprons delivering hearty cuisine, much of it based on the Franco-Germanic cooking of the Alsace region — think lots of *choucroute* (sauerkraut, usually served with sausages or other cuts of pork) and all manners of seafood. The downstairs dining room is ornately decorated with Art Nouveau flourishes and a glass-domed ceiling. Upstairs is cozier with wood paneling. It's owned by the Flo brasserie chain, which means that you'll see similar menus in the chain's other restaurants, which include Julien and Brasserie Flo. Service can be whirlwind. Brasseries are good for off-hours dining, tending to stay open until 1 a.m.

See map p. 142. 5–7 rue de la Bastille. ☎ **01-42-72-87-82.** *www.bofingerparis. com. Métro: Bastille. (Exit the station at boulevard Beaumarchais and turn left at rue de la Bastille.) Fixed-price menus (with half-bottle of wine): 32€ dinner daily and lunch Sat–Sun, 24€ lunch Mon–Fri. AE, DC, MC, V. Open: Mon–Fri noon to 3 p.m. and 6:30 p.m.–1 a.m., Sat–Sun noon to 1 a.m.*

Brasserie Balzar
$$ Latin Quarter (5e) ALSATIAN/BRASSERIE

Though it's now owned by the brasserie-buying titan Flo Group, locals still count this brasserie that opened in 1898 as a favorite and can regularly be seen in off hours sipping coffee and nibbling pastries. Choose from such hearty French classics (served by twinkly eyed waiters) as *steak tartare avec frites* (raw minced beef with french fries and salad) or roast leg of Quercy lamb. You can also get a good *foie de veau* (veal liver), *steak au poivre* (steak with crushed peppercorns), and a few fresh fish dishes. Portions are copious; french fries are crunchy, perfectly salted, and among the best in Paris.

See map p. 147. 49 rue des Écoles (on the corner of rue de la Sorbonne and rue des Écoles, less than a block south of the Musée de Cluny). ☎ **01-43-54-13-67.** *www. brasseriebalzar.com. Métro: Cluny-Sorbonne. Main courses: 15€–36€. AE, MC, V. Open: Daily noon to midnight. Closed Aug.*

Breakfast in America
$ Latin Quarter (5e) AMERICAN

Connecticut-born filmmaker Craig Carlson opened this diner in 2003 after years as an expat craving American-style big breakfasts. The food here is even better than what you get in the roadside spots back home, and it's been discovered by the locals: American travelers in need of a fix are often outnumbered by Parisians who pack the place for fluffy pancakes, crispy bacon, omelets, and a 2.50€ "bottomless mug o' joe." Breakfast is served all day every day except Sundays, but the menu also includes burgers, nachos, chicken wings, and sandwiches. A 9.95€ combo of burger, fries, and coffee is a good deal for Paris. Sunday's 16€ brunch is, of course, particularly busy. Service is efficient and friendly and in English; you may even be seated by Craig himself. There is another location in the Marais at 4 rue Mahler (Métro: Saint-Paul). ***Note:*** Tip is *not* included in the final tab here. The restaurants are very small and fill up quickly.

See map p. 147. 17 rue des Ecoles, 5e. ☎ **01-43-54-50-28.** *www.breakfast-in-america.com. Métro: Cardinal Lemoine or Jussieu. Main courses: 7.50€–12€. MC, V. Open: Daily 8:30 a.m.–11 p.m.; Mon–Sat lunch and dinner menu noon to closing, Sun brunch menu all day, Sun lunch and dinner menu 4 p.m. to closing.*

ChantAirelle
$$ Latin Quarter (5e)   AUVERGNE

If you happen to know any Parisians and want to impress them with a satisfying meal, ChantAirelle has equal parts charm and delicious peasant food from the Auvergne region of France. It's best during the warmer months to dine out back in high-walled garden. Appetizers may include *ardoise de salaisons de Haute-Loire* (a terrine served with regional meats including a variety of saucissons and country ham) or *oeuf pochés à la fourme d'Ambert artisanale* (poached eggs with regional cheese made by artisans). Main courses include a *dos de sandre poché sur lentilles vertes du Puy-en-Velay avec une sauce au Châteaugay* (poached perch back served over green Le Puy lentils — a delicacy — served with a wine sauce made from the region's best red wine), or a *la Truffade de Marie Rose* (a casserole of thinly sliced potatoes cooked in cream with Cantal cheese and Auvergne ham in the center). The restaurant also has packaged Auvergne products for sale, which could make great gifts for foodie friends. The door "moos" when opened and other wildlife sounds can be heard beneath the happy chatter of diners.

See map p. 147. 17 rue Laplace. ☎ *01-46-33-18-59. Métro: Maubert-Mutualité. (Take the street behind the Panthéon, rue Valette, and turn right onto rue Laplace.) Main courses: 16€–29€; prix fixe lunch menu (glass of wine included): 18€–23€. MC, V. Open: Mon–Fri noon to 2 p.m. and 7–10:30 p.m., Sat 7–10:30 p.m.*

Chateaubriand
$$–$$$ Oberkampf (11e)   MODERN BISTRO

A no-frills room in the eclectic Parmentier neighborhood, this place is the best example of the nouveau hip movement in the east of Paris. All kinds of folks pack the room tightly during dinner hours, from funky artists and creative types to television personalities. Mirroring the décor, raw cuisine leave no room for anything less than the fast service paired with fine ingredients and preparation. The courses making up the nightly fixed menu are deceptively simple, the combinations of flavors and textures so studied, they seem like they should have been obvious. A beef carpaccio under a leaf of Chinese radish was of the highest quality. Surely mackerel should always be served with cherries and a full scallion with stalk over a smoked eggplant puree? Book early.

See map p. 142. 129 av. Parmentier. ☎ *01-43-57-54-95. Reservations recommended. Métro: Goncourt. Lunch menu: 12€; tapas menu: 12€–35; dinner prix fixe menu 45€. AE, MC, V. Open: Tues–Fri noon to 2 p.m. and 8–11:30 p.m.*

Chez Casimir
$$ Gare du Nord (10e)   CLASSIC BISTRO

If you're arriving (or leaving) Paris via the Gare du Nord, schedule a lunch or dinner at this terrific restaurant not too far from the station. It's owned by Thierry Breton and on the same street as its sister restaurant, Chez

Michel (reviewed later). Both are well worth the trip, and reservations are strongly suggested. The rough interior churns up images of the original idea of bistros, with its yellowing walls, retro movie posters, and tables made of thick heavy wood — simple so as not to distract you from the food. The menu here consists of ingredients from the green market found that morning or the night before. Main-course options include the *filet de rascasse poêlé et ses petits legumes* (pan-fried scorpion fish served with chopped vegetables) and the adventurous *le fondant du joue du boeuf braisee et ses carottes* (braised tender ox cheek served with carrots). Allow yourself *pain perdu aux poires* (French toast served with pears — sure to invoke images of a French childhood you've secretly craved).

See map p. 142. 6 rue Belzunce. ☎ **01-48-78-28-80.** *Métro: Gare du Nord. (Exit the station on rue de Dunkerque and look for rue de Compiègne. Follow rue de Compiègne across boulevard Magenta, turn left on Magenta, and walk a few steps to the corner. This is rue Belzunce. Make a right here, and walk a block to the top of the street. The restaurant is on your right.) Main courses: 14€–22€; prix fixe lunch: 22€–26€; prix fixe dinner: 29€. MC, V. Open: Mon 7–11:30 p.m., Tues–Fri noon to 2 p.m. and 7–11:30 p.m., Sat 7–11:30 p.m.*

Chez Michel
$$ Gare du Nord (10e)   BRETON

You'll definitely have to reserve ahead of time here since crowds of Parisians come to this sister restaurant of Chez Casimir, run by a Breton chef whose name is actually Thierry Breton. The excellent, unusual food is served at very fair prices served in twin dining rooms decorated in simple wooden beams and low-key furniture. The menu may include *gibelotte de lapin* (a regional rabbit stew prepared with a lightly sweet cream sauce) or the ever-popular regional dish *kig ha farz* (a veal stew made with pork sausage, bacon bits, ham, leeks, buckwheat dumplings, herbs, and vegetables). A really unique treat is the *perdreau rouge rôtie,* or roasted red partridge served with cabbage and other vegetables cooked in lard. For dessert, ask if they have *kouign amann* (a Breton pastry made of layers of brioche dough, butter, and caramelized sugar). The cellar is more casual with wooden tables. Choose from more than 100 different wines at retail cost, a truly dizzying experience.

See map p. 142. 10 rue Belzunce. ☎ **01-44-53-06-20.** *Métro: Gare du Nord. Three-course prix fixe: 32€. Some entrées listed on the chalkboard add additional charges to the cost of the prix fixe. MC, V. Open: Mon 7 p.m. to midnight, Tues–Fri noon to 2 p.m. and 7 p.m. to midnight. Closed last week of July and first three weeks of Aug.*

Chez Omar
$$ Le Marais (3e)   NORTH AFRICAN

Believe it or not, Parisians are proud of the tradition of couscous restaurants sprinkled throughout their city. This North African delicacy arrived in France after the colonization of Morocco, Tunisia, and Algeria in the 19th century. Nowadays, most Parisians, including the ubiquitous

Le Fooding crowd, will point you in the direction of the often-crowded Chez Omar. Located in a traditional bistro setting on the edge of the Marais, the meal of choice is, of course, a huge steaming platter of couscous, served with chicken, *merguez* (lamb sausage), or beef. All platters come with stewed vegetables, spiced to perfection. Other *maghrebain* (North African) delights include *méchoui,* or spit-roasted lamb, and, of course, the mouthwatering desserts: a variety of layered pastries filled with almonds, pistachios, and sesame seeds, often sweetened with honey. Some fantastic French-Algerian wines are available as well. This place doesn't take reservations, so get there early for dinner to avoid lines.

See map p. 142. 47 rue de Bretagne. ☎ **01-42-72-36-26.** *Métro: Arts et Métiers. Couscous: 12€–26€; méchoui: 24€; main courses: 16€–18€. No credit cards. Open: Sun 7–10:30 p.m., Mon–Sat noon to 2:30 p.m. and 7–10:30 p.m.*

Fish La Boissonnerie
$$ Saint-Germain-des-Prés (6e)   CLASSIC BISTRO

On a street dotted with stalls selling produce, this funky but refined establishment made its home in a former fish shop at the heart of bohemian Saint-Germain. The freshest fish stars in most of their dishes either in a creative supporting role, such as in tagliatelle with cream of asparagus and smoked salmon, or playing a traditional leading role of sea bream filet with spring vegetables. Although the desserts are surely delicious, consider walking up the street to Grom or Amorino for some of the best gelati in town, as a refreshing complement to your meal.

See map p. 147. 69 rue de Seine. ☎ **01-43-54-34-69.** *Métro: Mabillon. Lunch menus: 13€ and 26€; dinner menus: 32€–37€. MC, V. Open: Tues–Sun 12:30–2:30 p.m. and 7–10:45 p.m. Closed the last weeks of Aug. and Dec.*

Frenchie
$$ Sentier (2e)   MODERN BISTRO

It's so easy to walk right past this shining gem hidden in a nondescript street in the garment district, but you would be missing out on one of Paris's prime culinary experiences: a menu changing daily to represent the chef's optimal combination of the freshest ingredients of the day. Chef Grégory Marchand (who christened his restaurant with the nickname he acquired working in world-class restaurants like the Gramercy Tavern in New York and Jamie Oliver's Fifteen in London) single-handedly produces daring and innovative dishes grounded in good taste and pure flavor. The result is at once subtle and rewardingly complex. On the day of my visit, I enjoyed a smooth cream of white bean with truffles, thick gnocchi in a fragrant lemon sauce, and an intense chocolate tart with salted caramel. Your best bet is to go there in person at the beginning of your stay to make a reservation, as getting through by phone is impossible due to their raging popularity.

See map p. 142. 5 rue de Nil. ☎ **01-40-39-96-19.** *www. frenchie-restaurant. com. Métro: Sentier. (Exit the station on rue Réaumur and continue east, turning left at rue des Petits Carreaux, and then right onto rue de Nil.) Lunch: 19€ (drinks not* *included); dinner: 21€–35€. AE, MC, V. Open: Tues 8–11:30 p.m., Wed–Sat noon to 2:30 p.m. and 8–11:30 p.m.*

La Bastide Odéon
$$ Saint-Germain-des-Prés (6e)   PROVENÇAL

Gilles Ajuelos has been serving delicious Provençal cooking since 1994 in a lovely cream-colored dining room accented with weathered wood and Provençal fabrics in shades of red. The menu changes regularly, but the dynamic creations may include starters of creamy artichoke soup with dried figs, *pain d'épices,* and a spectacular whipped cream made of goat cheese, or warm puff pastry stuffed with grilled eggplant seasoned in the chef's style. Main dishes may include milk lamb shoulder served with a blend of carrots, lemon, and *harissa* (a hot Tunisian pepper sauce), or perhaps a filet of sea bream served with black olives, roast pumpkin, and grilled *coppa* (Italian salami). Desserts are just as interesting, with a rhubarb tiramisu, a *mille-feuille* (multilayered pastry) with bourbon vanilla ice cream, or a stew of seasonal fruits served with Roquefort, goat cheese, and a spicy chutney. There's a nice, slightly pricey selection of wine. The restaurant is located on a narrow stretch of sidewalk next to the Théâtre de l'Odéon and a short walk from the Jardins du Luxembourg's place Edmond Rostand/boulevard Saint-Michel entrance.

See map p. 147. 7 rue Corneille. ☎ *01-43-26-03-65.* www.bastide-odeon.com. *Métro: Odéon. (Exit the station and take rue de l'Odéon south to place de l'Odéon, where the Théâtre de l'Odéon is located. To the left of the theater is rue Corneille; take this about 45m/150 ft. to the restaurant.) Main courses: 14€–22€. Lunch menu: 23€; three-course dinner menu: 41€. AE, MC, V. Open: Tues–Sat 12:30–2 p.m. and 7:30–10:30 p.m. Closed first three weeks in Aug and Dec 25–Jan 1.*

La Cigale Récamier
$$ Invalides (7e)   CLASSIC BISTRO

Located on rue Récamier, a stone-paved garden square, La Cigale has elegant outdoor dining during warm weather with some of the best food you can get in Paris for these prices. Though the original owner retired after 30 years, you can still get the delicious house specialty, delicate soufflés, beaten high and brimming with Camembert or tarragon cream (half-soufflés are available if you just want to taste). Try the Camembert and morels, a seasonal luxury. If you're not in the mood for a soufflé, other tempting entrees include *steak au poivre* (steak with coarsely ground peppercorns) or *filet de dorade* (filet of sea bream). For dessert try — you guessed it! — a soufflé made with, among other things, pistachios or salted butter caramel or Grand Marnier.

See map p. 147. 4 rue Récamier. ☎ *01-45-48-86-58. Reservations recommended. Métro: Sèvres-Babylone. (Exit the station at rue de Sèvres and cross over boulevard Raspail to the Hôtel Lutétia. Rue Récamier is the street just behind the hotel. The restaurant is about 24m/80 ft. down.) Main courses: 19€–28€. AE, DC, MC, V. Open: Mon–Sat noon to 2 p.m. and 7:30–11 p.m.*

La Fidélité
$$ Gare du Nord (10e)   MODERN BISTRO

What an appropriate name for a neighborhood haunt that increasingly throngs with perhaps not-so-local beautiful people. Now a vogue spot for *les branchés* (hip and trendy), this glitzy bar-cum-restaurant clearly loves contrasts: A kitschy neon sign and thick red curtains on an otherwise uninteresting street by the Gare de L'Est is met by the 1880s brasserie interior (striking high ceilings, moldings, and stucco), and its laid-back, almost goofy service is met by classy baby-bistro-style presentation. The lunch special offers one of the best deals in town for the quality and aesthetic of its dishes. Concoctions like skate wing served with a bitter grapefruit salad, filet of sea bream with a mousse-like foam of zucchini and fennel in saffron, or ox cheek in a *sauce vierge* (lemon, olive oil, chopped tomatoes and basil) are as fun to eat as they are to look at. Whether it's because it has the best *moelleux au chocolat* in Paris or because of its electric atmosphere, this place is sure to win your loyalty.

See map p. 142. 12 rue de la Fidélité. ☎ *01-47-70-19-34.* www.ladfidelite.com. *Métro: Gare de l'Est or Chateau d'Eau. Lunch prix fixe: 16€–21€; dinner prix fixe: 32€; main courses: 14€–26€. Open: Mon–Fri noon to 3 p.m. and 8 p.m.–1 a.m.*

L'Ambroisie
$$$$ Le Marais (4e)   HAUTE CUISINE

This gorgeous, three-Michelin-starred, spare-no-expense restaurant located in a 17th-century town house has been rated one of the best in France but has slipped a bit, and service is snobby but attentive. It counts among its diners former U.S. President Bill Clinton, who ate here as a guest of Jacques Chirac. Served in two mirrored and frescoed high-ceilinged dining rooms and a cozy back room (in summer there is an outdoor terrace), the seasonal specialties created by Chef Bernard Pacaud may include crawfish served in a *ravigote* (highly seasoned sauce) with peas and a coriander emulsion, or a *cassolette lutée d'homard aux penne et morilles* (shallow dish of lobster with penne and morels topped with puff pastry), and, if you're feeling wealthy, fresh Bresse squab smothered in a sweetened onion caramel sauce and sweet peas *à la française* (prepared with scallions, butter, and garlic). For dessert, try the *tarte fine,* which has won awards: It's a chocolate pie served with bitter chocolate and vanilla bourbon ice cream. If you can afford it, this restaurant just begs to be the setting for marriage proposals, anniversaries, and other special and romantic events.

See map p. 142. 9 place des Vosges. ☎ **01-42-78-51-45.** www.ambroisie-placedesvosges.com. *Reserve at least four weeks ahead. Métro: Saint-Paul. (Exit the station on rue Saint-Antoine and head east to rue de Birague, which leads into the place des Vosges. Turn left at the place des Vosges and follow the arcade around the corner to the restaurant.) Jacket and tie advised. Main courses: 84€–210€. AE, MC, V. Open: Tues–Sat noon to 1:30 p.m. and 8–9:30 p.m. Closed two weeks in Feb and three weeks in Aug.*

La Poule au Pot
$$ Les Halles (1er)   CLASSIC BISTRO

When Les Halles still was Paris's marketplace, its workers came to La Poule au Pot to share this signature dish, an old French recipe of chicken stewed with broth and vegetables, which has been served here since 1935 with much success — if the *livre d'or* (a gold book filled with the names of visiting celebrities) means anything. After the market's demise, visits from such celebrities as Maurice Chevalier, the Rolling Stones, and Prince kept this Parisian bistro on the map. The atmosphere created by the long zinc bar, *pots* of wine, red leather banquettes, a blackboard with the day's market specials, wood paneling, and waiters in long aprons transports you to another era, and traditional French fare is the name of the game here. Begin with a dozen escargot cooked Burgundy style with butter, garlic, and parsley or *oeufs cocotte à la crème* (eggs baked with cream), then try a filet of salmon cooked in a saffron cream sauce, scallops flambéed with whiskey, or the succulent house *poule au pot* with a tureen of the broth on the side. Finish with a velvety crème brûlée or the *Tarte Tatin,* an upside-down apple tart covered with caramelized sugar and served with flaming *Calvados* (an apple liqueur from Normandy).

See map p. 142. 9 rue Vauvilliers. ☎ **01-42-36-32-96.** www.lapouleaupot.fr. *Métro: Louvre-Rivoli. (Exit the station on rue de Rivoli and cross the street to rue du Louvre. Walk 2 blocks to rue Saint-Honoré and make a right. Proceed 2 blocks to rue Vauvilliers. The restaurant is near the end of the street, close to the gardens of the Forum des Halles.) Main courses: 24€–36€; prix fixe: 35€. MC, V. Open: Mon–Sat 7 p.m.–5 a.m.*

L'Aréa
$$ Le Marais/Bastille (4e)   MEDITERRANEAN/BRAZILIAN

Trendy artist types, musicians, and locals have been packing the house for Brazilian–Middle Eastern food at this inexpensive hip joint with a happening vibe near the place Bastille for 17 years. Owner Edward Chuaka was born in Brazil to Lebanese parents, and his menu not only shows it but attracts a big crowd of regulars. Choose such starters from either Brazil or Lebanon as *filezinho à Carioca* (ground beef marinated in red wine) or a *mezzé* plate of hummus, tabbouleh, and other assorted Lebanese salads, main courses like *Feijoada* (the Brazilian national dish, a stew of beef and pork served with black beans, cabbage, rice, and cassava flour) and *Grillades Libanaises* (skewers of Lebanese sausage, beef, lamb, and chicken served with tabbouleh and potatoes). Go early to get a seat; the place gets full later in the evening, with people waiting at the bar and spilling into the quiet rue des Tournelles.

See map p. 142. 10 rue des Tournelles. ☎ **01-42-72-96-50.** www.lareaforever. com. *Métro: Bastille. Main courses: 15€–22€; fixed-price dinner menu: 30€. AE, MC, V. Open: Tues–Sun noon to 3 p.m. and 6 p.m.–2 a.m.*

L'Atelier de Joël Robuchon
$$–$$$ Eiffel Tower (7e) MODERN BISTRO

This Michelin-starred place remains a *bonne adresse* among the dining chic. Joël Robuchon, arguably the most famous chef in France when he retired in the 1990s, came out of retirement in 2003 to open this chic red-and-black-lacquered restaurant that serves simple French and Asian fusion food in which the ingredients are the real stars. Seating is at a 36-person counter that wraps around the open kitchen. The idea is to give diners a "behind the line" experience, so you may see Robuchon giving orders, sous-chefs saucing main dishes, or a pig being roasted on a spit. The menu continually changes. Robuchon offers *tapas*-like tasting plates that diners are encouraged to share. Main dishes can include tempura soft-shell crab with a tangy avocado puree, a caramelized quail stuffed with foie gras and served with a puree of truffle potatoes, or milk-fed lamb cutlets with thyme. Desserts tend to range from whimsical, such as simple tarts, molten chocolate cake served with cocoa ice cream and an Oreo cookie, to seasonal fruits served with *fromage blanc* and *limoncello*. Robuchon accepts reservations only for lunch and early dinners (6:30 p.m. being early for Paris), so get here early if you want to score a decent place on the line for a table.

See map p. 147. In the Hôtel du Port-Royal, 5–7 rue de Montalembert. www.joel-robuchon.net. ☎ **01-42-22-56-56.** *Reservations accepted only for the first seating. Métro: Rue du Bac. Main courses: 19€–65€; prix fixe tasting menu: 150€. AE, DC, MC, V. Open: Daily. First seating 11:30 a.m.–12:30 p.m., second seating 2–3:30 p.m., dinner 6:30 p.m.*

Le Comptoir du Relais Saint-Germain
$$ Saint-Germain-des-Prés (6e) MODERN BISTRO

One of my favorite spots in Paris to have lunch, this tiny little bistro on a narrow sidewalk right off boulevard Saint-Germain is one of the main destinations for acolytes of *Le Fooding.* Chef Yves Camdeborde's constantly changing menus (he travels to the massive Rungis market in the suburbs every morning to get the freshest ingredients) have yet to disappoint, so show up early to grab an outdoor lunch table, or reserve well in advance for dinner. The always eye-pleasing choices could include a lobster cream soup served hot or cold, Provençal-style cooked tomato, stuffed with oxtail and pesto, or medallions of chicken with peppers and parsley. Also consider sampling any of the inspiringly arranged platters of meats and cheeses or terrines, all from diverse regions of France. During the week, Camdeborde does a five-course tasting menu for 50€. This place is perfectly situated in the carrefour de l'Odéon, where you can watch Left Bank habitués and students walk by, or wave to the people in the Horse's Tavern and Café les Éditeurs across the street.

See map p. 147. 9 carrefour de l'Odéon, 6e. ☎ **01-46-33-45-30.** *Métro: Odéon. Dinner reservations recommended. Starters: 5€–26€; main dishes: 12€–34€; weeknight tasting menu: 50€. Open: Daily 8:30 a.m.–11:30 p.m.*

A quick lunch

If you're tired of typical *boulangerie* sandwiches but not quite ready to sit down to a heavy noontime meal, there are some quality eateries that serve a familiar quick lunch. Inspired by the American-style eating, without skimping on quality or burning holes your pocket.

- ✔ **Class'Croute,** 166 rue Montmartre (2e and numerous locations): *For power-eaters.* A wide selection of tasty, well-prepared sandwiches, salads, quiches, and desserts. The "midi-bag" — a wholesome meal in a bag for under 10€ — includes soup or salad, main dish, dessert, drink, and small pastry.

- ✔ **Cococook,** 30 rue Charonne (3e with another location in the 6e): *For adventurous palates.* In small plastic containers, the salads not only create a well-balanced meal but also imaginatively combine fresh daily specials to achieve a delicious result. Go for Le Puy lentils, caramelized onion, goat cheese, and arugula.

- ✔ **Cojean,** 30 rue le Peletier (1er and numerous locations): *For green gourmets.* Mix-and-match from flavorful organic salads, sandwiches, and hot dishes, with nutritious ingredients. Try the Asian chicken salad with carrots, sprouts, and coriander.

- ✔ **Cuizines,** 46 rue de Provence, (9e with additional location in the 1er): *For serious foodies.* The focus here is on a gourmet and pleasurable eating experience on the run. Savor quality dishes, like salmon risotto, either there or to take away.

- ✔ **Jour,** 13 bd. Malesherbes (8e and numerous locations): *For salad lovers.* Choose a vegetable or grain base, as well as ingredients from a large and appetizing array to create your own salad, and pay for it by the kilo.

- ✔ **L'As du Falafel,** 34 rue des Rosiers (4e): *For veggies on the go.* The spicy sauces made in-house and the freshest of veggies are why, aside from the high-energy Israelis in charge, this hole-in-the-wall is Paris's most famous falafel shop.

- ✔ **Le Bar à Soupes,** 33 rue de Charonne (11e): *For soup-enthusiasts.* A trendy little outlet where soups are by no means a worst-case scenario. Choose from six different vegetable-based soups (try carrot and cumin, for example) every day either to eat in or take away. Perfect for a cold day in Paris.

- ✔ **Qualité & Co,** 7 Rue du Marché Saint-Honoré (1er and other locations): *For health nuts.* Nutritionally sound salads and sandwiches, with flavors that will pack a punch. Available organic choices include spiced quinoa, corn, tomato, and cucumber salad.

Le Cinq
$$$$ Champs-Elysées (8e) HAUTE CUISINE

Chef Philippe Legendre has earned two Michelin stars for this restaurant in the Four Seasons Georges V, where every element is in place, from the gray-and-gold dining room with its high ceilings and overstuffed chairs to the Limoges porcelain and Riedel stemware created for the restaurant. You may start with fresh morels and white asparagus with seasonal vegetables, potato puree, and sweet onion ravioli, and then move on to hand-caught sole served with a rustic brown butter and lime sauce garnished with ginger, garden peas, and watercress. For dessert, a ginger and lemon zest soufflé served with wild strawberries, or the chef's choice of assorted chocolate desserts may be on the menu. The wine list here is magnificent; if he has time, chief sommelier Thierry Hamon may even give you a tour of the cellar.

See map p. 142. 31 av. George V (in the Four Seasons George V Hotel). ☎ *01-49-52-71-54.* `www.fourseasons.com/paris/dining.html`. *Reservations required. Métro: George V. Light tasting menu: 155€; gourmet tasting menu (without beverage): 230€; main courses: 85€–240€. AE, MC, V. Open: Daily 12:30–2:30 p.m. and 7–10:30 p.m.*

Le 404
$$ Le Marais (3e)   NORTH AFRICAN

This is one happening place where patrons and staff may dance on the bar or in the aisles and the vibe is high energy and downright fun. Named for the Peugeot 404, one of the most popular models of car in Morocco in the 1960s, the restaurant is known as much for its fashionable clientele as its tasty *tagines,* couscous, and other North African dishes, all eaten in an atmospheric dining room with carved wooden screens in front of tall windows, low (and close-to-your-neighbor) seating, and exposed stone walls. You may start the evening with a *mezzé* tasting plate of hummus, a brick of salty North African cheese, or other regional appetizers and continue on to a flaky and tender chicken *tagine* stewed in lemon and olives (*tagine* is the clay pot in which everything is cooked) or couscous with seven vegetables. On the weekends, they do a "brunch berbère" with a special spicy "oriental" hamburger.

See map p. 142. 69 rue des Gravilliers. ☎ *01-42-74-57-81. Reservations required. Métro: Arts et Métiers. Main courses: 15€–24€. AE, MC, V. Open: Daily noon to 3 p.m. and 8 p.m. to midnight.*

Le Kokolion
$–$$ Montmartre (18e)   CLASSIC BISTRO

With its red facade and dimly-light ambience, the authenticity of this adorable French "resto" is hard to match. Glass spheres with light fixtures hang from the ceiling while kitschy movie posters, theater announcements and kitschy photographs crowd the walls. Open late and only for dinner, it feeds the grinning after-theater crowd from the nearby Théâtre de l'Atelie. The quality of the food and wine selection are much higher than the prices you pay. Starters will be classics such as escargots from Burgundy, foie gras with a fig confit (a glass of Sauterne is suggested at an addition price), or a more adventurous *os à moelle gratiné avec sel du cuve ronde et toast* (beef bone-marrow casserole made with reservoir salt) and main courses will include classics such as *confit de canard* (duck preserved in its own fat). Ice cream is fine for dessert, but the pastries are often frozen (you can't always have everything at these prices!).

See map p. 142. 62 rue d'Orsel. ☎ **01-42-58-24-41.** *Reservations suggested. Métro: Abbesses or Anvers. Dinner menu: 27€; main courses: 14€–24€. MC, V. Open: Tues–Sat 7:30 p.m.–12:30 a.m.*

Le Père Claude
$$ Eiffel Tower (15e) CLASSIC BISTRO

The family that runs Le Père Claude does it with much love, as evidenced by the thoughtfully rustic outside (empty champagne barrels, a wagon wheel, birch branches, and a bench) and the brown and cream interior where pictures of waitstaff through the years adorn some of the walls. (The restaurant even has its own jazz band with the names of its members on the front door.) Expect to tuck into enormous portions of red meat dishes here. Starters may include salads, made with fresh ingredients like crawfish tail and smoked salmon or duck heart, smoked duck breast, and foie gras served together. For dinner, the *panaché de viandes* is an assortment of perfectly roasted meats served with a comforting heap of mashed potatoes, or you can even have, yes, frog legs (sautéed with garlic and parsley). *Bouillabaisse* is the house special Thursday and Friday nights. Former President Jacques Chirac and Don King have been spotted (separately) chowing down here, but it's usually home to families and, to a lesser extent, tourists with big appetites. After dinner, you can stroll up the avenue de LaMotte-Picquet and take in a view of the spectacular illuminated Eiffel Tower.

See map p. 147. 51 av. de LaMotte-Picquet. ☎ **01-47-34-03-05.** www.lepere claude.com. *Métro: LaMotte-Picquet–Grenelle. (Exit the station on avenue de LaMotte-Picquet and head northeast about 0.4km/¼ mile, toward the Champ de Mars.) Main courses: 16€–75€. AE, MC, V. Open: Daily noon to 2:30 p.m. and 7–11:30 p.m.*

L'Epi Dupin
$$ Saint-Germain-des-Prés (6e) CLASSIC BISTRO

L'Epi Dupin is still one of the best of the bistros (see "Knowing the difference between a cafe and a bistro," earlier in this chapter) and a good value as well. Chef François Pasteau, pairs fine modern bistro cuisine with an antique French setting of hewn beams and stone walls (tables are quite close together). The food, which Pasteau buys fresh daily at the Rungis green market, runs to traditional rural French, with rabbit marinated in herbs with polenta and tomato-zucchini chutney, and a rhubarb strawberry tart topped with Verveine liquor ice cream for dessert. Service, though friendly, can be seriously rushed as staff scramble to accommodate three seatings a night.

See map p. 147. 11 rue de Dupin (between rue de Sèvres and rue du Cherche Midi). ☎ **01-42-22-64-56.** *Reservations strongly recommended. Métro: Sèvres Babylone. Fixed-price menus: 22€ lunch, 33€ dinner. AE, MC, V. Open: Mon 7–11 p.m., Tues–Fri noon to 3 p.m. and 7–11 p.m. Closed three weeks in Aug.*

A new wave to eat well

History has shown that the French love fighting revolutions, but Paris's latest has more to do with cooking eggs than cutting off heads. The newest movement, *Le Fooding* defies definition, but it's partly political — moving beyond the "old guard" of classic chefs and inexpensively bringing good food to the mouths of the people. But it's more about moving beyond traditions to spontaneously embrace the moment, a sort of culinary *carpe diem*. This movement was illustrated in a 2010 *New York Times* article by Christine Muhlke, who showed that a new flock of young and creative talent has established minimally decorated, no-frills restaurants in "popular" (now-gentrified) neighborhoods, offering either fixed or very limited menus. Thus, the prices remain pleasingly low as the creativity, quality, and preparation soar.

The following restaurants, some of which are reviewed in this chapter, are part of a list of high-quality, low-cost dining that keeps foodies worldwide still interested in how things are done in Paris. *—Emilie Abrams*

✔ **A l'Affiche,** 48 rue du Moscou, 8e (☎ 01-45-22-02-20; Métro: Rome), Vibrantly decorated with old movie posters, serves simple home-style dishes with a creative twist.

✔ **Chateaubriand** (see p. 150).

✔ **Frenchie** (see p. 152).

✔ **La Fidélité** (see p. 154).

✔ **L'Ami Jean,** 27 rue Malar, 7e (☎ 01-47-05-86-89; Métro: La Tour–Maubourg), a Basque restaurant run by Stéphane Jego, vanguard of Le Fooding.

✔ **Le Comptoir du Relais Saint-Germain** (see p. 156).

✔ **Le Hide,** 10 rue du Générale Lanrezac, 17e (☎ 01-45-74-15-81; Métro: Charles de Gaulle–Étoile), has traditional cuisine with a Japanese sensitivity as French-trained chef returns to his roots.

✔ **Le Repaire de Cartouche,** 8 bd. des Filles du Calvaire, 11e (☎ 01-47-00-25-86; Métro: Saint-Sébastien–Froissart), is a charmingly rustic room with equally rustic and hearty cuisine at fantastic countryside prices.

✔ **Le Square,** 227 bis rue Marcadet, 18e (☎ 01-53-11-08-41; Métro: Guy Môquet), is an unassuming neighborhood restaurant, where a fresh palette of delicate flavors is presented like a work of art on each plate.

Le Potager du Marais
$ Le Marais (3e)   VEGETARIAN

Make a reservation ahead of time, or you may have to wait for a while to get a seat at this popular organic vegetarian restaurant just a few steps from Centre Pompidou. The food, most of it organic (there are even some vegan dishes), is generally very good. The dining room is small with exposed stone walls, plants, and apricot tones. Most of the offerings are organic and vegans can be accommodated. You may start with a bowl of vegetarian French onion soup, Hungarian goulash or *moussaka* (eggplant pâté), and continue with a *croustillant des légumes* (a cutlet made of vegetables) or several vegan hamburgers, made from walnuts, mushrooms, or quinoa. It even has a *seitan bourguignon*. The desserts are great; try the *fondant au chocolat* with custard sauce, chocolate mousse, or various fruit tarts.

See map p. 142. 22 rue Rambuteau. ☎ *01-42-74-24-66. Métro: Rambuteau. Three-course prix fixe: 25€; main courses: 15€–23€. AE, MC, V. Open: Mon–Sat noon to 2:30 p.m. and 7–10:30 p.m.*

Les Bouquinistes
$$$–$$$$ Saint-Germain-des-Prés   HAUTE CUISINE

If you're going to get a tasting menu anywhere in Paris, this is the place to do it. This is the celebrated baby bistro of Michelin darling Guy Savoy, named after the booksellers near his restaurant on the Quay des Grands Augustins (originally spelled Les Bookinistes — the spelling changed mysteriously several years ago), is an amazing and relatively inexpensive way to enjoy some of Paris's most beautiful haute cuisine. The elegant dining room is staffed by top-notch, gracious waiters who cater to your every need. Although the menu is constantly changing, your starters could include a cream of red kuri squash served with a delicate chestnut biscuit, or a lovely platter of prawns flavored with lemongrass with carrots and ginger bathed in a coriander sauce; main courses could include cod served in a saffron broth with fresh vegetables and an orange-saffron custard, or a platter of *pigeo* served with zucchini and eggplant in a specially prepared lemon sauce. Desserts are always divine and usually dripping with exotic chocolates, although you may opt for the painstakingly selected cheeses. If you don't feel like shelling out the cash, their 26€ or 29€ lunch special is a huge bargain and certainly worth the extra coins. Reservations are strongly recommended.

See map p. 147. 53 quai des Grands Augustins. www.lesbouquinistes.com. ☎ *01-43-25-45-94. Métro: Saint-Michel. Lunch menus: 26€–29€; main courses: 24€–38€; tasting menus: 80€–100€. Open: Mon–Fri noon to 2:30 p.m. and 7–11 p.m., Sat 7–11 p.m.*

Maison Chardenoux
$$ Bastille (11e)   CLASSIC BISTRO

This restaurant's turn-of-the-20th-century décor is the very essence of old Paris (it has been appointed a Monument Historique), and though out of the way, a meal here by chef Cyril Lignac is worth the trek. A variety of French regional dishes are served in a dining room filled with swirling stucco decorations and brightened by etched windows with lacy curtains. All the dishes are classically prepared and lovely to gaze upon. You could start with girolle mushrooms fricasseed with ground hazelnut or terrine of duck foie gras with plum chutney. Main courses may include a sweet pork stew with a side of semolina sweetened with dates and a lemon jam, a top-quality tenderloin slathered in Béarnaise sauce, or a codfish casserole served with creamed scampi and sweet potato puree. Desserts are classically Gallic: French toast served with raspberries and pistachio ice cream, or a lemon tart covered in handmade meringue.

See map p. 142. 1 rue Jules-Valles. ☎ 01-43-71-49-52. www.restaurant lechardenoux.com. Métro: Charonne. (Exit the station on rue Charonne and walk 1 block to rue Jules-Valles. Turn left and walk to the end of the street. The restaurant is on the corner of rue Jules-Valles and rue Chanzy.) Three-course lunch menu: 25€; main courses: 20€–60€. AE, MC, V. Open: Daily noon to 2:30 p.m. and 7–10:30 p.m.

Restaurant du Palais-Royal
$$–$$$ Louvre (1er)   CLASSIC BISTRO

The elegant arcade that encircles the gardens inside the Palais Royal also surrounds this restaurant, making it one of the most romantic locations in Paris. Service is lacking during midday, because it's a favorite lunch spot for professionals working in the area; better to eat dinner here and avoid overworked waiters and waitresses. Sit at the terrace on warm, sun-filled days and begin your meal with starters such as a salmon and seaweed tartar or king crab served with diced vegetables. Main dishes vary with the season but may include roasted wild prawns served with lime and ginger or a sea bass *carpaccio* garnished with herbs and Parmesan cheese. Risottos are also a specialty here. Try the good house red wine, served Lyonnaise-style in thick-bottomed bottles. When dining outside just isn't an option, you can enjoy the dining room that shines in tones of gold, silver, and garnet.

See map p. 142. 43 rue Valois or 110 galerie Valois (on the northeast side of the Palais Royal arcade). ☎ 01-40-20-00-27. Métro: Palais Royal–Musée du Louvre. Main courses: 18€–40€. AE, DC, MC, V. Open: Mon–Fri noon to 2:30 p.m. and 7–10 p.m. Closed late Dec to late Jan.

Restaurant Plaza Athénée (Alain Ducasse)
$$$$ Champs-Elysées (8e)   HAUTE CUISINE

Multistarred Michelin chef Alain Ducasse divides his time between his restaurants in world-class destinations like London, Paris, Monaco, Hong Kong, Tokyo, and New York. His "modern and authentic" dishes reflect the room created by celebrated designer Patrick Jouin (the chandeliers have 10,000 crystal pendants) and contain produce from every corner of France — rare local vegetables, fish from the coasts, and dishes incorporating turnips, celery, turbot, cuttlefish, and Limousin veal. Specialties may include broiled Racan farm pigeon or Beluga caviar served with chilled prawns and a white wine reduction.

See map p. 142. In the Hotel Plaza Athénée, 25 av. Montaigne. ☎ 01-53-67-65-00. www.alain-ducasse.com. Reservations required. Métro: FDR or Alma-Marceau. Main courses: 75€–175€; fixed-price menus: 260€–360€. AE, DC, MC, V. Open: Mon–Wed 7:45–10:15 p.m., Thurs–Fri 12:45–2:15 p.m. and 7:45–10:15 p.m. Closed mid-July to mid-Aug.

Thomieux
$$$ Les Invalides (7e) MODERN BISTRO

A 1923 Parisian brasserie renovated with modern touches (imagine semi-private nooks in the form of wooden banquets, rounded glass lamp fixtures, red upholstered everything and huge mirrors), this former chic institution has been converted into a hip high-end eatery. Strong flavors and world influences have replaced traditional French cuisine (think sautéed shrimp and crunchy baby vegetables in a curry sauce or a French-style hamburger sprinkled with Parmesan cheese) presented by top-tier chef Jean-François Piège of the celebrated and very fancy Crillon. Mind you, this is another one of the many dining institutions invented by the ultrahip Costes brothers (Thierry, to be exact). The staff may be more interested in attending to the somewhat aged gentile locals of the fancy 7e. Go for a fun night of people watching and polite finger licking.

See map p. 147. 79 rue Saint-Dominique. ☎ *01-47-05-79-00.* www.thoumieux.fr. *Reservations strongly recommended. Métro: La Tour–Maubourg. (Walk along with Les Invalides on your right side up along boulevard de La Tour Maubourg or rue Fabert, and turn left onto rue Saint-Dominique.) Lunch prix fixe: 19€; dinner prix fixe: 65€; entrées: 37€–62€. AE, MC, V. Open: Daily noon to 2:30 p.m. and 7–11:30 p.m.*

Ze Kitchen Galerie
$$–$$$ Saint-Germain-des-Prés (6e) MODERN BISTRO

William Ledeuil opened this hip and sophisticated place in 2002 near the trendy Les Bouquinistes, where he once worked as chef de cuisine. It is indeed an art gallery and kitchen: Decorated with an eclectic collection of contemporary paintings and an expansive glass wall, the restaurant lives up to its name (and the neighborhood) as a private modern-art gallery with a kitchen (the paintings change every three months). The innovative, Asian-inspired menu changes every five weeks. The menu is broken down into soup and pasta starters and grilled main courses *(à la plancha)*. During each five-week run, Ledeuil will focus on a favorite ingredient, which occurs repeatedly in several dishes, and he plays with splashes of brightly colored and intensely flavored reductions. When I visited, he was particularly fond of lemongrass, which wonderfully lifted a succulent sea bream filet. Because portions are small, you'll more than likely have room for dessert, which may include tasty ginger-plum cake served with jasmine ice cream, or just a delightful lemongrass-melon sorbet. Reservations are recommended because this restaurant fills up fast.

See map p. 147. 4 rue des Grands Augustins. ☎ *01-44-32-00-32.* www.zekitchen galerie.fr. *Reservations recommended. Métro: Saint-Michel. Main courses: 21€–36€; tasting menu: 80€. AE, DC, MC, V. Open: Mon–Fri noon to 2:30 p.m. and 7–11 p.m., Sat 7–11 p.m.*

Dining and Snacking on the Go

Face it: Who can sit down to multicourse meals every day — even if they're cooked by legendary chefs? Fortunately, many alternatives to a

Light Meals in the Heart of the Right Bank

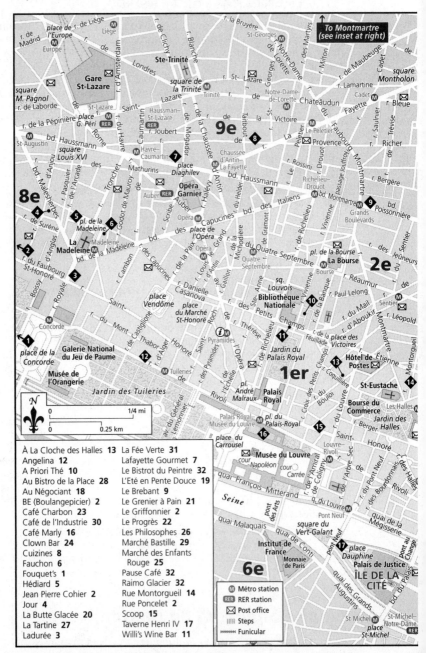

À La Cloche des Halles **13**	La Fée Verte **31**
Angelina **12**	Lafayette Gourmet **7**
A Priori Thé **10**	Le Bistrot du Peintre **32**
Au Bistro de la Place **28**	L'Eté en Pente Douce **19**
Au Négociant **18**	Le Brebant **9**
BE (Boulangepicier) **2**	Le Grenier à Pain **21**
Café Charbon **23**	Le Griffonnier **2**
Café de l'Industrie **30**	Le Progrès **22**
Café Marly **16**	Les Philosophes **26**
Clown Bar **24**	Marché Bastille **29**
Cuizines **8**	Marché des Enfants
Fauchon **6**	Rouge **25**
Fouquet's **1**	Pause Café **32**
Hédiard **5**	Raimo Glacier **32**
Jean Pierre Cohier **2**	Rue Montorgueil **14**
Jour **4**	Rue Poncelet **2**
La Butte Glacée **20**	Scoop **15**
La Tartine **27**	Taverne Henri IV **17**
Ladurée **3**	Willi's Wine Bar **11**

Ⓜ Métro station
ℝℰℝ RER station
⊠ Post office
ⅢⅢ Steps
⊶⊶⊶ Funicular

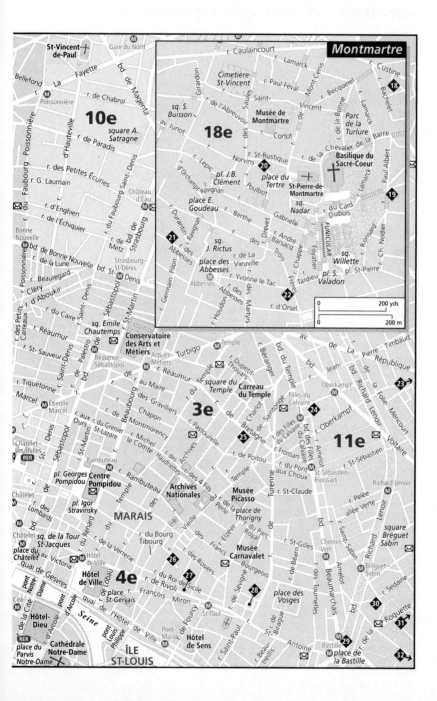

Light Meals in the Heart of the Left Bank

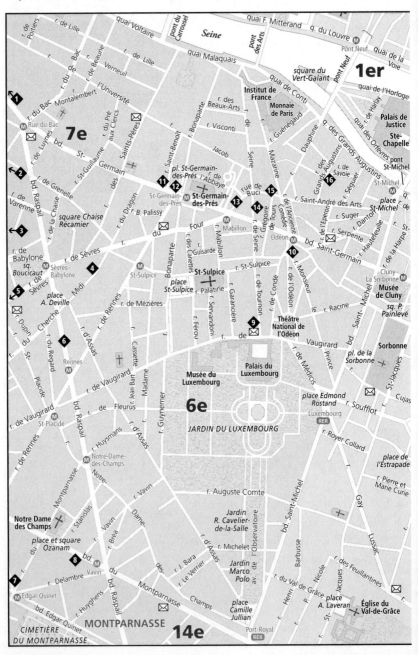

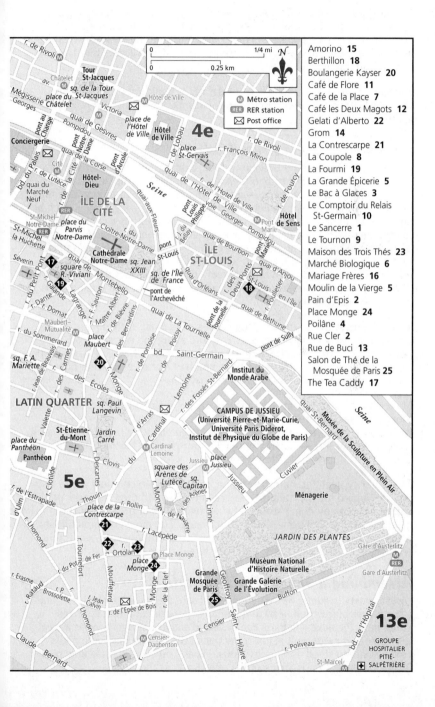

Amorino **15**
Berthillon **18**
Boulangerie Kayser **20**
Café de Flore **11**
Café de la Place **7**
Café les Deux Magots **12**
Gelati d'Alberto **22**
Grom **14**
La Contrescarpe **21**
La Coupole **8**
La Fourmi **19**
La Grande Épicerie **5**
Le Bac à Glaces **3**
Le Comptoir du Relais
   St-Germain **10**
Le Sancerre **1**
Le Tournon **9**
Maison des Trois Thés **23**
Marché Biologique **6**
Mariage Frères **16**
Moulin de la Vierge **5**
Pain d'Epis **2**
Place Monge **24**
Poilâne **4**
Rue Cler **2**
Rue de Buci **13**
Salon de Thé de la
   Mosquée de Paris **25**
The Tea Caddy **17**

full meal are available. Choose from street carts, sandwich places, and tea salons. And of course, there's that Parisian institution, the cafe. Listed here are some of Paris's best cafes and their more sophisticated sisters, the wine bars where you, too, can join in the great French art of people watching!

See the "Light Meals in the Heart of the Right Bank" and "Light Meals in the Heart of the Left Bank" maps for locations of establishments in this section.

Partaking of Paris street food

Some street vendors sell Belgian waffles, called *gaufres,* served warm with powdered sugar or chocolate sauce, but the Parisian street food you see the most is the *crêpe* — a thin wheat pancake stuffed with a filling that's either salty or sweet. When served with savory fillings, such as cheese or mushrooms, a street vendor may call it either a *crêpe salé* (salted or savory) or a *galette.* A true *galette,* a specialty from Normandy, is made with buckwheat and is cooked only on one side (unlike a traditional crêpe, which is cooked on both sides). However it's cooked, it's delicious and constitutes a meal. Sweet crêpe fillings include plain powdered sugar, chocolate-hazelnut spread, ice cream, or jam (called *compote*). Talk about a sugar rush!

You can find stalls or carts selling crêpes near most of the major attractions, in the parks and bigger gardens, and along the rue de Rivoli between the Marais and the place de la Concorde. When you buy a crêpe from a street vendor, you won't have much of a choice of sweet fillings; for a more extensive menu visit a *crêperie.*

Make a meal of crêpes at one of the many good establishments on rue du Montparnasse, where you can settle down in a peaceful atmosphere with a bowl of cider (a Breton specialty), a *galette* for a main course, and a crêpe for dessert — usually under 12€ per person (Métro: Edgar Quinet or Montparnasse-Bienvenüe).

The other typical Parisian street food, panini, is also sold just about anywhere. Named for the Italian-style bread with which they're made, panini can be almost any filling stuck between two slices of bread, and then flattened and grilled between two hot plates. The most common fillings are mozzarella, basil, and sun-dried tomatoes (a pizza sandwich, if you will). Panini are cheap, tasty, and easy to eat on the run.

Assembling a picnic, Parisian style

Grab a crusty baguette or two, some dried sausage, a wedge of cheese, and a few pieces of fruit and head to the nearest park or garden that strikes your fancy. Picnicking in Paris can be as fun and as unforgettable as a meal in a three-star restaurant at just a fraction of the cost. In this section, discover where to stock up on provisions. (***Note:*** You can also assemble picnic fixings cheaply at Parisian supermarkets all across the city.)

The traiteurs (gourmet food shops)

Look for the word *traiteur,* which designates a food shop that sells ready-made meat, pasta, and salad dishes. The two most famous, **Fauchon** and **Hédiard,** have main stores at place de la Madeleine, 8e (Métro: Madeleine), and branches all across Paris. Every neighborhood has several good *traiteurs* so be on the lookout, and don't hesitate to ask your hotel staff for recommendations.

- ✔ **Fauchon,** 30 place de la Madeleine, 8e (☎ 01-70-39-38-00; Métro: Madeleine; see map p. 164), was founded in 1886. This is *the* high-end food shop with everything from foie gras and Norwegian smoked salmon to caviar to fancy breads and cheeses. Their *épicerie* and *cave* together will entirely stock your picnic basket. Open Monday through Saturday 9 a.m. to 8 p.m.

- ✔ **Hédiard,** 21 place de la Madeleine, 8e (☎ 01-43-12-88-88; Métro: Madeleine; see map p. 164), is a gourmet food shop that sells upscale products, wine, and ready-made food to go. Open Monday through Saturday 9 a.m. to 10 p.m.

- ✔ **Lafayette Gourmet,** 48 bd. Haussmann, 9e (☎ 01-42-82-34-56, or 01-42-81-25-61; Métro: Havre-Caumartin; see map p. 164), is another wonderful grocery store that has everything you need for a picnic. It's located smack in the middle of the Galeries Lafayette complex (in the men's store). Open Monday through Saturday from 9:30 a.m. to 7:30 p.m. and until 9 p.m. on Thursday).

- ✔ **La Grande Épicerie,** Le Bon Marché, 38 rue de Sèvres, 7e (☎ 01-44-39-81-00; Métro: Sèvres-Babylone; see map p. 167), may be the best grocery store on the Left Bank. It has large *traiteur* and wine departments and sells everything from cleaning supplies to gourmet chocolate to fresh fish. Picnics just aren't complete without fresh salad expertly measured and mixed from this foodie wonderland. Open Monday through Saturday from 8:30 a.m. to 9 p.m.

The street markets

Every neighborhood in Paris has its street market, and it's probably the best place to find the freshest produce, cheeses of excellent quality, and other picnic supplies. Even when you don't buy anything, visiting one or two is worth the authentic reflection of Parisian society you encounter. Markets are generally open from Tuesday through Saturday, from around 7 a.m. to 1 p.m., and of course, the pickings are better the earlier you go. The ones open on Sunday are indicated. Some of the most well known include the following:

- ✔ **Marché Bastille,** 11e (Métro: Bastille; see map p. 164): This huge market sells everything from game, cheese, and vegetables to fish and condiments. Open Thursday from 7 a.m. to 2:30 p.m. and Sunday 7 a.m. to 3 p.m.

- ✔ **Marché Biologique,** boulevard Raspail between rue du Cherche-Midi and rue de Rennes, 6e (Métro: Rennes; see map p. 167): This all-organic market features greengrocers, winemakers, butchers, and bakers. Open Sunday 9 a.m. to 2 p.m. An "inorganic" market takes place here Tuesday and Friday from 7 a.m. to 2:30 p.m.

✔ **Place Monge,** 5e (Métro: Monge): One of the oldest markets in Paris on one of the city's more interesting streets. Sing along with accordion players on Sunday mornings. Open Wednesday and Friday 7:30 a.m. to 2:30 p.m., Sunday 7 a.m. to 3 p.m.

✔ **Marché des Enfants Rouge,** 39 rue de Bretagne, 3e (Métro: Arts et Métiers): Originally created in 1615, this small market boasts being the oldest in Paris. Find fresh fish, vegetables, cheese and meats here, or eat at one of the several restaurants on the perimeter. Open Tuesday through Sunday 8:30 a.m. to 1 p.m., Tuesday through Thursday 4 to 7:30 p.m., and Friday and Saturday 4 to 8 p.m.

✔ **Rue Cler,** 7e (Métro: Ecole-Militaire; see map p. 167): See how diplomats shop for their dinner in this chic market. Open Tuesday through Saturday from 8:30 a.m. to 1 p.m. and 5 to 7 p.m., Sunday 8:30 a.m. to noon.

✔ **Rue de Buci,** 6e (Métro: Odéon; see map p. 167): This lively market is close to all the Latin Quarter action. Open Tuesday through Sunday from 8 a.m. to noon.

✔ **Rue Montorgueil,** 1er (Métro: Les Halles/Châtelet; see map p. 164): Have breakfast at one of the many sidewalk cafes before choosing your produce. Open Tuesday through Saturday from 8 a.m. to 1 p.m. and 4 to 7 p.m.

✔ **Rue Poncelet,** 17e (Métro: Ternes; see map p. 164): The Poncelet market is especially renowned for its fresh fruit stalls. It's also close to Parc Monceau of Marcel Proust fame. Open Tuesday through Saturday 8:30 a.m. to noon and 2:30 to 6 p.m.

The best bakeries

You want a fresh baguette for your picnic, and you can find bakeries *(boulangeries)* on nearly every corner in residential neighborhoods. Keep in mind that the quality of the breads varies considerably.

Long lines of locals on weekend mornings or evenings before dinner give away the best bakeries. Here are some of Paris's best bakeries:

✔ **BE (Boulangepicier),** 73 bd. de Courcelles, 8e; ☎ 01-46-22-20-20. Open Monday through Saturday 7 a.m. to 8 p.m. Métro: Courcelles or Ternes; see map p. 164.

✔ **Boulangerie Kayser,** 8 rue Monge, 5e; ☎ 01-44-07-01-42. Open Wednesday through Monday 6:30 a.m. to 8:30 p.m. Métro: Maubert Mutualité; see map p. 167.

✔ **Jean Pierre Cohier,** 270 rue Faubourg Saint-Honoré, 8e; ☎ 01-42-27-45-26. Open Monday through Saturday 7:30 a.m. to 8 p.m. Metro: Ternes; see map p. 164.

✔ **Le Grenier à Pain,** 38 rue des Abbesses, 18e; ☎ **01-46-06-41-81.** Open Friday through Tuesday 7:30 a.m. to 8 p.m. Métro: Abbesses.

✔ **Moulin de la Vierge,** 166 av. de Suffren, 15e; ☎ **01-47-83-45-55.** Open Friday through Wednesday 7 a.m. to 8 p.m. Métro: Sèvres-Lecourbe; see map p. 167.

✔ **Pain d'Epis**, 63 av. Bosquet, 7e; ☎ **01-45-51-75-01.** Open: Sunday through Friday 7 a.m. to 8 p.m. Metro: Ecole Militaire; see map p. 167.

✔ **Poilâne,** 8 rue du Cherche-midi, 6e;. ☎ **01-45-48-42-59.** Open: Monday through Saturday 7:15 a.m. to 8:15 p.m. Métro: Saint-Sulpice or Sèvres Babylone; see map p. 167.

There are so many different types of bread available in these bakeries that a complete list would probably be impossible to compile accurately. However, the most common is the *baguette* — long, fat, and crispy. If you're feeling a little adventurous, spend a few extra centimes, on a *baguette de campagne, à l'ancienne,* or *de tradition.* These names mean that the baguette dough contains only flower, water, salt, and yeast and is prepared by hand, mixed, kneaded, and left overnight in order to let the yeast develop without ever being frozen. The result is a much more flavorful and chewier interior with an off-white, more rustic look than the simple white-interior baguettes. Look for *boulangeries* that say artisinal, which means that they prepare all their goods on the spot: These places sell pastries and bread with a mouthwatering taste that cannot be described in any language!

C'est quoi, un cupcake?

With little more than a *Sex and the City* reference to guide them, Parisians have now become addicted to cupcakes. Following the New York City trend, since 2008 several bakeries have opened dedicated to the frosting-topped delights (*"Mais c'est quoi ce truc?"* ["What is this thing?] is still a common reaction). Even famed pastry shop Ladurée offers its spin on the American classic. Expect to find Frenchified flavor combinations like *caramel au beurre sale,* rose water, *spéculoos* (think graham cracker), or pistachio in otherwise familiar cupcake form. — *Bryan Pirolli*

✔ **Berko,** 23 rue Rambuteau, 4e: Classic French combos meet the New York cupcake.

✔ **Chloé's,** 40 rue Jean-Baptiste Pigalle, 9e: Gluten-free and organic products, very a la mode.

✔ **Cupcake & Co,** 25 rue de la Forge Royale, 11e: Two French sisters started it all with this boutique in 2008.

✔ **Synie's,** 23 rue de l'Abbé Grégoire, 6e: British meets French in kitschy pink tearoom.

Watching the world go by at a cafe

Compiled here are some of my favorite cafes — places where you'll be comfortable reading the paper, writing postcards, people-watching, and soaking up the city's atmosphere while relaxing with a cup of coffee, a glass of wine or beer, or a sandwich, salad, or traditional French specialty like *pot-au-feu* (beef boiled with vegetables). Cafes are generally open from 8 a.m. until 1 a.m., and most take MasterCard and Visa.

If you miss having a regular cup of joe (not the dark and especially strong espresso) with some milk on the side (and not frothy steamed milk mixed in) ask for *un café américain*. But if they can't help or don't seem to understand, ask them for *un café allongé avec du lait froid à côté* (uhn ca-*fay* ah-lohn-*jay* a-vek doo lait *frwah* a koh-*tay*). It's a mouthful, but you'll get an espresso diluted with water and a jug of milk on the side.

Au Bistro de La Place

This square on the place du Marché Sainte-Catherine is a pedestrian zone on the site of an 18th-century market, and this cafe's plant-covered terrace is the prettiest of all the bistros here. The food is terrific; you may find fresh vegetable soup served hot or cold or an artichoke pâté with salad, topped off with butter-browned salmon served with a saffron sauce. Even if you don't come here for a meal, visit during the afternoon to enjoy a leisurely drink or pastry on the terrace.

See map p. 164. 2 place du Marché Sainte-Catherine, 4e (between rue de Turenne and rue de Sévigné). ☎ *01-42-78-21-32. Métro: Saint-Paul. Closed Fri.*

Café Charbon

The ultimate hipster hangout in the now-trendy Oberkampf neighborhood, wooden banquets, vaulted ceilings, and distressed mirrors give this former turn-of-the-20th-century dance hall the right kind of off-the-beaten-path atmosphere, while still being in the middle things. The typical cafe fare is tasty and simple, with tarts, nicely arranged platters of charcuterie, and fresh salads that will pep you up for your late-night bar crawl in the area.

See map p. 164. 109 rue Oberkampf, 11e. ☎ *01-43-57-55-13. Metro: Parmentier.*

Café de Flore

In the heart of Saint-Germain-des-Prés, this cafe will always be popular, even though the famous writers have moved on and its prices are high. Sartre is said to have written *Les Chemins de la Liberté (The Roads to Freedom)* at his table here, and he and Simone de Beauvoir saw people by appointment here. Other regulars included André Malraux and Guillaume Apollinaire. Paris's leading intellectual bookstore, La Hune, is right next door.

See map p. 167. 172 bd. Saint-Germain, 6e. ☎ *01-45-48-55-26. Métro: Saint-Germain-des-Prés.*

Café de la Place

If you're headed out of Paris via the Gare Montparnasse and you have a bit of extra time, skip the train station food stalls and come to this old-fashioned cafe overlooking small, tree-lined place Edgar Quinet, just around the corner and down the street. It's a calm and popular spot for young neighborhood residents. Browse the menu of inexpensive bistro specialties, or opt for a simple sandwich and a glass of wine. If you're lucky, there will be a *brocante* (flea market) or art fair in the square across the street.

See map p. 167. 23 rue d'Odessa, 14e. ☎ *01-42-18-01-55. Métro: Edgar-Quinet.*

Café de l'Industrie

This cafe is young, friendly, casual, and extremely popular; so much so that at night the crowd constantly overflows to the sidewalks next door and even across the street. To capitalize on its popularity, Café de l'Industrie bought its next-door neighbor and the former Moroccan restaurant across the street. Mod meets retro meets country in the spacious rooms that also have a vaguely colonial flavor. Hip Bastille denizens drift in and out all day. Bartenders like to mix "specialties," and if you ask for one with a winning smile, you may get a reduced price.

See map p. 164. 15–17 rue Saint-Sabin, 11e (at the corner of rue Sedaine and rue Saint-Sabin). ☎ *01-47-00-13-53. Métro: Breguet-Sabin or Bastille.*

Café les Deux Magots

Like its neighbor, Café de Flore, Café les Deux Magots was a hangout for Sartre and Simone de Beauvoir. The intellectuals met here in the 1950s, and Sartre wrote at his table every morning. Hemingway also haunted this place (when he had the money to do so, at least). With prices that start at 4.40€ for coffee, the cafe is an expensive place for literary-intellectual pilgrims, but a great spot to watch the nightly promenade on the boulevard Saint-Germain.

See map p. 167. 6 place Saint-Germain-des-Prés, 6e. ☎ *01-45-48-55-25. Métro: Saint-Germain-des-Prés.*

Café Marly

This is one of the prettiest cafes in Paris, and its location can't be beat. Sinking into one of the plush red chairs here amid high ceilings, warmly painted pastel walls, and luxurious sofa chairs with a drink or cup of tea is the best antidote to Louvre fatigue! This stunning cafe has a gorgeous view of the glass pyramid that is the museum's main entrance. You almost forget food is served here, but that would be a mistake — it's very good, if not abundant. It's on the expensive side, but that is normal considering your location. Enjoy the exquisite lighting on the pyramid and surrounding 18th-century facades from the outdoor balcony. After 8 p.m., seating is for dinner only.

See map p. 164. 93 rue de Rivoli, cour Napoléon du Louvre, 1er. ☎ *01-49-26-06-60. Métro: Palais Royal–Musée du Louvre.*

Fouquet's

This 20th-century Parisian institution is the place with the red umbrellas on the Champs-Elysées, not far from the Arc de Triomphe, and counts such patrons as James Joyce, Charlie Chaplin, Marlene Dietrich, Winston Churchill, Franklin D. Roosevelt, François Truffaut, Claude Chabrol, and Jean-Luc Godard. Opened in 1899, it's now registered as a historic monument.

See map p. 164. 99 av. des Champs-Elysées, 8e. ☎ *01-47-23-50-00. Métro: George V.*

La Contrescarpe

The dimly lit book-filled interior here is perfect for an intimate tête-à-tête, while the tables outside, which overlook four lilac trees and a fountain, seem to seat a more boisterous clientele. This is a good place to take a break after marketing on rue Mouffetard or visiting the nearby Panthéon.

See map p. 167. 57 rue Lacépède, 5e. ☎ *01-43-36-82-88. Métro: Cardinal Lemoine.*

La Coupole

The more things change, the more they stay the same at this Lost Generation cafe that has been packing them in for nearly a century. Henry Miller came here for his morning porridge, and now Japanese business-people, French yuppies, models, tourists, and neighborhood regulars keep the frenzied waiters running until 2 a.m. The food is good, too, though prices are high. There's dancing downstairs on the weekends.

See map p. 167. 102 bd. Montparnasse, 14e. ☎ *01-43-20-14-20. Métro: Vavin.*

La Fée Verte

This cafe/restaurant near Bastille is full of personality, from the friendly, good-humored waitstaff to the beaux-arts interior. However, the main theme of this neighborhood watering hole is absinthe, the infamous beverage that has gained much popularity in the last decade since its consumption was made legal in 2006. Order one of the steampunk-esque glass contraptions that serves shots of "the Green Fairy" (one of many nicknames for the drink, which the cafe takes its name from) through little spigots. Or if you're hungry, order the truly mind-boggling cheeseburger à la française. Delicious, but impossible to pick up with your hands!

See map p. 164. 108 rue de la Roquette, 11e. ☎ *01-43-72-31-24. Métro: Voltaire.*

Le Brebant

One of my personal favorites, Le Brebant's fantastic terrace overlooks the Grands Boulevards, one of the best spots for people watching in a non-touristy part of the city. Although not the cheapest place for a drink, Le Brebant boasts charming décor, a combination of colorful prints, copper tubing (which delivers cooling mists during the hot season), and brightly mismatched chairs. Customers are often young local professionals, and if you're feeling like a sweet Moroccan mint tea, Le Brebant's can't be beat!

See map p. 164. 32 bd. Poissonnière, 9e. ☎ *01-47-70-01-02. Métro: Grands Boulevards.*

Le Progrès

Situated near the footsteps of Sacré-Coeur, Le Progrès is quirky and simple and almost always packed. The benches and closely arranged tables put funky and bohemian locals next to tourists, all served by a youthful staff who yell jokes back and forth over the midday din. A *croque jeune homme* (their tongue-in-cheek name for a croque-monsieur) is only 8€, or you can just sip wine while watching the denizens of Montmartre pass you by. During the winter, their *vin chaud* (hot wine, with spices) will chase away the Parisian chill.

See map p. 164. 7 rue des Trois Frères, 18e. ☎ **01-42-64-07-37.** *Métro: Abbesses or Anvers.*

Le Sancerre

This is one of Montmartre's cheaper cafes located on rue des Abbesses where you can sit and watch the passing citizens of Montmartre in their hipster gear. They have great croque-monsieurs if you're hungry, or order a *café* and contemplate your next artistic endeavor like the other people sitting at neighboring tables. This lively place can get packed, so you may want to stop by in the late afternoon when things are calm.

See map p. 167. 35 rue des Abbesses, 18e. ☎ **01-42-58-0-20.**

Les Philosophes

This friendly, stylish place (the waiters wear vests and ties) in the heart of the Marais is always packed. Maybe that's because it's the perfect spot to refuel after visiting the Musée Picasso. It serves enormous salads, imaginative sandwiches, and thick *tartes* to a local crowd sprinkled with tourists in the know. The menu and kitchen here are the same as another cafe just around the corner, la Chaise au Plafond, an equally lovely place with more calm and elbow room, but less people watching.

See map p. 164. 28 rue Vieille du Temple, 4e. ☎ **01-48-87-49-64.** *Métro: Hôtel-de-Ville.*

L'Eté en Pente Douce

To find this cute cafe away from Montmartre's tourist hordes, turn right after exiting the *funiculaire,* and take the first set of steps leading down to a leafy square facing a small park. The terrace here looks out on stairs and iron lamps once painted by Montmartre artist Utrillo, and someone almost always performs here for the captive audience. The interior is brightly decorated with painted borders of leaves and plants, mosaics, unusual objets d'art, and a painted ceiling. Between lunch and dinner, the restaurant serves tea, pastries, and sandwiches.

See map p. 164. 23 rue Muller, 18e. ☎ **01-42-64-02-67.** *Métro: Chateau-Rouge.*

Pause Café

This *cantine du quartier* (neighborhood canteen) with lemon-colored outdoor tables is almost always full, and if it's nighttime, the patrons are most likely stopping in for drinks on their way to a night of dancing. Featured in Cédric Klapisch's 1996 film *Chacun cherche son chat (When the Cat's Away),* it attracts both tourists and neighborhood residents (and, admittedly, the occasionally rude waiter). A bright-colored, modern interior with hanging light fixtures also features found art, while outdoors is made tropical with cloth and bamboo umbrellas and potted palms. The food is fresh and tasty.

See map p. 164. 41 rue de Charonne, 11e. ☎ *01-48-06-80-33. Métro: Lédru-Rollin.*

Steeping and sipping at a tea salon (salons de thé)

Sitting down to tea in Paris can be an elegant and refined undertaking, or a relaxing break between bouts of shopping and *musée*-hopping. The tea salons have a wide range of blends, steeped to perfection, and the pastry selections are usually excellent (Ladurée's macaroons are world-famous). Save your full meals, however, for a restaurant because tea salons tend to be expensive.

- ✔ **Angelina,** 226 rue de Rivoli, 1er; ☎ **01-42-60-82-00.** Open daily 9 a.m. to 7 p.m.; breakfast is served 9 to 11:30 a.m. Métro: Concorde or Tuileries; see map p. 164.

- ✔ **A Priori Thé,** 35–37 Galerie Vivienne (enter at 6 rue Vivienne, 4 rue des Petits-Champs, or 5 rue de la Banque), 2e; ☎ **01-42-97-48-75.** Open Monday through Friday 9 a.m. to 6 p.m., Saturday 12:30 to 6:30 p.m., and Sunday noon to 6:30 p.m. Métro: Bourse, Palais Royal–Musée du Louvre, or Pyramides; see map p. 164.

- ✔ **Ladurée,** 16 rue Royale, 8e; ☎ **01-42-60-21-79.** Open Monday through Saturday 8:30 a.m. to 7 p.m. Métro: Concorde; see map p. 164. Also in Saint-Germain, 21 rue Bonaparte, ☎ **01-44-97-64-87.**

- ✔ **La Fourmi Ailée,** 8 rue du Fouarre, 5e; ☎ **01-43-29-40-99.** Open daily noon to midnight. Métro: Maubert-Mutualité; see map p. 167.

- ✔ **Maison des Trois Thés,** 1 rue Saint-Médard, 5e. ☎ **01-43-36-93-84.** Open Tuesday through Friday 1 to 6:30 p.m. Métro: Place Monge.

- ✔ **Mariage Frères,** 13 rue Grands Augustins, 6e; ☎ **01-40-51-82-50.** Open daily noon to 7 p.m. Métro: Saint-Michel; see map p. 167. Also at 30 rue du Bourg-Tibourg, 4e; ☎ **01-42-72-28-11.** Métro: Hôtel de Ville.

- ✔ **Salon de Thé de la Mosquée de Paris,** 39 rue Geoffroy-Saint-Hilaire, 5e; ☎ **01-43-31-18-14.** Open daily 10 a.m. to midnight. Métro: Place Monge; see map p. 167.

- ✔ **The Tea Caddy,** 14 rue Saint-Julien-le-Pauvre, 5e; ☎ **01-43-54-15-56.** Open daily noon to 7 p.m. Métro: Saint-Michel; see map p. 167.

A heady mix of wine bars

Paris's wine bars have a good selection of wines by the glass, and tasty light meals served all day in pleasant surroundings. These places are often a cozy and sophisticated alternative to the cafe.

À La Cloche des Halles

Look closely at the exterior for the bell that once tolled the opening and closing of the vast food market for which this neighborhood was named. This tiny bar and cafe is packed at lunchtime so you might want to go late afternoon. Patrons dine on plates of *jambon* (ham) or homemade quiche accompanied by a carafe of wine, and maybe the *Tarte Tatin* for dessert. It's convivial and fun, but very noisy and crowded, just like the rest of the quarter during the day. If you can't find a seat, you can usually stand at the bar and eat.

See map p. 164. 28 rue Coquillière, 1er. ☎ **01-42-36-93-89.** *Métro: Les Halles or Palais Royal–Musée du Louvre. Mon–Fri 8 a.m.–10 p.m., Sat 10 a.m.–5 p.m.*

Au Négociant

You may walk right past this tiny wine bar the first time, so make sure to retrace your steps. Wine by the glass is reasonable, and the excellent pâtés and terrines are homemade and served with fresh, chewy bread. Photographer Robert Doisneau *(Le Baiser de l'Hôtel de Ville)* was a regular.

See map p. 164. 27 rue Lambert, 18e. ☎ **01-46-06-15-11.** *Métro: Château-Rouge or Lamarck-Caulaincourt. Mon–Fri noon to 2:30 p.m., Tues–Thurs 6:30–10:30 p.m.*

Clown Bar

Founded in 1904, this place became a second home three years later to circus people working at the Cirque de l'Hiver next door who would congregate here and drop off letters to be mailed. There's a zinc bar decorated with a mélange of circus posters and circus-themed ceramic tiles and statues — although somewhat creepy to look at while eating pâté. The wine list features an extensive selection of French offerings from the Rhone and Languedoc.

See map p. 164. 114 rue Amelot, 11e. ☎ **01-43-55-87-35.** *Métro: Filles du Calvaire. Mon–Sat noon to 2:30 p.m. and 7 p.m.–1 a.m.*

La Tartine

A historic place with some very interesting and aged regular clientele, La Tartine underwent a renovation is the early 2000s (causing a loss of character, according to some), but the gorgeous zinc bar remained. Although it's not the same, the location is ideal. La Tartine is perfectly relaxed and comfortable — a mix of working class and well heeled frequent it. You can get a light lunch of goat cheese salad, or a pick-me-up of *tartine* (open-faced sandwich), cheese, or *charcuterie* (assorted sliced meats) plate along with one of many wines by the glass.

See map p. 164. 24 rue de Rivoli, 4e. ☎ **01-42-72-76-85.** *Métro: Saint-Paul. Wed–Mon noon to 10 p.m.*

Le Bistrot du Peintre

The doors are Art Nouveau and the bar is zinc at this cozy place where painters, actors, and night crawlers hang out. The delicious and reasonably priced food, wood paneling, large terrace, and superb belle époque atmosphere make this wine bar a highlight. The wine selection is affordable — an added bonus.

See map p. 164. 116 av. Ledru-Rollin, 11e. ☎ **01-47-00-34-39.** *Métro: Ledru-Rollin. Daily 9 a.m.–2 a.m. (the kitchen closes at midnight).*

Le Griffonnier

Chef Cédric Duthilleul delivers first-rate cuisine, and the wine cellar is superb. Sample the entree du jour or try a hearty plate of *charcuterie* (regional sliced meats), terrines, and cheese, usually from the Auvergne region of central France, and ask your waiter to recommend the wine. Hot meals are served at lunchtime Monday through Friday (until 3:30 p.m.) and Monday nights.

See map p. 164. 8 rue des Saussaies, 8e. ☎ **01-42-65-17-17.** *Métro: Champs-Elysées–Clemenceau. Mon–Fri 8 a.m.–9 p.m.*

Le Sancerre

Don't be put off by the unstylish interior, which consists of a wooden bar with stools losing some of their caning. Le Sancerre is a wonderful place to unwind for a light meal or glass of wine after visiting the Eiffel Tower. Loire wines are the specialty here, including, of course, Sancerre. Jean-Louis Guillaume, the friendly manager and bartender will discuss the best accompaniments for his wines. The more adventurous can sample the ubiquitous *andouillette,* the sausage that is decidedly an acquired taste.

See map p. 164. 22 av. Rapp, 7e. ☎ **01-45-51-75-91.** *Métro: Alma Marceau. Mon–Fri 8 a.m.–10 p.m., Sat 8 a.m.–4 p.m.*

Le Tournon

Two steps from the Jardin de Luxembourg, this bar has a fantastic selection of wines, albeit not the cheapest in this book. Casually frequented for more than 100 years, Le Tournon has touches of 1950s chic in the décor, and plenty of cheeses, tartines, and other delicacies to sample.

See map p. 167. 18 rue de Tournon, 6e. ☎ **01-43-26-16-16.** *Métro: Odéon. Sun 9 a.m.–7 p.m., Mon–Sat 8 a.m.–11 p.m.*

Taverne Henri IV

You can visit this authentic, old-fashioned bar for a quick pick-me-up after a Seine boat cruise. Although on the expensive side, the wine and food are excellent. The variety of wines by the glass can accompany open-faced sandwiches, pâtés, and such cheeses as Cantal and Auvergne blue.

See map p. 164. 13 place du Pont Neuf, 1er. ☎ *01-43-54-27-90. Métro: Pont Neuf. Mon–Fri 11:30 a.m.–10:30 p.m., Sat noon to 5 p.m. Closed Aug.*

Willi's Wine Bar

This has been a favorite of tourists and locals since its opening in 1980. An upscale crowd has sampled more than 250 different varieties of wine while seated at the polished oak bar or dined in the high-ceilinged oak-beamed dining room from a *prix fixe* menu starting at 20€. Each year, the owners commission an image relating to wine from an artist, and the colorful paintings are available for sale as prints.

See map p. 164. 13 rue des Petits-Champs, 1er. ☎ *01-42-61-05-09. Métro: Bourse, Pyramide, or Palais Royale. Mon–Sat noon to 2:30 p.m. and 7–11 p.m.; bar open Mon–Sat noon to midnight.*

Getting the scoop on Paris ice cream

If Paris doesn't have the best ice cream flavors in the world, it must run a close second. Such flavors (rhubarb, plum, cassis, honey nut . . .)! Ask for a *cornet seule* (kor-*nay* sul; single-scoop cone) or *cornet double* (kor-*nay* doobl; double scoop) — even the cone is yummy. Parisians cite **Berthillon,** 31 rue Saint-Louis-en-l'Île, 4e (☎ **01-43-54-31-61;** Métro: Cité; see map p. 167) as the best in the city, but the following establishments also put soft-serve to shame. Although Berthillon closes from July 15 through the first week in September, a note on the door directs customers to other nearby shops that sell its ice cream. **Le Flore en l'Île,** 42 quai d'Orléans, 4e (☎ **01-43-29-88-27;** Métro: Cité), a restaurant and *salon de thé,* always has an outside station to buy Berthillon ice cream. A chain of ice cream parlors called **Amorino** (see the following list) also boasts excellent ice cream in numerous flavors (for pure ingenuity try the grapefruit).

- ✔ **Amorino,** 4 rue de Buci, 6e; ☎ **01-43-26-57-46;** Métro: Odéon; see map p. 167. Other locations exist around the city.

- ✔ **Gelati d'Alberto,** 45 rue Mouffetard, 5e; ☎ **01-43-37-88-07;** Métro: Monge.

- ✔ **Grom,** 81 rue de Seine, 6e; ☎ **01-40-46-92-60;** Métro: Mabillon; see map p. 167.

- ✔ **La Butte Glacée,** 14 rue Norvins, 18e; ☎ **01-42-23-91-58;** Métro: Abbesses; see map p. 164.

- ✔ **Le Bac à Glaces,** 109 rue du Bac, 7e; ☎ **01-45-48-87-65;** Métro: rue du Bac; see map p. 167.

✔ **Raimo Glacier,** 59 bd. de Reuilly, 12e; ☎ **01-43-43-70-17;** Métro: Daumesnil; see map p. 164

✔ **Scoop,** 154 rue Saint-Honoré, 1er (behind the Louvre des Antiquaires); ☎ **01-42-60-31-84;** Métro: Louvre-Rivoli; see map p. 164.

Index of Establishments by Neighborhood

Louvre, Les Halles (1er)
À La Cloche des Halles (Wine Bar, $)
Angelina (Tea Salon, $)
Au Pied de Cochon (Classic Bistro, $$)
Café Marly (Cafes, $)
Cojean (Soup and Sandwiches, $)
Cuizines (Soup and Sandwiches, $)
Fauchon (Traiteurs, $)
La Poule au Pot (Classic Bistro, $$)
Qualité & Co (Soup and Sandwiches, $)
Restaurant du Palais-Royal (Classic Bistro, $$–$$$)
Scoop (Ice Cream, $)
Taverne Henri IV (Wine Bar, $)
Willi's Wine Bar (Wine Bar, $)

Sentier (2e)
A Priori Thé (Tea Salon, $)
Class'Croute (Soup and Sandwiches, $)
Frenchie (Modern Bistro, $$)

Le Marais, Île Saint-Louis/Île de la Cité (3e, 4e)
Au Bascou (Basque/Southwest, $$)
Au Bistro de la Place (Cafes, $)
Berko (Patisseries, $)
Berthillon (Ice Cream, $)
Chez Omar (North African, $$)
Cococook (Soup and Sandwiches, $)
L'Ambroisie (Haute Cuisine, $$$$)
L'Aréa (Mediterranean/Brazilian, $$)
L'As du Falafel (Soup and Sandwiches, $)
La Tartine (Wine Bar, $)
Le 404 (North African, $$)
Le Potager du Marais (Vegetarian, $)
Les Philosophes (Cafes, $)

Latin Quarter (5e)
A.O.C. (Classic Bistro, $$)
Auberge Le Pot de Terre (Classic Bistro, $)
Boulangerie Kayser (Boulangeries, $)
Brasserie Balzar (Alsatian/Brasserie, $$)
Breakfast in America (American, $)
ChantAirelle (Auvergne, $$)
Gelati d'Alberto (Ice Cream, $)
Hédiard (Traiteurs, $)
La Contrescarpe (Cafes, $)
La Fourmi Ailée (Tea Salon, $)
Maison des Trois Thés (Tea Salon, $)
Salon de Thé de la Mosquée de Paris (Tea Salon, $)
The Tea Caddy (Tea Salon, $)

Saint-Germain-des-Prés (6e)
A La Petite Chaise (Classic Bistro, $$)
Amorino (Ice Cream, $)
Café de Flore (Cafes, $)
Café les Deux Magots (Cafes, $)
Fish La Boissonnerie (Classic Bistro, $$)
Grom (Ice Cream, $)
La Bastide Odéon (Provençal, $$)
La Grande Épicerie (Traiteurs, $)
Le Comptoir du Relais Saint-Germain (Modern Bistro, $$)
L'Epi Dupin (Classic Bistro, $$)
Les Bouquinistes (Haute Cuisine, $$$–$$$$)
Le Tournon (Wine Bar, $)
Mariages Frères (Tea Salon, $)
Poilâne (Boulangeries, $)
Synie's (Patisseries, $)
Ze Kitchen Galerie (Modern Bistro, $$–$$$)

Eiffel Tower and Invalides (7e, 15e)

Au Bon Accueil (Modern Bistro, $$)
La Cigale Récamier (Classic French, $$)
L'Atelier de Joël Robuchon (Modern Bistro, $$–$$$)
Le Bac à Glaces (Ice Cream, $)
Le Père Claude (Classic French, $$)
Le Sancerre (Wine Bar, $$)
Moulin de la Vierge (Boulangeries, $)
Pain d'Epis (Boulangeries, $)
Thomieux (Modern Bistro, $$$)

Champs-Elysées and Ternes (8e and 17e)

A l'Affiche (Modern Bistro, $$)
BE (Boulangepicier; Boulangeries, $)
Fouquet's (Cafes, $)
Ladurée (Tea Salon, $)
L'Ami Jean (Basque/Southwest, $$)
Le Cinq (Haute Cuisine, $$$$)
Le Griffonnier (Wine Bar, $)
Le Hide (Modern Bistro, $$)
Jean Pierre Cohier (Boulangeries, $)
Jour (Soup and Sandwiches, $)
Restaurant Plaza Athénée (Alain Ducasse; Haute Cuisine, $$$$)

Opéra/Gare du Nord/Grands Boulevards (9e, 10e)

Chez Casimir (Classic Bistro, $$)
Chez Michel (Breton, $$)
Chloé's (Patisseries, $)
Lafayette Gourmet (Traiteurs, $)

La Fidélité (Modern Bistro, $$)
Le Brebant (Cafes, $)

Bastille/Oberkampf (4e, 11e, 12e)

Bofinger (Alsatian/Brasserie, $$)
Café Charbon (Cafes, $)
Café de l'Industrie (Cafes, $)
Chateaubriand (Modern Bistro, $$–$$$)
Clown Bar (Wine Bar, $)
Cupcake & Co. (Patisserie, $)
La Fée Verte (Cafes, $)
Le Bar à Soupes (Soup and Sandwiches, $)
Le Bistrot du Peintre (Wine Bar, $)
Le Repaire de Cartouche (Modern Bistro, $$)
Maison Chardenoux (Classic Bistro, $$)
Pause Café (Cafes, $)
Raimo Glacier (Ice Cream, $)

Montparnasse (14e)

Café de la Place (Cafes, $)
La Coupole (Cafes, $)

Montmartre (18e)

Au Négociant (Wine Bar, $)
La Butte Glacée (Ice Cream, $)
Le Grenier à Pain (Boulangeries, $)
Le Kokolion (Classic Bistro, $–$$)
Le Progrès (Cafes, $)
Le Sancerre (Cafes, $)
Le Square (Modern Bistro, $)
L'Eté en Pente Douce (Cafes, $)

Index of Establishments by Cuisine

Alsatian/Brasserie

Bofinger ($$, Bastille)
Brasserie Balzar ($$, Latin Quarter)

American

Breakfast in America ($, Latin Quarter)

Auvergne

ChantAirelle ($$, Latin Quarter)

Basque/Southwest

Au Bascou ($$, Le Marais)
L'Ami Jean ($$, Champs-Elysées)

Boulangeries and Patisseries

BE (Boulangepicier; $, Champs-Elysées)
Berko ($, Marais)
Boulangerie Kayser ($, Latin Quarter)
Chloé's ($, Opéra)

Cupcake & Co ($, Oberkampf)
Jean Pierre Cohier ($,
Champs-Elysées)
Le Grenier à Pain ($, Montmartre)
Moulin de la Vierge ($, Eiffel Tower)
Pain d'Epis ($, Eiffel Tower)
Poilâne ($, Saint-Germain-des-Prés)
Synie's ($, Saint-Germain-des-Prés)

Breton
Chez Michel ($$, Gare du Nord)

Cafes
Au Bistro de la Place ($, Le Marais)
Café Charbon ($, Oberkampf)
Café de Flore ($,
Saint-Germain-des-Prés)
Café de la Place ($, Montparnasse)
Café de l'Industrie ($,
Bastille-Oberkampf)
Café les Deux Magots ($,
Saint-Germain-des-Prés)
Café Marly ($, Louvre)
Fouquet's ($, Champs-Elysées)
La Contrescarpe ($, Latin Quarter)
La Coupole ($, Montparnasse)
La Fée Verte ($, Bastille)
Le Brebant ($, Opéra)
Le Progrès ($, Montmartre)
Le Sancerre ($, Montmartre)
Les Philosophes ($, Le Marais)
L'Eté en Pente Douce ($, Montmartre)
Pause Café ($, Bastille)

Classic Bistro
A La Petite Chaise ($$,
Saint-Germain-des-Prés)
A.O.C. ($$, Latin Quarter)
Auberge Le Pot de Terre ($, Latin
Quarter)
Au Pied de Cochon ($$, Les Halles)
Chez Casimir ($$, Gare du Nord)
Fish La Boissonnerie ($$,
Saint-Germain-des-Prés)
La Cigale Récamier ($$, Invalides)
La Poule au Pot ($$, Les Halles)
Le Kokolion ($–$$, Montmartre)

Le Père Claude ($$, Eiffel Tower)
L'Epi Dupin ($$,
Saint-Germain-des-Prés)
Maison Chardenoux ($$, Bastille)
Restaurant du Palais-Royal ($$–$$$,
Louvre)

Haute Cuisine
L'Ambroisie ($$$$, Le Marais)
Le Cinq ($$$$, Champs-Elysées)
Les Bouquinistes ($$$–$$$$
Saint-Germain-des-Prés)
Restaurant Plaza Athénée (Alain
Ducasse; $$$$, Champs-Elysées)

Ice Cream
Amorino ($, Saint-Germain-des-Prés)
Berthillon ($, Île de la Cité)
Gelati d'Alberto ($, Latin Quarter)
Grom ($, Saint-Germain-des-Prés)
La Butte Glacée ($, Montmartre)
Le Bac à Glaces ($, Eiffel Tower)
Raimo Glacier ($, Daumesnil)
Scoop ($, Louvre)

Mediterranean/North African
Chez Omar ($$, Le Marais)
L'Aréa ($$, Le Marais/Bastille)
Le 404 ($$, Le Marais)

Modern Bistro
A l'Affiche ($$, Champs-Elysées)
Au Bon Accueil ($$, Eiffel Tower)
Chateaubriand ($$–$$$, Oberkampf)
Frenchie ($$, Sentier)
La Fidélité ($$, Gare du Nord)
L'Atelier de Joël Robuchon ($$–$$$,
Eiffel Tower)
Le Comptoir du Relais Saint-Germain
($$, Saint-Germain-des-Prés)
Le Hide ($$, Champs-Elysées)
Le Repaire de Cartouche ($$, Modern
Bistro, Oberkampf)
Le Square ($, Montmartre)
Thomieux ($$$, Eiffel Tower)
Ze Kitchen Galerie ($$–$$$,
Saint-Germain-des-Prés)

Provençal

La Bastide Odéon ($$,
Saint-Germain-des-Prés)

Soup and Sandwiches

Class'Croute ($, Sentier)
Cococook ($, Marais)
Cojean ($, Louvre)
Cuizines ($, Louvre)
L'As du Falafel ($, Marais)
Le Bar à Soupes ($, Bastille)
Jour ($, Madeleine)
Qualité & Co ($, Louvre)

Tea Salons

Angelina ($, Louvre)
A Priori Thé ($, Sentier)
Ladurée ($, Champs-Elysées)
La Fourmi Ailée ($, Latin Quarter)
Maison des Trois Thés ($, Latin
Quarter)
Mariage Frères ($, Champs-Elysées)
Salon de Thé de la Mosquée de Paris
($, Latin Quarter)
The Tea Caddy ($, Latin Quarter)

Traiteurs

Fauchon ($, Louvre)
Hédiard ($, Latin Quarter)
Lafayette Gourmet ($, Opéra)
La Grande Épicerie ($,
Saint-Germain-des-Prés)

Vegetarian

Le Potager du Marais ($, Le Marais)

Wine Bars

À La Cloche des Halles ($, Louvre/Les
Halles)
Au Négociant ($, Montmartre)
Clown Bar ($, Bastille)
La Tartine ($, Le Marais)
Le Bistrot du Peintre ($, Bastille)
Le Griffonnier ($, Champs-Elysées)
Le Sancerre ($$, Eiffel Tower)
Le Tournon ($,
Saint-Germain-des-Prés)
Taverne Henri IV ($, Louvre)
Willi's Wine Bar ($, Louvre)

Index of Establishments by Price

$

À La Cloche des Halles (Wine Bar,
Louvre/Les Halles)
Amorino (Ice Cream,
Saint-Germain-des-Prés)
Angelina (Tea Salon, Louvre)
A Priori Thé (Tea Salon, Sentier)
Auberge Le Pot de Terre (Classic
Bistro, Latin Quarter)
Au Bistro de la Place (Cafes, Le
Marais)
Au Négociant (Wine Bar, Montmartre)
BE (Boulangepicier; Boulangeries,
Champs-Elysées)
Berko (Patisseries, Marais)
Berthillon (Ice Cream, Île de la Cité)
Boulangerie Kayser (Boulangeries,
Latin Quarter)
Breakfast in America (American, Latin
Quarter)

Café Charbon (Cafes, Oberkampf)
Café de Flore (Cafes,
Saint-Germain-des-Prés)
Café de la Place (Cafes,
Montparnasse)
Café de l'Industrie (Cafes,
Bastille-Oberkampf)
Café les Deux Magots (Cafes,
Saint-Germain-des-Prés)
Café Marly (Cafes, Louvre)
Class'Croute (Soup and Sandwiches,
Sentier)
Chloé's (Patisseries, Opéra)
Clown Bar (Wine Bar, Bastille/
Oberkampf)
Cococook (Soup and Sandwiches,
Marais)
Cojean (Soup and Sandwiches,
Louvre)

Cuizines (Soup and Sandwiches, Louvre)
Cupcake & Co (Patisseries, Oberkampf)
Fauchon (Traiteurs, Louvre)
Fouquet's (Cafes, Champs-Elysées)
Frenchie (Modern Bistro, Sentier)
Gelati d'Alberto (Ice Cream, Latin Quarter)
Hédiard (Traiteurs, Latin Quarter)
Jean Pierre Cohier (Boulangeries, Champs-Elysées)
Jour (Soup and Sandwiches, Madeleine)
La Butte Glacée (Ice Cream, Montmartre)
La Contrescarpe (Cafes, Latin Quarter)
La Coupole (Cafes, Montparnasse)
Ladurée (Tea Salon, Champs-Elysées)
Lafayette Gourmet (Traiteurs, Opéra)
La Fée Verte (Cafe, Bastille)
La Fourmi Ailée (Tea Salon, Latin Quarter)
La Grande Épicerie (Traiteurs, Saint-Germain-des-Prés)
L'As du Falafel (Soup and Sandwiches, Le Marais)
La Tartine (Wine Bar, Le Marais)
Le Bac à Glaces (Ice Cream, Eiffel Tower)
Le Bar à Soupes (Soup and Sandwiches, Marais)
Le Bistrot du Peintre (Wine Bar, Bastille/Oberkampf)
Le Brebant (Cafe, Opéra)
Le Grenier à Pain (Boulangeries, Montmartre)
Le Griffonnier (Wine Bar, Champs-Elysées)
Le Kokolion (Classic Bistro, Montmartre)
Le Potager du Marais (Vegetarian, Le Marais)
Le Progrès (Cafes, Montmartre)
Le Sancerre (Cafes, Montmartre)
Les Philosophes (Cafes, Le Marais)
L'Eté en Pente Douce (Cafes, Montmartre)

Le Tournon (Wine Bar, Saint-Germain-des-Prés)
Maison des Trois Thés (Tea Salon, Latin Quarter)
Mariage Frères (Tea Salon, Champs-Elysées)
Moulin de la Vierge (Boulangeries, Eiffel Tower)
Pain d'Epis (Boulangeries, Eiffel Tower)
Pause Café (Cafes, Bastille-Oberkampf)
Poilâne (Boulangeries, Saint-Germain-des-Prés)
Qualité & Co (Soup and Sandwiches, Louvre)
Raimo Glacier (Ice Cream, Daumesnil)
Salon de Thé de la Mosquée de Paris (Tea Salon, Latin Quarter)
Scoop (Ice Cream, Louvre)
Synie's (Patisseries, Saint-Germain-des-Prés)
Taverne Henri IV (Wine Bar, Louvre)
The Tea Caddy (Tea Salon, Latin Quarter)
Willi's Wine Bar (Wine Bar, Louvre)

$$

A l'Affiche ($$, Champs-Elysées)
A La Petite Chaise (Classic Bistro, Saint-Germain-des-Prés)
A.O.C. (Classic Bistro, Latin Quarter)
Au Bascou (Basque/Southwest, Le Marais)
Au Bon Accueil (Modern Bistro, Eiffel Tower)
Au Pied de Cochon (Classic Bistro, Les Halles)
Bofinger (Alsatian, Bastille)
Brasserie Balzar (Alsatian/Brasserie, Latin Quarter)
ChantAirelle (Auvergne, Latin Quarter)
Chateaubriand (Modern Bistro, Oberkampf)
Chez Casimir (Classic Bistro, Gare du Nord)
Chez Michel (Breton, Gare du Nord)
Chez Omar (North African, Le Marais)

Fish La Boissonnerie (Classic Bistro, Saint-Germain-des-Prés)

Frenchie (Modern Bistro, Sentier)

La Bastide Odéon (Provençal, Saint-Germain-des-Prés)

La Cigale Récamier (Classic Bistro, Invalides)

La Fidélité (Modern Bistro, Gare du Nord)

L'Ami Jean (Basque/Southwest, Champs-Elysées)

La Poule au Pot (Classic Bistro, Les Halles)

L'Aréa (Mediterranean/Brazilian, Le Marais/Bastille)

L'Atelier de Joël Robuchon (Modern Bistro, Eiffel Tower)

Le Comptoir du Relais Saint-Germain (Cafes, Saint-Germain-des-Prés)

Le 404 (Moroccan, Le Marais)

Le Kokolion (Classic Bistro, Montmartre)

Le Hide (Modern Bistro, Champs-Elysées)

Le Père Claude (Classic Bistro, Eiffel Tower)

L'Epi Dupin (Classic Bistro, Saint-Germain-des-Prés)

Le Repaire de Cartouche (Modern Bistro, Oberkampf)

Le Sancerre (Wine Bar, Eiffel Tower)

Le Square (Modern Bistro, Montmartre)

Maison Chardenoux (Classic Bistro, Bastille)

Restaurant du Palais-Royal (Classic Bistro, Louvre)

Ze Kitchen Galerie (Modern Bistro, Saint-Germain-des-Prés)

$$$

Chateaubriand (Modern Bistro, Oberkampf)

L'Atelier de Joël Robuchon (Modern Bistro, Eiffel Tower)

Les Bouquinistes (Haute Cuisine, Saint-Germain-des-Prés)

Restaurant du Palais-Royal (Classic Bistro, Louvre)

Thomieux (Modern Bistro, Eiffel Tower)

Ze Kitchen Galerie (Modern Bistro, Saint-Germain-des-Prés)

$$$$

L'Ambroisie (Haute Cuisine, Le Marais)

Le Cinq (Haute Cuisine, Champs-Elysées)

Les Bouquinistes (Haute Cuisine, Saint-Germain-des-Prés)

Restaurant Plaza Athénée (Alain Ducasse; Haute Cuisine, Champs-Elysées)

Part IV
Exploring Paris

"Now THAT was a great meal! Beautiful presentation, an imaginative use of ingredients, and a sauce with nuance and depth. The French really know how to make a 'Happy Meal.'"

In this part . . .

So many things to see in Paris . . . what do you do first . . . and how long will it take? Chapter 11 tells you a bit about what's worth seeing; lists some more cool things to see and do for kids, teens, history buffs, and art and literature lovers; and suggests gardens and parks to relax in after visiting all those museums. You also find here guided-tour options, from buses to bicycles. Chapter 12 describes today's shopping scene in Paris, previews four great shopping neighborhoods, covers the outdoor markets, and provides reviews of local shops of interest. In Chapter 13, you have the chance to discover Paris in four itineraries and a walking tour. And just when you're getting used to Paris, Chapter 14 sends you away on one of five popular day trips in the Île-de-France region.

Chapter 11

Discovering Paris's Best Attractions

In This Chapter
▶ Exploring Paris's top attractions
▶ Finding sights and activities for all types of interests
▶ Considering a guided tour

*I*n Paris, you're never at a loss for something to see, and this chapter starts you off with a succinct review of 20 of the city's top attractions, giving you the lowdown on when to go, how to get there, and why to visit it in the first place.

 Before you leave, log onto www.weather.com and look at the extended forecast for Paris. Or when you arrive, pick up a copy of the *International Herald Tribune* or *USA Today*'s international edition for extended weather forecasts and save museum visits for rainy days. (Keep in mind that most museums close on Mon or Tues and admission is free the first Sun of the month at national museums. On free days, be prepared to wait in long lines.)

Paris's Top Sights

Paris is synonymous with the Eiffel Tower, the Louvre, and the Arc de Triomphe, and you're probably planning to see at least one of them. A word of advice: Figure out which sights you'd be heartbroken to miss, and plan to do those first. After that, if you have the flexibility, improvise! There's so much to see that you'll reorder your itinerary daily. This chapter gives you an idea of what's out there.

Paris's Top Attractions

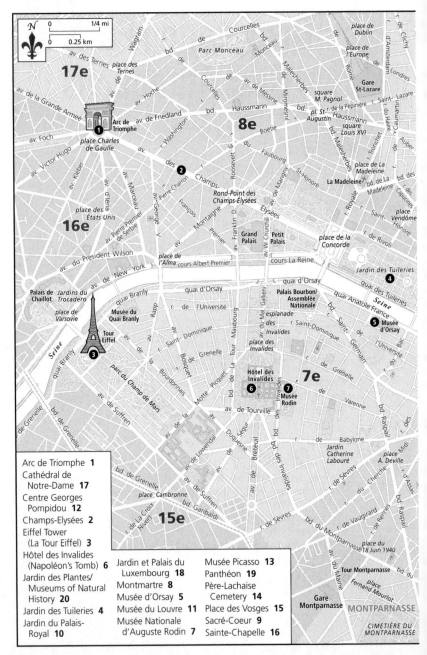

Arc de Triomphe **1**
Cathédral de
    Notre-Dame **17**
Centre Georges
    Pompidou **12**
Champs-Elysées **2**
Eiffel Tower
    (La Tour Eiffel) **3**
Hôtel des Invalides
    (Napoléon's Tomb) **6**
Jardin des Plantes/
    Museums of Natural
    History **20**
Jardin des Tuileries **4**
Jardin du Palais-
    Royal **10**

Jardin et Palais du
    Luxembourg **18**
Montmartre **8**
Musée d'Orsay **5**
Musée du Louvre **11**
Musée Nationale
    d'Auguste Rodin **7**

Musée Picasso **13**
Panthéon **19**
Père-Lachaise
    Cemetery **14**
Place des Vosges **15**
Sacré-Coeur **9**
Sainte-Chapelle **16**

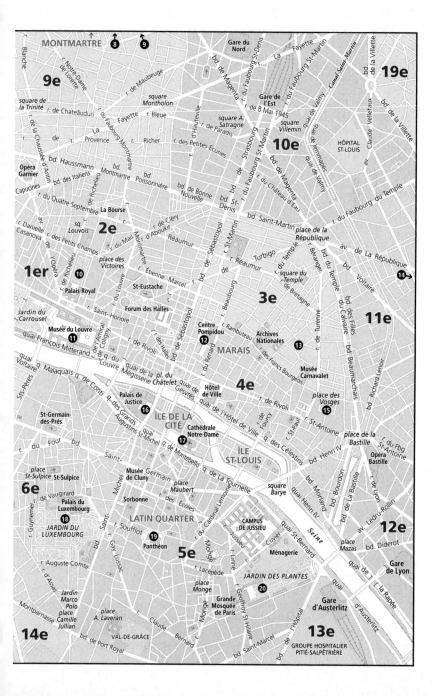

Saving on seeing the sights

One of the best bargains for tourists visiting Paris is the *Paris Museum Pass,* which offers free and unlimited admission to over 60 of the top sights of Paris and the Île-de-France. The card also promises no waiting in admission lines, but you still have to stand in line for security checkpoints at the museums that have them. ***Note:*** The pass is *not* accepted at the Eiffel Tower. It's offered in three versions: a two-consecutive-day pass (32€), a four-consecutive-day pass (48€), and a six-consecutive-day pass (64€). The biggest benefit is that you don't have to wait in line at most museums and monuments! You just saunter up to a separate window, and they wave you through. If you love planning ahead, buy the pass online (http://en.parismuseumpass.com). You can also buy the pass at Charles de Gaulle Airport in the tourist information areas in Terminal 1 and in Terminals 2C, 2D, 2E, and 2F, as well as at any branch of the tourist office, at most museums and monuments, and at any Fnac (a French chain store selling electronics and music), one of which is located conveniently at 74 Champs-Elysées.

Arc de Triomphe
Champs-Elysées (8e)

The Arc de Triomphe represents victory to the French, although it has also witnessed the agony of defeat, as in 1871 when Paris was seized by the Prussians during the Franco-Prussian War, and in 1940 when Nazi armies marched victoriously through the Arc and down the Champs-Elysées. Napoléon commissioned the Arc to honor his army and its 128 victorious battles. Today it houses the Tomb of the Unknown Soldier, which was dedicated in 1921 to honor the 1,500,000 French soldiers who died during World War I. The panoramic view is the real attraction for visitors to the Arc de Triomphe, where joyous French citizens have celebrated everything from the end of World War II and their liberation to winning the World Cup (for soccer) in 1998. From the top, 49m (162 ft.) up, you can see in a straight line the Champs-Elysées, the obelisk in the place de la Concorde, and the Louvre. Twelve streets and avenues, named for Napoleonic battles and war heroes, radiate out from the Arc. That big cube at the far end is the Grande Arche de la Défense in Saint-Denis, built to be the modern equivalent to this arch. Every year, the last day of the Tour de France sees the racers riding up the Champs and around the Arc in a series of laps before the victor is declared. An eternal flame beneath the Arc pays tribute to the lost soldiers and is symbolically relit every evening at 6:30 p.m. Allow an hour to visit, an hour and a half in high season.

Don't try to cross to the Arc de Triomphe on surface streets! Attempting to dodge the warp-speed traffic zooming around the Arc will likely get you seriously hurt. Instead, use one of the clearly marked entrances to the underpass beneath the Arc, which you find on surrounding streets.

Buy your ticket at the end of the underpass from a clerk in a small booth, and then climb the stairs to find yourself standing at the base of the Arc near the Tomb of the Unknown Soldier. You have two choices to reach the top: a set of more than 250 winding steps or an elevator. The line for the stairs is always shorter. Both stairs and elevator lead to the small interior museum and store on the Arc's top floor. To get to the outdoor viewing platform, you need to climb another flight of narrow steps; the viewing platform is *not* wheelchair accessible.

 Keep in mind that on busy days, there will be a line of people in the underpass waiting to buy tickets. Go early if you're visiting during the height of tourist season.

See map p. 190. Place Charles-de-Gaulle. ☎ *01-55-37-73-77.* www.monuments-nationaux.fr. *Métro: Charles de Gaulle–Étoile. Bus: 22, 30, 31, 52, 73, or 92. Admission: 9€ adults, 5.50€ seniors and students, free for children 17 and under. Open: Apr–Sept daily 10 a.m.–11 p.m., Oct–Mar daily 10 a.m.–10:30 p.m. Closed major holidays.*

Cathédrale Notre-Dame de Paris
Île de la Cité (4e)

"Our Lady of Paris" is the heart and soul of the city, the Gothic church constructed between the 12th and 14th centuries that dominates the Seine and the Île de la Cité, as well as the history of Paris. Notre-Dame is a study in Gothic beauty and gargoyles, at once solid with squat, square facade towers and graceful with flying buttresses around the sides. It's been remodeled, embellished, ransacked, and restored so often that it's a wonder it still has any architectural integrity at all (during the Revolution, it was even stripped of its religion and rechristened the Temple of Reason).

Construction of Notre-Dame (see the nearby "Notre-Dame de Paris" map) started in 1163 when Pope Alexander III laid the cornerstone; it was completed in 1330. Built in an age of illiteracy, the cathedral windows tell the stories of the Bible in its portals, paintings, and stained glass. Angry citizens pillaged Notre-Dame during the French Revolution, mistaking religious statues above the portals on the west front for representations of kings and beheading them. (To see the statues removed by revolutionaries visit the Musée de Cluny; see "Especially for history buffs," later in this chapter.)

Nearly 100 years later, after Notre-Dame had been turned into a barn, writer Victor Hugo and other artists called attention to its dangerous state of disrepair and architect Viollet-le-Duc began the much-needed restoration. He designed Notre-Dame's spire, a new feature, and Baron Haussmann (Napoléon III's urban planner) tore down the houses cluttering the views of the cathedral.

Visiting Notre-Dame takes a good hour to 90 minutes. The highlight for kids will undoubtedly be climbing the 387 narrow and winding steps to the top of one of the towers for a fabulous view of the gargoyles and of Paris (set aside at least 45 minutes for this, more during high season). And note that the entrance to the towers is outside the cathedral on the left side of the facade on rue du Cloître Notre-Dame. If you plan to visit the tower, go early in the morning! Lines stretch down the square in front of the cathedral and outside the towers' entrance during the summer. Before entering, walk around to the east end of the church to appreciate the spectacular flying buttresses. Visit on a sunny morning to catch the giant rose windows — which retain some of their 13th-century stained glass — in all their glory. Of interest to history buffs will be the cathedral's Treasury (on the Seine side of the building), which houses such valuable items as gold and jeweled chalices and other items from Notre-Dame's long history.

See map p. 190. 6 Parvis Notre-Dame. ☎ *01-42-34-56-10.* www.notredamede paris.fr. *Métro: Cité or Saint-Michel. RER: Saint-Michel. Bus: 21, 24, 38, 47, 85, or 96. Admission (you must have exact change for the towers and undergo a bag search): The cathedral is free; towers 8€ adults, 5€ students 18–25, free for children 17 and under. Open:* **Cathedral** *daily 8 a.m.–6:45 p.m. (until 7:15 p.m. Sat–Sun);* **treasury** *Mon–Fri 9:30 a.m.–6 p.m., Sat 9:30 a.m.–6:30 p.m., Sun 1:30–6:30 p.m.;* **towers** *Oct–Mar daily 10 a.m.–5:30 p.m., Apr–Sept daily 10 a.m.–6:30 p.m. (until 11 p.m. Sat–Sun in June–Aug);* **crypt** *daily 10 a.m.–6 p.m. Free* **museum tours in English,** *Wed, Thurs, Sat 2:30 p.m.; visits start inside at the great organ.*

Centre Georges Pompidou
Le Marais (4e)

British architect Richard Rogers and Italian architect Renzo Piano designed this futuristic "guts-on-the-outside" building in the late 1960s as part of a redevelopment plan for the neighborhood, and since its opening in 1966, the Centre National d'Art et de Culture Georges Pompidou has been a surprisingly popular attraction — so popular that the wear and tear of about 160 million visitors caused the building to begin crumbling and it closed for a three-year renovation in 1997. It's a wonderfully spacious haven in which to view, touch, or listen to modern art and artists. The newer of Paris's two modern art museums, the Centre Georges Pompidou includes two floors of work from the Musée National d'Art Moderne, France's national collection of modern art. The Centre Pompidou also houses a cinema, a huge public library, spaces for modern dance and music, temporary exhibits that often include video and computer works, and nearly 150 drawings, paintings, and other works by Romanian sculptor Constantin Brancusi in the Brancusi Atelier, a small building near the Pompidou's entrance. Plan on spending at least two hours to do the works and a half-hour buying souvenirs here.

Sadly, taking a free escalator ride to the top for the breathtaking panoramic view of Paris is no more; you can pay 3€ to take the ride (free for people 26 and under on the first Sun of every month), otherwise the view is included when you purchase admission to the museum. However, if all you're interested in is the view, consider stopping at the Pompidou's ultrahip top-floor restaurant Georges. For the same price as an adult's full-package admission to the museum (10€), you can relax with a glass of wine and enjoy the 360-degree view from indoors.

Notre-Dame de Paris

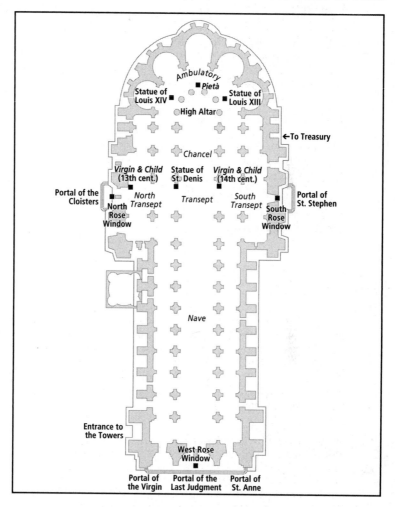

As a bonus, visit the nearby Igor Stravinsky fountain (informally *la Fontaine des automats*), which is free. Its animated sculptures by Jean Tinguely and Niki de Saint Phalle include red lips spitting water, a multicolored treble-clef symbol, a mermaid squirting water from strategic body parts, and a twirling grinning skull, all representations of Stravinsky's compositions.

See map p. 190. Place Georges Pompidou. ☎ **01-44-78-12-33.** www.centre pompidou.fr. *Métro: Rambuteau. Admission: 10€ adults (12€ May–Aug), 8€ students 18–25 (9€ May–Aug), free for ages 17 and under. Open: Wed–Mon 11 a.m.– 9 p.m. Last admission 8 p.m. Closed May 1.*

Champs-Elysées
Champs-Elysées (8e)

This is the avenue where the military march on Bastille Day, where cinephiles line up for French and American movies playing in the many theaters, where tourists wander the broad sidewalks and browse some of the same stores that can be found back home, where the Tour de France crowns the winner. But this isn't just a boulevard; if you happen to be in Paris during a major soccer competition (like when the French won the World Cup and Euro Cup soccer championships, in 1998 and 2000, respectively), you understand what the Champs-Elysées means to the French. They come here to celebrate victory and freedom. When close to a million singing, flag-waving Parisians spilled into the avenue, it was said that the country hadn't experienced such group euphoria since the days following the Liberation of Paris by the Allies in 1944. The scene on France's most famous street is liveliest at night, with people lining up for the numerous cinemas (see English-language films here by looking for *v.o.* for *version originale* on schedules and movie posters) and floodlights illuminating the Arc de Triomphe and place de la Concorde. Restaurants consist mainly of standard chain cafes (Chez Clément, Hippo) and American-style fast-food (McDonald's, Planet Hollywood), although good restaurants abound on the streets surrounding the avenue (see Chapter 10). You can shop at reasonably priced stores, such as Zara, get good deals on T-shirts at Petit Bateau, pick up what all of Europe is listening to at Fnac or Virgin, search for chic souvenirs at Le Drugstore, wander the very luxe (Louis Vuitton, whose flagship "cultural space" and store opened in 2006), and pass chain stores that you'd see in any American mall (the Disney Store, Quiksilver). Some of the stores are open on Sunday. Allow at least an hour to walk from top to bottom, longer if you want to shop, eat, or dawdle.

See map p. 190. Métro: Concorde, Champs-Elysées–Clemenceau, Franklin D. Roosevelt, George V, or Charles de Gaulle–Étoile. Bus: Many lines cross it, but only no. 73 travels its entire length.

Eiffel Tower (La Tour Eiffel)
Eiffel Tower/Les Invalides (7e)

Paris's most famous symbol weighs 7,300 tons, soars 324m (1,062 ft.), is held together with 2.5 million rivets, and was due for destruction 20 years after the World's Fair of 1889 for which it was built. (Its usefulness as a communications tower saved it, and all the major television stations and many radio stations still broadcast from it today.) Praised by some and criticized by others, the tower created as much controversy in its time as did I. M. Pei's pyramid at the Louvre 100 years later. Upon completion, the Eiffel Tower was the tallest structure in the world. People have climbed it, bungee-jumped from it, and cycled down the tower's steps. Since 2003, the year the tower welcomed its 200 millionth guest, 20,000 lights sparkle for ten minutes an hour each evening until 2 a.m. in summer and 1 a.m. in winter. Parisians often comment that the final lighting hour is the best one, because the yellow ambient lighting on the tower's structure is turned off, and only the sparkling white lights can be seen.

Keeping an eye on your wallet while eyeing the goods

You won't be able to avoid pesky (and illegal) vendors trying to cajole you into buying everything from Eiffel Tower key chains to postcards to mechanical butterflies; they constantly approach tourists standing in line for Eiffel Tower admission tickets. Be attentive — some of these vendors work in tandem with pickpockets who will rip you off while you're busy looking at the displays. As for the quality of the merchandise — it's pretty bad. Buy your souvenirs from shops and licensed vendors. (See Chapter 4 for advice on what to do if you get pickpocketed.)

But what you really want to know are the practicalities: Do I have to climb stairs? Do elevators go to the top? Are there bathrooms? Do they have snacks? Can I ascend in a wheelchair? The answers: The Tower has three levels that are accessible by elevator. No elevator goes directly from ground level to the top; you must change elevators at the second level. Although you can take stairs from the ground to the first and second levels, you can't take stairs from the second level to the top. Most likely you'll wait for elevators on the first and second levels in specially roped-off lines. In high season, the wait sometimes is as long an hour for each line. Restrooms are located on each level, and snack bars and souvenir stands are on the first and second levels. The tower is wheelchair accessible to the second level but not to the top.

Some advice: Over six million people visit the Eiffel Tower each year. To avoid *loonnnggg* lines, go early in the morning or in the off season and take the stairs to Level 2 to avoid waiting in line for the elevators there (you can only get to the top by elevator, however, and you'll have to wait in line for it). If this isn't possible, allow about three hours for your visit: one hour to line up for tickets and another two to access the elevators on levels 1 and 2.

Food is available at the Altitude 95 restaurant on the first floor, which is simply gorgeous after its 2009 total renovation, but overpriced for the quality of its meals. A first-floor snack bar and second-floor cafeteria are open, but again, they're not the best values (you'll pay about 7.50€ for a slice of pizza or a sandwich and a drink). The best food at the Eiffel Tower is also its most expensive, without a doubt: The Michelin-starred Jules Verne, one of Paris's most celebrated restaurants, is on the Eiffel Tower's second level. (One of the pluses of dining here is that you get your own private elevator to the restaurant.)

If you have the patience to wait until sunset, the Eiffel Tower at night is recommended! Its lights frame the lacy steelwork beneath you in a way that daylight doesn't, and the Seine reflects it all.

See map p. 190. Champs de Mars. ☎ **01-44-11-23-23.** *www.tour-eiffel.fr.*
Métro: Trocadéro, Ecole-Militaire, or Bir-Hakeim. RER: Champ de Mars–Tour Eiffel.
Admission: First and second levels by stairs 4.50€ adults, 3.50€ children 4–11, free for
children 3 and under; first and second levels by elevator 8.10€ adults, 4€ children
4–11; to sommet (top) level 13€ adults, 9€ children 4–11. Open: Mid-June to late Aug
daily 9 a.m.–12:45 a.m., early Sept to mid-June daily 9:30 a.m.–11:45 p.m.

Hôtel des Invalides (Napoléon's Tomb)
Eiffel Tower/Les Invalides (7e)

Louis XIV, who liked war and waged many, built Invalides, one of Europe's
architectural masterpieces, as a hospital and home for all veteran officers
and soldiers "whether maimed or old or frail." It still has offices for departments of the French armed forces, and part of it is still a hospital. The best
way to get the sense of the awe that the Hôtel des Invalides inspires is to
walk to it by crossing the Alexander III bridge. The dome of the **Église du
Dôme** (gilded with 12kg/27 pounds of real gold), is one of the high points
of classical art, with a skylight rising 107m (351 ft.) from the ground.
Sixteen green copper cannons point outward in a powerful display.

Enemy flags captured during the military campaigns of the 19th and 20th
centuries hang from the rafters in two impressive rows at the **Église de
Saint-Louis,** known as the Church of the Soldiers, but most visitors come to
see the **Tomb of Napoléon** where the emperor is buried in six coffins, one
inside the other, under the great dome. The first coffin is iron, the second
mahogany, the third and fourth lead, the fifth ebony, and the outermost oak.
The emperor's remains were transferred here 20 years after his death in
1820 on the island of St. Helena, where he was exiled following his defeat at
Waterloo. Buried along with Napoléon in smaller tombs are the emperor's
two brothers, his son Napoléon II of France, Claude Rouget de Lisle (author
of *La Marseillaise,* the French national anthem), and Henri de la Tour
d'Auvergne, Viscount de Turenne — one of France's greatest military leaders. Napoléon was so respected that even the 1793 extremist revolutionaries, who scattered the remains of the other deceased French leaders
interred at Saint-Denis, preserved his bones until their final resting place in
les Invalides. A must-see is the **Musée de l'Armée,** one of the world's greatest military museums; admission is included when you buy your ticket for
Napoléon's tomb. It features thousands of weapons from prehistory to
World War II including spearheads, arrowheads, maces, cannons, and guns
in addition to battle flags, booty, suits of armor, and uniforms from around
the world. The Charles de Gaulle wing tells the story of World War II on
video touch screens, a decoding machine, and other artifacts. Admission
here allows access to Napoléon's Tomb, the Musée de l'Armée, a scale
models museum, and the Order of the Liberation museum. Set aside two
hours for a complete visit or a half-hour to see only the tomb.

See map p. 190. Place des Invalides. ☎ **01-44-42-38-77.** *www.invalides.org.*
Métro: La Tour Maubourg, Invalides, or Varenne. Bus: 28, 49, 63, 69, 83, 87, or 92.
Admission: 9€ adults, 7€ seniors and students 18–26, free for children 17 and under
and for all on July 14. Open: Oct–Mar Wed–Mon 10 a.m.–5 p.m., July–Aug Wed–Mon
10 a.m.–6 p.m. Every Tues 10 a.m.–9 p.m. reduced admission: 7€ adults, free for

students and seniors after 5:30 p.m. Tomb of Napoléon open until 6:45 p.m. July–Aug. Closed the first Mon of every month (except July–Sept), Jan 1, and Dec 25.

Jardin des Plantes/Museum of Natural History

One of the best attractions in Paris for parents and children alike, the Jardin des Plantes is an extensive garden full of local and exotic plants, carefully manicured and lovingly maintained. Straight and broad paths, both in and out of shade, are perfect for strolls (you can also just sit on any the numerous benches while the kids play). Best of all is the Musée National d'Histoire Naturelle, a wonderful place children have visited for centuries to gape at bugs, bones, minerals, meteorites, dinosaurs, fossils, and endangered species. On the site of the former royal medicine garden, the cavernous Grand Gallery of Evolution traces life and humankind's relationship to nature. A giant squid, Wheke (6m/19¾ ft. long and donated by the National Institute of Water & Atmospheric Research in 2008), floats overhead in the area devoted to cephalopods, and holds the distinct title of being the first giant squid ever preserved and displayed in a museum. The endangered and extinct-species room displays (stuffed versions of) Gabonese monkeys, Sumatran tigers, lemurs of Madagascar, and a mock-up of the dodo bird. English explanations of some exhibits are available. Also part of the Museum of Natural History in separate buildings are the Entomological Gallery (1,500 insect specimens for bug-loving kids), the Paleontology and Anatomy Gallery (the relationship between humans and animals shown with lots of skeletons), and the Mineralogy and Geology Gallery (1,800 minerals, meteorites, and precious stones). *Note:* At the time of writing the Mineralogy Gallery was closed for renovations, scheduled to re-open by mid-2011. Walk outside amid 2,000 mountain plants from the Alps and the Himalayas in the Alpine garden, see the cacti in the Mexican garden, the greenhouse with tropical plants and rows of trees, beds of herbs and flowers, a 17th-century maze, and a carousel. Save for last the medium-size *ménagerie* (zoo), one of the oldest in the world (it opened in 1794 with animals from the zoo at Versailles), housing live bears, buffalo, big cats, apes, antelope, reptiles (including an alligator found in a room at the Hôtel de Paris), tortoises, small Przewalski horses (which no longer exist in the wild), and birds. Don't overlook the super-cool Vivarium — the spiders and insects are remarkable, especially the bugs that look like living tree branches! — or the Microzoo, where kids use microscopes to get a look at the life of the tiniest animals. A small restaurant on the zoo's premises offers pick-me-ups for the tired and cranky. Allow at least two hours.

See map p. 190. 57 rue Cuvier, 5e. ☎ *01-40-79-30-00.* www.mnhn.fr. *Métro: Gare d'Austerlitz (exit from the rue Buffon side; you're right next to the Gallery of Anatomy and Paleontology) or Jussieu (walk up rue Geoffroy Saint-Hilaire to the Grande Galerie de l'Evolution). Admission:* **Grande Galerie and other galleries** *7€ adults, free for ages 26 and under;* **ménagerie (zoo)** *8€ adults, 6€ students ages 4–26, free for children 3 and under;* **gardens** *free. A single ticket for entry to all exhibition halls, galleries, and the menagerie is available for 20€. Open: Park 8 a.m.–8 p.m.; Grand Galerie Wed–Mon 10 a.m.–6 p.m.; other galleries Wed–Mon 10 a.m.–5 p.m. (to 6 p.m. on weekends and holidays); ménagerie open daily Mon–Sat 9 a.m.–5 p.m. Most galleries and exhibitions are closed May 1.*

Jardin des Tuileries
Louvre (1er)

Come for a stroll here either before or after visiting the Louvre. Once a fashionable carriageway, today the Tuileries is Paris's most visited park and a great place to rest your feet and catch some rays on conveniently placed wrought-iron chairs surrounding the garden's fountains. In keeping with the French style of parks, trees are planted according to an orderly design and the sandy paths are arrow straight. Spread out across 25 hectares (63 acres), the gardens were originally laid out in the 1560s for Queen Mother Catherine de Medici in front of the Tuileries Palace, which was burned down during the 1871 Paris Commune. The Orangerie (a jewel among Paris's museums) and the Jeu de Paume are at the garden's western edge, and to the east you'll find 40 beautiful Maillol bronzes scattered among the trees, as well as four sculptures by Rodin, and works by Jean Dubuffet, Alberto Giacometti, David Smith, Max Ernst, Henry Moore, and Henri Laurens. You can sit down for a light snack at one of the outdoor cafes or pick up a sandwich from the Paul *boulangerie* stand ("Paul" is a classy chain of traditional-style bakeries). During the summer, a carnival features an enormous Ferris wheel (with great views of the city), a log flume, fun house, arcade-style games, snacks, and machine-made soft ice cream (but I find the best ice cream in the Tuileries is the homemade ice cream sold from a stand right beyond the Arc de Triomphe du Carrousel at the entrance to the Tuileries).

See map p. 190. Quai des Tuileries. Entrances on rue de Rivoli and place de la Concorde, 1er. ☎ **01-30-20-90-43.** *Métro: Concorde or Tuileries. Bus: 21, 24, 27, 39, 42, 48, 68, 69, 72, 73, 81, 84, or 94. Admission: Free. Open: June–Aug daily 7 a.m.–11 p.m., Sept daily 7 a.m.–9 p.m., Oct–Mar daily 7:30 a.m.–7:30 p.m., Apr–May daily 7 a.m.–9 p.m.*

Jardin du Palais Royal
Louvre (1er)

In past centuries, gamblers and those seeking more lascivious pleasures flocked to this garden where Cardinal Richelieu ordered the Royal Palace built in 1629 as his personal residence, complete with grounds landscaped by the royal gardener. Today the palace is no longer open to the public, but its statue-filled gardens, including Daniel Buren's wonderful prison-striped columns of staggered heights built in 1986 (which make for a great photo op), remain one of the most restful places in the city. The square is also ringed by restaurants, art galleries, and expensive specialty boutiques (the additional buildings that house these were added in 1780), and it's home to the Comédie-Française.

See map p. 190. Entrances on rue de Rivoli and place de la Concorde. ☎ **01-47-03-92-16.** *Métro: Concorde or Tuileries. Bus: 21, 27, 39, 48, 69, 72, 81, or 95. Admission: Free. Open: June–Aug daily 7 a.m.–11 p.m., Sept daily 7 a.m.–9:30 p.m., Oct–May daily 7:30 a.m.–8:30 p.m. Closing times may vary depending on the season.*

Jardin et Palais du Luxembourg
Saint-Germain-des-Prés (6e)

No matter which entrance you walk through, you'll fall in love with this beloved park not far from the Sorbonne and just south of the Latin Quarter. It's the sixth arrondissement's **Jardin du Luxembourg,** one of Paris's most popular parks. Children love it for its playground, pony rides, puppet theater, and the Fontaine de Médicis (the central Médici Fountain) where they can sail toy boats and watch the ducks. Besides pools, fountains, and statues of queens and poets, there are tennis and boules courts (*boule* literally means ball; in this game also known as *pétanque,* players compete to see who can roll their small steel ball closest to a larger steel ball that lies farther down the court). Certain areas of lawn are available for seating, where many of the vibrant (and often impossibly beautiful) Parisians come to suntan, picnic, and read during the warmer months. Free classical music concerts often take place in the afternoons during this time as well. In recent years, art has been exhibited on the wrought-iron fence at the garden's northwestern entrance near boulevard Saint-Michel and rue de Médicis.

The park was commissioned by King Henri IV's queen, Marie de Medici, who also had the **Palais du Luxembourg** built at the northern edge of the park. The Palais resembles the Palazzo Pitti in Florence, where Marie spent her childhood and for which she was homesick. When the queen was banished in 1630, the palace was abandoned until the Revolution in 1789, when it was used as a prison. Now the seat of the French Senate, it is not open to the public.

Orchards in the park's southwest corner contain 360 varieties of apples, 270 kinds of pears, and various grapevines. Members of the French Senate get to eat the fruit, but leftovers go to a soup kitchen. Walk north and you come across a bevy of beehives behind a low fence. A beekeeping course is taught here on weekends. See whether you can find the Statue of Liberty tucked away nearby.

See map p. 190. Main entrance at the corner of boulevard Saint-Michel and rue des Médicis. ☎ **01-43-29-12-78.** *Métro: Odéon. RER: Luxembourg, Port-Royal. Bus: 38, 82, 84, 85, or 89. Admission: Free. Open: Daily dawn to dusk.*

Montmartre
On the Right Bank

This neighborhood/village is for anyone who admires the work of Toulouse-Lautrec, is interested in one of Picasso's earliest studios, or loved the films *Le Fabuleux Destin d'Amélie Poulain* or *Moulin Rouge.* You can get to Montmartre by taking the Métro to the Anvers, Blanche, Pigalle, or Abbesses stop, the entrance of which is graced by a fabulous Art Nouveau Métro sign. You can either walk to the top of the *butte* (hill) or take the *funiculaire* (outdoor small railway) up. (To take the *funiculaire,* walk from the Anvers Métro station the short distance from rue Steinkerque and turn left onto rue Tardieu, where, for a Métro ticket, the *funiculaire* whisks you from the base of the Montmartre butte to the road right beneath Sacré-Coeur.) After visiting Sacré-Coeur and the touristy but fun place du Tertre, a square with overpriced restaurants and artists clamoring to sketch your portrait, wander down the hill where you eventually stumble across Paris from another era: Surprisingly unspoiled lanes, quiet squares, ivy-clad shuttered houses with gardens, and even Paris's only vineyard. Altogether, it creates a sense of the rustic village it once was. (*Note:* See Chapter 13 for a detailed walking itinerary through Montmartre.)

Musée d'Orsay
Les Invalides (7e)

This stone and iron former train station is one of the world's greatest museums of 19th-century art, with an unsurpassed collection of Impressionist masterpieces. Opened in 1900 by the Compagnie des Chemins de Fer d'Orléans, it was virtually abandoned 39 years later. (You can see its sorry state in Orson Welles's film *The Trial.*) In 1979, it was classified as a historical monument to prevent its demolition and its transformation into a museum began in 1983. Paris's collections of 19th-century art, which had been scattered among many museums, now had a single home, and the Musée d'Orsay opened to the public in 1986.

Normally, there are three floors of collections, with the world-famous Impressionist paintings on the upper levels. At the time of writing, renovations on the upper floors were underway, with a tentative end date of somewhere in mid-2012. However, the museum assures its guests that the popular Impressionist works will remain on display in the lower-level exhibition galleries (unfortunately, the Café des Hauteurs on the fifth floor, with its fabulous view of the Seine through its clock window, is closed — a crowded first-floor café replaces the sandwiches, drinks, and light fare, and the beautiful second-floor restaurant remains open). Traditionally displayed on the ground floor are Ingres's *La Source,* Millet's *L'Angelus,* the Barbizon school, Manet's *Olympia,* and other works of early Impressionism. Impressionism continues on with Renoir's *Le Moulin de la Galette,* Manet's *Déjeuner sur l'Herbe,* Degas's *Racing at Longchamps,* van Gogh's *Self-Portrait,* and Whistler's *Portrait of the Artist's Mother.* Works by Gauguin and the Pont-Aven school, Toulouse-Lautrec, Pissarro, Cézanne, and Seurat also are exhibited. Symbolism, naturalism, and Art Nouveau are represented on the middle level; the international Art Nouveau exhibit is worth a look for its wonderful furniture and objets d'art as well as Koloman Moser's *Paradise,* a beautiful design for stained glass. Give yourself three hours, including a lunch break in the museum's gorgeous, turn-of-the-20th-century Musée d'Orsay restaurant on the middle level. In 2010, admission to the Musée d'Orsay and the Musée Rodin was sold in a "passport" for 12€, saving you 6€ (the museums must be visited in the same day); a similar passport for Orsay and Musée de l'Orangerie can be purchased at either museum for 13€, to be used within four days of visiting the first museum of choice.

See map p. 190. 1 rue Bellechasse or 62 rue de Lille. ☎ **01-40-49-48-14.** *www. musee-orsay.fr. Métro: Solférino. RER: Musée d'Orsay. Admission: 8€ ages 26 and over, 5.50€ ages 18–25 and for everyone after 4:15 p.m. (from 6 p.m. on Thurs), free for ages 17 and under and for everyone on the first Sun of each month. Open: Tues–Wed and Fri–Sun 9:30 a.m.–6 p.m., Thurs 9:30 a.m.–9:45 p.m. Last admission 30 minutes before close.*

Cruising the Seine river

Is there anything more fulfilling than lazing down one of the world's most romantic and well-known rivers? Well, perhaps killing the canned PA sightseeing commentary and getting rid of all the other camera-clicking tourists would help the romantic mood, but if it's mood you're after, you can always take a more refined, though wildly expensive, dinner cruise.

Three companies offer similar tours in the same price range with recorded commentaries. The most well known are the **Bateaux-Mouches** that sail from the Right Bank and have huge floodlit boats. **Bateaux-Parisiens** sail from the Left Bank, while **Vedettes Pont Neuf** sail from the Île de la Cité. Vedettes boats are smaller, more intimate, and not all of them are covered.

Bateaux les Vedettes du Pont Neuf, square du Vert-Galant, 1er (☎ **01-46-33-98-38;** www.vedettesdupontneuf.com; Métro: Pont-Neuf), sail from the riverside where the Pont Neuf crosses the Île de la Cité. Departures: March 15 through October 31 daily at 10:30 a.m., 11:15 a.m., noon, and then every half-hour from 1:30 to 10:30 p.m.; November 1 through March 14 every 45 minutes Monday through Thursday from 10:30 a.m. to noon and 2 to 6:30 p.m., and at 8 p.m. and 10 p.m. Saturday and Sunday tours leave every 45 minutes from 10:30 a.m. to noon, every half-hour from 2 to 6:30 p.m., and at 8 p.m., and every half-hour from 9 to 10:30 p.m. Rates: 12€ adults, 6€ children 12 and under. Cheaper rates — 8€ for adults, 4€ for children — are available online.

Bateaux-Mouches, pont de l'Alma, Right Bank, 8e (☎ **01-42-25-96-10;** www.bateaux-mouches.fr; Métro: Alma Marceau), embark from the Port des Champs-Elysées, on the Right Bank between Pont de l'Alma and the Pont des Invalides, passing by the major monuments along the Seine in both directions. Departures: In summer high season (approximately Apr–Sept) every 30 minutes from 10:15 a.m. to 11 p.m.; in winter (Oct–Mar) boats leave anywhere from 45 minutes to an hour between departures from 11 a.m. to 9 p.m. Rates: 10€ adults, 5€ seniors 65 and over and kids 4 to 12, free for kids 3 and under.

Bateaux-Parisiens, port de la Bourdonnais, Left Bank, 7e (☎ **01-44-11-33-44;** www.bateauxparisiens.com; Métro: Bir-Hakeim), leave from the Eiffel Tower or Notre Dame, and make a complete circuit of the monuments along either side of the Seine. Departures: April through September every half-hour from 10 a.m. to 10:30 p.m.; October through March every hour, some half-hourly from 10 a.m. to 10 p.m. Rates: 11€ adults, 5€ children 3 to 12, free for children 2 and under.

A cheaper alternative to the daytime tour is the **Batobus** (☎ **08-25-05-01-01** at a charge of 0.15€ per minute; www.batobus.com), a water taxi with no piped-in commentary that stops every 25 minutes at eight major points of interest: the **Eiffel Tower,** the **Musée d'Orsay, Saint-Germain-des-Prés, Notre-Dame,** the **Jardin des Plantes, Hôtel de Ville,** the **Louvre,** and the **Champs-Elysées.** A day ticket costs 13€ for adults, 7€ for children 15 and under; Batobus runs June through August from 10 a.m. to 9:30 p.m., September from 10 a.m. to 7 p.m., November through Christmas 10:30 a.m. to 4:30 p.m., December 26 through January 2 from 10:30 a.m. to 5:30 p.m.

Musée du Louvre
Louvre (1er)

The three steps to an enjoyable Louvre experience are to:

1. Buy your tickets in advance. Visitors from the United States and Canada can purchase tickets online from www.ticketweb.com (don't be put off by the Paris, CA, location denoted on the Web site; this is the Louvre in Paris, France) and have them delivered to their homes before departure. Visitors from other countries can use www.fnac.com or www.ticketnet.com. If you're already in France upon reading this, some Métro stations have tickets for sale at the window or you can buy tickets from the distributors on the second floor of the Carrousel du Louvre. Take the escalator near the Nature et Découverte store to the second floor; distributors are on the left However, the simplest way to get your advance tickets is to buy them from the *billetterie* (ticket desk) at any Fnac store (except Fnac photo shops). A 1.50€ commission is charged by Fnac. A nearby branch is at Forum des Halles, 1 rue Pierre Lescot.

2. Grab a free map of the Louvre at the Information Desk under the Pyramid or get a free guide. The Louvre bookstore in the Carrousel du Louvre sells many comprehensive guides and maps in English; you can also grab brochures for "Visitors in a Hurry," or a guide-book, *The Louvre, First Visit.*

3. Take a guided tour. You can try a 90-minute tour by a museum guide (☎ 01-40-20-52-63) that covers the most popular works (*Venus de Milo, The Wedding Feast at Cana,* the *Mona Lisa, The Raft of the Medusa,* and the Galerie d'Apollon) and gives you a quick orientation to the museum's layout. Times and prices for more detailed tours vary, but the tour of the most celebrated works is 9€ for adults and 6€ for students 26 and under; it's offered every day at 11 a.m. and 2 p.m. If you prefer to set your own pace, you can rent an audio tour (6€) at the entrance to any of the wings.

I. M. Pei's glass pyramid is the main entrance to the museum; pregnant women, visitors with children in strollers, and those with disabilities have priority. Avoid this entrance and its long lines by using the **99 rue de Rivoli/Carrousel du Louvre** entrance, or take the stairs at the **Porte des Lions** near the Arc de Triomphe du Carrousel (the arch resembling a smaller Arc de Triomphe). Those who already have tickets or have the Carte Musées et Monuments can use the special entrance to the Louvre at the **passage Richelieu** between rue de Rivoli and the courtyard.

Tickets are valid all day so you can enter and exit the museum as many times as you prefer. Admission is reduced after 6 p.m. on Wednesday and Friday, and free the first Sunday of each month.

The Louvre palace (see "The Louvre" map) evolved during several centuries, first built as the Château du Louvre in 1190 by Philip Augustus. It first opened as a museum in 1793, and it would take you a month of visits to see the more than 30,000 treasures it now houses. But a visit to the Louvre

The Louvre

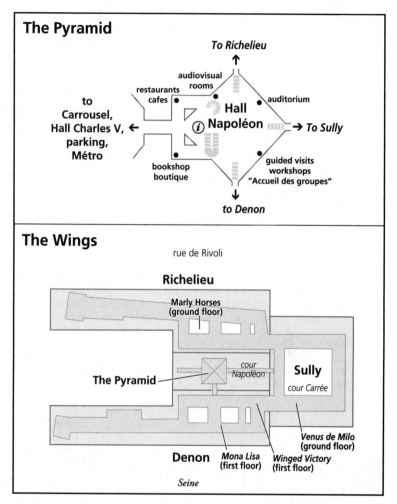

doesn't have to be overwhelming. The museum is organized in three wings — Sully, Denon, and Richelieu — over four floors exhibiting art and antiquities from Oriental, Islamic, Egyptian, Greek, Etruscan, Roman, Oceanic, European, and North and South American civilizations. It also includes galleries of sculpture, objets d'art, paintings, prints, drawings, and the moats and dungeon of the original medieval Louvre fortress.

When you're in a hurry, but you want to do the Louvre on your own, do a quick, "best of the Louvre" tour on either Wednesday or Friday when the museum is open until 9:45 p.m. Start with Leonardo da Vinci's *Mona Lisa* (Denon wing, first floor); on the same floor nearby are two of the Louvre's most famous French paintings, Géricault's *The Raft of Medusa* and Delacroix's *Liberty Guiding the People*. Next, visit the *Winged Victory* and Michelangelo's *Slaves* (both Denon wing, ground floor) before seeing the *Venus de Milo* (Sully wing, ground floor). After that, let your own interests guide you. Consider that only Florence's Uffizi Gallery rivals the Denon wing for its Italian Renaissance collection, which includes Raphael's *Portrait of Balthazar Castiglione* and Titian's *Man with a Glove*. And the revamped Egyptian antiquities department is the largest exhibition of Egyptian antiquities outside Cairo. The Greek and Roman portions also have undergone reorganizations, while the large format paintings are truly astounding.

See map p. 190. ☎ *01-40-20-53-17 for the information desk, or 08-92-68-46-94 to order tickets.* www.louvre.fr. *Métro: Palais Royal–Musée du Louvre. Admission: 9.50€ adults (6€ after 6 p.m. on Wed and Fri), free for ages 17 and under and for everyone (but crowded) the first Sun of each month. Open: Wed–Mon 9 a.m.–6 p.m. (until 10 p.m. Wed and Fri). The entrance or entresol, with its information desks, medieval Louvre exhibit, cafes, post office, and shops, stays open daily until 9:45 p.m.*

Musée Picasso
Le Marais (3e)

This mansion in the Marais houses the world's largest collection of Spanish master Pablo Picasso's art, and you can pay a visit here on each trip to Paris and see something different each time because the works are constantly rotated (there are more works than space available!). Located in the renovated Hôtel Salé, which was built in the mid-17th century for a salt tax collector (hence, the name, which translates as the "salted mansion"). The museum was created in 1973 by Picasso's heirs, who donated his personal art collection to the state in lieu of paying outrageous inheritance taxes after his death. The spectacular collection includes more than 200 paintings, nearly 160 sculptures, 88 ceramics, and more than 3,000 prints and drawings. Every phase of Picasso's prolific 75-year career is represented. Works can be viewed chronologically; particularly interesting is seeing how his paintings were influenced by the women he loved at the time: his first wife, Olga; Marie-Thérèse Walter, mother of his daughter, Maya; Françoise Gilot, mother of Paloma and Paul; and Dora Maar, among others. Budget at least two hours here, if not more. It's best to go early in the morning, as the narrow corridors in parts of the museum get particularly crowded during the afternoon (they need every square inch of wall space to exhibit this enormous collection). The museum also displays works by other artists collected by Picasso, including Corot, Cézanne, Braque, Rousseau, Matisse, and Renoir. A visit here is well worth the trip; make sure to walk around the neighborhood afterward to shop the trendy boutiques and fill up on falafel from one of the numerous stands on and around rue des Rosiers.

See map p. 190. 5 rue de Thorigny (in the Hôtel Salé). ☎ *01-42-71-25-21.* www.musee-picasso.fr. *Métro: Chemin-Vert, Saint-Paul, or Filles du Calvaire. Admission: 8.50€ adults 26 and over, 6.50€ adults 18–25, free for ages 17 and under. Admission during special exhibitions may be slightly higher. Open: Apr–Sept Wed–Mon 9:30 a.m.–6 p.m., Oct–Mar Wed–Mon 9:30 a.m.–5:30 p.m.*

Musée Rodin
Eiffel Tower/Les Invalides (7e)

If you ask an jet-setting art fanatic to name his or her favorite museum in Paris, more often then not, you'll be met by gushes about this wonderful place. It's a large house with just 16 rooms surrounded by bucolic gardens in one of Paris' most premier neighborhoods. Auguste Rodin, often regarded as the greatest sculptor of all time, lived and worked here from 1908 until his death in 1917, an era when his legendary sculptures were labeled obscene. This collection includes all his greatest works. In the courtyard, *Burghers of Calais* is a harrowing commemoration of the siege of Calais in 1347, after which the triumphant Edward III of England kept the town's six richest burghers as servants. Also in the courtyard is *The Thinker.* The *Gates of Hell* is a portrayal of Dante's *Inferno.* Intended for the Musée des Arts Décoratifs, the massive bronze doors were not completed until seven years after Rodin's death. Inside the most popular attraction is *Le Baiser (The Kiss),* which immortalizes in white marble the passion of doomed 13th-century lovers Paolo Malatesta and Francesca da Rimini. Studies done by Rodin before he executed his sculptures take up some of the 16 rooms. Particularly interesting is the evolution of his controversial nude of Balzac rising from a tree trunk. Don't miss the works of Camille Claudel, a top-rated artist and Rodin's student and lover for many years. The museum is in the 18th-century Hôtel Biron, which was a convent before it became a residence for such writers and artists as Matisse, Isadora Duncan, Jean Cocteau, and the poet, Rainer Maria Rilke. Count on spending at least an hour and a half here.

If you don't have much time or money, pay the 1€ admission to visit just the gardens, where Rodin's works stand among 2,000 rosebushes, bubbling springs, and other plants. A playground is also hidden within the grounds. Allow at least an hour to visit the garden, longer if you want to break for coffee in the garden cafe.

See map p. 190. 77 rue de Varenne (in the Hôtel Biron). ☎ **01-44-18-61-10.** www. musee-rodin.fr. *Métro: Varenne or Saint François Xavier. Admission: 6€ ages 26 and over (10€ with temporary exhibitions), 5€ ages 18–25 (7€ with exhibitions), 10€ for families of two adults and children 17 and under (including exhibitions), free for children 17 and under. Open: Tues–Sun 10 a.m.–5:45 p.m. Last admission 30 minutes before close.*

Panthéon
Latin Quarter (5e)

Is it a church? Is it a museum? Is it a tomb? Perhaps the best description would be: The Panthéon is to France what Westminster Abbey is to England — a final resting place for many of the nation's greatest men and one woman, Marie Curie. Few other monuments in Paris have had as versatile a career as the neoclassical Panthéon, whose huge dome is one of the landmarks of the Left Bank. Inside the domed church's barrel-vaulted crypt are the tombs of Voltaire, Rousseau, Hugo, Braille, and Zola. French writer, politician, and adventurer André Malraux was the last to be entombed here in 1996. Louis XV originally built the Panthéon as a church in thanksgiving to Saint-Geneviève after his recovery from gout. Construction started in 1755, but after the French Revolution, the church was renamed the Panthéon, in remembrance of ancient Rome's Pantheon, and rededicated as a burying ground for France's heroes. All Christian elements were removed and windows were blocked. From 1806 to 1884, officials turned the Panthéon back into a church two more times before finally declaring it what it is today. Along with historical information of the great figures buried here, a small wing is devoted to explanation of the scientific theories and experiments discovered by Pierre and Marie Curie. A pendulum suspended from the central dome re-creates Jean-Bernard Foucault's 1851 demonstration proving the rotation of the earth. A plaque here is dedicated to 2,600 "righteous" people who helped save French Jews from deportation during World War II. The views from the top here are some of the best in Paris.

See map p. 190. Place du Panthéon. ☎ *01-44-32-18-00.* http://pantheon. monuments-nationaux.fr. *Métro: Cardinal-Lemoine or Maubert-Mutualité. Bus: 21, 27, 38, 82, 84, 85, or 89. Admission: 8€ ages 26 and over, 5€ ages 18–25, free for children 17 and under. Open: Apr–Sept daily 10 a.m.–6:30 p.m., Oct–Mar daily 10 a.m.–6 p.m.*

Père-Lachaise Cemetery
Montmartre and beyond (20e)

On a high hill overlooking Paris, this "city" is the final resting ground for some of the world's most illustrious composers, artists, writers, poets, singers, and philosophers. Chopin, Bizet, Proust, Balzac, Corot, Delacroix, Pissarro, Modigliani, Molière, Oscar Wilde, Isadora Duncan, Simone Signoret, Yves Montand, and of course, Jim Morrison (framed pictures of him grace the walls of neighboring brasseries, but his bust has been removed due to vandalism) have been laid to rest in this, the world's most visited cemetery. No wonder Parisians have always come here to stroll and reflect; with its winding, cobbled streets, park benches, and street signs, the 44-hectare (110-acre) Père-Lachaise is a minicity unto itself. Many visitors leave flowers or notes scrawled on Métro tickets for their favorite celebrity residents. The tombs are artistic works, decorated with exquisite marble and stone statuettes or chiseled around diminutive stained-glass windows.

Legends abound. The 18th-century bronze tomb of murdered journalist Victor Noir is reputed to make women fertile when rubbed (the polished sheen of certain parts of his statue is testament to its lore!). Oscar Wilde's impressive tomb here, carved by Sir Jacob Epstein, is covered with lipstick-spots from the kisses of his admirers. The tragic 12th-century love story of Abélard and Héloïse (she was his student and her uncle castrated him when he found out about their affair) has faded, but in the 19th century, their tombs were magnets for disappointed lovers. You can obtain a free map from the gatekeeper at the main entrance, but the better map is one sold outside the entrance for 3€. Guided visits are available for 6€ per person (inquire at the main entrance). Or you can just use the

"Père-Lachaise Cemetery" map provided in this chapter. Allow at least two hours to visit.

See map p. 190. 16 rue du Repos. ☎ **01-55-25-82-10.** *Main entrance on boulevard du Ménilmontant. Métro: Père-Lachaise. Bus: 61, 69, or 102. Admission: Free. Open: Mar 16–Nov 5 Mon–Fri 8 a.m.–6 p.m., Sat 8:30 a.m.–6 p.m., Sun and holidays 9 a.m.–6 p.m.; Nov 6–Mar 15 Mon–Fri 8 a.m.–5:30 p.m., Sat 8:30 a.m.–5:30 p.m., Sun and holidays 9 a.m.–6 p.m. Last entry to the cemetery is allowed 15 minutes before closing time.*

Place des Vosges
Le Marais (3e)

The place des Vosges sits right in the middle of the Marais — a symmetrical block of 36 rose-colored town houses, nine on each side, with handsome slate roofs and dormer windows. At ground level is a lovely arcaded walkway that's now home to galleries, cafes, antiques dealers, and smart boutiques. In the early 17th century, Henri IV transformed this area into the most prestigious neighborhood in France, putting his royal palace here, and the square quickly became the center of courtly parades and festivities. After the Revolution, it became place de l'Indivisibilité. Victor Hugo lived at no. 6 for 16 years (see "More Fun Things to See and Do," later in this chapter). This is one of the places in Paris where you can enjoy a sandwich in front of the fountain, and catch some rays alongside local students and older residents. Allow 30 minutes to walk all the way around the square under the arcades and a brief stroll in the park.

See map p. 190. Métro: Saint-Paul. Bus: 20, 29, 69, 76, or 96.

Sacré-Coeur
Montmartre (18e)

The white Byzantine-Romanesque basilica dominating Paris's highest hill — the one that you can see from all around the city — is Basilique du Sacré-Coeur. Built from 1876 (after France's defeat in the Franco-Prussian War) to 1919, the church's interior is not as striking as its exterior and is, in fact, vaguely depressing. The best reason to come here is for the city-spanning views from its dome — visibility is 48km (30 miles) across the rooftops of Paris on a clear day. Conserve your pre-dome climbing energy by using the *funiculaire* to take you to Sacré-Coeur. Simply take the Métro to the Anvers station, and then ride the elevator to exit the station. Walk the short distance from rue Steinkerque and turn left onto rue Tardieu, where, for the price of a Métro ticket, the *funiculaire* whisks you from the base of the Montmartre butte to an area right below the church (if you purchased a weekly Navigo pass, the ride costs nothing).

To reach the dome and crypt, face the church and walk around to its left side, following the signs. You walk down a set of stairs and follow a walkway about 15m (50 ft.) to an iron gate. The entrance and ticket machine are on your right.

The climb from the church floor to the dome is up a flight of nail-bitingly steep corkscrew steps.

Père-Lachaise Cemetery

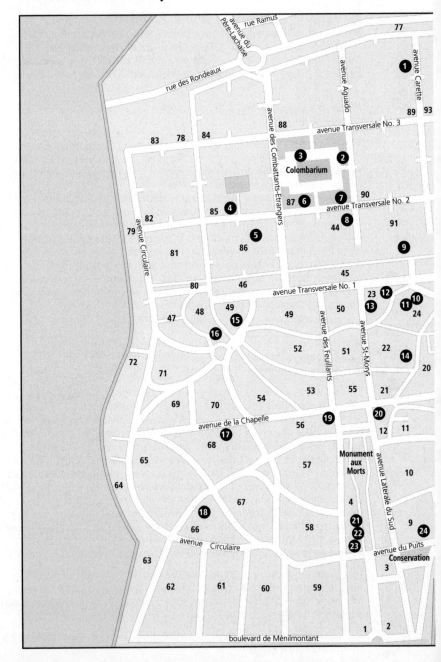

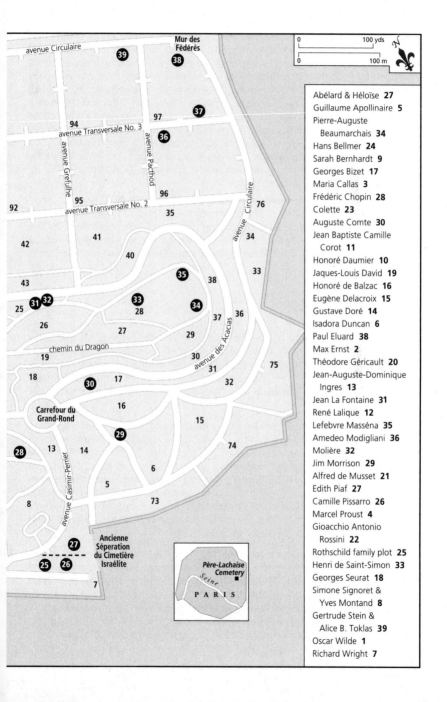

0		100 yds
0		100 m

Abélard & Héloïse **27**
Guillaume Apollinaire **5**
Pierre-Auguste
   Beaumarchais **34**
Hans Bellmer **24**
Sarah Bernhardt **9**
Georges Bizet **17**
Maria Callas **3**
Frédéric Chopin **28**
Colette **23**
Auguste Comte **30**
Jean Baptiste Camille
   Corot **11**
Honoré Daumier **10**
Jaques-Louis David **19**
Honoré de Balzac **16**
Eugène Delacroix **15**
Gustave Doré **14**
Isadora Duncan **6**
Paul Eluard **38**
Max Ernst **2**
Théodore Géricault **20**
Jean-Auguste-Dominique
   Ingres **13**
Jean La Fontaine **31**
René Lalique **12**
Lefebvre Masséna **35**
Amedeo Modigliani **36**
Molière **32**
Jim Morrison **29**
Alfred de Musset **21**
Edith Piaf **27**
Camille Pissarro **26**
Marcel Proust **4**
Gioacchio Antonio
   Rossini **22**
Rothschild family plot **25**
Henri de Saint-Simon **33**
Georges Seurat **18**
Simone Signoret &
   Yves Montand **8**
Gertrude Stein &
   Alice B. Toklas **39**
Oscar Wilde **1**
Richard Wright **7**

On the other side of Sacré-Coeur is the **place du Tertre,** where Vincent van Gogh once lived; he used it as a scene for one of his paintings. The place is usually swamped by tourists and quick-sketch artists in the spring and summer. Don't let the artists push you around too much: Their sketched likenesses of you or your companions may leave something to be desired, especially at their prices. Following any street downhill from the place du Tertre leads you to the quiet side of Montmartre. The steps in front of the church come alive around dusk, when street musicians entertain the crowd that gathers to watch the city's lights come on. Be alert: Pickpockets love Montmartre. Young men often hang around Sacré-Coeur and try to sell made-on-the-spot bracelets to tourists, tied directly onto your wrist — this is a classic way of partially incapacitating you while they rifle through the pockets of you or your fellow travelers. Don't stop for them; just give them a polite *"non, merci."*

See map p. 190. Place du Parvis du Sacré-Coeur. ☎ **01-53-41-89-00.** *www.sacre-coeur-montmartre.com. Métro: Anvers. Take elevator to surface and follow signs to funiculaire, which runs to the church; fare: one Métro ticket. Bus: The only bus that goes to the top of the hill is the local Montmartrebus. Admission: Basilica free, dome and crypt 5€. Open: Basilica daily 6 a.m.–10:30 p.m., dome and crypt daily 9 a.m.–5:45 p.m.*

Sainte-Chapelle
Île de la Cité (4e)

There are two ways to appreciate Sainte-Chapelle. Save it for the early afternoon on a sunny day, because the effect of its 15 perfect stained-glass windows soaring 15m (50 ft.) high to a star-studded vaulted ceiling is purely kaleidoscopic. Or, if you have the time, catch a classical music concert here, when light from the chandeliers dancing off the windows is magical.

Built between 1246 and 1248 by Louis IX, the only French king to become a saint, Sainte-Chapelle, the "Holy Chapel," was a shrine to house relics of the Crucifixion, including the Crown of Thorns that Louis bought from the Emperor of Constantinople. Building Sainte-Chapelle certainly cost less than the outrageously expensive Crown of Thorns, which was said to have been acquired at the crucifixion. (Louis purchased the Crown from his cousin, Emperor Baldwin II of Constantinople, at a sum of 135,000 *livres tournois* — meanwhile Sainte-Chapelle cost only 40,000 to construct.) The Crown now resides in the vault at Notre-Dame.

Sainte-Chapelle actually consists of two chapels, one on top of the other. Palace servants used the *chapelle basse* ("lower chapel"), ornamented with fleur-de-lis designs. The *chapelle haute* ("upper chapel," accessed by 30 winding steps) is one of the highest achievements of Gothic art. If you spend the time (which can take hours or even a day!), you can see that the 1,134 scenes in the stained-glass windows trace the Biblical story from the Garden of Eden to the Apocalypse. St. Louis is shown several times.

Most evenings at 7 p.m. and 8:30 p.m. Sainte-Chapelle hosts wonderful classical chamber music concerts. The world-class acoustics alone are reason enough to try to see one of these, but the beauty of the setting is unforgettable (as is, however, the fact that the church is not air-conditioned). A board outside announces the upcoming concerts, however tickets can be purchased at any Fnac store, as well as through the ClassicTic Web site (www.classictic.com/en/Special/Concerts-in-La-Sainte-Chapelle) or by calling the chapel's information line (see the next paragraph).

See map p. 190. 4 bd. du Palais (in the Palais de Justice on the Île de la Cité). ☎ *01-53-40-60-80.* http://sainte-chapelle.monuments-nationaux. fr. *Métro: Cité, Châtelet–Les Halles, or Saint-Michel. RER: Saint-Michel. Admission: 8€ ages 26 and over, 5€ ages 18–25, free for children 17 and under. Open: Mar–Oct daily 9:30 a.m.–6 p.m., Nov–Feb daily 9 a.m.–5 p.m.* **Note:** *On most weekdays, Sainte-Chapelle is closed 1–2 p.m.*

More Fun Things to See and Do

After you hit all the city's top attractions, you may want to search out some of its lesser known sights that are worth visiting. This section introduces you to some of those spots. Organized with specific interests in mind, it gives you ideas about how to make Paris truly your own. The "More Fun Things to Do in Paris" map can help you locate the fun zones.

Especially for kids

If you're a kid visiting Paris, there are so many things to do and see, from zoos and boat rides to a city of science and magic museums! There's the fun Parisian tradition of *les guignols* (puppet shows) that, even though they're conducted in French, are pretty easy to figure out. You can find the shows in the Jardin du Luxembourg, the Champ de Mars, outside of Sacré-Coeur and the Jardin des Tuileries. All Parisian parks, in fact, are wonderful for children, even without the puppet shows; one of the best is the **Bois de Vincennes,** located at the most eastern edge of the city. You can rent a boat for a leisurely row on the lake, or a bike to ride on the park's miles of bike paths, or visit the great zoo with 1,200 animals (sadly, due to renovation, it closed for four years at the end of 2008). Wander the wonderful maze at the more centrally located **Jardin des Enfants des Halles,** 105 rue Rambuteau (☎ **01-45-08-07-18;** access is free, generally open from 10 a.m. to 4 or 6 p.m.; Métro: Châtelet). The French love well-behaved children and are happy to welcome them, especially in the following locations that have been designed with kids in mind.

Paris d'Enfants (☎ **01-48-74-92-80;** www.parisdenfants.com) organizes treasure hunts, guided tours, and other excursions to help introduce touring families to the city. Your kids receive an activity booklet on each tour to help them make the most of their discoveries, from the Louvre to the Luxembourg gardens. Call or e-mail in advance to find out what itineraries will be available during your stay; your kids will thank you for it.

More Fun Things to Do in Paris

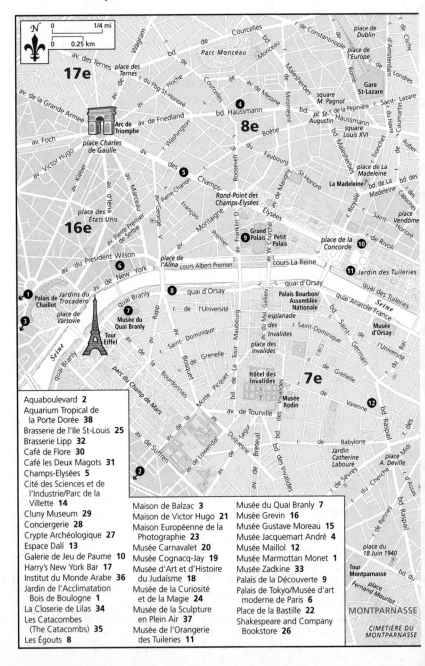

Aquaboulevard **2**
Aquarium Tropical de
  la Porte Dorée **38**
Brasserie de l'Ile St-Louis **25**
Brasserie Lipp **32**
Café de Flore **30**
Café les Deux Magots **31**
Champs-Elysées **5**
Cité des Sciences et de
  l'Industrie/Parc de la
  Villette **14**
Cluny Museum **29**
Conciergerie **28**
Crypte Archéologique **27**
Espace Dalí **13**
Galerie de Jeu de Paume **10**
Harry's New York Bar **17**
Institut du Monde Arabe **36**
Jardin de l'Acclimation
  Bois de Boulogne **1**
La Closerie de Lilas **34**
Les Catacombes
  (The Catacombs) **35**
Les Égouts **8**

Maison de Balzac **3**
Maison de Victor Hugo **21**
Maison Européenne de la
  Photographie **23**
Musée Carnavalet **20**
Musée Cognacq-Jay **19**
Musée d'Art et d'Histoire
  du Judaïsme **18**
Musée de la Curiosité
  et de la Magie **24**
Musée de la Sculpture
  en Plein Air **37**
Musée de l'Orangerie
  des Tuileries **11**

Musée du Quai Branly **7**
Musée Grevin **16**
Musée Gustave Moreau **15**
Musée Jacquemart André **4**
Musée Maillol **12**
Musée Marmottan Monet **1**
Musée Zadkine **33**
Palais de la Découverte **9**
Palais de Tokyo/Musée d'art
  moderne de Paris **6**
Place de la Bastille **22**
Shakespeare and Company
  Bookstore **26**

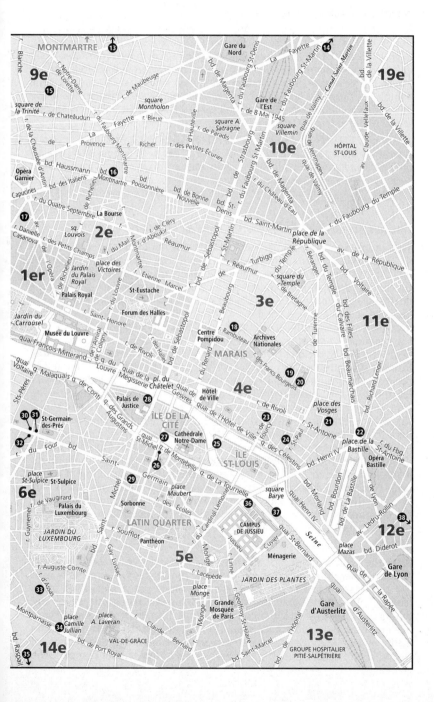

Aquarium Tropical de la Porte Dorée

It's a little off the beaten path, but it's still a fascinating place to visit either before or after a visit to the nearby Parc Zoologique de Paris. Aquatic life is grouped by theme and by oceanographic region in 80 aquariums. Your kids will love the circular aquarium where the Nile crocodiles live, and be excited to view sharks in natural-looking environments. The most recent exhibition, through March 2011, was titled *In the Wake of Sharks*, featuring colorful explanations of different species of sharks and a wall of enormous teeth. Allow at least 90 minutes.

See map p. 214. 293 av. Daumesnil, 12e. ☎ **01-53-59-58-60**. *Métro: Porte Dorée. Admission: During special exhibits 6.50€ ages 26 and over, 5€ ages 4–25, free for children 3 and under; not during special exhibits 4.50€ ages 26 and over, 3€ ages 4–25, free for children 3 and under. A special family rate of 6€–8€ may also be available Open: Tues–Fri 10 a.m.–5:15 p.m., Sat–Sun and certain holidays 10 a.m.–7 p.m.*

Cité des Sciences et de l'Industrie/Parc de la Villette

This simply enormous, science-oriented theme park has interactive exhibits on everything from outer space to genetically manipulated plants, all in an incredibly cool setting. There's a planetarium, movie cinemas, ten themed gardens, and an aquarium, as well as an adventure playground designed specifically for 3- to 12-year-olds. On the complex's east side is **Explora,** which features exhibits, models, robots, and interactive games; demonstrates scientific techniques; and presents subjects that include the universe, the earth, the environment, space, computer science, and health (in one experiment, you can test your sense of smell). The **Cité des Enfants (Children's City)** was recently remodeled and expanded and is divided into exhibits for 2- to 7-year-olds, and 5- to 12-year-olds. Kids will learn how their bodies work in a variety of ways by seeing themselves from every angle, exploring mazes, discovering the properties of water through experiments — the list of activities for children is simply endless here. The gigantic **Géode** sphere, on the complex's south side, is a wonder, with a huge hemispheric IMAX screen on which six or so films are shown daily. Another theater, the **Cinaxe,** is a simulator that projects movies on a screen while accelerating and moving the audience in different directions (children 2 and under, pregnant women, and those with disabilities are not allowed). Kids can climb aboard an actual submarine in the **l'Argonaute** exhibit (on the complex's south side next to Géode) and participate in technology demonstrations at the **Science Actualités (Science Today).**

After the visit, let your kids run wild in the expansive, green **Parc de la Villette,** where they can play in one of the ten gardens — especially neat are the **Garden of Childhood Terrors,** a blue spruce and silver birch "forest" where eerie music plays, and the **Dragon Garden** where kids and adults can cruise down the tongue of a dragon, an enormous slide. There are restaurants in the complex and food stands in the park. This could easily be an all-day visit. The Cité des Sciences et l'Industrie is bordered by La Villette canal basin. Directly across is another smaller complex, the

Cité de la Musique, accessible by a bridge; its exhibits, museums, and concerts are also worth a stop.

See map p. 214. 30 av. Corentin-Cariou, 19e. ☎ **01-40-05-80-00.** www.cite-sciences.fr. *Métro: Porte de la Villette. Admission:* **Explora exhibitions** *8€ adults, 6€ seniors and students 6 to 25, free for children 5 and under;* **Cité des Enfants** *6€;* **Géode** *11€ ages 26 and over, 9€ ages 25 and under and per person in large families or groups;* **Cinaxe Theater** *5.40€ (children must be 3 or over to enter Cinaxe);* **Argonaute submarine** *3€. Check Web site for special combination tickets and seasonal deals. Open: Géode Tues–Sun and some Mon 10:30 a.m.–8:30 p.m.; everything else Tues–Sat 9:30 a.m.–6 p.m., Sun 10 a.m.–7 p.m.*

Jardin d'Acclimatation Bois de Boulogne

A fond childhood memory for many Parisians, this place is like an amusement park from another era, small enough to be manageable with such low-tech attractions as a petting zoo and a house of mirrors, a big chair swing, and mechanized boats. And after a half-day at this 10-hectare (25-acre) park, your children will sleep well! The park's layout is simple: Just follow its circular road in either direction, and it eventually gets you back to where you started. Attractions also include bumper cars, an archery range, a shallow pool with water games, a miniature golf course, individual mechanical horses that take "riders" on a little circuit, a farm, a protected pavilion of exotic birds, a mirror maze, a quick little roller coaster, an American-style bowling alley, a playground, pony rides, and a "City of Merry-Go-Rounds," where young "citizens" can drive cars, fire trucks, and planes; try their hand at carnival games; and ride the carousel. Kids and their parents can also take in a puppet show. The park has an "enchanted river," a lake bordered by a bright blue-topped Korean pavilion, a restaurant, and snack and ice cream stands. The most fun way to get here is to take the Petit Train from the Métro's Porte Maillot exit (2.70€ round-trip). Pay for rides by buying a *carnet* of 15 tickets for 32€.

See map p. 214. 16e. ☎ **01-40-67-90-82.** www.jardindacclimatation.fr. *Métro: Les Sablons (exit on rue d'Orléans; entrance is about 150m/500 ft. away). Bus: 43, 73, 82, or 174. Or take the open-air Petit Train from the Bois de Boulogne's Porte Maillot exit; 2.70€ round-trip. Admission: 2.90€ adults and children 3 and over, free for children 2 and under. Open: May–Sept daily 10 a.m.–7 p.m., Oct–Apr daily 10 a.m.–6 p.m.*

Musée de la Curiosité et de la Magie

It's a bit dusty at this easy-to-miss museum in an old building next to the Village Saint-Paul, but kids won't care. Bona fide magicians escort you through vaulted rooms containing a collection of trick mirrors, animated paintings, talking genies, and the history of illusion in general. Who amongst you is brave enough to risk sticking a hand in the mouth of a lion to see if it's really an illusion? Although they won't disclose any secrets, you and your kids will have your senses tickled through many interactive displays. Live magic shows performed throughout the afternoon are also highly entertaining. The museum shop sells all the tools your kids need to cast (benevolent) spells back home.

See map p. 214. 11 rue Saint-Paul, 4e. ☎ **01-42-72-13-26.** www.museedela
magie.com. *Métro: Saint-Paul. Admission: 9€ adults, 7€ children 12 and under.
Open: Wed and Sat–Sun 2–7 p.m. and daily during national school breaks in winter,
over Easter, Toussaint/All Saints Day (Nov 1), and Christmas.*

Musée Grevin

London, New York, and Hong Kong have Madame Tussauds, but Paris has
its very own wax museum (and one of the few private museums listed here).
Although it's kitschy and cheesy at times, this museum is not only entertaining but a great introduction to French history and culture for those who are
still learning. Entering the museum is a trip in itself, thanks to the six-minute
introductory presentation, Le Palais des Mirages (the hall of mirrors), an
optical illusion installation created by Eugène Hénard for the World's Fair
in 1900. The very-popular exhibit was moved to the Musée Grevin in 1906
and revived in 2001 to show off the (at the time, very exotic) "Maharajah's
temple" with its endless rows of columns, animatronic elephants, and somewhat dated representation of far away cultures. The rest of the museum
includes very lifelike wax sculptures of luminaries ranging from current
world leaders (look for U.S. President Barack Obama and French President
Nicolas Sarkozy), French actors and performers like Gerard Depardieu and
a 1960s-era Brigitte Bardot perched on a kitchen table, and world-recog-
nized celebrities such as Naomi Campbell, Jimi Hendrix, and Louis
Armstrong. Probably unique in wax museums is the wonderful reverse-
chronological browse through French history: beginning with philosophers
and writers like Jean-Paul Sartre, Emile Zola, and Ernest Hemingway. You'll
be eye to eye with famous political figures, kings, religious leaders, and even
a screaming medieval torture victim (could be a little scary for young children!). The colorful history lesson is ultimately charming and makes an
otherwise fun hour and a half equally educational.

See map p. 214. 10 Boulevard Montmartre, 9e. ☎ **01-47-70-85-05.** www.grevin.
com. *Métro: Grands Boulevards. Admission: 20€ adults; 17€ seniors, students, and
children 15–18; 12€ children 6–14; 10€ children 5 and under. Open: Mon–Fri 10 a.m.–
6:30 p.m., Sat–Sun and holidays 10 a.m.–7 p.m.*

Palais de la Découverte

This museum is a full funhouse of science brought to life for kids. Here,
you can explore a planetarium, a room devoted to the earth's geology
from its beginnings to the future, a mathematics atelier that promises a
fun experience, and lots of live experiments on weekends. Your hair will
stand on end in the electrostatics room; kids can light up displays, test
their muscle reactions on special machines, see experiments about elec-
tromagnetism in an annex off the Electricity Room, and learn about DNA
in the Life Sciences wing. A popular exhibit in 2010 displayed unusual
marine animals, with plenty of bright colors and weird shapes that curious
children boisterously enjoy. Count on spending at least two hours here.

See map p. 214. Grand Palais Av. Franklin D. Roosevelt, 8e. ☎ **01-56-43-20-21.** www.
palais-decouverte.fr. *Métro: Franklin D. Roosevelt. Admission: 7€ ages 26*

and over, 4.50€ ages 6–25, free for children 5 and under; planetarium supplement 3.50€. Some workshops may cost an additional 1.50€ per person. Open: Tues–Sat 9:30 a.m.–6 p.m., Sun 10 a.m.–7 p.m. Closed major holidays.

Especially for teens

The kid-friendly sights in the previous section are appropriate for teenagers, but here are a few more suggestions for kids who are a bit older.

Aquaboulevard

If your teens are bored in Paris (and you're not visiting during July and Aug when the banks of the Seine become a beach), go to Aquaboulevard, which claims to be the biggest water park in Europe. Its seven water slides, wave pool, against-the-current river, indoor and outdoor pools, spas and Jacuzzis, whirlpool, geysers, water cannons, walls of water, water bed with bubbles, and waterfall make it a fun substitute, and it's safer than swimming in the Seine. A McDonald's, an Oh! Poivrier!, a pizza place, a Hippopotamus, and a first-run movie theater are located on the premises as well.

See map p. 214. 4 rue Louis-Armand, 15e. ☎ *01-40-60-10-00.* www.aquaboulevard. fr. *Métro: Balard (head down avenue de la Porte de Sèvres; just after you walk under the overpass, you'll see Aquaboulevard straight ahead). Admission: 25€ ages 12 and older Apr–Sept, 20€ ages 12 and older Sept–Mar, 12€ children 3–11 (who must be accompanied by an adult). Open year-round: Mon–Thurs 9 a.m.–11 p.m., Fri–8 a.m. to midnight, Sat 9 a.m. to midnight, Sun 8 a.m.–11 p.m. Children 2 and under are not admitted.*

Les Catacombes (The Catacombs)

This is the coolest, creepiest, most macabre attraction in Paris. *"Arrête, c'est ici l'Empire de la Mort"* ("Stop, here is the Empire of Death") reads the inscription over the door of the Catacombs, and if they're open when you visit (Les Catacombes seem to undergo repairs at the most inopportune times), you're in for a spooky visit like no other. This attraction is truly not for the faint of heart, so it's perfect for hardy kids older than 10, because the tunnels are dark, damp, and, frankly, a bit scary. A former quarry, Les Catacombes began housing bones in 1785 from the Cimetière des Innocents and an assortment of other overstocked Parisian cemeteries. Now Les Catacombes are the final resting place for about six million skulls and skeletons stacked in thousands of yards of tunnels.

It's helpful to have a flashlight (*lampe de poche,* lahmp duh *puhsh*) to navigate the tunnels. Your best bet is to bring one from home, but if you haven't, you can buy one in one of the stores on boulevard Raspail or the pedestrian rue Daguerre off avenue Général Leclerc. Before you buy, however, first check to see if the Catacombs are closed for repairs.

Those prone to claustrophobia should think twice about entering. The deep, dark tunnels close in rapidly and tightly. A flashlight will help navigate the poorly lit corridors and allow you to see the inscriptions. Wear non-slip shoes (such as hiking boots) to avoid a misstep on the rocky, often damp passageways and a hood to protect yourself from the water dripping overhead. The visit takes about an hour. Les Catacombes earned the nickname *place d'Enfer* ("Hell Square"), which later became *place Denfert-Rochereau*, and you can take Métro line 4 or 6, or RER B to the stop of the same name.

See map p. 214. 1 place Denfert-Rochereau, 14e. ☎ 01-43-22-47-63. www. catacombes-de-paris.fr. Métro: Denfert-Rochereau. The entrance is an unassuming small door where a plate reads entrée des catacombes. Admission: 8€ ages 27 and over, 4€ ages 14–26, 6€ seniors, free for children 13 and under. Open: Tues–Sun 10 a.m.–5 p.m. (last entry at 4 p.m.).

Les Égouts

One of Paris's more offbeat but still-popular tours is through the sewers — oh yes! The tour starts with a short film about the history of sewers: Though the tunnels here were laid out in the 1850s during the reign of Napoléon III, at the same time that Haussmann was designing the Grands Boulevards, Paris's sewers date all the way back to Roman times. The film is followed by a visit to a small museum, and finally the short trip through the maze. Paris's sewers are laid out like an underground city, with streets clearly labeled and each branch pipe bearing the name of the building to which it's connected. Don't worry; you won't trudge through anything *dégoutant* (disgusting), but the visit may leave your clothes smelling a bit ripe. Make this the last of the day's attractions, and wear something you don't plan to wear again until after the next wash day. The ceiling occasionally drips water, but the tour guides insist that it's only condensation and thus clean. Guided tours are free, and most are in French, but English and Spanish are available in summer. Toward the end, a long montage of the evolution of the city's drainage system also gives a beautiful timeline of the entire city's development as a whole, from the pre-Roman period until present day. Plan on spending an hour and a half to two hours.

See map p. 214. 7e. ☎ 01-53-68-27-81. Métro: Alma-Marceau (then walk across the bridge to the Left Bank). RER: Pont de l'Alma. The entrance is a stairway on the Seine side of the Quai d'Orsay, facing no. 93; look for a free-standing ticket booth. Admission: 4.30€ adults, 3.50€ ages 6–16, free for children 5 and under. Open: May–Sept Sat–Wed 11 a.m.–5 p.m., Oct–Apr Sat–Wed 11 a.m.–4 p.m. Closed between Christmas and the second week in Jan.

Especially for history buffs

The city is filled with wonderful museums to satisfy even the pickiest buff's thirst for knowledge. Blue plaques on buildings tell you the names of famous people and the dates that they lived there. Brown-and-orange signs in French give you an overview of an area's particular story. (For those who have learned some French for the voyage, don't despair if you don't recognize some of the verb endings in these signs! Any historical writing makes use of a nonspoken literary past tense, the *passé simple*. It's used to make people think of the described events as truly historical, although, personally, it seems a bit pretentious!). This section gives a rundown on places worth a visit.

Musée de Cluny

This is one of the jewels of Paris museums, and a tranquil place to visit in the heart of the Latin Quarter. It's home to the famous tapestry series *The Lady and the Unicorn.* Officially called the Musée National du Moyen Age/Thermes de Cluny, this is no dull Dark Ages museum. It houses ancient Roman hot and cold baths, the original statues that furious revolutionaries tore from Notre-Dame in 1790 (thinking they represented royalty), one of the most beautiful tapestry series in the world, and a peaceful garden that makes reference to it. You also find remnants of clothing that royalty wore in the Middle Ages, coins, leatherwork, and Gothic furniture, as well as church art — jeweled crosses, statues, sculptures, clothing, tapestries, and paintings of saints.

In the 19th century, the Hôtel de Cluny belonged to a collector of medieval art; upon his death in the 1840s, the government acquired the house and its contents. You enter through a medieval cobblestone courtyard, the Cour d'Honneur (Courtyard of Honor) — be sure to take in the turreted building and its gargoyles; this is one of the only medieval residences left in Paris. After paying for admission in the tiny lobby, turn left past the gift shop (save it until last) and try to take it all in. The fascinating Roman baths and the Notre-Dame statues are one floor down; one floor up is *The Lady and the Unicorn.* The tapestries hang in a dimly lit room by themselves. You can sit in one of the cushioned seats and try to figure out the meaning of the sixth tapestry. (The first five are an allegory representing the five senses; the meaning of the sixth tapestry remains a mystery.) In one of the medieval-period chambers being renovated, you can find a detailed miniature model of the Cluny hotel, which anyone can touch — it was placed there to give blind visitors the opportunity to feel the shapes and construction used in the medieval architecture. The gift shop is a wonderful place for souvenirs, and the renovated gardens are an oasis of calm off one of the Latin Quarter's busiest streets. Every plant (except two) in *The Lady and the Unicorn* tapestries was extensively researched and tracked down to be planted here.

See map p. 214. 6 place Paul-Painlevé, 5e (between rue du Sommerard and rue des Écoles). ☎ *01-53-73-78-00.* www.musee-moyenage.fr. *Métro: Cluny-Sorbonne. Admission: 8€ ages 27 and over, 6€ ages 18–26, free for children 17 and under and for all first Sun of month. Open: Wed–Mon 9:15 a.m.–5:45 p.m. Closed Jan 1, May 1, and Dec 25.*

Conciergerie

This was once one of the most elegant palaces in Europe, commissioned by Philippe le Bel in the 14th century. But the kings moved to the Louvre, and the building was left to be administrative offices of the Crown. It was turned into a prison in the 15th century, and it's probably most famous for its days during the terror years of the French Revolution, when 4,164 "enemies of the people," including Marie Antoinette and her husband, Louis XVI, resided here before meeting their fate. Visitors pass through the Tour d'Argent (the Silver Tower), where the crown jewels were once stored, and the Tour César to the Salle des Gardes (Guard Room) entrance.

Probably the most popular exhibit is Marie Antoinette's 1-sq.-m (11-sq.-ft.) cell. More than 4,000 of those imprisoned here headed for the guillotine on the place de la Révolution (now the place de la Concorde), including revolutionary ringleaders Danton and Robespierre, assassin Charlotte Corday, and the poet André Chénier. The far western tower, the Tour Bonbec, came to be known facetiously as the Tower of Babel because of the frequent screams from the many prisoners tortured there. Marie Antoinette's cell is now a chapel, and the other cells have been transformed with exhibits and mementos designed to convey a sense of prison life in a brutal era. Of welcome relief after the prison walls is the Women's Courtyard, with a small central garden and a fountain that was originally a bathhouse. Plan on spending two hours both here and in Sainte-Chapelle, the high-Gothic chapel and one of Paris's top sights (mentioned earlier in this chapter) with 15 spectacular stained-glass windows that are simply awe-inspiring. *Note:* A "twin ticket" is available to visit both the Conciergerie and l'Église Sainte-Chapelle for 11€.

See map p. 214. Palais de Justice, Île de la Cité, 1er. ☎ **01-53-73-78-50.** http://conciergerie.monuments-nationaux.fr. *Métro: Cité, Châtelet–Les Halles, or Saint-Michel. (Exit the Métro at Cité, which is between rue de la Cité and boulevard du Palais; the Palais is directly across boulevard du Palais.) RER: Saint-Michel. Admission: 7€ ages 26 and over, 5.50€ ages 18–25, free for children 17 and under. Open: Mar–Oct daily 9:30 a.m.–6 p.m., Nov–Feb daily 9 a.m.–5 p.m. Closed Jan 1, May 1, and Dec 25.*

Crypte Archéologique

This may be one of the best reasons to stop construction on a parking lot — ever. In 1965, excavations for a new parking lot under the *parvis* (a portico in front of the church) of Notre-Dame revealed Gallo-Roman ramparts, third-century Gallo-Roman rooms heated by an underground furnace system called a *hypocaust,* and cellars of houses dating back to medieval times. The parking lot project was abandoned, and the excavations were turned into this neat archaeological museum. Over the centuries, builders erected new structures over the ruins of previous settlements, raising the island about 7m (23 ft.). To help you visualize the buildings that once stood here, scale models show how Paris grew from a small settlement to a Roman city, and photographs show the pre-Haussmann parvis. Allow about 45 minutes, longer if you're a history buff.

See map p. 214. Place du parvis Notre-Dame, 4e (about 60m/200 ft. directly in front of Notre-Dame, accessed by downward-leading stairs). ☎ **01-55-42-50-10.** *Métro: Cité. RER: Saint-Michel–Notre-Dame. Admission: 4€ adults, 3€ ages 13 to 26, free for children 12 and under. Open: Thurs–Tues 10 a.m.–6 p.m.*

Institut du Monde Arabe

Founded by a partnership of the French state, led by President François Mitterrand, and 22 Arab countries, this institute, including a museum and academic library, was inaugurated in 1987 for the study and presentation of Arab culture across the world. The striking Jean Nouvel–designed monolith pays homage to Arab architecture with its facade made up of 240 round windows that resemble *mashrabiyas,* a type of traditional lattice-work that filters out sunlight (Nouvel designed the windows so that they automatically open and close based on the intensity of the sun). The museum's collection comprises historic Arab and Islamic art, as well as contemporary artists and exhibitions on ethnography. Originally, all of this was laid out chronologically; however, while these permanent collections are still being exhibited (the museum's three levels were being renovated at the time of writing), the collection and artistic mission is transitioning to a more global presentation of Arab culture and art with more weight on contemporary expression and thematic observations, rather than chronology. Still, the Institute continues to host a plethora of concerts, conferences, workshops, and temporary art exhibitions relating to the Arab world; 2010 saw a display of some of the finest works from the private collection of British-Iranian billionaire David Khalili, which at more than 20,000 unique pieces is reportedly the largest of its kind in the world. Allow at least two hours for your visit, and definitely stop in the cafe across the courtyard for steaming cups of sweet mint tea, prepared and served in the traditional North African style.

See map p. 214. 1 rue des Fossés-Saint-Bernard, 5e (walk toward the Seine on rue des Fossés-Saint-Bernard until it becomes Place Mohammed V; the museum is on the right side near the intersection of boulevard Saint-Germain). ☎ *01-40-51-38-38.* www.imarabe.org. *Métro: Jussieu, Cardinale-Lemoine. Bus: 24, 63, 67, 86, 87, or 89. Admission: 6€ adults, 4€ students 26 and under. Open: Sept–June Tues–Sun 10 a.m.–6 p.m., July–Aug Tues–Sun 1–6 p.m.; guided visits available at 3 p.m. daily during the week and with an additional tour at 4:30 p.m. on weekends. Closed May 1 and major holidays.*

Musée Carnavalet

Housed inside two beautiful Renaissance mansions, Paris history comes alive here through an incredible selection of paintings, reassembled rooms in all their period glory, and other items from daily life long ago. The blue-and-yellow rooms of Louis XV and Louis XVI are here in all their ornately furnished glory. The chess pieces that Louis XVI played with while awaiting his beheading are here, as are Napoléon's cradle, Marie Antoinette's personal items, and a replica of Marcel Proust's cork-lined bedroom. The Cabinet Doré de l'hotel La Rivière room has a spectacular gilded, ceiling painting of Apollo and Aurora by Charles Le Brun; his other ceiling painting is of Psyche with the Muses. Many salons depict events related to the Revolution, and the paintings of what Paris used to look like are fascinating. Numerous models of the Bastille prison are represented, including one depicting the peasant revolt itself. There is a wing devoted to the archaeology of Paris's earliest settlements (some artifacts, such as the fishing boats used by settlers, date back to between 2200 and 4400 B.C.). Visitors can even touch some of the exhibits here. A beautiful garden with access only from the museum is a nice place to revive afterward. The courtyard houses bas-reliefs of the season by celebrated architect François Mansart (who enlarged the buildings) and next to it are zodiac signs carved in the 16th century by Jean Goujon. The statue in the center is Louis XIV, by Coysevox. You may want to buy an English-language guidebook in the museum's gift shop, because audio guides are in French. *See map p. 214. 23 rue de Sévigné, 3e.* ☎ **01-44-59-58-58.** *http://carnavalet. paris.fr. Métro: Saint-Paul. (Turn left on rue de Sévigné.) Admission: Free for permanent collections; temporary exhibits vary in price. Open: Tues–Sun 10 a.m.–6 p.m.*

Musée d'Art et d'Histoire du Judaïsme

The beautiful 17th-century mansion Hôtel de Saint-Aignan houses this enormous collection tracing the development of 2,000 years of Jewish culture in France and also in Europe, from life in the Middle Ages to the 20th century. In addition to beautifully crafted religious objects, including several copies of the Torah, with breastplates, crowns, and cloth coverings from different Jewish communities throughout the world, there are shofars, menorahs, ark curtains, and spectacular velvet cloaks reflecting both the Sephardic and Ashkenazi traditions throughout Europe and North Africa. The museum has medieval gravestones and 20th-century paintings and sculptures. The museum also presents very thoroughly the newly available documents relating to the Dreyfus affair, the notorious scandal that falsely accused a Jewish army captain of providing secret military information to the German government in 1894. The free audio tour is very informative. The exhibits end with a collection of works by Jewish artists, including paintings by Modigliani, Soutine, Zadkine, and Chagall. In 2010, the museum featured a charming exhibition on the development of klezmer music in New York during the 20th century. Allow at least two hours. Security is tight here; you'll have to pass through metal detectors.

See map p. 214. 71 rue du Temple, 3e (between rue Rambuteau and rue de Braque). ☎ **01-53-01-86-60.** *www.mahj.org. Métro: Rambuteau, Hôtel de Ville. Bus: 29, 38, 47, or 75. Admission: 6.80€ ages 27 and over, free for ages 26 and under. Open: Mon–Fri 11 a.m.–6 p.m., Sun 10 a.m.–6 p.m.*

Place de la Bastille

Ignore the traffic and try to imagine the place de la Bastille just more than 200 years ago, when it contained eight towers rising 30m (100 ft.). It was here, on July 14, 1789 (now commemorated in France as Bastille Day), that a mob attacked the old prison, launching the French Revolution. Although the Bastille had long since fallen into disuse, it symbolized the arbitrary power of a king who could imprison anyone for any reason, while the citizenry paid high taxes for his follies, his biggest being the maintenance of the court at Versailles. Prisoners of means could buy a spacious cell and even host dinner parties, but the poor disappeared within the prison's recesses and sometimes drowned when the Seine overflowed its banks. The attack on the prison was therefore a direct assault on royal power. The Bastille was razed in 1792. In its place stands the Colonne de Juillet, a 51m (171-ft.) bronze column built between 1830 and 1849 to commemorate Parisians killed in civil uprisings in 1830 and 1848.

11e. Métro: Bastille. (The Colonne de Juillet is across from the Métro.)

Especially for art lovers

From galleries in the Marais, Bastille, Saint-Germain-des-Prés, and near the Champs-Elysées, through Egyptian, Assyrian, and Greco-Roman art at the Louvre, realism, Impressionism, and Art Nouveau at the Musée d'Orsay, to the modern international masters at the Centre Pompidou, it's an understatement to say that Paris offers a vast wealth of art.

But art in Paris is not merely French art. Though French movements began or developed here, generations of artists from all parts of the world have thrived in Paris, and the city's museums and galleries hold enough art for several lifetimes of daily viewing. If you're an art lover and happen to be in town in October, Paris presents the enormous Foire Internationale d'Art Contemporain (www.fiac.com), one of the largest contemporary art fairs in the world with stands from more than 150 galleries, half of them foreign. The following museums are often less crowded than their larger and more famous counterparts, but each has plenty of wonders in store.

Espace Dalí

Tucked away on top of Montmartre, this fantastically eerie place is devoted entirely to the surrealist work of Salvador Dalí, who is one of many 20th-century artists who had a studio in Montmartre. Included in more than 300 of his works is the largest collection of Dalí sculptures in France as well as a complete collection of his signed works of lithography and engraving. Aside from the recognizable melting clocks, look for his oddly metamorphosed elephants, snails, and other creatures while being serenaded by phantasmagoric music and the voice of the artist himself. There are even photographic self-portraits with his twisted and iconic mustache styles (he would be happy to know that they're becoming en vogue again) and a fantastic gift shop that's hard to match. The museum is small and potentially a lot of fun for children who aren't bothered by weird imagery. Allow at least an hour for a complete visit.

See map p. 214. 11 rue Poulbot, 18e (about 30m/100 ft. from Place du Tertre, follow rue du Calvaire to the top of the stairs that descend south, turn right and follow rue Poulbot). ☎ **01-42-18-56-60.** *www.daliparis.com. Métro: Abbesses or Anvers. Admission: 10€ adults, 6€ students 26 and under, 7€ seniors 60 and over, free for children 7 and under. Open: Daily 10 a.m.–6 p.m.*

Galerie de Jeu de Paume

One of the two museums in Paris dedicated to photography, the Jeu de Paume is named for the French precursor to modern tennis. Built in 1861 under the regime of Napoléon III, it once housed the royal practice courts. During World War II, it served as storage for Jewish cultural objects and "degenerate" art offensive to the Nazis. Up through 1986, it served as a museum for impressionist works (most of which now can be found at the Musée d'Orsay). Originally la Galerie Nationale du Jeu de Paume, the gallery merged with the original Centre Nationale de la Photographie (first housed at the Palais de Tokyo, then in the Hôtel de Rothschild) to form simply Jeu de Paume, an association celebrating all forms of photographic images, including leading contemporary work and Internet-based art. The exhibitions are constantly rotating; in 2010, the gallery presented the first-ever retrospective of groundbreaking Hungarian photographer André Kertész. Allow an hour for visiting.

See map p. 214. 1 place de la Concorde, 8e (next to the Musée de l'Orangerie at the southern edge of the Jardin des Tuileries). ☎ *01-47-03-12-50.* www.jeudepaume. org. *Métro: Concorde. Admission: 7€ adults, 5€ students 26 and under. Free entrance for students 26 and under last Tues of every month 5–9 p.m. Open: Tues noon to 9 p.m., Wed–Fri noon to 7 p.m., Sat–Sun 10 a.m.–7 p.m.*

Maison Européenne de la Photographie

Two renovated 18th-century town houses contain this sleek museum, which has the goal of making the three fundamental mediums of photography — exhibition prints, the printed page, and film — accessible to all. It succeeds on all fronts. A first-floor gallery exhibits original period prints such as Irving Penn's photo of Colette; the vaulted 18th-century basement displays cutting-edge photography, film projections, and installations. There is a space for young photographers to show their work, and the Roméo Martinez library displays some 12,000 titles spanning the last 50 years of photography. Martinez was editor-in-chief of *Camera* magazine for 20 years. There are permanent collections of Polaroid art and an excellent video library that allows you to look up thousands of photographs. Past highlights have included an exhibition celebrating 15 years of work by famed American photographer Annie Leibovitz, and an exhibition of photographic work from famed designer Karl Lagerfeld — himself a photographer since 1987. Allow at least an hour and a half including a pick-me-up in the cozy vaulted 18th-century basement cafe.

See map p. 214. 5–7 rue de Fourcy, 4e. ☎ *01-44-78-75-00.* www.mep-fr.org. *Métro: Saint-Paul or Pont-Marie. Bus: 67, 69, 76, or 96. Admission: 7€ adults, 4€ seniors 60 and over and students 8–26, free for children 7 and under, free for all Wed 5–8 p.m. Free guided tours are available on certain dates, which can be verified by calling or visiting the Web site; reservations necessary. Open: Wed–Sun 11 a.m.–8 p.m.*

Musée Cognacq-Jay

La Samaritaine department store founder Ernest Cognacq and his wife Marie-Louise Jay amassed at the turn of the 20th century this collection of 18th-century rococo art that features works by François Boucher, Jean-Honoré Fragonard, Peter Paul Rubens, Louis-Michel van Loo, Jean-Antoine Watteau, Elisabeth Vigée-LeBrun, and Giambattista Tiepolo, displayed in elegant Louis XV and Louis XVI paneled rooms. There is a collection of everyday objects, such as dance cards, and snuff and candy boxes, shelves of porcelain and porcelain figures, rich wood cabinets, and furniture. The building housing it all is the beautifully preserved Hôtel Donon, built in the 16th century. You can walk through a little manicured garden, open May through September, to enjoy sunny days.

See map p. 214. 8 rue Elzévir, 3e (between rue des Francs Bourgeois and rue Barbette). ☎ *01-40-27-07-21. Métro: Saint-Paul. Admission: Permanent collections are free. Open: Tues–Sun 10 a.m.–6 p.m.*

Musée Jacquemart André
Champs-Elysées (8e)

This kid-friendly museum is very much worth a visit, not only for the Italian and Flemish masterpieces by Bellini, Botticelli, Carpaccio, Uccello, Rubens, Rembrandt, and van Eyck, but also to see how very rich Parisians lived in the 19th century. Highlights of the collection include Rembrandt's *Docteur Tholinx,* Van Dyck's *Time Cutting the Wings of Love,* a fresco by Jean Baptiste Tiepolo, Domenico Ghirlandaio's naturalistic *Portrait d'un Vieillard,* and a portrait of *Catherine Skavronskaia* by Elisabeth Vigée-LeBrun, one of Marie Antoinette's favorite artists, and a fascinating person in her own right. As you wander the ornate gilt-ridden rooms, pause in the "winter garden," a tour de force of marble and mirrors flanking an unusual double staircase. For kids, the museum has organized a special activity: At the beginning of the visit, kids receive a free booklet with word mysteries, led by a little comic-book mouse named Filou. The kids use the contents of the museum to solve the puzzles, aided by clues spread throughout the museum, and find out the "secret letters." It is all worthwhile, especially for the surprise! Take advantage of the free interactive audio that guides you through the mansion with fascinating narrative. Visit at 11 a.m., allow at least an hour, then take a break in what was Madame Jacquemart's lofty-ceilinged dining room, now a pretty tearoom serving light lunches (the salads are all named for artists) and snacks.

See map p. 214. 158 bd. Haussmann. ☎ *01-45-62-11-59.* www.musee-jacquemart-andre.com. *Métro: Miromesnil. Bus: 22, 28, 43, 52, 54, 80, 83, 84, or 93. Admission: 10€ adults, 8.50€ students and children 7–17, free for ages 6 and under. For families, a second child may enter free for the price of one children's admission. Open: Museum daily 10 a.m.–6 p.m., cafe daily 11:45 a.m.–5:30 p.m.*

Musée de la Sculpture en Plein Air

You may wander through this open-air sculpture garden on the Left Bank of the Seine between the Institut du Monde Arabe and the Jardin des Plantes and not realize that this is an actual museum. Works are from 29 artists, including César, Ossip Zadkine, and François Stahly.

See map p. 214. Quai Saint-Bernard, 5e (on the quay of the Seine between the Institut du Monde Arabe and the Jardin des Plantes). Métro: Sully-Morland or Gare d'Austerlitz. Admission: Free. If you go on a summer Thurs evening around 8 p.m., you can see outdoor dancing nearby.

Musée de l'Orangerie des Tuileries

Since spring, 2006, visitors have been delighting in the at-last renovated Musée de l'Orangerie, which had been undergoing repairs for close to a decade. The highlight of the Orangerie is most definitely its two oval rooms wrapped nearly 360 degrees with Monet's *Nymphéas,* the water-lily series he painted especially for the Orangerie, and these rooms were the primary focus of the renovations. The immense and awe-inspiring murals simply pop from their spotless cream-white walls, lit brightly enough to accentuate all the beautifully emotional colors. But don't make the water-lily paintings your sole reason to visit. Since 1984, the museum has also housed the remarkable John Walter and Paul Guillaume art collection, comprising works by Cézanne, Renoir, Rousseau, Matisse, Modigliani, Dérain, Picasso, and Soutine, among other artists. The temporary exhibitions are also fantastic; recently the museum exhibited 26 works of Swiss painter Paul Klee, including loans from the Beyeler Foundation; at the time of writing, an exhibition of Frida Kahlo and Diego Rivera was scheduled for fall of 2011.

See map p. 214. Jardin des Tuileries, 1er. ☎ 01-44-77-80-07. Métro: Concorde. Admission: 7.50€ adults, 5€ students 26 and under, free for all first Sun of month. Open: Wed–Mon 9 a.m.–6 p.m. (until 9 p.m. Fri). Closed May 1 and Dec 25.

Musée du Quai Branly

Premiere French architect Jean Nouvel (also responsible for the Fondation Cartier and the Institut du Monde Arabe) designed Paris's newest big museum, which is just a few blocks from the Eiffel Tower. Housed in four spectacular buildings (one has a wall of living plants) with a garden off from the quai Branly, are the art, sculpture, and cultural materials of a vast range of non-Western civilizations, separated into different sections that represent the traditional cultures of Africa, East and Southeast Asia, Oceania, Australia, the Americas, and New Zealand. The pieces here come from the now defunct Musée des Arts Africains et Océaniens, from the Louvre and the Musée de l'Homme. Some of the most impressive exhibits present tribal masks of different cultures; the cultural objects seem to emanate powerful, lifelike emotion. Allow two hours for a full visit. There are numerous entrances to the museum grounds from the area near the Eiffel Tower; the main entrance is on quai Branly.

See map p. 214. 27 or 37 quai Branly and 206 or 218 rue de l'Université, 7e. ☎ 01-56-61-70-00. www.quaibranly.fr. Métro: Alma-Marceau (cross le pont d'Alma, turn right, and follow along the Seine until you come across a large glass-paneled wall, which among other things, will say "Musée du Quai Branly"). RER: Pont d'Alma. Admission: Permanent collection 8.50€ adults, 6€ seniors and students 18–26, 10€ adults and 7€ students for access to permanent collection and temporary exhibitions, free for children 17 and under and for all first Sun of the month. Open: Tues, Wed, and Sun 11 a.m.–7 p.m.; Thurs, Fri, and Sat 11 a.m.–9 p.m.

Musée Gustave Moreau

Although this is a national museum with a great reputation among Parisians, it's not often at the top of the list for visits, which is a shame. Some of the paintings could be described as bizarre and even creepy, but there is elegant beauty in the many works on display here by symbolist painter Gustave Moreau. Influenced by the English pre-Raphaelites and better known as Henri Matisse's teacher, Moreau painted mythological fantasies in a sensuous, romantic style with work that looks as if it is encrusted with jewels. Many of the images, with its layering of clean lines over landscapes, evoke the haunting, spectral images that define his brand of symbolist work. The artist himself established and designed this duplex museum studio so that his oeuvres could be displayed the way he wanted long after his death. Although not a painting, one of the most stunning parts of the town house is the wrought-iron staircase designed by Albert Lafon in 1895 that connects the two levels of the duplex. More than 6,000 of Moreau's works can be found here. Among them are *The Pretenders, The Life of Humanity, The Apparition, Orpheus by the Tomb of Eurydice,* and *Jupiter and Semele.* Moreau taught at the École des Beaux-Arts; his museum's first curator, Georges Rouault, was his favorite student, among other famous artists such as Henri Matisse. The artist's apartment is also preserved here and worth a quick visit. An hour and a half should be plenty.

See map p. 214. 14 rue de la Rochefoucault, 9e (between rue la Bruyère and rue Saint-Lazare). ☎ **01-48-74-38-50.** www.musee-moreau.fr. *Métro: Trinité d'Estienne d'Orves. Bus: 32, 43, 49, 68, or 74. Admission: 5€ adults; 3€ seniors 60 and over, students, and adults 18–25; free for children 17 and under. Open: Wed–Mon 10 a.m.–12:45 p.m. and 2–5:15 p.m.*

Musée Maillol

Curvaceous, bold, and graceful bronze statues of Aristide Maillol's favorite model, Dina Vierny, are on vibrant display as are the works of Impressionist and Postimpressionist artists in this renovated 18th-century convent, now reopened after a renovation during the summer of 2010. Outside is the sculpted fountain of the four seasons by Edme Bouchardon. But it is the important modern-art collection inside that rightly draws the most notice. The elegant upper floors of the museum display crayon and pastel sketches of Vierny, who Maillol discovered when she was only 15 years old. He believed her voluptuous figure was the personification of femininity and she served as his exclusive model for ten years. Maillol's personal collection includes the work of his friends, Matisse and Bonnard, as well as two sculptures by Rodin, and works by Gauguin, Dégas, Rousseau, Odilon Redon, Maurice Denis, Kandinsky, and Renoir. Vierny, who collected art most of her life, has an important collection of modern primitives that include Douanier, Rousseau, and Camille Bombois, as well as drawings by Suzanne Valadon, Dégas, Picasso, and Foujita. The museum features splendid temporary exhibits; it has shown the work of photographer duo Pierre et Gilles as well as English artist Damien Hirst. In late 2010, a featured exhibition showed collected treasures of the historic Medici family.

See map p. 214. 61 rue de Grenelle, 7e. ☎ **01-42-22-59-58.** www.museemaillol. com. *Métro: Rue du Bac. Admission: 11€ adults, 9€ ages 11–25, free for children 10 and under. Open: Wed–Mon 10:30 a.m.–7 p.m. (last ticket sold at 6:15 p.m.).*

Musée Marmottan Monet

It's a little off the beaten path — out in the 16e in an area of beautiful buildings between the Ranelagh garden and the Bois de Boulogne — but if you have the time and the weather's on your side, this exquisite museum devoted to the works of Claude Monet is worth the trip. It contains the world's largest collection of Monet's work, including his water lily paintings as well as his more abstract representations of the Japanese Bridge at Giverny. The painting that coined the term describing the painting style and artistic movement, *Impression: Sunrise,* is located here. Monet's personal collection can also be found here, with paintings and sculpture by his contemporaries Pissarro, Manet, Morisot, and Renoir.

The museum is in a 19th-century mansion that belonged to the art historian Paul Marmottan. He donated his house and collection of Empire furniture and Napoleonic art to the Académie des Beaux-Arts upon his death in 1932.

Donations have expanded the collection to include more Impressionist paintings and the stunning Wildenstein collection of late medieval French, Italian, English, and Flemish illuminated manuscripts. Allow at least an hour and a half for a visit.

See map p. 214. 2 rue Louis-Boilly, 16e. ☎ **01-44-96-50-33.** *www.marmottan.com. Métro: La-Muette. (Exit the station and follow where rue de Passy becomes Chaussée de la Muette; continue straight onto Avenue de Ranelagh, turning right at Avenue Raphaël. The museum is on the left corner of Rue Louis-Boilly and Avenue Raphaël.) Admission: 9€ adults, 5€ ages 8–25, free for children 7 and under. Open: Daily 11 a.m.–6 p.m. (until 9 p.m. Tues). Closed Jan 1, May 1, and Dec 25.*

Musée Zadkine

Head to this tranquil small museum before or after a trip to the Jardin du Luxembourg; it's located across the street from the park on the rue d'Assas. It's the perfect spot to view the works — about 300 sculptures and more than 350 drawings — of Belarusian sculptor Ossip Zadkine. The small statue garden is sheltered within walls of Virginia creeper, and Japanese cherry, maple, and birch trees lend shade to the garden's changing artwork. The garden and museum are free, the temporary exhibits don't cost much, and it's worth a visit if you like contemporary sculpture or if you're familiar with the artist's work. Zadkine moved to Paris around 1909 and lived and worked in this house and studio from 1928 until his death in 1967. His art, books, tools, and furniture are all on display, as well as many of his works in brass, wood, and stone. His bronze, *Destroyed City* (1953), is considered a masterpiece; the model is exhibited here (the original is in Rotterdam). The museum is accessed through an alleyway.

See map p. 214. 100 bis rue d'Assas, 6e. ☎ **01-55-42-77-20.** *Métro: Notre-Dame-des-Champs or Vavin. Bus: 38, 82, 83, or 91. Admission: Free for permanent exhibits; temporary exhibits 4€ adults, 3€ students 18–26, 2€ children 17 and under. Open: Tues–Sun 10 a.m.–6 p.m.*

Palais de Tokyo/Musée d'Art Moderne de Paris

This neoclassical palace, built in 1937, takes its name from the site that it now occupies, originally known as the quai de Tokyo. Known also as *une site de création contemporaine* (a site for the creation of contemporary art), the palace is host to nationally funded exhibitions showing the works of emerging French and European contemporary artists. The palace's east wing is also host to the Musée d'Art Moderne de la Ville de Paris (not to be confused with the Centre Pompidou), which hosts an impressive (and free to view!) permanent collection of 20th-century modern art, including works by Picasso, Matisse, Utrillo, Yves Klein, and Georges Braque. Although even Parisians are a bit confused by the existence of two centers of contemporary art in the city, the Palais de Tokyo exhibits conceptual artwork items that the Centre Pompidou will not — not yet, anyway. Nonetheless, swing by when traipsing around the 16e, if for no other reason than the view of the Eiffel Tower from its outdoor terrace.

See map p. 214. 13 avenue du Président Wilson, 16e. (Entrance to the Musée d'art Moderne at no. 11.) ☎ *01-47-23-54-01.* www.palaisdetokyo.com. *(Musée d'Art Modern: 01-53-67-40-00 and* http://mam.paris.fr.*) Métro: Iéna. Bus: 32, 42, 63, 72, 80, 82, or 92. Admission: 9€ adults, 6€ seniors 61 and over and students 18–25, free for children 17 and under; Musée d'Art Moderne free for permanent collection, 5€–10€ for temporary exhibitions.*

Especially for the literary

Paris's literary landmarks aren't all connected to Ernest Hemingway, F. Scott Fitzgerald, and the Lost Generation, though it sure can seem that way sometimes.

Brasserie de l'Île Saint-Louis

If you're a fan of *From Here to Eternity* or *The Thin Red Line,* pay a visit to this brasserie (see also Chapter 10 for a review of the food), where novelist and regular customer James Jones kept his own *chope* (mug) at the bar. Not only is the location excellent — the building is situated directly off the footbridge from Île de la Cité to Île Saint-Louis with a gorgeous view of the eastern tip of Île de la Cité (including the back of Notre-Dame and the Panthéon in the distance) — but this eatery is one of the last remaining independent brasseries in Paris. Jones lived with his family around the corner on Île de la Cité, and the film about their lives, *A Soldier's Daughter Never Cries,* was filmed in the neighborhood.

See map p. 214. 55 quai de Bourbon. ☎ *01-43-54-02-59. Métro: Pont Marie. Main courses: 18€–32€ lunch and dinner. V. Open: Thurs–Tues noon to midnight.*

Brasserie Lipp and Café les Deux Magots

You can't talk about literary Paris without mentioning Ernest Hemingway, and two of his favorite hangouts are just across the street from each other on boulevard Saint-Germain-des-Prés. Brasserie Lipp is where Hemingway lovingly recalls eating potato salad in *A Moveable Feast,* and the Café les Deux Magots is where Jake Barnes meets Lady Brett in *The Sun Also Rises.* Tourism has driven up prices, so just go for a glass of wine or a coffee (and remember that it's cheaper standing up at the bar than sitting down at a table). The people watching will undoubtedly be good. Refrain, if you can, from snapping flash photos; the regulars can get mighty annoyed!

See map p. 214. **Brasserie Lipp:** *151 bd. Saint-Germain, 6e.* ☎ *01-45-48-53-91. Open: Daily 9 a.m.–1 a.m.* **Café les Deux Magots:** *170 bd. Saint-Germain, 6e.* ☎ *01-45-48-55-25. Open: Daily 7:30 a.m.–1:30 a.m. Both are less than 46m (151 ft.) from the Saint-Germain-des-Prés Métro stop.*

Café de Flore

Next door to Les Deux Magots is this other infamous Saint-Germain-des-Prés cafe. Sartre is said to have written *Les Chemins de la Liberté (The Roads to Freedom)* at his table, and he and Simone de Beauvoir saw people by appointment here. Other regulars included André Malraux and Guillaume Apollinaire. Since 1994, the cafe has each autumn awarded the approximately 6,000€ Prix de Flore to a young writer of promising talent.

See map p. 214. 172 bd. Saint-Germain, 6e. ☎ **01-45-48-55-26.** *Métro: Saint-Germain-des-Prés.*

Harry's New York Bar

This place is still going strong all these years after — guess who? — Ernest Hemingway and F. Scott Fitzgerald went on a few famous benders. It has a cabaret in the cellar, and the Bloody Mary was said to have been invented here, but Harry's high prices may dissuade you. If cost is no concern, kick back and have what might just be the best martini in Paris.

See map p. 214. 5 rue Danou, 2e. ☎ **01-42-61-71-14.** *Métro: Opéra (head down the rue de la Paix and take the first left). Open: Daily 10:30 a.m.–4 a.m.*

La Closerie de Lilas

Lilac bushes still bloom here (the name means the "courtyard of lilacs"), and the place is just as crowded as it was in the 1930s, although its high, high prices are geared toward a tourist crowd. Notable luminaries were author John Dos Passos, Picasso, and Leon Trotsky. The Closerie's true claim to fame, however, is that Hemingway completed *The Sun Also Rises* on the terrace here in just six weeks. Much of the novel also takes place here.

See map p. 214. 171 bd. du Montparnasse, 6e. ☎ **01-40-51-34-50.** *Métro: Vavin. RER: Line B to Port-Royal. (Exit onto boulevard du Port-Royal and walk west. Cross avenue de l'Observatoire. Boulevard du Port-Royal turns into boulevard du Montparnasse. The restaurant is on the north corner of avenue de l'Observatoire and boulevard du Montparnasse.) Open: Daily noon to 1 a.m.*

Maison de Balzac

Novelist Honoré de Balzac wrote some of his most famous novels while living in this rustic cabin in the very posh residential Passy neighborhood from 1840 to 1847. He lived under a false name (M. de Breugnol) to avoid creditors and allowed entrance only to those who knew the password. He wrote some of his *La Comédie Humaine (The Human Comedy)* here. See his preserved study with portraits, leather-bound books, letters, and manuscripts on display. You can also see his jewel-encrusted cane (why spend on bills when you can have jewels?) and the Limoges coffeepot that bears his initials in mulberry pink. Expect to spend about 45 minutes here.

See map p. 214. 47 rue Raynouard, 16e. ☎ **01-55-74-41-80.** http://balzac.paris.fr. *Métro: Line 6 to Passy (walk 1 block away from the river and turn left* *onto rue Raynouard). Bus: 32, 50, 70, or 72. Admission: Permanent collections free; temporary exhibits 4€ adults, 3€ seniors, 2€ students 14–26, free for children 13 and under. Open: Tues–Sun 10 a.m.–6 p.m. Closed holidays.*

Maison de Victor Hugo

Here's your chance to explore one of those gorgeous place des Vosges apartments! Of course, if you or your kids have read *The Hunchback of Notre-Dame* or *Les Misérables,* you may want to visit here anyway. Victor Hugo lived on the second floor of this town house (built in 1610) from 1832 to 1848. The museum was designed to reflect the way Hugo structured his life: Before Exile, During Exile, and After Exile. (He fled the country after an unsuccessful revolt against President Louis Napoléon, who later became Napoléon III, and returned to Paris 16 years later, after the collapse of the Second French Empire.) You can see some of his furniture, samples of his handwriting, his inkwell, first editions of his works, and a painting of his 1885 funeral procession at the Arc de Triomphe. Portraits of his family adorn the walls, and the fantastic Chinese salon from Hugo's house on Guernsey where he was exiled is reassembled here. The highlight is more than 450 of Hugo's drawings, illustrating scenes from his own works. Plan to spend an hour here.

See map p. 214. 6 place des Vosges, 4e (between rue des Tournelles and rue de Turenne, nearer to rue de Turenne). ☎ *01-42-72-10-16.* http://musee-hugo. paris.fr. *Métro: Saint-Paul. Bus: 20, 29, 65, 69, or 96. Admission: Free; some temporary exhibitions may have a charge but are free for children 14 and under. Open: Tues–Sun 10 a.m.–6 p.m. (ticket window closes at 5:15 p.m.).* **Note:** *Though admission is free, you still must stand in line for a ticket from the cashier in the gift shop (enter on the right).*

Shakespeare & Company

The newest of the Shakespeares was opened by George Whitman in the mid-1960s and named in honor the original Shakespeare & Co. (he also named his daughter, Sylvia Beach Whitman, after the original proprietor, and she now manages the place with her father). It serves as a haven for Americans and English speakers, playing the dual role of gathering place and bookstore. Poetry readings take place on Sunday nights, and Whitman will give lodging to a (debatably) lucky few writers or poets in exchange for work in the store. Note that this is *not* the original Shakespeare & Company. The original opened in 1919 at 6 rue Dupuytren (take the Métro to Odéon, walk through the square there, and turn left) by Sylvia Beach. Two years later, Beach moved the shop to 12 rue de l'Odéon (the building is no longer there) and stayed until the United States entered World War II (in German-occupied Paris, Beach was considered an enemy alien and was forced to abandon shop).

See map p. 214. 37 rue de la Bûcherie, 5e. ☎ **01-43-26-96-50.** *Métro or RER: Saint-Michel.*

Especially for nature lovers

Most parks are open until sunset, unless otherwise noted. Count on spending at least an hour (much of that relaxing in the beautiful surroundings).

Bois de Boulogne

This huge park on the west side of Paris was once a royal forest and hunting ground. Napoléon III donated it to the city and Baron Haussmann transformed it, using London's Hyde Park as his model. Today the Bois is a vast reserve of more than 880 hectares (2,200 acres) with jogging paths, bridle trails, bicycling (bike rental available Apr–Oct near the Les Sablons entrance to the park), and boating on its Lac Inférieur and Lac Supérieur (boat rental available at the northern edge of the Lac Inférieur). Also here are the **Parc de la Bagatelle** (see listing later); the famous **Longchamp** and **Auteuil** racecourses; the **Stade Roland Garros,** where the French Open is held; the **Musée National des Arts et Traditions Populaire** (which documents French everyday life from the year 1000 to the present); and the beautiful **Pré Catalan,** a lovely park in which it is said the copper beech has a span wider than any other tree in Paris. The Pré Catalan contains the **Jardin Shakespeare** in which you can find many of the plants and herbs mentioned in Shakespeare's plays and the Pré Catalan restaurant, one of Paris's prettiest and most expensive restaurants. The **Jardin d'Acclimatation** (see "Especially for kids" earlier in this chapter) is one of Parisian children's favorite amusement parks. **Les Serres d'Auteuil,** at the southeastern edge of the Bois, are the municipal greenhouses and gardens that supply Paris with its flowers and plants. Open to the public, the greenhouses are especially nice to visit in winter; they provide a taste of the Caribbean with orchids, tropical plants, and palm trees. As the sun sets, prostitutes in parked cars and vans line the road on each side of the Porte Dauphine entrance, so the Bois is best enjoyed in daylight. This park is so big that you can spend an entire afternoon here.

See map p. 214. 16e. Métro: Porte Dauphine or Les Sablons.

Bois de Vincennes

Once a hunting ground for kings, this is the largest green space in Paris. Rent a boat at the two lakes here: **Lac Daumesnil,** on the west side of the park has two islands connected by a bridge; **Lac des Minimes** is located on the northwestern edge of the Bois. The Bois de Vincennes is home to the **Parc Zoologique** (which will be closed until 2012 for renovations); a **Buddhist center** right next to the bridge at Lac Daumesnil, complete with temple and Buddha effigy; and the **Château de Vincennes,** in which early monarchs Charles V and Henri III sought refuge from war and where Mata Hari was executed in 1917. The Bois de Vincennes houses the spectacular **Parc Floral de Paris** (see listing later), the **Hippodrome de Vincennes** for harness racing, and the **Aquarium Tropical de la Porte Dorée** (see the "Especially for kids" section, earlier in this chapter). This is also a big park where you can enjoy spending an entire afternoon.

12e. Métro: Porte Dorée or Chateau de Vincennes.

Parc de Belleville

If you visit the bustling neighborhood of Belleville, stop in this park for its beautiful views of western Paris. Topped by the Maison de l'Air, a museum with displays devoted to the air that we breathe, there are fountains, a children's play area, and an open-air theater with concerts during the summer. Rock formations and grottoes evoke the days when the hill was a strategic point for fighting enemies such as Attila the Hun. Access the park by taking the rue Piat off rue de Belleville and enter through an iron gate spelling out the words Villa Ottoz. A curved path leads you to tree-lined promenades (more than 500 trees are here), with the first of the magnificent Left Bank views peeping through the spaces between pretty houses. Beds of roses and other seasonal flowers line walks, and views of the city's Left Bank become more pronounced the higher up the terraced pathways you go.

20e. Métro: Pyrénées (walk down rue de Belleville and turn left onto rue Piat where you see arched iron gates leading into the park) or Couronnes (cross boulevard de Belleville and turn left onto rue Julien Lacroix to find another entrance).

Parc de la Bagatelle

Located in the Bois de Boulogne, the Parc de la Bagatelle is known for its gardens, which reveal the art of gardening through the centuries. The rose garden was planted by Monet's friend, Jean-Claude-Nicolas Forestier, whose claim to fame was as designer of the Champs de Mars and other gardens. His 10,000 roses of 1,200 varieties peak in June. You can enjoy bulbed plants (tulips, hyacinths, and so on) in March; peonies, clematis, and irises in May; water lilies in June; dahlias and autumn foliage in October; and winter-flowering trees, shrubs, and snowdrops during the cold months. A water-lily pond pays homage to that certain famous painter of water lilies. Forestier was inspired by the Impressionists and their way of showing flowers by species and emphasizing the effects of mass planting. The *orangerie* here is home to the Festival Chopin à Paris from mid-June to mid-July. The château, which you can view from the outside only, was built by the Comte d'Artois in 1775, after he made a bet with his sister-in-law, Marie Antoinette, that he could do it in less than 90 days; it took 66 days. Under Napoléon, it was used as a hunting lodge.

16e. Métro: Porte Maillot. Exit at av. Neuilly. Bus: 244 to the Bagatelle–Pré Catalan stop.

Parc de la Villette

This modern park is part of the grounds of the Cité des Sciences et de l'Industrie and has a series of themed gardens, including an exotic bamboo garden and one featuring steam and water jets. Scattered throughout the park are playgrounds and other attractions (see "Especially for kids," earlier in this chapter). In the summer, you can catch an outdoor movie or listen to a concert, and kids can play on a giant dragon slide. You can get to the Parc de la Villette by Métro, but a fun, alternative route worth trying is the guided canal trip to the park from Pont l'Arsenal or Musée d'Orsay with **Paris Canal** (☎ **01-42-40-96-97**; Métro: Bastille) or **Canauxrama**

(☎ 01-42-39-15-00; Métro: Jaurès). See "Paris by Guided Tour," later in this chapter.

See map p. 214. 19e. Métro: Porte de la Villette.

Parc des Buttes-Chaumont

Although this park is no secret, it's really one of the most amazing the city has to offer, if not for its distance from the center. A former gypsum quarry and centuries-old dump, it's one of four man-made parks Napoléon III commissioned to resemble the English gardens he grew to love during his exile in England. It features bucolic cliffs, a suspension bridge, waterfalls, a lake, and a cave topped by a temple. The waterfall cave is musty, but romantic — it's listed in *Où S'Embrasser à Paris (Where to Kiss in Paris)* as one of the top hidden make-out spots in the city (in the mornings you may even have it to yourselves). The stunning views of the temple and all of Paris as viewed from the west are great reasons to come here for a stroll or a picnic. And if you need more convincing, the restaurant–cum–dance bar Rosa Bonheur, located in a building at the northeastern edge of the park hosts some of the best parties in town.

19e. Métro: Buttes-Chaumont. (The station is located within the park.)

Parc Floral de Paris

The Bois de Vincennes houses the spectacular Parc Floral de Paris, with a butterfly garden, library, and miniature golf course, as well as the Parc Zoologique de Paris. You can rent bikes here and ride around the extensive grounds, or row a rented canoe around a winding pond. (You can even rent quadricycles — bicycles built for four — for around 10€.)

12e. ☎ 01-55-94-20-20. Métro: Château de Vincennes. (Exit at cours des Maréchaux and walk south; the château is on the right. Cross avenue des Minimes into the park.) Open: Daily 9:30 a.m. to dusk.

Parc Monceau

This was Marcel Proust's favorite park. A Dutch windmill, a Roman temple, a covered bridge, waterfall, farm, medieval ruins, and a pagoda, all designed by Carmontelle, are some of the oddities in this park in that borders Paris's ritzy 8e and 17e arrondissements. It contains what is said to be Paris's largest tree, an Oriental plane tree with a circumference of almost 7m (23 ft.). Have a picnic on a bench here with supplies from the nearby markets at rue Poncelet or rue de Levis and watch the English nannies from the nearby palatial apartment buildings stroll with their charges.

Boulevard de Courcelles, 8e. Métro: Monceau. (The Métro station is at the edge of the park.)

Promenade Plantée

New York City's new High Line green space took as its example this old railroad bridge that was converted, starting in 1987, into a clever

5-km-long (3-mile) garden that begins behind the Opéra Bastille and runs along the length of avenue Daumesnil, the Reuilly Garden, and the Porte Dorée to the Bois de Vincennes (it makes a great jogging path). Beneath the promenade, artisans have built boutiques and studios into the bridge, collectively known as the Viaduc des Arts. Check them out for eclectic, unusual gifts.

12e. Métro: Bel Air or Dugommier. Walk from the Métro to avenue Daumesnil. The elevated railroad bridge above avenue Daumesnil is the Promenade Plantée.

Houses of the holy

Paris has had a tradition of worship since the first settlers on the Isle of Parisii in the third century B.C. In fact, many of Paris's churches were built on the ruins of pagan temples. Today Paris's churches are treasure-troves of fine art, stained glass, and architecture. Included here are some of those worth a visit.

La Madeleine

Resembling a Roman temple, the Madeleine is one of Paris's minor land-marks. Although construction started in 1806, the Madeleine wasn't con-secrated as a church until 1842. The building was originally intended as a temple to the glory of the Grande Armée (Napoléon's idea, of course). Climb the 28 steps leading to the facade and look back: You'll be able to see rue Royale, place de la Concorde and the obelisk, and, across the Seine, the dome of Invalides. Inside, Rude's _Le Baptême du Christ_ is on the left as you enter.

Place de la Madeleine, 8e. ☎ **01-44-51-69-00.** _Métro: Madeleine. Open: Daily 9:30 a.m.–7 p.m. Closed Sun 1:30–3:30 p.m._

La Mosquée de Paris

Built from 1922 to 1926 in the Hispano-Moorish style and overlooked by a green-and-white minaret, this is one of the newer religious establishments in Paris. The complex is divided into three sections for study, leisure, and worship. At the heart is a patio surrounded by finely carved arcades, mod-eled on the Alhambra in Granada, Spain. The Salon du Thé here is a lovely place for refreshment, as popular for its Arabian Nights décor as it is for its mint teas and baklava. Fountains, North African music, plush ban-quettes, and mosaics create an exotic but casual hangout for the local student population. The _hammam_ (steam baths) are a popular place with trendy types and older Arab men who get massaged and exfoliated here (painful but oh-so-worth it!).

39 rue Geoffroy-Saint-Hilaire, 5e. ☎ **01-43-31-18-14.** _Métro: Monge. Open: Daily 10 a.m.–10 p.m._

Saint-Etienne du Mont

Standing directly behind place du Panthéon, this is one of Paris's most extraordinary churches. Completed and consecrated in the 17th century, on the site of a 13th-century abbey, the church is a unique blend of late Gothic and Renaissance styles. Preserved near the chancel and set in an ornate copper-trimmed shrine is the sarcophagus stone for Paris's patron saint, Geneviève, who saved the city from the Huns in the fifth century. The most impressive attraction here, however, is the 16th-century rood screen, embraced by twin spiraling marble staircases — a stunning display of Renaissance design. The tombs of Pascal and Racine are also here.

1 place Saint-Geneviève, 5e. ☎ *01-43-54-11-79. Métro: Cardinal Lemoine. Open: Daily Sept–June Mon–Sat 8:30 a.m. to noon and 2–7 p.m., Sun 9 a.m. to noon and 3:30–7:30 p.m.; July–Aug Tues–Sun 10 a.m. to noon and 4–7:15 p.m.*

Saint-Eustache

This massive church at the heart of Les Halles was built between 1532 and 1637, combining a Gothic structure with Renaissance decoration. Molière and Mme. de Pompadour were baptized here, and Molière's funeral was held here in 1673. This was the first church to contain the tombs of celebrated Parisians, most notably Louis XIV's finance minister, Colbert. The organ is one of the finest in Paris and has been entirely restored and modernized. Franz Liszt used to play the organ here, and there is a free concert every Sunday at 5:30 p.m. There are also free jazz and piano concerts from time to time.

2 Impasse Saint-Eustache, 1er. ☎ *01-42-36-31-05. www.saint-eustache.org. Métro: Les Halles. Open: Mon–Fri 9:30 a.m.–7:30 p.m.*

Saint-Germain-des-Prés

This is the most famous church in the 6e and one of the most important Romanesque monuments in France. Built in the 11th century, Saint-Germain-des-Prés was an important abbey and center of learning during the Middle Ages. At the time of the French Revolution, the monks were expelled and the church was vandalized. But much still remains, including the large tower, the oldest in Paris. King John Casimir of Poland is buried at the church, as is the heart of René Descartes. A small square at the corner of place Saint-Germain-des-Prés and rue de l'Abbaye contains Picasso's small sculpture of the head of poet Guillaume Apollinaire.

3 place Saint-Germain-des-Prés, 6e. ☎ *01-55-42-81-33. Métro: Saint-Germain-des-Prés. Open: Daily 8 a.m.–8 p.m.*

Saint-Julien le Pauvre

One of the oldest churches in Paris, this small example of Gothic splendor sits in the lovely square René Viviani. Originally constructed in the 12th century, it lies on the original pilgrimage route of Saint-Jacques de Compostelle to Spain. The oldest tree in Paris, an acacia reputedly planted in 1602, still stands in its garden. The church contains a stunning wooden screen, which encloses a beautiful chancel. Many classical concerts take place here throughout the year.

79 rue Galande, 5e. ☎ *01-43-54-52-16. Métro: Saint-Michel. Open: Mon–Sun 9:30 a.m.–1 p.m.*

Saint-Roch

This 17th-century church has the richest trove of painting and sculpture in Paris outside a museum. Beginning on the right aisle, notice the bust of *Maréchal François de Créqui* by Geneviève, *Cardinal Dubois and Priests* by Coustou, and paintings by Louis Boulanger in the fourth chapel. The celebrated statue by Falconet, *Le Christ au Jardin des Oliviers,* is at the entrance to the choir. Other highlights include *La Nativité* by Anguier (on the altar), the bust of Le Nôtre by Coysevox, and the monument to the painter Mignard by Girardon (both on the left side). Classical music concerts are played here on Tuesdays, often featuring compositions by Bach and Vivaldi, starting around 12:30 p.m.

296 rue Saint-Honoré, 1er. ☎ *01-42-44-13-20. Métro: Tuileries or Palais Royal– Musée du Louvre. Open: Mon–Sat 8 a.m.–7:30 p.m., Sun 8:30 a.m.–7:30 p.m.*

Saint-Séverin

A religious building has stood here since the sixth century. The current building, begun in the 13th century, is in flamboyant Gothic style. The west portal came from the church of Saint-Pierre-aux-Boeufs on the Île de la Cité before it was demolished in 1837. The dramatic palm-tree-shaped vaulting only serves to enhance the brilliant stained-glass windows behind the altar, depicting the seven sacraments. Also notable is the chapel to the right of the altar, which was designed by Mansart and contains an intensely moving series of etchings by Georges Rouault and an extraordinary rendering of the Crucifixion by G. Schneider.

1 rue des Prêtres-Saint-Séverin, 5e. ☎ *01-42-34-93-50. Métro: Saint-Michel. Open: Mon–Sat 11 a.m.–7:30 p.m., Sun 9 a.m.–8:30 p.m.*

Saint-Sulpice

This church, unfinished since the funds ran out in the mid-18th century, houses three of Eugène Delacroix's greatest masterpieces: *Jacob Wrestling with the Angel, Heliodorus Driven from the Temple,* and *St. Michael Vanquishing the Devil.* And that's not all: During both equinoxes and at the midday winter solstice, sunlight hits the bronze meridian line running along the north–south transept, climbs the obelisk to the globe on top, and lights the cross. The organ here is one of the grandest in Paris, built in 1781. More recently, and to the chagrin of the church caretakers, Saint-Sulpice has become a tourist hot spot due to its feature in Dan Brown's *The Da Vinci Code.* Among other things, the book suggests that the church had been built on the site of a round pagan temple, with the meridian line as the original outline of its boundaries. This is all untrue; however, it doesn't make this beautiful and grand church any less interesting to visit.

Place Saint-Sulpice, 6e. ☎ *01-42-34-59-65. Métro: Saint-Sulpice. Open: Daily 7 a.m.– 7:30 p.m.*

Paris's Bridges

When you buy Métro tickets, have a look at the logo. What looks like the profile of a woman in a circle is actually an artistic rendering of the Seine as it meanders through Paris. Here are just a few of the works of art spanning that river.

Petit Pont

A bridge has spanned the Seine from the Left Bank to the Île de la Cité since the times of Julius Caesar, who wrote about one in his *Commentaries.* The current incarnation is the Petit Pont (Little Bridge), which was built in 1853.

Pont des Arts

The Pont des Arts is one of Paris's prettiest bridges. It's a seven-arched pedestrian-only footbridge connecting the Louvre and the Académie Française that originally opened in 1804 and was the first iron bridge on the Seine. It suffered much bomb damage during World War I and World War II, and barges often ran into it. It finally collapsed in 1979 and was replaced with this steel version in 1984. You see plenty of artists painting the views of the northern tip of Île de la Cité, the Louvre, and the Académie Française, as well as pedestrians navigating the potted plants on their way to the Louvre. In warm weather, it's a popular picnic spot. Art exhibits are occasionally displayed. This is one place perfect for photo ops.

Pont Neuf

The 12-arched Pont Neuf (New Bridge) is probably Paris's most famous bridge, and its design marks the end of the Middle Ages. Started in 1578, it was finally completed in 1603 and opened to the public by Henri IV in 1603. A statue of Henri IV astride a horse divides the bridge into its two spans, which are anchored on the tip of Île de la Cité.

Métro: Pont Neuf.

Pont Saint-Michel

The Pont Saint-Michel has three arches and is decorated with a large letter *N*, which causes some to mistake it for the Pont Neuf. The *N* refers to Napoléon III, who had it built in 1857 to replace the crumbling bridge that preceded it. Up until 1808, people lived in houses on the bridge.

Métro: Saint-Michel.

Paris by Guided Tour

If you're a newcomer to the wonders of Paris, an orientation tour can help you understand the city's geography. But even if you've been coming to Paris for ten years or more, one of the various tours can introduce you to sides of the city you never knew existed. As you see in this chapter, you have many good reasons for taking a guided tour. In fact, being shown around by guides whose enthusiasm makes the city come to life can be the high point of your entire trip.

Embarking on a bus

Paris is the perfect city to explore on your own, but if time is a priority, or your energy is at low ebb, consider taking an introductory bus tour. The top tour-bus company in town is Grayline's **Cityrama** (☎ **01-44-55-60-00;** www.cityrama.com), which has a 1½-hour, top-sights tour daily at 10 a.m., 11:30 a.m., and 2:30 p.m. during the winter and at 10 a.m., 11:45 a.m., and 2:45 p.m. during the summer. The cost is 20€ adults, 10€ children 4 to 11, free for children 3 and under. Cityrama also offers various full-day tours of Paris from 81€ to 180€, and three- and four-hour historic and major-sights tours starting at 44€. The four-hour "Seinorama" tour (daily at 2:30 p.m.) includes a drive up the **Champs-Elysées,** a one-hour cruise on the Seine, and a stroll to the second-floor of the **Eiffel Tower.** It costs 50€ for adults, 25€ for children 11 and under.

Cityrama also offers a variety of "Paris by Night" tours with bus trips around the illuminated city and perhaps a dinner and Seine Cruise starting from 40€; more deluxe packages include a show at the **Moulin Rouge** or **Paradis Latin** or dinner in the **Eiffel Tower** (prices start at 81€). Cityrama offers free pickup from some hotels, or you can meet at their office at 2 rue des Pyramides (Métro: Pyramides), between rue Saint-Honoré and rue de Rivoli (across from the **Louvre**).

Paris L'OpenTour, 13 rue Auber, 9e (☎ **01-42-66-56-56;** www.paris-open-tour.com; Métro: Havre-Caumartin), from Paris's public transportation system (the RATP), was originally a rival of Cityrama; however, now you can book your tickets through the latter's Web site. Its bright yellow-and-green convertible double-decker buses take you to four different areas, and you listen to recorded commentary in English through a set of headphones given to you when you board. The best part about L'OpenTour is that you can buy a one- or two-day pass and hop on and off to see the city's destination at your own pace. There are four available routes:

✔ The "Paris Grand Tour" covers Paris's most central sights, minus the Islands: La Madeleine, Opéra, the Louvre, Notre-Dame, Saint-Germain-des-Prés, Musée d'Orsay, place de la Concorde, Champs-Elysées, Arc de Triomphe, Trocadéro, Eiffel Tower, and Invalides.

✔ The "Montmartre-Grands Boulevards" tour goes to the Montmartre *funiculaire* (but not up the Montmartre hill), the Gare du Nord, Gare de l'Est, and the Grands Boulevards.

✔ The "Bastille-Bercy Tour" goes east to Notre-Dame, the Bibliothèque Nationale de François Mitterrand, Gare de Lyon, and Parc Bercy.

✔ The "Montparnasse-Saint-Germain-des-Prés" tour goes to the Jardin du Luxembourg, the Observatory, the Tour Montparnasse, the Catacombes, Invalides, and Saint-Germain-des-Prés.

L'OpenTour makes its stops at regular city bus stops marked with the L'OpenTour logo. You can board at any of these stops and buy a pass right on the bus. The pass is also for sale at any branch of the Paris Tourist Office, L'OpenTour kiosks near the Malesherbes (8e) and Anvers (9e) bus stops, the RATP office at place de la Madeleine (8e), the main Batobus docks on the Seine, the offices of Paris L'OpenTour at 13 rue Auber (9e), and even the Cityrama office (address listed earlier). Your hotel may also have the passes for sale; ask at the reception desk.

A one-day pass costs 29€ for adults, 15€ for children 4 to 11; a two-day pass costs 32€ for adults, 15€ for children 4 to 11, and 22€ for holders of the Paris Visite pass. You can get on or off the bus as many times as you want, which, in my opinion, makes this the more worthwhile tour. The buses run daily every 15 to 30 minutes throughout the year from about 9:15 a.m. to 6:30 p.m.

The **RATP** also runs the **Balabus** (☎ 01-58-76-16-16 or 32-46 in France), a fleet of orange-and-white buses that runs only on Sundays and holidays from 12:30 to 8 p.m., April through September. The name is a portmanteau of *balade* (meaning a stroll) and a bus. According to the RATP Web site, the Balabus hits all the important Paris sites between the two ends of the line. Routes run between the Gare de Lyon and the Grand Arche de La Défense, in both directions, and cost just one Métro ticket. Look for the *Bb* symbol across the side of the bus and on signs posted along the route.

Touring by boat

One of the most beautiful ways to see Paris is by taking a sightseeing boat cruise up and down Paris's waterways. In addition to the Seine River cruises (see the "Cruising the Seine river," sidebar earlier this chapter), try a longer and more unusual tour with **Paris Canal** (☎ 01-42-40-96-97; www.pariscanal.com; Métro: Bastille). Its 2½-hour cruises leave the Musée d'Orsay or areas near the Canal Saint-Martin at 9:30 a.m. and ends at several locations — the most popular (and original) tour being Orsay to the Parc de la Villette. The boat passes under the Bastille and enters the Canal Saint-Martin for a lazy journey along the tree-lined quai Jemmapes. You cruise under bridges and through many locks. The boat leaves the Parc de la Villette at 2:30 p.m. for the same voyage in reverse, in front of the folie des visites du parc sign and returns to quai d'Orsay at 5 p.m. Other trips include full tours of the Seine outside the city limits, some heading to the Stade de France (Paris's ever-popular sports stadium) and even onto the Marne River, giving a taste of the local suburbs and countryside. Reservations are essential. The trip costs 18€ for adults 26 and over, 15€ for seniors 60 and over and adults and kids 12 to 25, and 11€ for kids 4 to 11.

If you have restless young children, the wait for the water to rise at each lock may prove too long. You may want to consider one of the shorter Seine boat trips mentioned earlier or take the canal cruise one way and travel back by Métro.

Canauxrama (☎ 01-42-39-15-00; www.canauxrama.com; Métro: Jaurès) offers 2½-hour tours similar to Paris Canal's at 9:45 a.m. and 2:30 p.m., leaving from Port l'Arsenal in the 12e and ending at the Parc de la Villette in the 19e, as well as through the Canal Saint-Denis, the Marne River, and the typical Seine boat cruise. The cost is 16€ for adults, 8.50€ for children 4 to 11, free for children 3 and under. Reservations are required.

Horsing around: A guided tour at 2 horsepower

Cruising around Paris in a tiny car with an open roof and a hilarious tour guide is a terrific way to see the city! The Citroën 2CV (meaning 2 *chevaux,* or 2 horsepower) was to France what the VW Beetle was to the United States, and it was France's most popular car from its debut before World War II up to 1990, when Citroën stopped production. Now you can tour Paris in its best-loved car with **4 Roues Sous 1 Parapluie (Four Wheels Under an Umbrella;** ☎ 08-00-80-06-31 inside France or 06-67-32-26-68 outside France; www.4roues-sous-1parapluie.com). One to three people can choose from numerous tours that introduce essential monuments such as the Eiffel Tower, Notre-Dame, and the Place de la Concorde, or see plazas and sites not normally frequented by tourists, but that are still very much a part of the city's charm: a *Da Vinci Code* tour, an *Amélie Poulain* tour through Montmartre, a tour of different gardens throughout the city, a shopping tour, a secret Paris insider tour, a romantic evening for two that throws in dinner and dessert, a cosmopolitan escapade four-hour tour. You can even custom-design your own tour. Prices start at 19€ for a half-hour trip to 144€ per person in a group of three for the four-hour Versailles or Chantilly tour. There are a variety of tours lasting a half-hour up to four hours for trips outside the city. The chauffeur/tour guides are very funny and full of knowledge, and each speaks English and French. These are not big cars, so a three-hour three-person (adult) tour could get uncomfortable. Reservations are required by telephone or online.

Walking your way across Paris

Paris Walks (☎ 01-48-09-21-40; www.paris-walks.com) is a popular English-language outfit offering fascinating two-hour guided walks with such themes as Paris during the Revolution, Hemingway's Paris, the Marais, the Village of Montmartre, Chocolate Tour, the Latin Quarter, and the Two Islands. Call for tours being offered during your visit and for where and when to meet — usually at a Métro station entrance at 10:30 a.m. and again at 2:30 p.m. Tours cost 12€ adults, 10€ students 15 to 21, and 8€ children 14 and under. They also offer weekend jaunts to places such as **Fontainebleau** or **Monet's Gardens** at Giverny.

French Links (☎ 01-45-77-01-63; www.frenchlinks.com) is run by Rachel Kaplan, the author of numerous guidebooks about living in Paris, such as *Best Buys to French Chic in Paris,* as well as the continuously updated *Paris Insider Guides,* who lets you customize your tour from a two-hour walking tour, to a full-day cultural tour. Trained, experienced guides with degrees in art and history lead you on such walks as Paris in a Basket: Gourmet Market Tour, Gastronomical Paris Tour, Parisian Art Nouveau, The Liberation of Paris, Photographer's Walking Tour, and many others. And they're happy to help you design your own tour. The talks are entertaining and fun, geared to everyone from high-school and college-age students to retirees. Four-hour tours without transportation start at 425€ for one to four people. All tours must be prebooked and prepaid with a U.S. bank check or by credit card (American Express, MasterCard, or Visa) using their secure server.

Lire et Partir (☎ 01-48-08-00-42; www.lireetpartir.com), meaning "Read and Go," was founded by Patrick Maunand, a French former engineer whose passion for literature pushed him to write three books on "literary Paris" and share his knowledge with tourists. This collective of five knowledgeable tour guides — all longtime American residents of Paris — offers tours that retrace the history of famous Parisian authors and literature. Past programmed tours of French authors have included Molière at the Louvre, Rimbaud in the Latin Quarter, and Balzac in the Marais. Tours regarding the Lost Generation writers like Gertrude Stein and Ernest Hemingway are included as well. This group is constantly updating the scope and focus of their excursions, which start at around 15€ per person for a half-day tour, with full-day tours around 30€. Most recently Lire et Partir began a Moveable Feast tour, which brings the restaurants, meals, and homes described by literary greats like Colette and Cocteau to the visitors firsthand. At 360€ per person, the three-hour tour is accompanied by readings from great works of literature and includes a coffee break in a famous literary cafe and a five-course author-inspired meal (including champagne!) cooked by Charlotte Puckette, a Cordon Bleu–trained chef and the author of *The Ethnic Paris Cookbook.*

Paris en vélo (by bike)

One of the best ways to see Paris — and burn off some of those rich dinners — is from the seat of a bike. Mayor Bertrand Delanoë, a huge proponent of improving the city's air quality, has introduced two initiatives. The first, **Paris Respire (Paris Breathes),** opens the roadways, streets and thoroughfares all across the city to bikers, inline skaters, runners, and walkers (in other words, no cars or motorbikes allowed) on Sundays between 10 a.m. and 5 p.m. Areas include on the banks of the Seine in the 1er, 4e, and 7e; the banks of the Canal Saint-Martin in the 10e; roads in the 6e near Jardin du Luxembourg (Mar–Nov); popular streets like la rue Mouffetard in the 5e or rue de la Roquette near Bastille; near Montmartre in the 18e; and the two big parks flanking the city, the Bois de Vincennes (12e) and the Bois de Boulogne (16e). There are more Paris Respire streets free during the spring and summer than during the colder seasons, check out the mayor's office Web site (www.paris.fr) for the latest updates regarding the program.

Now wildly popular, the **Velib'** bicycle-rental program brings 20,000 bikes into the city and places them in specially built bike racks in more than 1,200 stations in high-pedestrian destinations. You can spot regular Velib' users riding around the city at all hours of the day and night. The name of the program is a combination of the words *vélo* (bicycle) and *liberté* (freedom or liberty).

After you purchase your short-term subscription card (see the next paragraph), you can use any Velib' for free as long as you return it to any of the stations before a 30-minute interval. Afterward, you'll be charged 1€ for the next 30 minutes, then 2@eu for the next 30 minutes, then an additional 4€, and so on.

Buy a one-day (1€) or seven-day (5€) short-term ticket *(abonnement courte durée)* at any Velib' station or *tabac*. You'll need a valid credit card (in order to charge a temporary security deposit).

Only cards with a microchip *(une puce)* will work at the automated Velib' stations. At the time of writing, only a few American debit and credit cards carried a chip — American Express Blue cards have one, as well as Blink debit cards released by Chase Manhattan Bank. Look for a small symbol depicting waves or a chip — your credit or debit card may have one already.

Bike About Tours (☎ 06-18-80-84-92; www.bikeabouttours.com) fulfills your dreams of coasting through Parisian neighborhoods on a bicycle, led by a local English-speaking guide who feels more like a friend than a herd leader. The 3½-hour tours cost 30€ per person and includes helmet, bicycle, and insurance. All tours, which range from the big monuments to personalized "hidden Paris" adventures, leave from the statue of Charlemagne in front of Notre-Dame at 10 a.m. (and 3 p.m. during the summer). Best of all, they're led by real Parisian residents and French speakers who know Paris intimately — more than can be said for some of the competitors (some hire visiting American college students with little experience riding through the winding streets). This company also organizes private tours and rents bikes at a reasonable 15€-per-day rate. With small groups (12 people maximum), you won't get lost in the crowd, or worst, left all alone on the often-confusing maze of boulevards. The cheery tour leaders feel more like friends showing their favorite city spots to you, rather than automatically hitting really obvious sights that you can find on your own. Leisurely paced with a coffee break, but impressively complete, the tour is only enhanced by the gel-padded seats which are most welcome when speeding over cobbled streets!

Chapter 12

Shopping the Local Stores

. . . .

In This Chapter

▶ Getting an overview of Paris's shopping scene
▶ Understanding Customs and the VAT
▶ Finding the best department stores, street markets, and bargain shops
▶ Searching the prime shopping neighborhoods

. . . .

*W*ith the way the economy is in many English-speaking parts of the world, shopping in Paris may not be high on your list of things to do when visiting the city. Fortunately (or maybe not), even the window shopping is exquisite: Enticing goods are arranged just so in windows — and the prices are listed. Believe it or not, bargains *do* exist here. From the toniest haute couture shop to the hidden *dépôt-vente* (resale shop) selling last year's Yves Saint Laurent at fabulously reduced prices, even nonshoppers can find something. This chapter gives you an overview of the Parisian shopping scene, providing hints about where to find the bargains, how to get it all home, and even how to get some of your money back.

Surveying the Scene

The cost of shopping in Paris isn't always astronomical. If you plan only to buy haute couture clothing, then yes, you'll pay top prices. However, Paris has many stores that sell clothing and goods at prices comparable to what you'd pay in the United States. And some items in Paris are even cheaper than they are in your hometown, including some French and European brands of perfume and cosmetics, shoes, clothing from French-based companies such as Petit Bateau and Lacoste, and French-made porcelain, cookware, and glassware. You'll obviously pay more for any name brand imported from the United States, such as Donna Karan and Calvin Klein, and for any souvenirs in areas heavily frequented by tourists.

Keep in mind that a 19.6 percent value-added tax (VAT) is tacked on to the price of most products, which means that most things cost less at home. (For details on getting a VAT refund, see the next section "Getting the VAT back.") Appliances, paper products, housewares, computer supplies, electronics, and CDs are notoriously expensive in France, but checking out prices of French products before your trip can help you recognize a bargain.

Probably the best time to find a bargain in Paris is during the government-mandated twice-annual sales *(soldes)* in January and July when merchandise gets marked down at least 30 percent and up to 70 percent during the final week. You'll often see lines of Parisians outside their favorite stores the first days of the sales. If you can brave the crowds, you just may find the perfect designer outfit at a fraction of its retail price. *Note:* Though the sales are supposed to last two weeks, they often run much longer, often into the next month, according to the amount of merchandise left.

Generally, store hours are Monday through Saturday from 9:30 a.m. (sometimes 10 a.m.) to 7 p.m., and later on Thursday evenings, without a break for lunch. Some smaller stores are closed Monday or Monday mornings, and break for lunch for one to three hours, beginning at around 1 p.m., but this schedule is becoming increasingly rare. Small stores also may be closed for all or part of August and on some days around Christmas and Easter. Sunday shopping is gradually making inroads in Paris but is limited mostly to tourist areas; try the Carrousel du Louvre at the Louvre, rue de Rivoli across from the Louvre, rue des Francs-Bourgeois in the Marais, and the Champs-Elysées. The department stores are open the five Sundays before Christmas, and occasionally one or two Sundays during the annual sales.

Politeness is imperative when you shop in Paris. Always greet salespeople at smaller stores with *"Bonjour, madame"* or *"Bonjour, monsieur"* when you arrive (Appendix B can help with pronunciation). And regardless of whether you buy anything, say, *"Merci, au revoir"* ("Thank you, goodbye") when you leave.

Clothing sizes are different around the world. In French men's trousers, for example, add 10 to the waist size you wear in U.S. clothing to get the French size. To determine what size you need to look for, check out Table 12-1, which lists conversions for U.S. and Continental sizes.

Paris Shopping

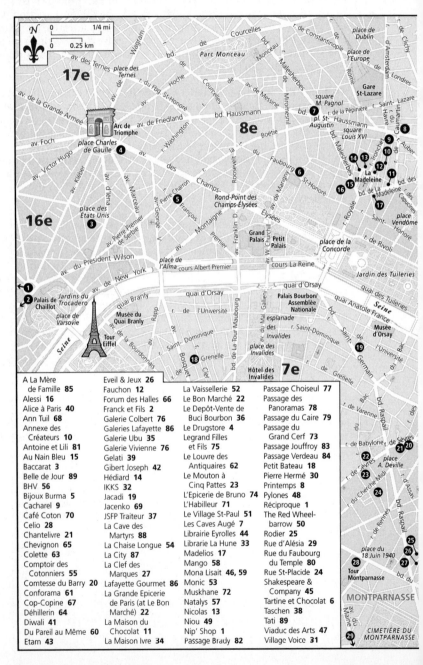

A La Mère
de Famille **85**
Alessi **16**
Alice à Paris **40**
Ann Tuil **68**
Annexe des
Créateurs **10**
Antoine et Lili **81**
Au Nain Bleu **15**
Baccarat **3**
Belle de Jour **89**
BHV **56**
Bijoux Burma **5**
Cacharel **9**
Café Coton **70**
Celio **28**
Chantelivre **21**
Chevignon **65**
Colette **63**
Comptoir des
Cotonniers **55**
Comtesse du Barry **20**
Conforama **61**
Cop-Copine **67**
Déhillerin **64**
Diwali **41**
Du Pareil au Même **60**
Etam **43**

Eveil & Jeux **26**
Fauchon **12**
Forum des Halles **66**
Franck et Fils **2**
Galerie Colbert **76**
Galeries Lafayette **86**
Galerie Ubu **35**
Galerie Vivienne **76**
Gelati **39**
Gibert Joseph **42**
Hédiard **14**
IKKS **32**
Jacadi **19**
Jacenko **69**
JSFP Traiteur **37**
La Cave des
Martyrs **88**
La Chaise Longue **54**
La City **87**
La Clef des
Marques **27**
Lafayette Gourmet **86**
La Grande Epicerie
de Paris (at Le Bon
Marché) **22**
La Maison du
Chocolat **11**
La Maison Ivre **34**

La Vaissellerie **52**
Le Bon Marché **22**
Le Depôt-Vente de
Buci Bourbon **36**
Le Drugstore **4**
Legrand Filles
et Fils **75**
Le Louvre des
Antiquaires **62**
Le Mouton à
Cinq Pattes **23**
L'Epicerie de Bruno **74**
L'Habilleur **71**
Le Village St-Paul **51**
Les Caves Augé **7**
Librairie Eyrolles **44**
Librarie La Hune **33**
Madelios **17**
Mango **58**
Mona Lisait **46, 59**
Monic **53**
Muskhane **72**
Natalys **57**
Nicolas **13**
Niou **49**
Nip' Shop **1**
Passage Brady **82**

Passage Choiseul **77**
Passage des
Panoramas **78**
Passage du Caire **79**
Passage du
Grand Cerf **73**
Passage Jouffroy **83**
Passage Verdeau **84**
Petit Bateau **18**
Pierre Hermé **30**
Printemps **8**
Pylones **48**
Réciproque **1**
The Red Wheel-
barrow **50**
Rodier **25**
Rue d'Alésia **29**
Rue du Faubourg
du Temple **80**
Rue St-Placide **24**
Shakespeare &
Company **45**
Tartine et Chocolat **6**
Taschen **38**
Tati **89**
Viaduc des Arts **47**
Village Voice **31**

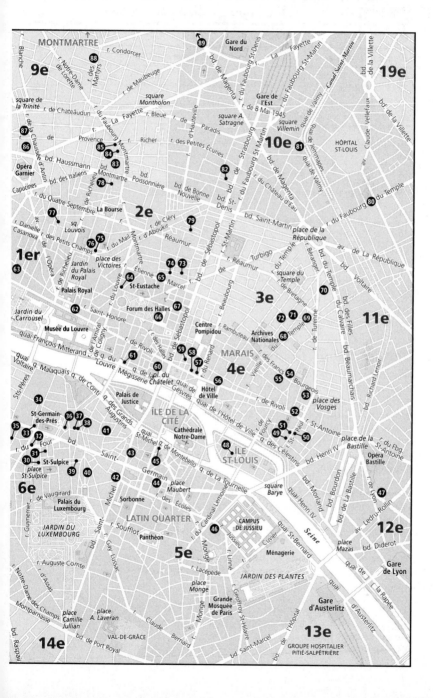

Table 12-1		The Right Fit: Size Conversions	
U.S.	*Continental*	*U.S.*	*Continental*
Women's Clothes		*Women's Shoes*	
4	36	5	36
6	38	6	37
8	40	7	38
10	42	8	39
12	44	9	40
14	46	10	41
Men's Shirts		*Men's Shoes*	
14½	37	7	39½
15	38	8	41
15½	39	9	42
16	41	10	43
16½	42	11	44½
17	43	12	46

Getting the VAT back

Whenever you spend more than 175€ in a single store, you're entitled to a partial refund on the value-added tax (VAT), also referred to in France as TVA. The refund, however, isn't automatic. Food, wine, and tobacco don't count, and the refund is granted only on purchases that you take out of the country — not on merchandise that you ship home. The amount of the refund varies; it's 12 percent in Galeries Lafayette and Printemps, and it may be anywhere from 15 percent to 18 percent at smaller boutiques.

When applying for a refund, you must show the store clerk your pass-port to prove your eligibility. You're then given an export sales document (in triplicate — two pink sheets and a green one), which you must sign, and usually an envelope addressed to the store.

Two private tax refund companies operate in Paris: the bigger **Global Blue** (www.global-blue.com) and **Premier Tax Free** (www.premier taxfree.com).

When you spend more than 175€ in a store that participates in Global Blue's Europe Tax-Free shopping program (indicated by the tax-free sticker in the store's windows), you're given a Tax-Free Shopping Cheque that shows the amount of refund owed to you when you leave the country. Have this check stamped by a Customs officer in the airport, and then take it to the special Global Blue counter for an instant refund. Global Blue offices are located in Travelex boutiques at the Charles de Gaulle Airport at Terminal 1, arrivals level; Terminal 2A, departures level; Terminal 2B, arrivals; Terminal 2C, departures level; Terminal 2F, departures, transit, and arrivals levels; and in Terminal 3 on the departures level. In Orly Airport, there are two Global Blue offices, in Orly South, Terminal 1, and at arrivals Gate H.

It works the same way with Premier Tax Free. Look for premier tax free stickers in the windows of stores participating in this program, and spend more than 175€ to get your refund. Premier Tax Free offices are located at Kanoo desk in the American Express building, 11 rue Scribe, 9e (Métro: Opéra); the Kanoo desk on the basement level, Women's Fashion & Accessories in Printemps, 64 bd. Haussmann (Métro: Saint-Lazare); at two I.G.E. locations on the Champs-Elysées: no. 26 and no. 79 (Métro: Franklin D. Roosevelt and Charles de Gaulle–Étoile, respectively); at the MultiCHANGE bureaus at 7 rue de Castiglione (Métro: Tuileries), 8 bd. de la Madeleine (Métro: Madeleine), 161 rue de Rennes (Métro: Montparnasse-Bienvenüe), and 180 bd. Saint-Germain (Métro: Saint-Germain-des-Prés); in Charles de Gaulle Airport Travelex offices (see the Global Blue section earlier); and in the Travelex desks in Orly South and West.

Department stores that cater to foreign visitors, such as Au Printemps, Le Bon Marché, and Galeries Lafayette, have special *détaxe* areas where clerks prepare your invoices for you. You must present your passport. Otherwise, when you leave the country, bring all documents to the airport's *détaxe* booth and have a Customs official stamp them. Enclose the appropriate document (the pink one) in the store envelope the clerk provided when you bought your merchandise and mail it from the airport from which you're leaving the European Union. Although the wait for a refund in a check can be anywhere from one to six months, some of the big department stores can give you your rebate immediately, either in cash or by crediting your credit card. Travelers leaving from Charles de Gaulle Airport can visit the *détaxe* refund point in Terminal 1 on level 1 (boarding) or in Terminal 2 at halls A, B, C, or F near the most central departures entrance. At Orly, the *détaxe* booth is in Orly West on the departure level.

 Whenever you're claiming a tax refund, try to arrive at the airport as early as possible because you must show everything you're declaring to a Customs official, and you may have to wait in line. Plus, after you finish with *détaxe,* you must stand in line again to check your luggage.

If you're traveling by train, go to the *détaxe* area in the station before boarding because you can't have your refund documents processed on the train. Give the three sheets to the Customs official, who stamps them and returns a pink and a green copy to you. Keep the green copy and mail the pink copy to the store.

Your reimbursement is either mailed as a check (in euro) or credited to your credit card account, which is better, because you may find it difficult to cash a check for euro in your home country. If you don't receive your tax refund within six months, write to the store, giving the date of purchase and the location where the forms were given to Customs officials. Include a photocopy of your green refund sheet.

Getting your goodies through Customs

Returning **U.S. citizens,** who've been away for 48 hours or more, are allowed to bring back, once every 30 days, $800 worth of merchandise duty-free (a *duty* is a tax). You're charged a flat duty of 3 percent on the next $1,000 worth of purchases; on gifts, the duty-free limit is $100 (any item that costs more than $100 is subject to the full tax). U.S. citizens have the right to bring back up to 200 cigarettes, 100 cigars, and 1 liter of alcohol duty free; any larger amount will be taxed regardless of whether you've reached the $800 limit. You can't bring fresh food into the United States (ignore what the people in the Paris duty-free stores tell you — fresh meats and cheeses are *not* allowed); canned foods, however, are allowed.

Citizens of the United Kingdom and **Ireland** who are returning from a European Union (EU) country have no limit on what they can bring back from an EU country, as long as the items are for personal use (including gifts), and the necessary duty and taxes have been paid. Limits are set at: 3,200 cigarettes, 200 cigars, 3kg (6.6 pounds) of smoking tobacco, 10 liters of spirits, 90 liters of wine, and 110 liters of beer.

Canada allows its citizens a once-a-year C$750 exemption after spending seven days out of the country, and you're allowed to bring back duty free: 200 cigarettes, 50 cigars, 200 grams of smoking tobacco, and 1.5 liters of wine or 1.14 liters of liquor. In addition, you can mail gifts to Canada from abroad at a value of up to C$60 a day, provided they're unsolicited and don't contain alcohol, tobacco, or advertising matter. Write on the package "Unsolicited Gift, under $60 Value." All valuables need to be declared on Form Y-38 before your departure from Canada, including serial numbers of valuables you already own, such as expensive foreign cameras.

The duty-free allowance in **Australia** is A$900 (A$450 for those 17 and under) and does not include tobacco or alcohol. Upon returning to Australia, citizens can bring in 250 cigarettes or 250 grams of loose tobacco, and 2.25 liters of alcohol. If you're returning with valuable goods that you already own, such as foreign-made cameras, you need to file Form B263.

The duty-free allowance for **New Zealand** is NZ$700. Citizens 18 and older can bring in 200 cigarettes or 50 cigars, or 250 grams total of tobacco products, plus 4.5 liters of wine or beer, or up to three bottles of liquor products that don't exceed 1.125 liters.

Checking Out the Big Names

Check out the "Paris Shopping" map for the locations of the stores listed here.

BHV

This store near the Marais and next door to the Hôtel de Ville has become an unsung hero of good deals and great selection of all different kinds of merchandise. BHV (Bazar de l'Hôtel de Ville) sells the usual clothing, cosmetics, luggage, and leather ware at decent prices, but it's really worth a visit because of its giant basement-level hardware store with everything you need to fix up your home. After a recent expansion, a whole separate BHV Homme building has clothing and accessories exclusively for men. You can also check out its very cute pet store, BHV La Niche, at 42 rue de la Verrerie (it has some of the best small dog and cat carriers I've ever seen!), or its new BHV Cave at 13 rue des Archives, which has every gadget and knickknack ever invented for the die-hard wine enthusiast.

See map p. 248. 52 rue de Rivoli, 1er. ☎ *01-42-74-90-00.* www.bhv.fr. *Métro: Hôtel de Ville.*

Forum des Halles

This was the site of the original wholesale market of Paris, where merchants would come from kilometers away to set up tables of fruits, vegetables, dairy products, and so forth. In 1971 the market was formally moved to a suburb outside the city limits, and a major RER and Métro stop — Les Halles — and a mall complex were built. The forum is the closest thing to a "mall" shopping center that you can find in Paris. In the place where once stood fishmongers and butchers of Emile Zola's *Le Ventre de Paris* (les Halles market is a centerpiece of the story), you can go clothes-shopping in the Gap, Celio, and H&M; buy CDs and DVDs at Fnac; buy furniture at Habitat; get lunch; and even see a movie at the UGC theaters on the lowest underground level. In 2007, architects Patrick Berger and Jacques Anziutti won the bid for the total redesign of the Forum des Halles, however the plans have yet to be enacted or any improvements made at the time of writing. Parisians have regarded this central area of the shopping mall as an eyesore since its redesign in 1975. Beware that the area can be seedy later on at night.

See map p. 248. 101 Porte Berger, 1er. ☎ *01-44-76-96-56.* http://en.forum deshalles.com. *Access from numerous doors surrounding the complex, on rue Rambuteau, rue Berger, and rue de Pierre Lescot; or enter directly from Métro station. Métro: Les Halles.*

Franck et Fils

Those in the know refer to this store in the chic Passy neighborhood as "Paris's smallest department store," but its size is by no means a measure of its quality. A bit off the beaten path and owned by the same group as Le Bon Marché, Franck et Fils for years was an adorably petite and classically designed department store with areas selling Chanel, Burberry, and Pierre Cardin to the bourgeois area residents and the occasional tourist. However, in 2010, it was totally renovated with a new look (think 21st-century boutique hotel) and a new bevy of hip and youthful designers. The top floor features urban couture favorites such as ACNE, Alexander Wang, APC, and Helmut Lang, while the ground floor has haute boutiques like Stella McCartney and Lanvin. Fashionistas will not be disappointed.

See map p. 248. 80 rue de Passy, 16e. ☎ *01-44-14-38-74.* www.francketfils. fr. *Métro: La Muette.*

Galeries Lafayette

Of the three major Paris department stores, Galeries Lafayette is probably the most-visited by a hair due to its prolific advertising campaigns — usually huge, colorful posters featuring French supermodels, often in avant-garde clothing and whimsically styled to match the season. Merchandise here ranges from good to excellent with lots of deals during the sales. Look for women's clothing from Sonia Rykiel, Comptoir des Cotonniers, and agnès b. And check out the gourmet grocery store, Lafayette Gourmet, in the men's store. Main store restaurants include Häagen-Dazs; Lina's gourmet sandwiches; Fauchon tearoom and restaurant; McDonald's; Café Sushi; and Lafayette Café on the sixth floor, which has great views of Paris (it's a self-serve cafeteria and a personal favorite). If you don't already have one, ask at the front desk for the 10 percent discount coupon, good in most departments. All the advertising has only benefited Galeries Lafayette: This store gets downright crowded, and if you visit during the sales, pace yourself or you can become thoroughly fatigued. *Détaxe* is 12 percent here.

See map p. 248. 40 bd. Haussmann, 9e. ☎ *01-42-82-34-56.* www.galeries lafayette.com. *Métro: Opéra or Chaussée-d'Antin.*

Le Bon Marché

The oldest department store in France (and, purportedly, the world) and is Left Bank's only *grand magasin,* and it's a wonderful respite from the multibuilding, crowded shopping experience of Au Printemps and Galeries Lafayette. Elegant, but small enough to be manageable, much of the store's merchandise is exquisite and includes designers such as Sonia Rykiel, Bensimon, Vivienne Westwood, Burberry, and Yohji Yamamoto. The main store's third floor is particularly renowned for its large shoe selection and grand lingerie department (where dressing rooms have phones to summon your salesperson). The basement features a beautiful bookstore and upscale toys as well; in fact, many bourgeois Parisians head to Le Bon Marché for their every shopping need. Thus, rarely is anything cheap. Make sure to visit Le Grand Épicerie next door (is there anything you can't get at Le Bon Marché?), where you can buy everything from toilet paper to truffles. The Café de la Grand Épicerie, found on the second floor in the Home Décor section in the main store, features selections chosen by this gourmet grocery store's food, wine, and pastry professionals.

See map p. 248. 24 rue de Sèvres, 7e. ☎ *01-44-39-80-00.* www.lebonmarche. com. *Métro: Sèvres-Babylone.*

Le Drugstore

Though not a department store (it's more a mini-mall), Le Drugstore Publicis (as is it officially known) is included here because it was an important part of Parisian culture in the 1960s, and its owner, ad giant Publicis, is hoping to regain that status with a stunningly modern glass renovation that cost millions of euros. Inside is a brasserie run by a disciple of multistarred French chef Alain Ducasse (waitstaff is clothed by French designer Jean-Charles Castelbajac); an international newsstand; a gift shop; a drugstore (naturally); gourmet food, wine, and cigar stores; a Kiehl's store; and a Shu Uemura beauty products shop. Also here are movie theaters and a bar with a terrace overlooking the Champs and the Arc de Triomphe. Owned by Publicis since the late '50s, Le Drugstore was the height of cool in the 1960s when it was one of the few places in Paris you could pick up a pack of cigarettes or a magazine at 2 a.m. (and in a sense, it still is since most *tabacs,* not to mention newsstands, are closed by 11 p.m.). Although its new revamping did not make it the hip place it once was, there are plenty of history and luxury items to go around while stomping around the Champs-Elysées.

See map p. 248. 131 av. du Champs-Elysées, 8e. ☎ *01-44-43-79-00. Métro: Georges V, Charles de Gaulle–Étoile. Open: Daily 10 a.m.–2 a.m.*

Monoprix

These Target-like stores are Paris's best-kept secret, where you can find wonderful clothing, much of it fashion-forward, at reasonable prices along with accessories, low-priced cosmetics, lingerie, and housewares. Most of the locations also have large grocery stores (although prices tend to be higher than other supermarkets; see the following Tip). The Champs-Elysées branch at no. 52 is open until midnight Monday through Saturday.

Various locations. ☎ *08-10-08-40-00.*

For those looking for grocery stores that are a little more reasonable than Monoprix, **Le Marché Franprix** is an inexpensive grocer that still sells good-quality vegetables, fruits, cheeses, mustards, and all the normal French sundries. Its stores are on practically every other street throughout the city.

Printemps

Printemps (formally and formerly known as *Au Printemps*) is one of Paris's largest department stores. Merchandise is sold in three different buildings: Printemps de l'Homme (menswear), Printemps de la Maison (furniture and accessories), and Printemps de la Mode (women and children's fashion). Well-known designers represented here include (but are certainly not limited to) Dolce & Gabbana, Armani, and Burberry. Fashion shows take place under the 1920s glass cupola (seventh floor) at 10 a.m. every Tuesday year-round, and every Friday from March through October. You can easily spend a day here, and there are eight restaurants scattered throughout the three buildings. The beauty department in the main building is, according to Printemps, the largest in the world. There is a fabulous selection of lingerie in the basement level of the main building, as well. *Détaxe* is offered at 12 percent here.

See map p. 248. 64 bd. Haussmann, 9e. ☎ *01-42-82-50-00.* www.printemps.com. *Métro: Havre-Caumartin. Open: Mon–Sat 9:35 a.m.–7 p.m. (until 10 p.m. Thurs).*

Tati

Quite frankly, Tati is a tacky store full of cheap clothing, but where else can you find the a perfectly funky going-out top for 2€? Or wear-for-one-season shoes at 10€? In fact, you never know what you may find here if you dig; the occasional gem rewards those who are persistent. Tati also has a jewelry branch called Tati Or, an eyewear store known as Tati Optic, and a travel agency called Tati Vacances. Although this purveyor of cheap things has been threatened with bankruptcy in the past, the perpetual existence of bargain seekers and a global recession has kept these rock-bottom deals happily available.

See map p. 248. 4 bd. Rochechouart, 18e. ☎ *01-55-29-52-20.* www.tati.fr *Métro: Barbès-Rochechouart. Other branches are located at 68 av. du Maine (*☎ *01-56-89-06-80; Métro: Gaîté) and 30 av. d'Italie (*☎ *01-53-80-97-70; Métro: Place d'Italie).*

Taking It to the Street (Markets)

The huge **Marché aux Puces de la Porte de Saint-Ouen** (18e), purportedly the largest flea market in the world, is a real shopping adventure and although you probably won't snag a bargain, it's still well worth the visit. It features several thousand stalls, carts, shops, and vendors selling everything from vintage clothing (see if you can find the vendor whose specialty is wearing her merchandise from the mid-1800s) to antique chandeliers, paintings, furniture, and toys. You need to arrive early to snag the deals — if you can find any. The best times for bargains are right at opening time and just before closing time. To reach the market, take the Métro to the Porte de Clignancourt stop; exit onto avenue de la Porte de Clignancourt. (You also can exit onto boulevard Ornano, which turns into avenue de la Porte de Clignancourt.) Head north a block and cross beneath an underpass; the markets begin on your left. It's open Saturday through Monday 9 a.m. to 8 p.m.

Starting at the underpass just past the Clignancourt Métro stop, you'll see stalls selling cheap junk, but don't stop here! Turn left onto rue des Rosiers, the market's main street. Be alert — pickpockets roam the markets, especially the stalls on the periphery.

Don't pay the ticketed price or the price the vendor first quotes you; always haggle. You can usually get at least 10 percent off.

Visitors to Paris usually choose the Clignancourt market over the convivial market at **Porte de Vanves** (14e), a gem still waiting to be discovered. Probably the smallest of the fleas, it's nevertheless a good place to browse among friendly dealers. To reach the market, take the Métro to the Porte de Vanves stop, exit at boulevard Brune, follow it east to avenue Georges Lafenestre, and turn right. It's open Saturday and Sunday 8:30 a.m. to 1 p.m. A cheap clothing market takes its place after 1 p.m. Other flea markets include one at **Porte de Montreuil** (Métro: Porte de Montreuil) and another at **place d'Aligre**, 14e (Métro: Ledru-Rollin; open: 9 a.m. to noon). Much more downscale, these markets give the term *junk* a whole new meaning.

Scoring Bargains in Paris

The savvy Parisian waits for sales, knows the addresses of discounters, and knows that some of the best fashion deals are found in resale shops that deal directly with designer showrooms for half-price designer clothing that has been worn on a runway or used in a fashion shoot. And four words are the key to her world: *soldes* (sales), *dégriffés* (designer wear with the labels cut out), *stock* (overstock), and *dépôt-vente* (resale). Most *dépôts-ventes* are on the Right Bank in the 8e, 16e, and 17e arrondissements. If you're itching for a bargain after shopping for full-price items, visit one of the streets where discount stores abound:

- ✔ **Rue d'Alésia**, 14e (Métro: Alésia), is filled with French designer discount outlets selling last year's overstock at up to 70 percent below retail and boutiques that buy overstock and sell name brands at big discounts. The stock boutiques are more downscale than their sister shops; be prepared to rifle through the racks to find the gems. Outlets include **Chevignon** at no. 122, **Cop-Copine** at no. 118 **Darjeeling** (a French lingerie brand) at no. 68, **Evolutif** (selling brands like Kenzo and Canali) at no. 98, **Marrionaud** at no. 70, **Nafnaf** at no. 143, **Rodier** at no. 82, **Tout Compte Fait** at no. 101 bis, **Via Veneto** at no. 72 (for Dior, Armani, and other designer menswear), **Jacadi** at no. 116, and **Sonia Rykiel** at no. 65.

- ✔ **Rue du Faubourg du Temple**, 11e (Métro: Goncourt), in up-and-coming Oberkampf and Belleville, is still a secret to some Parisians, but not to those looking for trendy and fashionable clothes of all styles at rock-bottom prices. Search through many of the stores for gems, but know that **Samrina et Louis Mod** at no. 54 has funky clothes for women, usually synthetic but still a huge bargain. **Kxana** at no. 89 is a big store with clothing and accessories (and even changing rooms!).

- ✔ **Rue Saint-Placide**, 6e (Métro: Sèvres-Babylone), is also a street of dreams with many discount stores, including **Le Mouton à Cinq Pattes** (8 rue Saint-Placide) and **La Générale de Pharmacie** (no. 58), which sells French cosmetics and skincare products at up to half the normal prices. Discounted no-name shoes and housewares are also sold on this street. Perpendicular to Le Bon Marché, Saint-Placide is quite a relief on the pocketbook after perusing the wares at the luxury department store.

You can also try these discount stores spread throughout the city.

Annexe des Créateurs

This is made up of two stores — one devoted to selling gently worn designer daywear, the other to barely worn evening wear. If you don't mind wearing resale togs, you could save yourself between 40 percent and 75 percent off the retail price of the items. The store has been described as an Ali Baba's cave entirely devoted to luxury, and the description is apt. You find names like Chanel, Dior, Thierry Mugler, Louis Vuitton, Hermès, Vivienne Westwood, and Jean-Paul Gaultier.

See map p. 248. 19 rue Godot de Mauroy, 9e. www.annexedescreateurs.com. ☎ *01-42-65-46-40. Métro: Havre-Caumartin or Madeleine.*

La Clef des Marques

This pair of huge and fairly disorganized stores sells everything from baby clothes to grown-up couture by big names like Paul & Joe, Helmut Lang, and Versace. Women can find Diesel jeans here for under 50€, while men might score a Gianfranco Ferré button-down for 30€. They also sell shoes, lingerie, sports clothes, and accessories. Racks are overfull so you have to hunt a bit for a bargain.

See map p. 248. 124 bd. Raspail, 6e. ☎ *01-45-49-31-00. Métro: Notre-Dame des Champs.*

Le Dépôt-Vente de Buci Bourbon

This resale store is actually two shops right next to each other with vintage and not-so-old clothing and accessories for men and women along with gently used furniture.

See map p. 248. 4 and 6 rue Bourbon Le Chateau, 6e. ☎ *01-46-34-45-05 and 01-46-34-28-28. Métro: Saint-Germain-des-Prés or Mabillon.*

Le Mouton à Cinq Pattes

Visit "the sheep with five legs" when you're feeling energetic — racks at this *dégriffé* store are simply packed and the store is often crowded. It carries extremely wellknown designer names (most of the tags are ripped out) on women's, men's, and children's clothing, shoes, and accessories. The stock changes constantly, so if you see something you like, grab it; it won't be there the next time.

See map p. 248. 8 and 18 rue Saint-Placide, 6e. ☎ *01-45-48-86-26 for all stores. Métro: Sèvres-Babylone. Another branch is located at 138 bd. Saint-Germain (*☎ *01-43-26-49-25).*

L'Habilleur

For those who love soft things and delicate drapings, this sprawling loft-like space has a great selection of sweaters, jeans, scarves, and most other desirable items for men and women. You can find 50-percent-off discounts from brands like Issey Miyake, Fake London, Paul & Joe, and Roberto Collina.

See map p. 248. 44 rue de Poitou, 3e. ☎ **01-48-87-77-12.** *Métro: Saint-Sébastien–Froissart.*

Nip' Shop

Yves Saint Laurent, Max Mara, Paula Ka, Sonia Rykiel, and Guy Laroche are big labels here, but lesser-known designers are also represented. It's in the same neighborhood as Réciproque (see below) but much more intimate. Ask the smiling woman who runs this shop for suggestions and advice; she knows her wares and will find the item that has been waiting for you all along.

See map p. 248. 6 rue Edmond-About, 16e. ☎ **01-45-04-66-19.** *Métro: Rue de la Pompe.*

Réciproque

This series of *dépôts-ventes* (resale shops) on rue de la Pompe claims to be the largest in Paris, with over 6,970 sq. m (7,500 sq. ft.) devoted to clothing for men, women, and children. Exhaust yourself among the jewelry, furs, belts, antiques, scarves, and designer purses (Hermès, Dior, Gucci, and Louis Vuitton are just a few of the names I've seen). A careful search can result in Hermès scarves and ties at a third of their normal price, as well as gently-worn Chanel suits that begin around 800€ (that's about a quarter of the price of a new one).

See map p. 248. 89, 92, 93, 95, 97, and 101 rue de la Pompe, 16e. ☎ **01-47-04-30-28.** *No. 89 is a shop of "objets" with small accessories and jewels; nos. 93, 95, and 101 are the different categories of women's clothing and shoes; and the men's shop is across the street at no. 92. Métro: Rue de la Pompe. Closed Mon.*

Hitting the Great Shopping Neighborhoods

You don't need beaucoup bucks to afford to shop in Paris (except for certain stores in the 8e!). Great deals for every taste and dollar amount can be found. Read this section to get a significant head start in the hunt for that perfect item.

The cost of high fashion: The 8e

Head for the 8e to see why people like Carrie Bradshaw and Saudi princes in need of a luxury shopping spree jet to Paris. Nearly every French designer is based on two streets — **avenue Montaigne** (Métro: Alma-Marceau, Franklin D. Roosevelt) and **rue du Faubourg Saint-Honoré** (Métro: Concorde) — where bills of more than 1,000€ are expected, and snooty sales clerks are par for the course. You can still have a good time window-shopping here (and get an idea of what's in style), even if you don't have a platinum card.

Although avenue Montaigne and rue du Faubourg Saint-Honor boast some of the same big designer names, they're completely different in temperament. Avenue Montaigne is wide, graceful, lined with chestnut trees, and undeniably hip, attracting the likes of **Dolce & Gabbana** at no. 54 (☎ 01-42-25-68-78) and **Prada** at no. 10 (☎ 01-53-23-99-40). Other designers on this street include **Céline**, no. 36 (☎ 01-56-89-07-92); **Chanel**, no. 42 (☎ 01-47-23-74-12); **Christian Dior**, no. 30 (☎ 01-40-73-73-73); **Salvatore Ferragamo**, no. 45 (☎ 01-47-23-36-37); **Georges Rech**, no. 2 (☎ 01-47-20-15-16); **Giorgio Armani**, no. 18 (☎ 01-42-61-55-09); **Gucci**, no. 60 (☎ 01-56-69-80-80); **Nina Ricci**, no. 39(☎ 01-40-88-67-60); **Emanuel Ungaro**, no. 2 (☎ 01-53-57-00-00); **Valentino**, no. 17 (☎ 01-47-23-64-61); and **Versace**, no. 45 (☎ 01-47-42-88-02).

Rue du Faubourg Saint-Honoré is jammed with shoppers walking along the small, narrow sidewalks. Begin at the rue Royale intersection and head west. **Prada** is located at no. 6 (☎ 01-58-18-63-30); **Yves Saint-Laurent** for women is at no. 38 (☎ 01-42-65-74-59), for men at no. 32 (☎ 01-53-05-80-80). Other high-quality or haute couture designers include **Comme des Garçons**, no. 54 (☎ 01-53-30-27-27); **Givenchy**, no. 28 (☎ 01-42-68-31-00); **Lanvin**, no. 22 (☎ 01-44-71-33-33); **Chloé**, no. 56 (☎ 01-44-94-33-00); **Sonia Rykiel**, no. 70 (☎ 01-42-65-20-81); **Pierre Cardin**, no. 59 (☎ 01-42-66-92-25); and **Missoni**, no. 1 (☎ 01-44-51-96-96).

Classically hip: The 3e and 4e

There's something for everyone in the Marais: Divide your time between culture (15 different museums are right here) and commercialism in this beautiful neighborhood crammed with magnificent Renaissance mansions, artists' studios, secret courtyards, and some of the most original shops in the city. **Rue des Francs-Bourgeois** (Métro: Saint-Paul or Rambuteau), the highlight of the area, is full of small shops selling everything from fashion to jewels. And its stores are open on Sunday! **Rue des Rosiers** (Métro: Saint-Paul) is a fashion destination in its own right, with hot designers flanking Jewish falafel joints. The Marais is a relatively small area, so don't be afraid to ramble down the tiniest lane whenever whim dictates. Part of the fun of this neighborhood is that it's such a mixed (shopping) bag.

Marais highlights include **Paule Ka**, 20 rue Mahler (☎ **01-40-29-96-03**), for the sort of 1960s clothing made famous by Grace Kelly, Jackie Onassis, and Audrey Hepburn; and **Autour du Monde**, 8 and 12 rue des Francs-Bourgeois (☎ **01-42-77-16-18**), which sells chic and comfortable men's and women's clothing, as well as tablecloths, tableware, linen, and other stylish home goods from the innovative French designer Bensimon. **Antik Batik**, 8 rue Foin (☎ **01-48-87-95-95**), is a reasonably well-known French company that features clothes inspired by world cultures; find African prints, Chinese silk outfits, colorful South American scarves and ponchos, and *salwar kameez* ensembles accompanied by Indian-pattern inspired scarves. **Noir Kennedy**, 22 rue Roi de Sicile (☎ **01-42-74-55-58**), has lots of black clothing, vintage tees, and skinny jeans for the hipster in all of us (who doesn't want Che Guevara underpants?), while **Barbara Bui,** 43 rue des Francs Bourgeois (☎ 01-48-04-05-94), has elegant, contemporary clothing at somewhat premium prices. Spanish sneaker brand **Camper,** 9 rue des Francs Bourgeois (☎ 01-48-87-09-09), has the latest in urban footwear with edgy patterns and color combinations. Also check out **Zadig et Voltaire,** 16 rue Pavée (☎ 01-44-59-39-06), a subtle and charming favorite of the well-dressed yet casual Parisian. **S. D. Spontini,** 29 rue des Francs Bourgeois (☎ 01-44-78-70-71), has chic and slim-fitting menswear that perfectly creates that trendy Euro silhouette, and **XOOS,** 39 Rue de Turenne (☎ 01-42-76-92-30), is another men's boutique if you're still searching for the perfect button-down. Covering your feet, **Jean-Claude Monderer,** 22 rue des Francs Bourgeois (☎ 01-48-04-51-41), sells stylish men's and women's sneakers, loafers, and sleek and slender going-out shoes for both sexes.

Smart and sophisticated: The 6e

Stylish young professionals with old family (called *Bon Chic Bon Genre* or BCBG) call this, one of the prettiest areas in Paris, home. Here you can shop with the BCBG amid bookstores, art and antiques galleries, high-end designer clothing shops, decently priced shoe and accessories stores, and sophisticated and trendy boutiques. You won't go thirsty with famed literary hangouts such as **Café de Flore, Les Deux Magots,** and **Brasserie Lipp** nearby.

Louis Vuitton has a huge luggage-specialized store behind Les Deux Magots on 6 place Saint-Germain (☎ 01-45-49-62-32), and **Christian Dior** is nearby at 16–18 rue de l'Abbaye (☎ 01-56-24-90-53). **Giorgio Armani** is at 149 bd. Saint-Germain (☎ 01-45-48-62-15); and **Céline** is at 58 rue de Rennes (☎ 01-45-48-58-55). Much more pleasing price-wise are Italian designers **Stefanel,** 54 rue de Rennes (☎ 01-45-44-06-07), and **Comptoir des Cotonniers,** 30 rue du Buci (☎ 01-43-54-56-73), where mothers and daughters can happily shop shoulder-to-shoulder. **The Kooples,** 61 rue de Rennes (☎ 01-42-22-41-86), a chain with exploding popularity, sells youthful and sophisticated monochrome clothing here and six other locations, much like **IKKS,** 32 rue du Four (☎ 01-45-48-73-88), whose clothing has more colors and equal sophistication. A bit more grown up is **Tara Jarmon,** 18 rue de Four (☎ 01-46-33-26-60) and 75 rue Saints Pères (☎ 01-55-44-36-14). A similar store that sells ubiquitous and authentic horizontal-striped sweaters of virile French sailors is **Saint James,** 66 rue de Rennes (☎ 01-53-63-09 82).

The **Marché Saint-Germain** at 14 rue Lobineau is a modern shopping mall that's a bit out of place in a neighborhood known for bookstores and upscale boutiques. Visit if you need to experience air-conditioning and use the restrooms; otherwise don't waste your time — why visit the Gap and Zara when the styles are the same at home but the prices higher?

The arcades

You can't speak of shopping without mentioning Paris's quaint arcades. In the 19th century, people, horses, and carriages crowded unpaved, dirty, badly lit streets. When it rained, everything turned to mud. Imagine shopping in these conditions! But one 19th-century shopkeeper looking for innovative ways to draw crowds to his store proposed displaying wares in pretty covered passageways with other merchants. And, thus, the first malls were born. These days, the charming iron and glass arcades are still shopping havens, and the 2e has Paris's greatest concentration, each with its own character.

✔ **Passage Choiseul,** 44 rue des Petits-Champs (Métro: Quatre-Septembre), dates from 1827 and is the longest and most colorful arcade, selling discount shoes and clothing and used books. French writer Céline grew up here and included it in the books *Journey to the End of Night* and *Death on the Installment Plan.*

✔ **Passage des Panoramas,** 11 bd. Montmartre and 10 rue Saint-Marc (Métro: Grands Boulevards), opened in 1800 and was enlarged with the addition of galleries Variétés, Saint-Marc, Montmartre, and Feydeau in 1834. Its stores sell stamps, clothes, and gifts, and it's the passage with the largest choice of dining options: Korean food, a cafeteria, tea salons, and bistros.

✔ **Passage Jouffroy,** across the street at 10 bd. Montmartre (Métro: Grands Boulevards), was built between 1845 and 1846. It became an instant hit as Paris's first heated gallery. After an extensive restoration of its tile floors, the gallery now houses a variety of arty boutiques, including a dollhouse store, and an Italian cafe that sells fancy kitchen gizmos such as espresso machines and vacuum-pump wine stoppers.

✔ **Passage Verdeau,** 31 bis rue du Faubourg-Montmartre (Métro: Le Peletier), was built at the same time as its neighbor, Passage Jouffroy. You can find old prints, movie stills, books, and postcards here.

✔ **Galerie Vivienne,** 4 place des Petits-Champs, 5 rue de la Banque, or 6 rue Vivienne (Métro: Bourse), is hands-down the most gorgeous of all the arcades. Its classical friezes, mosaic floors, and graceful arches have been beautifully restored. Built in 1823, this neoclassical arcade is now a national monument that attracts upscale art galleries, hair salons, and boutiques, including Jean-Paul Gaultier and a Louboutin display with heels so high that you might just gag.

✔ **Galerie Colbert** is linked to the adjoining Galerie Vivienne. It was built with a large rotunda and decorated in Pompeian style in 1826 to capitalize on the success of Galerie Vivienne.

✔ The pretty **Passage du Grand Cerf,** 10 rue Dussoubs (Métro: Etienne-Marcel), has more of a modern bent, with jewelry designers, trendy clothing stores, furniture stores with funky, "ethnic-inspired" pieces, decorative tchotchkes, and an ad agency.

For a complete change of pace, head over to the following arcades, but keep in mind that the neighborhoods aren't the nicest. The **Passage Brady,** 46 rue du Faubourg Saint-Denis (Métro: Strasbourg Saint-Denis), has become an exotic bazaar where Indian restaurants and spice shops scent the air; the passage opened in 1828. The **Passage du Caire,** 2 place du Caire (Métro: Sentier), is one of the oldest arcades built in 1798 to commemorate Napoléon's triumphant entry into Cairo; it reflects the Egyptomania of the time with fake columns and death masks of pharaohs on its exterior. In the heart of Paris's Sentier garment district, it's home to clothing wholesalers and manufacturers.

Young and edgy: The 2e

The second *arrondissement* has a spread of different kinds of stores that cater to Paris's most cutting-edge hip or *branché* (a synonym literally meaning "plugged in") and younger fashion crowd. The area sells a mix of high fashion, specialty niche stores, urban fashion, and discounted wares; you can find the Jean-Paul Gaultier boutique in the picturesque **Galerie Vivienne** on one end and Kookaï Le Stock on the other. The cheapest shopping is in the **Sentier area,** around the Sentier Métro stop, which is Paris's garment district, overlapping parts of the 3e and 1er. The best — but not the cheapest — shops are found within a square formed on the south by rue Rambuteau, on the west by rue du Louvre, on the north by rue Réaumur, and on the east by rue Saint-Martin. This area is where you can find hip secondhand clothes, funky club wear, and *stock boutiques* selling last season's designs at a discount.

 The neighborhood is considered to be chic and wealthy, but prostitutes still frequent the area later in the afternoon and evening, especially rue Saint-Denis.

For last year's unsold stock of women's and teen's clothing, visit **Kookaï Le Stock,** 82 rue Réaumur, 2e (☎ 01-45-08-93-69). **Espace Kiliwatch,** 64 rue Tiquetonne, 2e (☎ 01-42-21-17-37), seems like a never-ending tour through decades of vintage clothing and styles; persistence may reward you with a bargain. Meanwhile, the neighborhood mecca of club kids and design gurus is at British import **Kokon To Zai,** 48 rue Tiquetonne, 2e (☎ 01-42-36-92-41), selling well-known and emerging designers in a small store decorated in vibrant colors. **RoyalCheese,** 22 rue Tiquetonne (☎ 01-42-21-30-65), hawks streetwear like 2K T-shirts to jeans from brands like Cheap Monday. Neighboring boutiques **RoyalCheese X Vans** and **Bluecheese,** 24 rue Tiquetonne (☎ 01-40-28-06-56), specializes in the popular brand of skater sneakers and jeans only, respectively. For haute couture sophistication with an edge, head to **Jean-Paul Gaultier,** 6 rue Vivienne (☎ 01-42-86-05-05). Find clothes for all at **agnès b.,** 2, 3, 4, and 6 rue du Jour (☎ 01-40-39-96-88, 01-42-33-04-13, 01-40-13-91-27, and 01-45-08-56-56, respectively). This carefully designed store sells timelessly chic and carefully detailed outfits, with plenty of choices for the whole family (the men's store is at no. 3, children's at no. 2, women's at no. 6, and bags and accessories at no. 4).

Bohemian bourgeois: The 18e

There is some kinship between the Marais and Montmartre fashion, but les Montmartrois (citizens of Montmartre), with their offbeat outfits and offbeat jobs (artists, musicians, writers), have a style that's a little more vintage and little more hipster than the rapidly mainstreaming Marais. That said, Montmartre has an increasing number of chain shops, more than ever before. There are, however, many more bargain finds here than you would find in the Marais. The window-shopping shouldn't be missed: Be sure to check out rue d'Orsel (one of the consignment shops features a snow-white cat, sleeping on the shoes you might buy), rue Lépic, and rue des Abbesses.

The walking tour in Chapter 13 passes practically all the boutiques listed here!

Antoine et Lili, 90 rue des Martyrs (☎ 01-42-58-10-22), with its bright pink interior, sells whimsical clothing for teen and adult women and decorative household items. **Beauty Monop,** 28 rue des Abbesses (☎ 01-42-52-89-61), is a Monoprix outlet that sells hair care and beauty products at fantastic prices. **Chiffon et Basile,** 86 rue Martyrs (☎ 01-46-06-54-36), is a vintage and hip-kid clothing boutique with skinny jeans, colorful sneakers, and fun T-shirts (conceived by young, cheerful Basile, Chiffon is his costume-designer mother), while **Maje,** 92 rue des Martyrs ☎ 01-42-59-75-35), is a boutique clothing chain for stylish women who mean business. More women's clothes can be found in a former locksmith's shop at **Make My D,** 7 rue de la Vieuville (☎ 01-44-92-82-98), where owner Nathalie Bui (sister of designer Barbara Bui) personally helps customers choose pieces from her selection of quality designers. In a similar vein look for **Spree,** 16 rue de la Vieuville (☎ 01-42-33-41-40), much larger than it seems, inconspicuously tucked away as it is on the twisty street, and find good deals on the latest fashions from Marc Jacobs, Comme des Garçons, and smaller designers. For the guys, stop at **Jo.,** 47 rue d'Orsel (☎ 01-55-79-99-16), with slim-cut menswear from Emile Lafaurie (the best slacks in the city with reasonable price tags). **Jérémie Barthod,** 7 rue des Trois Frères (☎ 01-42-62-54-50), features unique costume jewelry — if twisted metal and glass beads could grow naturally out of the ground, this is how they would look. In her on-site studio and boutique, **Emmanuelle Zysman,** 81 rue des Martyrs (☎ 01-42-52-01-00), creates hand-made jewelry made to look like heirlooms from past generations; look for flat-pounded gold and silver bracelets and necklaces or flowery rings and earrings for younger ladies.

Shopping in Paris from A (ntiques) to W (ine)

Listed here are some of the best stores representing both economy and first-class shopping in the City of Light.

Antiques

Le Louvre des Antiquaires

This enormous mall is filled with all kinds of shops, selling everything from silverware to sketches by famous artists and Louis XIV furniture. Items are pricey, but rumors have it that some good deals exist here. A café and toilets are located on the second floor. *See map p. 248. 2 place du Palais-Royal, 1er.* ☎ *01-42-97-27-27.* www.louvre-antiquaires.com. *Métro: Palais Royal–Musée du Louvre.*

Le Village Saint-Paul

This indoor-outdoor arts and antiques fair was once a 17th-century village. Its shops display paintings, antiques, and other items, both inside and in the courtyard. It's easy to walk past the entrances, so look for the signs just inside the narrow passageways between the houses on rue Saint-Paul, rue Jardins Saint-Paul, and rue Charlemagne. The raw-food-leaning restaurant Cru can also be found in its depths. *See map p. 248. 23–27 rue Saint-Paul, 4e. No phone. Métro: Saint-Paul. Closed Tues–Wed.*

Bookstores

Chantelivre

Although most of the reading material here is in French, this place is a testament to the Gallic devotion to private bookshops. It has plenty of coffee-table books, art books, graphic novels, and beautiful kids' books. If you love books, even if don't read the language, you'll probably find something you like here. *See map p. 248. 13 rue de Sèvres, 6e.* ☎ *01-45-48-97-69.* www.chantelivre.com. *Métro: Sèvres Babylone or Saint-Sulpice.*

Gibert Joseph

Gibert Joseph is *the* Parisian students' bookstore, selling new and second-hand books, records, videos, and stationery on several floors and in several branches on boulevard Saint-Michel. If you're looking to learn some basic French vocabulary or grammar, there are small practice textbooks for English-speakers at rock-bottom prices. Late September, when students at the nearby colleges buy their textbooks, it can get very crowded. *See map p. 248. 26 and 30 bd. Saint-Michel, 6e.* ☎ *01-44-41-88-88.* www.gibertjoseph.com. *Métro: Odéon or Cluny-Sorbonne.*

Librairie Eyrolles

This convenient and charming bookstore has an extensive selection of books on every topic imaginable, as well as stationery, fancy pens, and even books in English, Spanish, and a handful of other languages. Its selling point for voyagers is the useful visitor information, like maps and neighborhood guides, and a whole assortment of gifts to bring home, including Paris flip-books for the kids and coffee-table book souvenirs for the grown-ups.

See map p. 248. 55, 57, 61, and 63 bd. Saint-Germain, 6e. ☎ *01-44-41-11-74.* www. eyrolles.com. *Métro: Maubert-Mutualité.*

Librairie La Hune

Sandwiched between cafes Les Deux Magots and de Flore, this bookstore has been a center for Left Bank intellectuals since 1945 when Sartre was among its clients. Most books are in French. It's open until midnight every night except Sunday.

See map p. 248. 170 bd. Saint-Germain, 6e. ☎ *01-45-48-35-85. Métro: Saint-Germain.*

Mona Lisait

The French hold their independent lifestyle very dear, and chain bookstores don't play a big part of the culture. Mona Lisait (a play-on-words of the famous painting by Da Vinci, it translates as "Mona was reading") is one of the chains, but a good one because a great number of used books are always on sale, and sometimes barely even used.

See map p. 248. 9 rue Saint-Martin, 4e. ☎ *01-42-74-03-02.* www.monalisait.fr. *Métro: Rambuteau. Other locations include 39 rue Jussieu, 5e (*☎ *01-40-51-81-22; Métro: Jussieu).*

The Red Wheelbarrow

Founded by Canadian bookseller Penelope Fletcher Le Masson in 2001, this cozy English-language bookstore not far from Le Village Saint-Paul (see "Antiques" earlier) stocks primarily contemporary and classic literature, with novels translated from French, general nonfiction, including a wide range of Paris- and France-related titles, and an extensive children's section. They also carry some French-English bilingual books and stories set in France.

See map p. 248. 22 rue Saint-Paul, 4e. ☎ *01-48-04-75-08.* www.theredwheel barrow.com. *Métro: Saint-Paul.*

Shakespeare & Company

No, this *isn't* the original (that was on rue l'Odéon), but English-speaking residents of Paris and backpackers still gather in this wonderfully dark and cluttered store, named after Sylvia Beach's legendary literary lair and run more and more these days by owner George Whitman's daughter, Sylvia Beach Whitman. There is a selection of new books, but most books are used. Backpackers and willing travelers can sleep in beds among the stacks, while working during the day to pay for a good night's sleep. A fat black cat lives there as well and has been sleeping on the same desk on the second level each time I visited — you can pet him; he's friendly. *Note:* Poetry readings are held on Sundays.

See map p. 248. 37 rue de la Bûcherie, 5e. ☎ *01-43-25-40-93.* www.shakespeare andcompany.com. *Métro: Saint-Michel.*

Taschen

While Taschen's gorgeous (and sometimes provocative) artistic coffee-table books can be found all over the world, there's something quite extraordinary about this boutique, full of nothing but their colorful photography and cultural insight.

See map p. 248. 2 rue de Buci, 6e. ☎ *01-40-51-79-22.* www.taschen.com. *Métro: Odéon.*

Village Voice

Quality fiction in English is the highlight of this small two-level store in Saint-Germain-des-Prés, along with an excellent selection of poetry, plays, nonfiction, and literary magazines. Owner Odile Hellier has been hosting free poetry and prose readings with celebrated authors and poets since 1982, and this is a wonderful place to attend an English-language reading. (Check *Paris Free Voice* for readings.)

See map p. 248. 6 rue Princesse, 6e. ☎ *01-46-33-36-47.* www.villagevoice bookshop.com. *Métro: Mabillon or Saint-Germain.*

Ceramics, china, and glass

Baccarat

This famous crystal production house museum, and boutique now officially resides in place des Etats-Unis in the 16e. The pieces are beautiful, but you'll pay dearly for what you get.

See map p. 248. 11 place des Etats-Unis, 16e. ☎ *01-40-22-11-00 museum,* ☎ *01-40-22-11-22 boutique. Métro: Boissière.*

La Maison Ivre

The Left Bank between Saint-Germain-des-Prés and the Seine is the unofficial antiques and art-gallery district, and this store sits right in the district's heart. It carries an excellent selection of handmade pottery from across France, emphasis on the Provence region, and ceramics from southern France. You can purchase beautiful, well-made pieces of ovenware, bowls, platters, plates, pitchers, mugs, and vases.

See map p. 248. 38 rue Jacob, 6e. ☎ *01-42-60-32-88.* www.maison-ivre.com. *Métro: Saint-Germain-des-Prés.*

Clothing for children

Alice à Paris

This small chain of children's clothing stores is not nearly as well known as the other stores listed in this section, but it has lovely, understated clothes for children 10 and under. With soft, supple fabrics, soothing prints and muted colors, kids can dress in grown-up style at actual kid prices, without sacrificing quality.

See map p. 248. 9 rue d l'Odéon, 6e. ☎ *01-42-22-53-89.* www.aliceaparis.com. *Another location is at 64 rue Condorcet, 9e (*☎ *01-48-78-17-31).*

Du Pareil au Même

Du Pareil au Même is *the* place to buy clothes for every child on your list — clothes are practical, *très mignons* (very cute), and very reasonably priced.

See map p. 248. 1 rue Saint-Denis, 1er. ☎ *01-42-36-07-57.* www.dpam.com. *Métro: Châtelet. Many branches are located throughout the city.*

Jacadi

When BCBG women (see the "Smart and sophisticated: The 6e" section earlier in this chapter) have children, Jacadi is where they buy their very proper children's clothes that feature rich fabrics and such gorgeous touches as hand-done smocking and pretty fabrics.

See map p. 248. 256 bd. Saint-Germain, 7e. ☎ *01-42-84-30-40.* www.jacadi.com. *Métro: Solférino. Many branches are located throughout the city.*

Natalys

Part of a French chain with a dozen stores in Paris, Natalys sells children's wear, maternity wear, and related products.

See map p. 248. 74 rue de Rivoli, 1er. ☎ *01-40-29-46-35.* www.natalys.com. *Métro: Hôtel de Ville. Other branches include 47 rue de Sèvres, 6e (*☎ *01-45-48-77-12).*

Petit Bateau

For years, women in the know have been stocking up on T-shirts from this very cute (and somewhat expensive) brand of clothing that uses simple patterns and color pairings to give a sense of delightful and well-made simplicity. The signature "little boat" icons grace the front of their tops or attach via little side-labels — anyone can feel like a small French kid chasing pigeons through the Jardins de Luxembourg. I say *anyone* because Petit Bateau, designed with infants, toddlers, and young children in mind, carries the same fun little-kid styles sized for adults!

See map p. 248. 24 rue Cler, 7e. ☎ *01-47-05-18-51.* www.petit-bateau.com. *Métro: La Tour Maubourg. A branch specializing in adult sizes can be found at 9 rue du 29 Juillet, 1e (*☎ *01-42-96-28-15).*

Tartine et Chocolat

This store features more typically French, precious, and pricey clothes.
See map p. 248. 105 rue du Faubourg Saint-Honoré, 8e. ☎ *01-45-62-44-04.* www.tartine-et-chocolat.fr. *Métro: Concorde.*

Clothing for men

Café Coton

Finding that perfect button-down shirt is no hassle at this chain of boutiques, where styles range from business and casual to clubby and "vogue." Attentive and polite staff will help you choose the best cut and colors to match your wishes and personal style, and the priciest shirt is only 150€.
See map p. 248. 52 rue de Saintonge, 3e. ☎ *01-48-04-00-86.* www.cafecoton.com. *Numerous locations, including 5 rue de Sèvres, 6e (*☎ *01-42-22-76-15).*

Celio

Dressing like a youthful Parisian man doesn't have to kill your wallet. I often call Celio "the French Gap," which refers to their prices and their menswear — shirts, polos, button-down pants, belts, jackets, and so forth — basically everything that the Gap sells but with a specifically French twist of small details and a bit more flair.
See map p. 248. 134 bd. Saint-Germain, 6e. ☎ *01-55-42-93-63.* www.celio.com. *Métro: Saint-Germain-des-Prés. Numerous locations.*

Chevignon

This fashionable men's store gives fashion-forward looks that have industrial detailing and nice colors that follow season trends *de la mode*. A chain that's sold in many countries, it's almost impossible to find in the United States, and when you do it's heavily marked up. Ironically, printed text on the clothing is often in English. Check out the scarves, sweaters, and zip-ups that are very slimming and very French-looking.
See map p. 248. 26 rue Etienne Marcel, 2e. ☎ *01-42-33-60-20. Métro: Etienne Marcel.*

Jacenko

Owner Fred Jacenko was an accessories designer at Hermès for ten years before opening this lovely boutique of stylish menswear, which sells clothing made of high-quality cotton and wool knits by top-notch, mostly independent designers (although you can find some coats by Givenchy on the racks). Look for jeans by French brand Notify, shoes by Pierre Hardy, jackets by London designers Holland Esquire, fine cottons by English company John Smedley, and an adorable Italian brand called Scallion.
See map p. 248. 38 rue de Poitou, 3e. ☎ *01-42-71-80-38. Métro: Saint-Sébastien–Froissart.*

Madelios

This huge store offers one-stop shopping for men, selling everything from overcoats to lighters to luggage. If companions get bored waiting, the store is part of a small mall that has some nice stores for browsing.

See map p. 248. 23 bd. de la Madeleine, 1er. ☎ *01-53-45-00-00. Métro: Madeleine.*

Clothing for teens and the young-at-heart

Antoine et Lili

If you're strolling the quays of the hip Canal Saint-Martin, have a peek into this magenta-themed store selling youngish bohemian clothes and accessories, and decorations that look great in dorm rooms or kitschy apartments. Some fun items include picture frames made from colorful scrap metal, or funky notebooks bound with hand-made paper. A garden and small canteen also are located here.

See map p. 248. 95 quai Valmy, 10e. ☎ *01-40-37-41-55. Métro: Gare de l'Est. Another branch can be found at 90 rue des Martyrs, 18e (*☎ *01-42-58-10-22).*

Cop-Copine

Cutting-edge and flattering, Cop-Copine makes great youthful clothes that enhance your good parts and disguise your not-as-good ones.

See map p. 248. 80 rue Rambuteau, 2e. ☎ *01-40-28-49-72. Métro: Les Halles. RER: Châtelet–Les Halles.*

IKKS

Although this brand of hip and trendy clothes now has lines for adults, originally it was conceived to clothe the *ados branchés* (hip adolescents). Serviced by skinny young French men and women wearing outfits picked out on the job, here you can find very reasonable deals on funky scarves, bags, form-fitting jeans, sweaters, T-shirts with abstract patterns (or whatever happens to be en vogue that season), and all forms of footwear.

See map p. 248. 32 rue du Four, 6e. ☎ *01-45-48-73-88.* www.ikks.com. *Métro: Saint-Germain-des-Prés. Several locations include a boutique at 6 rue des Rosiers (*☎ *01-42-78-16-90).*

Mango

With locations throughout the city, this store is popular with young Parisian women for its inexpensive, fashion-conscious, body-hugging (sometimes tacky) clothes.

See map p. 248. 82 rue de Rivoli, 1er. ☎ *01-44-59-80-37.* www.mango.com. *Métro: Hôtel de Ville or Louvre-Rivoli.*

Clothing for women

Ann Tuil

This small chain of boutiques specializes in the trendiest, up-to-the-minute women's footwear from designers like Marc Jacobs, Chloé, Kenzo, and Sergio Rossi. From comfortable flats to the highest of heels, all of them with lovely design and colors, Ann Tuil would surely get the Carrie Bradshaw nod of approval. The time of writing, a new boutique was about to open at no. 63 on the Champs-Elysées.

See map p. 248. 103 rue Vieille du Temple. ☎ **01-42-88-37-52.** *www.anntuil.com. Métro: Saint-Paul.*

Cacharel

Beautiful women's, children's, and men's clothes are featured at Cacharel, some in pretty Liberty-flower printed fabrics.

See map p. 248. 36 rue Tronchet, 9e. ☎ **01-42-68-38-88.** *Métro: Havre-Caumartin.*

Colette

This is Paris's most cutting-edge clothing store, and everything from designer clothes to cameras and beauty products is artistically arranged. You can also find artsy tchotchkes, art magazines, and avant-garde coffee-table books. Even if you don't buy (the prices are astronomical), just looking is fun, and you can break for a snack or drink from one of the extensive selection of waters at the basement Water Bar.

See map p. 248. 213 rue Saint-Honoré, 1er. ☎ **01-55-35-33-95.** *www.colette.fr. Métro: Tuileries.*

Comptoir des Cotonniers

This well-known designer has branches in the major department stores as well as boutiques scattered around the city. Clothes are fashionable without being too cutting-edge, and they're made well from cotton, wool, or silk. Their numerous boutiques market to women from young to middle aged. Styles, though not timeless, will last a few seasons at home.

See map p. 248. 33 rue des Francs-Bourgeois, 4e. ☎ **01-42-76-95-33.** *www.comptoirdescotonniers.com. Métro: Saint-Paul. Numerous locations.*

Etam

Women's clothing at Etam is made mostly from synthetic or synthetic-blend fabrics, but the fashions are recent and the stores are simply *everywhere*. Etam's lingerie, sold in regular Etam stores and separately at Etam Lingerie, has the best deals on pretty and affordable nightclothes, underwear, and other exciting apparel.

See map p. 248. 17 rue de l'Arrivée, 1er. ☎ **01-43-27-03-04.** *www.etam.com. Métro: Pont Neuf.*

Gelati

Paris is home to exquisite shoe designers such as Christian Louboutin, Robert Clergerie, and Maude Frizon, but if you can't afford their high, high prices, come to this fun shoe store that carries styles inspired by top designers but doesn't reflect their couture prices.

See map p. 248. 6 rue Saint-Sulpice, 6e. ☎ *01-43-25-67-44. Métro: Mabillon.*

La City

The clothes sold in numerous boutiques across Paris are perfect for work or for going out to dinner, and young women are the target audience. Although everything is synthetic, the prices are reasonable.

See map p. 248. 37 rue Chaussée d'Antin, 9e. ☎ *01-48-74-41-00.* www.lacity.fr. *Métro: Chaussée d'Antin.*

Rodier

For quality, stylish knitwear, Rodier is the upscale choice. Prices are high for ready-to-wear, but you can often find good bargains during the sales. A Rodier stock store can be found at 82 rue d'Alésia (☎ **01-45-42-06-24**).

See map p. 248. 46 rue Notre-Dames des Champs, 6e. ☎ *01-42-84-40-37.* www.rodiernew.com. *Métro: Notre-Dame-des-Champs.*

Crafts

Viaduc des Arts

When the elevated railroad cutting across the 12e was transformed into the Promenade Plantée, the space beneath was redesigned to accommodate a long stretch of artisan shops, galleries, furniture stores, and craft boutiques. Some of the glasswork artists here are absolutely superb. If you plan to visit the Bois de Vincennes via the Promenade Plantée, duck in for a look on any day except Sunday, when it's closed. The Viaduc Café here (43 av. Daumesnil) is a pleasant place for a light bite or a glass of wine.

See map p. 248. 9–147 av. Daumesnil, 12e. www.viaducdesarts.fr. *Métro: Bastille, Lédru-Rollin, Reuilly-Diderot, or Gare-de Lyon.*

Food

A La Mère de Famille

What other city has a candy store with over 240 years of experience? Founded in 1761 by Pierre Jean Bernard, this store sells the best chocolates, jams, herbal teas, sweet bonbons, candied fruits, and everything you know you shouldn't eat but will anyway (including, of course, ice cream). Still in its original location on a picturesque corner near Montmartre, try the rhubarb jam and pick up some candied chocolates that look exactly like olives. Of course, everything is fantastic, so a simple entry to inhale the perfume of a classic French candy store is the best way to begin.

See map p. 248. 35 rue du Faubourg Montmartre, 9e. ☎ *01-47-70-83-69.* www. lameredefamille.com. *Métro: Cadet or Grands Boulevards.*

Comtesse du Barry

Named for the infamous royal mistress of Louis XV, the midnight-blue facade of this chain of gourmet food shops definitely suggests a touch of royal taste. Parisians who don't feel like cooking order whole meals from here for dinner parties, but you can certainly pick up blocks of their foie gras (one of the most popular specialties), as well as other pâtés and terrines, which make great gifts for foodies. They also sell wine and champagne, sweets, chocolates, spices, seasonings, and a whole bevy of food items that you didn't realize you simply had to try.

See map p. 248. 1 rue de Sèvres, 6e. ☎ *01-45-48-32-04.* www.comtessedubarry. com. *Métro: Sèvres-Babylone. Numerous locations throughout the city.*

Fauchon

Paris's original gourmet store is still going strong, opening small branches all over the city. This is its flagship store, and here the signature pink-labeled cans of coffee, caviar, foie gras, biscuits, wines, oils, candy, and pastries fight for beautifully organized shelf space. If you're in the area, take a peek inside if only for its long history. Split into two parts, one section carries the many prepackaged gourmet delights, clearly meant to be gifts; the other carries staples. But save your shopping for other, cheaper grocery stores that may stock, incidentally, some of Fauchon's products.

See map p. 248. 26 place Madeleine, 8e. ☎ *01-70-39-38-00.* www.fauchon.com. *Métro: Madeleine.*

Hédiard

Across the street from rival Fauchon is Hédiard, a gourmet food shop that sells most of the same products as Fauchon, but packaged in red-and-black stripes (although I won't say that one is better than another, this year I got my food gifts at this store). Hédiard is slightly cheaper than Fauchon and has good prepared hot and cold food. If you must have foie gras with your baguette, then Hédiard is one of the places you can count on finding it. Branches are located throughout the city.

See map p. 248. 21 place de la Madeleine, 8e. ☎ *01-43-12-88-88.* www.hediard. fr. *Métro: Madeleine.*

JSFP Traiteur

If you're visiting the rue de Buci market, have a look inside this store (originally known as Jacques Papin, after the famous TV chef) if only to salivate over some of the most exquisite foods you may ever see, including trout in aspic, fine pâtés and salads, lobsters, and smoked salmon. The name has changed, but the quality remains the same in this busy pedestrian street in the Latin Quarter.

See map p. 248. 8 rue de Buci, 6e. ☎ *01-43-26-86-09.* www.jsfp-traiteur.com. *Métro: Odéon.*

Lafayette Gourmet

They keep this large, well-stocked supermarket well hidden in the men's building at Galeries Lafayette. Once you find it, you'll discover it's a terrific spot to browse for gifts or for yourself. It has a good selection of wines, and the house-brand merchandise, often cheaper than other labels, is of very good quality. Eat at the prepared-food counters or sit at the small bar for a glass of wine.

See map p. 248. 40 bd. Haussmann, 9e. (Enter through the men's department of Galeries Lafayette. It's on the mezzanine level, accessed by an escalator.) ☎ *01-42-82-34-56. Métro: Chaussée-d'Antin.*

La Grande Epicerie de Paris (at Le Bon Marché)

This is one of the best luxury (meaning it's not cheap) supermarkets in Paris and a great place to look for gourmet gifts, such as olive oils, homemade chocolates, fresh pastas, and wine. Food is artfully arranged in glass cases, and the produce is some of the freshest around. It makes for wonderful one-stop picnic shopping, too, offering a wide array of prepared foods and cheeses and terrific snack food (some of it from the U.S.!).

See map p. 248. 38 rue de Sèvres, 7e. ☎ *01-44-39-81-00.* www.lagrande epicerie.fr. *Métro: Sèvres-Babylone.*

La Maison du Chocolat

Each candy at this chain of fancy chocolate shops is made from a blend of as many as six kinds of South American and African chocolate, flavored with anything you could imagine. The salespeople here know everything there is about mixing chocolates and their fillings; ask them to help you with an assortment if you think you can contain yourself from stuffing them in your mouth all at once!

See map p. 248. 225 rue du Faubourg-Saint-Honoré, 8e. ☎ *01-42-27-39-44.* www. lamaisonduchocolat.com. *Métro: Ternes.*

L'Epicerie de Bruno

A spice store and gourmet grocery, owner and creative director Bruno seeks to broaden the palate of Parisians by introducing specially made curries, rare and particular spices, and impossible to find chilies from around the world. The spices are well organized and beautifully packaged; these would make a great gift for your gourmet friend who couldn't make it to Paris with you.

See map p. 248. 30 rue Tiquetonne, 2e. ☎ *01-53-40-87-33.* www.lepiceriede bruno.com. *Métro: Etienne Marcel.*

Pierre Hermé

Upscale and whimsical in character, the wildly popular Pierre Hermé clearly rivals the macaroons of the famous Ladurée with its unique meringue confections — lines to pick up a box often extend outside the doors of the boutique during busy hours. They also sell traditional pastries such as *mille-feuilles,* tarts in all flavors, and chocolate pastries that could cure any spiritual woes. The macaroon flavors range from classic, like praline and hazelnut, pistachio, Venezuelan chocolate, and the always-incredible *caramel au beurre salé* (salted butter caramel), to the more creative varieties, such a strawberry and balsamic vinegar or wasabi, jasmine, rose petal, or olive oil and vanilla. Definitely worth the wait!

See map p. 248. 72 rue Bonaparte, 6e. ☎ *01-43-54-47-77.* www.pierreherme. com. *Métro: Saint-Sulpice.*

Gifts and jewelry

Belle de Jour

This elegant shop at the footsteps of Sacré-Coeur sells antique glass perfume bottles, combs, mirrors, cosmetic cases, and other delicate toiletry items that are truly objets d'art. The gracious owners, Marie-Christine Muller-Vandame and Yann Schalburg, also sell old prints of perfume and beauty ads, as well as various other pretty art nouveau and art deco household knickknacks. These unique (but fragile!) items make wonderful gifts and keepsakes for those who enjoy little fine things in life.

See map p. 248. 7 rue Tardieu, 18e. ☎ *01-46-06-15-28.* www.belle-de-jour.fr. *Métro: Abbesses.*

Bijoux Burma

To make others whisper "Are they real or aren't they?" visit Bijoux Burma for some of the best costume jewelry in the city. (You can always reply: "They're real, and they're *fabulous!*")

See map p. 248. 50 rue François 1er, 8e. ☎ *01-47-23-70-93.* www.bijouxburma. com. *Métro: Franklin D. Roosevelt. Numerous locations, including one at 8 bd. des Capucines, 9e (*☎ *01-42-66-21-51).*

Diwali

For the fashionable pseudo-hippie in your life, Diwali will undoubtedly provide a fun and colorful keepsake. This chain of stores carries fashion accessories including colorful scarves handmade in Central America, West Africa, and South Asia), a huge assortment of bracelets, necklaces, and dangly earrings made of materials such as wood and seashells, and many other hand-luggage-size tokens from across the globe.

See map p. 248. 40 rue Saint-André-des-Arts, 6e. ☎ *01-43-29-10-09. Métro: Saint-Michel. Numerous locations.*

Galerie Ubu

This chain of jewelry stores sells simple, dangling silver bracelets inspired by Indian design, as well as earrings, rings, and necklaces that have simple and fun shapes. Some are decorated with beads made of colorful resin, and all, at close glance, are fairly unique. Street vendors of the world sell the cheap version of this kind of jewelry, but at Ubu the pieces have been carefully designed to last and are definitely real silver.

See map p. 248. 32 rue du Dragon, 6e. ☎ *01-45-49-37-11.* www.ububijoux.com. *Métro: Saint-Sulpice. Other locations include 83 rue des Martyrs (*☎ *01-42-23-40-92).*

La Chaise Longue

This bi-level gift shop is open on Sunday (when it gets very crowded) and is simply bursting at the seams with cool gifts such as dinnerware, designer teapots, three-dimensional picture frames, patterned drinking glasses, bath towels with fun prints, among many, many other things. It's very reasonably priced and definitely worth a visit — this is one of those stores where you find something you didn't know existed but cannot live without.

See map p. 248. 20 rue des Francs Bourgeois, 3e. ☎ *01-48-04-36-37. Métro: Saint-Paul. Another location is at 8 rue Princesse, 6e (*☎ *01-43-29-62-39; Métro: Saint Michel).*

Monic

There's so much to look at in this store in the Marais — open Sunday afternoons — that it's overwhelming! In business for over 30 years, here awaits a wide range of affordable costume jewelry and designer creations, many at discount prices.

See map p. 248. 5 rue des Francs-Bourgeois, 4e. ☎ *01-42-72-39-15.* www.bijoux-monic.com. *Métro: Saint-Paul. Another location can be found at 14 rue de l'Ancienne-comédie, 6e (*☎ *01-43-25-36-61; Métro: Odéon).*

Muskhane

This place is owned by a French woman who lives in Katmandu. She returns twice a year to Paris with beautiful wools that she uses to create all kinds of objects for this delightful boutique. You can find unbelievably soft cashmere sweaters, arm warmers, gloves, and berets dyed in beautiful muted colors. Additionally, there all sorts of fun objects made from felt wool, from whimsical decorative items like balls, mushrooms, and turtles, to storage baskets, tote bags, throw rugs, and other great items for around the home. It's the Himalayas seen through the lens of a true *Parisienne*.

See map p. 248. 3 rue Pastourelle, 3e. ☎ *01-42-71-07-00.* www.muskhane.com. *Métro: Rambuteau.*

Pylones

These boutiques sell Simpsons and Tintin collectibles, children's umbrellas that stand on their own, bicycle bells shaped like ladybugs, pastel-colored toasters, back massagers shaped like octopi, and a variety of other unusual and brightly colored gift items. It's a fun place to browse.

See map p. 248. 57 rue de Saint-Louis-en-l'île, 4e. ☎ *01-46-34-05-02.* www. pylones.com. *Métro: Cité. Branches at 7 rue Tardieu, 18e (*☎ *01-46-06-37-00), and 13 rue Sainte-Croix de la Bretonnerie, 4e (*☎ *01-48-04-80-10).*

Home and housewares

Alessi

Alessi offers bright and affordable kitchen implements, such as magnetized salt-and-pepper shakers and dish scrubbers that look a bit *human*. You can find some cutlery, dishes, and linens, too. Check out the Mr. Suicide drain plug — a yellow man chained to a blue stopper that floats to the surface when you take a bath.

See map p. 248. 31 rue Boissy d'Anglais, 8e. ☎ *01-42-66-31-00.* www.alessi.com. *Métro: Madeleine or Concorde.*

BHV

I've already listed the BHV once in this chapter, but it has some of the best selection and prices in the entire city for house and kitchenware. Head up to the fourth floor (niveau 3) to pick up any kind of kitchen item from Le Creuset sauté pans to champagne flutes and the perfect garlic press. Also don't forget all your wine supplies at BHV Cave, around the corner at 13 rue des Archives.

See map p. 248. 52 rue de Rivoli, 1er. ☎ *01-42-74-90-00. Métro: Hôtel de Ville.*

Conforama

This huge store sells everything for your home at reasonable prices: furniture, appliances, garden tools and accessories, and everyday china and glass. Check out its selection of kitchen tools: It always boggles my mind how many different gadgets the French have available for making delicious food.

See map p. 248. 2 rue de Pont Neuf, 1er. ☎ *01-42-33-78-58.* www.conforama.fr. *Métro: Pont Neuf.*

Dehillerin

Filled with high-quality copper cookware, glasses, dishes, china, gadgets, utensils, ramekins, pots, and kitchen appliances, this place makes cooks go wild — especially because the prices are discounted. With the current rate of exchange, don't be surprised when you find out how much a discounted price still turns out to be!

See map p. 248. 18 rue Coquillière, 1er. ☎ *01-42-36-53-13.* www.e-dehillerin. fr. *Métro: Les Halles.*

La Vaissellerie

These boutiques are always crammed full of very cute and inexpensive white porcelain tableware, placemats, and tablecloths in check-patterns or simple Provençal designs (think yellow and blue borders with pictures of olives and jugs). Don't miss the unique spice containers, labeled jars for *farine* and *sucre* (flour and sugar) — essentially anything you could need for a cute French kitchen. A set of espresso cups make a good gift and are easily portable.

See map p. 248. 92 rue Saint-Antoine, 4e. ☎ *01-42-72-76-77.* www.la vaissellerie.fr. *Métro: Saint-Paul. Numerous locations around the city.*

Toys

Au Nain Bleu

FAO Schwarz in Manhattan emulated this, the world's fanciest toy store. Translated as "at the blue dwarf's," for more than 150 years Au Nain Bleu has been selling toy soldiers, stuffed animals, games, and puppets in a gorgeous space. More modern toys, including airplanes and model cars, are also on hand. After over a century in its location on rue Faubourg Saint-Honoré, in 2007 the store moved to its new location on boulevard Malesherbes, near le parc Monceau. Obviously, this would be a terrific place to bring your kids!

See map p. 248. 5 bd. Malesherbes, 8e. ☎ *01-42-65-20-00.* www.aunainbleu. com. *Métro: Villiers or Monceau.*

Eveil & Jeux

Formerly a subsidiary of the Fnac, this chain of stores was recently purchased by the ID group, which also owns children's clothing store Jacadi. Still a great place for the kids and to pick up books, toys, educational games DVDs, and music for children.

See map p. 248. 19 rue Vavin, 6e. ☎ *01-56-24-03-46. Métro: Vavin.*

Niou

This little shop next to the Village Saint-Paul is chock-full of colorful items for the rug rats. In addition to books and board games, there are plenty of items made of wood and metal (think trains, soldiers, dolls, and much more), and none of the cheap plastic toys that lose their character or break within a few months of play. Not as big as Au Nain Bleu (see earlier), but certainly less pricey and with just as much quality.

See map p. 248. 11 rue Saint-Paul, 4e. ☎ *01-48-87-24-21. Métro:* www.niou.fr. *Saint-Paul.*

Wine

La Cave des Martyrs

Written on the window of this store on the fantastic Rue des Martyrs is *Les Cavistes Pas Ordinaires,* which, translated, reads "Not Your Ordinary Wine Store." The friendly staff members here have an extensive knowledge of the French national beverage and are more than happy to share their expertise. They'll pick out something fantastic in any price range and will happily pack a case for you to send home (however, you'll have to arrange the shipping yourself). They also carry spirits, liquors, and champagne, of course.

See map p. 248. 39 rue des Martyrs, 9e. ☎ *01-40-16-80-27. Métro: Notre-Dame de Lorette.*

Legrand Filles et Fils

In addition to fine wines, this store stocks brandies, chocolates, coffees, and *oenophile* (wine-lover) paraphernalia. It also conducts wine tastings one night a week.

See map p. 248. 1 rue de la Banque, 2e. ☎ *01-42-60-07-12.* www.caves-legrand.com. *Métro: Bourse.*

Les Caves Augé

Opened in 1850, this is the oldest wine shop in Paris, with a *sommelier* (wine steward) on-site who can advise you on the vintage French and international wines that this store carries. If you're looking for something delightful, you'll be very pleased; if you're looking for delightfully inexpensive, you may have a bit of trouble.

See map p. 248. 116 bd. Haussmann, 8e. ☎ *01-45-22-16-97.* www.cavesauge.com. *Métro: Saint-Augustin.*

Nicolas

This Nicolas is the flagship store of the almost 200-year-old wine chain that has more than 110 branches in and around Paris. It offers good prices for bottles you may not be able to find in the United States. Look for the maroon or wine-colored facade with yellow lettering; if you're going on a picnic, you can always depend on Nicolas.

See map p. 248. 31 place de la Madeleine, 8e. ☎ *01-42-68-00-16.* www.nicolas.com. *Métro: Madeleine.*

Chapter 13

Following an Itinerary

In This Chapter

▶ Visiting for three days
▶ Staying for five days
▶ Taking a tour of the Marais

*W*ith so much to see in Paris, where do you start first? The itineraries in this chapter help you figure it out. Branch out and explore Paris's interesting alleyways and pretty green spaces, which you'll encounter all around you. That is what is so much fun about Paris: It reveals itself in all kinds of ways.

Making the Most of Paris in Three Days

On **Day One,** start early by having coffee and croissants at a cafe or pick up a pastry at a *boulangerie* near your hotel to eat on the run, or if you just can't live a day without an American breakfast, take yourself to Breakfast in America in the Latin Quarter or Marais. Then begin at the true center of Paris: **Notre-Dame** on the **Ile de la Cité.** The cathedral is *the* starting point for any tour, and Paris's starting point, as well — you're at Kilomètre Zéro, from which all distances in France are measured. From there, take a short walk west to the island's other Gothic masterpiece — **Sainte-Chapelle** in the **Palais de Justice.** Afterward, cross the Seine to the **Louvre** on the Right Bank. Select just a few rooms in a particular collection for your first visit. The Louvre is one of the world's largest and finest museums, and it would take months to see everything — aside from the requisite *Mona Lisa* and *Venus de Milo,* consider the stupendous grand format paintings to see their amazing detail and massive scale. Take a well-deserved lunch break in the museum's comfortable **Café Marly** overlooking I. M. Pei's pyramid, or if you want more, cheaper food choices, try the food court on the Louvre's second floor (escalators in the Carrousel de Louvre where you enter give access).

From the museum, stroll west through the beautiful **Jardin des Tuileries** looking out for the beautiful statues by Maillol, Rodin, and others to the **place de la Concorde,** with its Egyptian obelisk and fountains. Continue west up the **Champs-Elysées,** browsing some of the same stores you can

find in your own hometown (though **Fnac** and **Virgin Megastore** a
good places to buy music, and each has a cafe on the premises for a
break; **Le Drugstore** has exquisite but pricey gifts and books), on either
side of the avenue until you come to the **Arc de Triomphe.** Pay it a visit,
and then find avenue Marceau on the south side of the Arc and walk
south or take bus no. 92 to Alma Marceau and board the **Bateaux-
Mouches** for a **Seine boat ride** (see Chapter 11). After you disembark,
have some delicious steak frites for dinner at the friendly and reasonably priced **Relais de l'Entrecôte,** 15 rue Marbeuf, 8e (from Pont L'Alma
walk down avenue George V to rue Marbeuf and make a right; L'Assiette
Lyonnaise is on your right).

Explore the **Left Bank** on **Day Two.** Take the Métro to LaMotte-Picquet-
Grenelle and stop into **Monoprix** just across the street for cheap picnic
food from its grocery store. Walk north up avenue de Suffren until you
reach the **École-Militaire.** Facing it is the **Eiffel Tower** and its front lawn,
the **Champs-de-Mars,** where you can spread out to have a picnic after
visiting the tower. Afterward, head east on quai Branly (which turns into
quai d'Orsay), until you reach the grounds of Invalides and visit the
gold-topped **Église du Dôme** (which contains the **Tomb of Napoléon**).
Admission also includes entrance to the **Musée de l'Armée.** Across boulevard des Invalides is the **Musée Rodin,** where you can enjoy a slow
walk around the beautiful gardens before gazing at the artwork inside.

Still have energy? Great! Stop at the **Café Varenne,** 36 rue de Varenne,
7e, for a quick pick-me-up espresso or snack; then head up rue du Bac,
turn left onto boulevard Saint-Germain, right onto rue de Bellechasse
and arrive at **Musée d'Orsay.** Afterward, walk over to the Métro's
Assemblée Nationale station at the intersection of boulevard Saint-
Germain and rue de Lille. Take the Métro two stops to rue du Bac and
exit onto boulevard Saint-Germain, making sure to walk in the direction
traffic is heading, all the while browsing in upscale shops and art galleries. At place Saint-Germain-des-Prés, look for one of the famous cafes,
Café de Flore, Café Les Deux Magots (see Chapter 10), or **Brasserie
Lipp,** and have a well-deserved drink. When you finish, take rue
Bonaparte (which intersects Saint-Germain-des-Prés) south to Parisians'
favorite park, the **Jardin du Luxembourg.** Stroll through the park (keeping an eye out for beehives and a mini Statue of Liberty) and exit at the
boulevard Saint-Michel gates on the park's east side. Walk north on boulevard Saint-Michel toward the river. You'll be in the **Latin Quarter.** The
Panthéon is at the top of the hill on rue Soufflot. You can enjoy a nice
meal at one of the many inexpensive restaurants located behind the
Panthéon on rue Mouffetard.

On **Day Three,** get up early and hop on the Métro to Saint-Paul, in the
heart of the **Marais.** Head east on rue Saint-Antoine, and then turn north
onto rue de Birague, which will take you right to Paris's oldest square,
the aristocratic **place des Vosges,** bordered by 17th-century town
houses. Exit on rue des Francs-Bourgeois (for some great but a bit
pricey shopping), and then turn north onto rue Vieille du Temple until
you see the **Musée Picasso.** Try to arrive when it opens at 9:30 a.m., and

allow two hours for your visit. Afterward double back on rue du Vieille du Temple to rue des Rosiers and pick up a filling lunch from **L'As du Falafel,** 34 rue des Rosiers, 4e. Browse the stores here and head west on rue des Francs Bourgeois (pause at your leisure for some fantastic window-shopping), which eventually turns into rue Rambuteau. Follow rue Rambuteau west to rue Beaubourg, where you'll face the back of the wonderful **Centre Georges Pompidou.** Spend two hours exploring it.

Afterward, hop on the Métro at the Rambuteau station and get off at Place de la République. Follow rue du Faubourg du Temple until you hit le Quai de Valmy, and then turn right. Spend a leisurely 90 minutes walking along the **Canal Saint-Martin,** and perhaps stop at **Hôtel de Nord** on the other side of the canal at 102 Quai Jemmapes, 10e, for another great pick-me-up espresso. Once you've seen the length of the canal, get on the Jaurès Métro stop and take Line 2 toward Charles de Gaulle–Étoile, getting off at the Anvers station. Walk north on rue Tardieu to the base of **Sacré-Coeur.** Take the funicular (one Métro ticket) to the top and then spend 15 to 20 minutes inside Sacré-Coeur before climbing to its dome. After climbing down, head behind the church to the **place du Tertre,** which still looks like an old-fashioned Parisian square, despite artists begging to paint your picture (some can be quite persuasive, but they're too expensive, and it's better to just politely tell them, *"Non, merci"*). Even though the cafes are picturesque — and more expensive — save your appetite for **Le Kokolion,** 62 rue d'Orsel, for dinner.

Planning a Five-Day Visit

Spend the first three days as outlined in the "Making the Most of Paris in Three Days" itinerary. Add the **Conciergerie** to your tour of île de la Cité on Day One; the entrance is on the Seine side of the Palais de Justice.

On **Day Four,** visit **Versailles.** On **Day Five,** take the Métro to Opéra to visit the stunning **Opéra Garnier** with its mural by Marc Chagall. Then head north to boulevard Haussmann to shop the rest of the afternoon away at department stores **Printemps** and **Galeries Lafayette.** The sixth-floor cafeteria at Galeries Lafayette offers plenty of lunch or dinner choices — from a salad bar to grilled steaks and dessert.

A Walking Tour through the Marais

The **Marais** (translation: "swamp," which it used to be), the old Jewish quarter of Paris, is also now one of its hippest, chicest neighborhoods with the new edging out a population that has called this area home since the Middle Ages. Jo Goldenberg, a kosher deli, restaurant, and Paris institution, closed its doors in 2006, and as rents skyrocket, the family-run kosher pizza places, delis, and religious shops are giving way to designer boutiques and restaurants. There is still a Jewish presence here; the rue Pavée Orthodox Synagogue is the heart of the community, but the beloved working-class neighborhood is much changed. Some Jewish residents are adapting, and others are moving to Paris's farther reaches in the 19e and 20e *arrondissements.* The mix of old and new only enhances this quarter's attractions, however, making the Marais one of the best places to visit for tourists and locals alike.

Take the Métro to the Saint-Paul station and, after climbing the steps from the station, turn right (or east) along the rue Saint-Antoine. On your right will be the baroque church of **Saint-Paul–Saint-Louis** (badly in need of restoration), where Victor Hugo was a parishioner and donated the holy water fonts on each side of the entrance. Delacroix's *Christ in the Garden of Olives* is in the left transept, if you want to take a peek inside.

Turn right when leaving the church and walk across rue Saint-Antoine to the **Hôtel de Sully,** a 17th-century mansion commissioned by Henri IV, that houses the **Caisse Nationale des Monuments Historiques et des Sites,** which features some great photography exhibits. Walk through the front courtyard into lovely formal gardens. This is a popular place for locals to catch some sun on warm days. Walk through the courtyard in the direction of the building's *orangerie,* passing a bookstore on the left side (inside you can see the building's original painted wood beams) and exit on the right side of the *orangerie* to **place des Vosges** (see Chapter 11).

Thirty-six brick and stone pavilions rise from graceful arcades surrounding a gorgeous central plant- and flower-filled square. This used to be the court of Henri IV, and the buildings were constructed according to strict plan: The height of the facades equals their widths, and triangular roofs are half as high as the facades. In the southeastern corner here is the **Maison de Victor Hugo** (see Chapter 11), the prolific author of *Les Misérables* and *The Hunchback of Notre-Dame.* After a quick (and free) visit to his house, leave the square at the end opposite the entrance and make a left onto **rue des Francs-Bourgeois** for some window shopping (don't miss the mouthwatering women's clothing at, **Zadig & Voltaire** at no. 42 and **Barbara Bui** at no. 43, or the smartest of men's attire at **S.D. Spontini** at no. 29) before hitting the **Musée Carnavalet** (see Chapter 11) on the corner of rue de Sévigné. Facing the Musée Carnavalet, turn right and continue up rue de Sévigné. Turn left at rue du Parc-Royal, continue to place de Thorigny and make a right onto rue de Thorigny. At no. 5 is the **Musée Picasso.**

This is one of the must-see museums of Paris, one of the largest collections of the master's paintings (if not the largest) in the world. When finished, retrace your steps to the corner of rue du Parc-Royal and rue Payenne. Turn right onto rue Payenne and stop by the pretty square Georges-Cain on the left, where you can see remnants from some of the city's demolished mansions. Follow rue des Francs-Bourgeois to no. 38, the **Allée des Arbalétriers,** a typical medieval street with large paving stones and overhanging floors. This was where Louis d'Orléans, King Charles V's brother, was hacked to death by goons for the duc de

Bourgogne. Make a right onto rue Vieille-du-Temple. On the corner is the late Gothic turret that is the only remnant of a mansion (the **Hôtel Hérouet**), built around 1510. At no. 87 is the Hôtel de Rohan-Strasbourg; no. 60 is the **Hôtel de Guénegaud des Brosses,** which houses the Musée de la Chase et Nature; and at no. 58 are the towers of the **Hôtel de Clisson,** a 14th-century mansion. No. 60 is the **Hôtel de Soubise,** where the **Musée de l'Histoire de France** is located. Cross rue des Francs-Bourgeois, continuing on rue Vieille-du-Temple for the **Hôtel Amelot-de-Bisseuil** at no. 47, where Beaumarchais wrote *The Marriage of Figaro* in 1784. If you feel like some window shopping, the area around this street, including gorgeous cashmere creations at **Muskhane** at 3 rue Pastourelle, 3e, or stylish menswear at **Jacenko,** 38 rue de Poitou. At the Hôtel Amelot-de-Bisseuil take a right and then turn left onto the **rue des Rosiers,** the heart of the old Jewish quarter.

Much of the Jewish community here dates back to the 13th century and references to the "street of rosebushes" *(rosiers)* appeared as early as 1230. This is where you'll want to grab something filling, like a falafel from **L'As du Falafel** at no. 34. If you turn right onto rue Pavée at the end of rue des Rosiers, you'll see the **synagogue** at no. 10, built by Hector Guimard, artisan of the Art Nouveau subway entrances. At the end of the street is the Saint-Paul Métro station across rue Saint-Antoine. If you still have energy, cross rue Saint-Antoine, take a right and walk to rue Saint-Paul. At no. 10 is the **Musée de la Curiosité et de la Magie** (see Chapter 11), and a bit farther down is the Village Saint-Paul, a secluded 17th-century village–cum–outdoor art and antiques fair. It's easy to walk past the entrances, which are tucked between rue Saint-Paul, rue Jardins Saint-Paul, and rue Charlemagne (look for the signs just inside the narrow passageways between houses). You'll find yourself in a cluster of interlocking courtyards lined with shops selling antiques, paintings, and bric-a-brac. The haphazard arrangement of courtyards dates from the 14th century when they were the walled gardens of King Charles V. Also on rue Saint-Paul, for those travelers who miss the United States, is **Thanksgiving,** a store selling such items as Marshmallow Fluff and Fritos at no. 20. The English-language Little Red Wheelbarrow bookstore is next door at no. 22. Retrace your steps up rue Saint-Paul to rue Saint-Antoine to catch the Métro to your next destination.

Take a Stroll through a Parisian Village

Montmartre has been long on its way to becoming hip and trendy, but it still retains a certain separatist, village charm compared to the rest of Paris. Its twisted streets and ivied walls are still just as charming as the days before it was incorporated into the city, when it was a village known for its cheap wines and artistic inhabitants (many artists left Paris proper for Montmartre at night precisely because of the cheap drinks). The twisting streets here can sometimes mean very confused voyagers, but fear not! This half-day's tour of Montmartre will have you walking around like a local in no time.

Bring a map that has a good rendering of the 18th *arrondissement.* Though getting lost is part of the fun of Montmartre, it's getting out that can get a bit frustrating.

✔ **Scoping Abbesses, Part One:** Start out at Place Blanche, to see what might be the world's most famous nightclub, the **Moulin Rouge.** Take the requisite picture (lit up at night, it is most impressive!), and walk up **rue Lepic.** Open during the day are great cheese shops and small produce shops. At no. 12 is **Lux-Bar,** which opened a century ago and continues to give locals a place to soothe their palates. Across the street at no. 15 is **Café des Deux Moulins** of *Amélie* fame. The interior remains mostly the same, with the glass toilettes sign and the copper-topped bar (the cigarette counter was removed a while ago for more space). A big *Amélie* poster graces the back wall. Turn right and walk down **rue des Abbesses.** Here is some great shopping (check out Comptoir des Cotonniers at no. 41). You'll also pass the fantastic *boulangerie* **Le Grenier du Pain,** at no. 38, and a good people-watching cafe, **Le Sancerre,** at no. 35, eventually ending up in place des Abbesses. Here you'll see the **Eglise Saint-Jean-de-Montmartre,** which was built in 1904, and also the beautiful Art Deco entrance to the Abbesses stop, designed by Hector Guimard. It is one of the last two original Métro entrances left in the city.

A good place to have a picnic lunch if you buy your sandwich from Le Grenier à Pain is next to the "I love you wall," located in the square Jehan Rictus (just off of place des Abbesses, on the other side of the Métro entrance and the merry-go-round). In this small green space is a wall with the words *I love you* (*Je t'aime* in French) written in over a hundred different languages. *Comme c'est romantique!*

✔ **Scoping Abbesses, Part Two:** The next part of the tour leads up to everyone's favorite Montmartre landmark: Sacré-Coeur. However, the streets leading up to it are quite important — especially if you like shopping. Walk along rue des Abbesses until you cross **rue des Martyrs.** You'll see an **Antoine et Lili** at no. 90, a shop perfect for interesting little gifts for the college crowd. Then take a quick left and right onto rue Yvonne le Tac. At no. 9 you pass the entrance to the chapel built on the supposed spot of the beheading of Saint-Denis, for whom all of Montmartre (the word *Montmartre* comes from mountain, or *mont,* of the martyr) is named. At no. 8 is a lovely ivied building, while around the corner you pass the local cafe **Au Progrès,** at 7 rue des Trois Frères, perfectly situated in a four-way crossroads, with the ideal panoramic view of Parisian streets. Make another right and traverse rue d'Orsel. Here are art galleries, a great shop that sells antique books, and some really ugly modern furniture shops. If it's later at night, a great restaurant on this street is **le Kokolion,** at no. 62. For menswear, go to **Jo.,** at no. 47, and **S. D. Spontini,** just up the street at 1 rue de Trois Frères. A real circus supply store (fun gift ideas!) is at **Bonjour l'Artiste,** at no. 35.

✔ **Sacré-Coeur and place du Tertre:** Climb the lamppost-divided stairs famously depicted in the photograph by Brassaï, or for the price of a Métro ticket, take the *funiculaire* (walk from the Anvers Métro station the short distance to rue Steinkerque and turn left onto rue Tardieu). Enjoy the fantastic, free view for which you don't have to wait in line. Work started on this basilica in the 1870s and the building is a pastiche of Romanesque and Byzantine styles. Renoir, Picasso, Seurat, Degas, Van Gogh, and Zola all hung out in Pigalle and Montmartre. And there was no keeping Toulouse-Lautrec away, of course. Follow around the western side of the basilica, passing the dwarfed Église Saint-Pierre du Montmartre, and wander around place du Tertre without letting yourself get too abused by the painters dying to paint your picture. Here you can truly see how this place was once its own village, with adorable houses, old paned windows, and tiny cobblestone passageways (not to mention some of the highest rents in the city). Walk around the edges of the place du Tertre area to the **Espace Dalí,** 11 rue Poulbot, a small museum dedicated to Dalí's work, of which there is a plethora to see (and hear — his voice plays over eerie ambient music). Then wander up rue des Saules, passing the famous cabaret **Au Lapin Agile** at no. 22, a famous haunt of artists Picasso, Modigliani, and Utrillo (they still have music shows here, but they're vastly overpriced). Around the corner is the **Musée de Montmartre,** at 12 rue Cortot, where you can learn all about the history and art associated with this beloved part of Paris.

✔ **There and back again:** Once you've had enough of the hilltop, make your way down through place Jean Baptiste Clément and down rue de la Mire to rue Ravignan, where you can see a beautiful house (built in 1911), located right across the street from 49 rue Gabrielle, where Picasso had his first studio in Paris. On this street are more art studios and funny narrow passages, as well as the very fairly priced **Chez Marie** (no. 27). Continue east to the upper portion of rue Lepic, where you can catch a glimpse of the oldest and only remaining windmill in Montmartre, **Le Moulin de la Galette** (unfortunately, you can't visit it). Descend farther past rue Berthe and onto rue Androuet, where you'll find the little Collignon grocery store from *Amélie* — she really did live in Montmartre! You're again on rue des Trois Frères. Follow it along and you'll shortly pick up rue Ravignan again. Here you can find the **Bateau Lavoir,** another studio haunted by the likes of Picasso and Modigliani, at 11 bis place Emile Godeau. In this spot, there are benches where you can rest before you end up back at Abbesses, enjoying another quick view of the Paris skyline.

Chapter 14

Going Beyond Paris: Five Day Trips

In This Chapter

▶ Enjoying the excesses of Versailles
▶ Reliving history at Fontainebleau
▶ Basking in the stained-glass light at Chartres's cool cathedral
▶ Hanging out with "Le Mickey" at Disneyland à la français
▶ Lingering at the lilies in Monet's gardens

The day trips outlined in this chapter are well worth tearing yourself away from Paris for, even though it may be difficult. Don't worry — you'll be back in the city in time to enjoy a nightcap in a cafe. The "Day Trips from Paris" map can help you plan your excursions.

The Château de Versailles

Sofia Coppola's movie version of the life of Marie Antoinette, "teen queen," generated renewed interest in the opulent Austrian import, but even if you haven't seen the film, you'll discover that there's more to Versailles (☎ 01-30-83-78-00; www.chateauversailles.fr) than its incredible château, of which the term *awe-inspiring* doesn't begin to do justice. This palace is a small city on more than 800 hectares (2,000 acres) that houses formal and fanciful gardens, meadows (with sheep), a mile-long Grand Canal modeled on the one in Venice, the Grand and Petit Trianon mansions, a hamlet (the Hameau) where Marie Antoinette played peasant, the restored royal stables, a coach museum, fountains, and woods. All this attests to the power royalty once had and to one king who truly believed he deserved it: Louis XIV. The king hired the best to build Versailles: Louis Le Vau and Jules Hardouin-Mansart, France's premier architects; André Le Nôtre, designer of the Tuileries gardens; and Charles Le Brun, head of the Royal Academy of Painting and Sculpture, who fashioned the interior. Construction got underway in 1661.

In 1682, Louis XIV transferred the court to Versailles to live with him and thus prevent plots against him. Historians estimate that anywhere from 3,000 to 10,000 people, including servants, lived at Versailles in the 100 years between the rules of Louis XIV and Louis XVI, and court etiquette grew to be absurd. (Sometimes attendants engaged in power struggles about who ranked high enough to dress Marie Antoinette while the young queen waited, shivering. And Versailles's female royalty gave birth before a live audience; the higher the rank, the better the seat.) When you see all this over-the-top magnificence and try to estimate the cost, you may have a better understanding of the anger of the revolutionaries a century later.

Louis XIV enjoyed an incredibly long reign of 72 years (though he was only 5 years old when he inherited the title). When he died in 1715, he was succeeded by his great-grandson, Louis XV, who continued the outrageous pomp and ceremony and made interior renovations and redecorations until lack of funds forced him to stop. Louis XV's son and daughter-in-law, Louis XVI and Marie Antoinette, made no major changes at Versailles, but by then it was too late. On October 6, 1789, a mob voicing the feelings of the average French citizen sick of bearing the brunt of the costs of royalty's foibles marched on the palace and forced the royal couple to return to Paris. This was the beginning of the French Revolution. The royal family eventually lost their lives, save one daughter (though some report that the young *dauphin,* or heir to the throne, never really died in prison, but was spirited away from the country), and Versailles ceased to be a royal residence.

The monarchy was reinstated in 1830, and Louis-Philippe, who reigned from 1830 to 1848 and succeeded Louis XVIII, prevented Versailles's destruction by donating his own money to convert it into a museum dedicated to the glory of France. In the mid-20th century, John D. Rockefeller also contributed to the restoration of Versailles, and the work from that contribution continues to this day. The nearby "Versailles" map shows the current configuration.

Getting there

Catch the **RER Line C** to Versailles from one of the stops at the Gare d'Austerlitz, Saint-Michel, Musée d'Orsay, Invalides, Ponte d'Alma, Champ de Mars, or Javel and take it to the Versailles Rive Gauche station (take "direction Versailles-rive-gauche-château"), from which there's a shuttle bus to the château. Or, you can take the 15-minute walk through the town, which is very pretty on its own. A one-day **Mobilis** ticket will cost you 9.80€, which covers not just there and back but also your Métro ride to the RER station. The trip takes about 35 minutes. Eurailpass holders travel free on the RER but must show their Eurailpass at the kiosk near any RER entrance to receive a ticket that opens the turnstile leading to and from the RER platforms.

An alternative method of reaching Versailles from central Paris involves regular **SNCF Transilien trains,** which make frequent runs from two

Day Trips from Paris

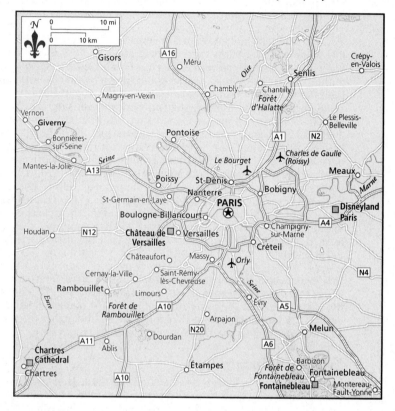

railway stations — Gare Saint-Lazare and Gare Montparnasse — to Versailles. Trains departing from Gare Saint-Lazare arrive at the Versailles Rive Droit railway station; trains departing from Gare Montparnasse arrive at Versailles Chantiers. The cost of the tickets is the same as the RER. Both stations lie within a ten-minute walk of the château, which is a wonderful way to orient yourself with the town, its geography, its scale, and its architecture. If you can't or don't want to walk, you can take bus H, X, or G, or (in midsummer) a shuttle bus marked either tri or château from any of the three stations directly to the château for a fee of 3€ each way. Because of the vagaries of the bus schedules, it may be easier to walk. Directions to the château are clearly signposted from each railway station. Another method of arrival for the adventurous is to take bus no. 171 toward Versailles–place d'Armes. The bus leaves from the Pont de Sèvres Métro station, at the southern end of Line 9. The journey is roughly 25 minutes this way.

To reach Versailles by car, drive west on the A13 highway from Porte d'Auteuil toward Rouen. Take the Versailles-Château exit, about 23km

(14 miles) from Paris. Park in the visitors' parking lot at place d'Armes for 5.50€ Monday through Friday, 6.50€ on weekends. The drive takes about 30 minutes, though in traffic it can take more than an hour.

You can also take advantage of the Versailles **Passeport** (☎ **01-30-83-78-00**), a one-day pass to visit the entire Château de Versailles and all the surrounding attractions within the city. This includes audio-guided tours in the château, the chapel, the King and Queen's Grand Apartments, the Dauphin's (Crown Prince) Apartments, and the Appartements de Mesdames (ladies-in-waiting, open only on weekends during the low season). The opera house reopened after two years of renovations ending in 2009, and is now hosting concerts and official functions. After this massive opulent castle visit, you have free rein of the parks, gardens, and forest groves, the **Grand Trianon** (the nearby private retreat of Louis XIV), the **Domaine de Marie-Antoinette** (Marie Antoinette's private fields, open Apr–Oct), and all the temporary exhibits. If you use the Passeport during the high season, the spectacle of **Les Grands Eaux Musicales** (see the next section) is also included. The tickets cost 25€ for adults, 18€ for visitors 18 and under. Keep in mind that seeing each attraction separately requires purchasing your ticket at an Fnac or SNCF ticket booth.

Don't want the hassle of getting to Versailles yourself? You can also take a tour bus there. **Cityrama,** 2 place des Pyramides, 1er (☎ **01-44-55-61-00**; www.cityrama.fr), has different trips to Versailles ranging from 54€ to 162€ for adults, 27€ to 152€ for children (the higher-priced tickets also include trips to Giverny, Fontainebleau, and Barbizon).

Exploring Versailles

I cannot be more serious when I lay down two words of advice — arrive early! If you really want to beat the crowds, get there at 8 a.m. when it opens. More than three million tourists visit Versailles each year, and you'll want to have as much of a head start as possible. Also, don't be surprised by various renovations taking place in public areas that have not been announced: It seems that a lot of repair work is going on, which may affect your visit.

The first rooms you see in the palace are the six Louis XIV–style **Grand Appartements,** which kings used for ceremonial events, and the **Petit Appartements,** where they lived with their families. Louis XV stashed his mistresses, Madame du Barry and Madame de Pompadour, in his second-floor apartment, which you can visit only with a guide (the Petit Trianon was built as a retreat for the king's mistress, but Madame de Pompadour died before it was completed). Attempts have been made to restore the original décor of the queen's bedchamber, which Marie Antoinette renovated with a huge four-poster bed and silks in patterns of lilacs, her favorite flower, and peacock feathers. Look for the secret door through which she attempted to escape.

Versailles

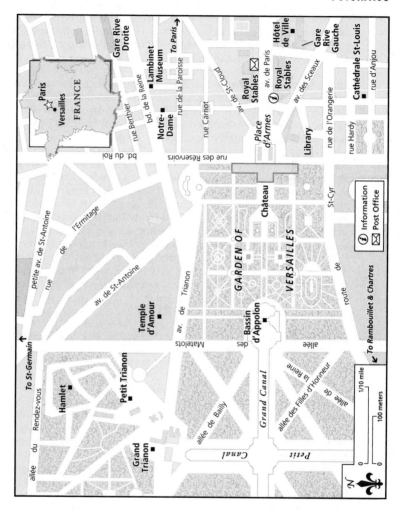

Other magnificent rooms include the **Salons of War and Peace,** which flank the palace's most famous room, the 71m-long (236-ft.) **Hall of Mirrors.** Hardouin-Mansart began work on the hall in 1678, and Le Brun added 17 large windows and corresponding mirrors. The ceiling paintings represent the accomplishments of Louis XIV's government. Jacques-Ange Gabriel designed the **Library** with its delicately carved panels. The **Clock Room** contains Passement's astronomical clock, which took 20 years to make; it's encased in gilded bronze.

Gabriel also designed the **Royal Opéra** for Louis XV. Try to imagine it the way it used to be during a concert — bearskin rugs under foot and the light of 3,000 powerful candles. Hardouin-Mansart built the gold-and-white **Royal Chapel** between 1699 and 1710. After his father's death, Louis XVI and Marie Antoinette prayed for guidance here, fearing they were too young to run the country.

After you see the château, plan to spend at least an hour strolling through the **Formal Gardens,** spread across 100 hectares (250 acres). Here Le Nôtre created a Garden of Eden, using ornamental lakes and canals, geometrically designed flowerbeds, and avenues bordered with statuary. Louis XV, imagining he was in Venice, would take gondola rides with his lover of the moment on the mile-long Grand Canal. The restored vegetable gardens *(le Potager de Roi)* are here, as well. If you visit on a weekend in the summer, try to take in **Les Grands Eaux Musicales,** a show in which the fountains move in time to the classical music of Bach, Mozart, or Berlioz. Cost is 8€ adults, 6€ ages 6 to 18, free for children 5 and under. Another spectacle is **Les Grandes Eaux Nocturnes,** a variety of breathtaking shows, combining sound-and-light displays with fireworks, but also featuring dance, puppetry, and high-quality theatrics that the French do well. Held between June and September, the kids will definitely enjoy these as much as you. Prices range from 25€ for adults to 17€ for children 10 to 18; seniors and children 9 and under are free. (For reservations to either show, see www.chateauversailles spectacles.fr or call ☎ 01-30-83-78-89).

Because of the crowds and long lines, most guests are content to visit only the château and gardens, but you can see much more at Versailles if you have the stamina. The most important of the remaining sights are the **Grand Trianon** and the recently renovated **Petit Trianon.** Trianon was the name of the town that Louis bought and then razed in order to construct a mansion, le Grand Trianon, where he could eat light meals away from the palace. Designed in 1687, again by Hardouin-Mansart, the Grand Trianon has traditionally served as a residence for the country's important guests, although former President Charles de Gaulle wanted to turn it into a weekend retreat for himself. Napoléon I spent the night here, and U.S. President Richard Nixon slept in the room where Madame de Pompadour (Louis XV's mistress) died. Gabriel, the designer of the place de la Concorde, built the Petit Trianon in 1768 for Louis XV, who used it for trysts with Madame du Barry, his mistress after de Pompadour. Marie Antoinette adopted it as her favorite residence, where she could escape the constraints of palace life.

Behind the Petit Trianon is the **Hameau,** or hamlet, a collection of small thatched farmhouses and a water mill, a setting where Marie Antoinette pretended she was back at her family's country retreat in Austria. Near the Hamlet is the **Temple of Love,** built in 1775 by Richard Mique, Marie Antoinette's favorite architect. In the center of its Corinthian colonnade is a reproduction of Bouchardon's Cupid shaping a bow from the club of Hercules.

Louis XIV's stables, **La Grande Écurie,** are newly restored and open to the public. Also designed by Hardouin-Mansart, the stables held as many as 600 horses owned by the king. These days, you'll see 20 ivory-colored Lusitano horses from Portugal. A morning tour here includes a dressage demonstration with riders in costume on horses performing to music. Near the stables is the entrance to **Le Musée des Carrosses,** which houses horse-drawn coaches from the 18th and 19th centuries, among them one used at the coronation of Charles X and another used at the wedding of Napoléon I and his second wife, Marie-Louise. One sleigh rests on tortoiseshell runners. A ticket to the Petit Trianon also admits you to this museum, and to the **Salle du Jeu de Paume.** Constructed by Louis XIV, this museum space was originally an indoor court intended for *le jeu de paume,* a sport that was the precursor to tennis. It has historical significance, because it's the place where, on June 20, 1789, the French Revolution began: Representatives of the Third Estate, unsatisfied with the reforms of Louis XVI, met at the Jeu de Paume and swore they would not leave the chamber until they were given a Constitution.

Admission to La Grande Écurie is 6€ adults, 5€ children 17 and under. It is open on specific Tuesdays and Thursdays at 11 a.m. Admission to the coach museum is 3€, free for ages 17 and under. The Musée des Carrosses and the Salle du Jeu de Paume are open only on certain weekends and holidays; you must call ahead to the Versailles info line to see if they're available for viewing.

Admission to the palace is 15€ for adults. It's free for ages 17 and under and for everyone on the first Sunday of every month from November through March. Combined admission to the Grand and Petit Trianons is 10€ for adults, free for those 17 and under. Audio guides are available in iPods for free. Admission to the gardens is free except for the days of Grands Eaux Musicales (see earlier for prices).

Lecturer-led one-hour tours of the palace are 16€, or the admission price including the Trianon and the Domaines de Marie Antoinette plus 7€. Tours are free for children 9 and under.

From April through October, the palace is open Tuesday through Sunday from 9 a.m. to 6:30 p.m. The rest of the year, the palace is open Tuesday through Sunday from 9 a.m. to 5:30 p.m. From May through September the Grand Trianon and Petit Trianon are open daily noon to 6:30 p.m.; from October through April, the Grand Trianon and Petit Trianon are open daily noon to 5:30 p.m. The park and the gardens are open daily, except in bad weather, from 7 a.m. in summer and 8 a.m. in winter until sunset (between 5:30 and 9:30 p.m., depending on the season).

Dining options

The town of Versailles has no shortage of places where you can break for lunch, but after you're on palace grounds, you may find it infinitely more convenient just to stay put — otherwise you have to hike back into town and back out to the palace again. In the château, you can eat at Le Grand Café d'Orléans, a snack bar just off the Cour de la Chapelle. In the Formal Gardens is an informal restaurant, **La Flotille,** on Petite Venise (www.laflottille.fr). (To get there from the château, walk directly back through the gardens to where the canal starts. Petite Venise and the restaurant are to your right.) There is La Petite Venise, a wood-beamed restaurant, brasserie, and tearoom with outdoor seating between the Grand Canal and the Apollo Fountain. Finally, several **snack bars** and fresh-squeezed orange juice stands are located in the gardens near the Quinconce du Midi and the Grand Trianon. In the gardens there are a few food stands as well, some of which have fantastic ice cream.

Note: For those with limited mobility, electric cars are available at the south entrance (☎ **01-30-83-75-05**).

The Palais de Fontainebleau

Fontainebleau is much less crowded than Versailles, and you can combine culture and outdoor activities. It's a terrific day trip from Paris. After you tour the castle, hike the trails, rock-climb, or rent bikes to ride in the 16,800-hectare (42,000-acre) Forêt (Forest) de Fontainebleau that 13 million guests visit each year. The palace (☎ **01-60-71-50-70;** check out the nearby "Fontainebleau" map) is probably most famous as the site of Napoléon's farewell to his imperial guard before he went into exile. It also contains more than 700 years of royal history from the enthronement of Louis VII in 1137 to the fall of the Second Empire in 1873. And artist Leonardo da Vinci played a small role in its history.

Tickets for access to the Grands Appartements are 10€ for adults, free for children 18 and under. Access to Les Petits Appartements are an additional 6.50€ for adults, and 5€ for children 18 and under. Guided visits cost an additional 6.50€ for adults, and 5€ for children 18 and under.

Getting there

To reach Fontainebleau by train, take the SNCF Montargis line to Fontainebleau Avon station; it departs hourly from the Gare de Lyon in Paris. The trip takes 35 to 60 minutes and costs 8.05€. Fontainebleau Avon station is just outside the town in Avon, a suburb of Paris. From the station, the town bus (direction Château) makes the 3km (2-mile) trip to the château every 10 to 15 minutes Monday through Friday, and every 30 minutes on Saturday and Sunday. A Mobilis ticket for one day between zones 1 and 2 (Paris) and zone 6 (Avon–Fontainebleau) costs 17€ — this will allow you to ride the bus to and from the chateau without worrying about buying individual tickets.

You can also reach Fontainebleau on a tour bus. **Cityrama,** 4 place des Pyramides, 1er (☎ **01-44-55-61-00;** www.cityrama.fr), combines both Fontainebleau and the nearby artist's village of Barbizon (see "Dining options," later); prices run 69€ for adults and 35€ for children.

Fontainebleau

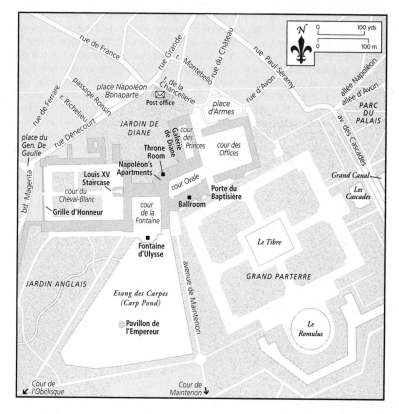

Exploring Fontainebleau

Fontainebleau was built for love. François I transformed a run-down royal palace into Fontainebleau in 1528 for his mistress, and his successor, Henri II, left a beautiful memorial to the woman he loved — a **ballroom** decorated with the intertwined initials of his mistress, Diane de Poitiers, and himself.

The *Mona Lisa* once hung here, and it is said that its creator, Leonardo da Vinci, personally brought the painting to its buyer, his friend François I. The *Mona Lisa* remained in the royal family for years before it was gifted to the Louvre. Stucco-framed paintings now hanging in the **Gallery of François I** include *The Rape of Europa* and depict mythological and allegorical scenes related to the king's life. Make sure to see the racy ceiling paintings above the **Louis XV Staircase,** which was originally painted for the bedroom of a duchess. The stairway's architect simply ripped out the bedroom floor, using its ceiling to cover the stairway. One fresco depicts the Queen of the Amazons climbing into Alexander the Great's bed.

When Louis XIV ascended the throne, Fontainebleau was largely neglected because of his preoccupation with Versailles, but it found renewed glory under Napoléon I. You can walk around much of the palace on your own, but most of the Napoleonic rooms are accessible only on guided tours, which are in French. Napoléon had two bedchambers; mirrors adorn either side of his bed in the grander chamber (look for his symbol, a bee), while a small bed is housed in the aptly named **Small Bedchamber.** A red-and-gold throne with the initial *N* is displayed in the **Throne Room.** You can also see Napoléon's **offices,** where the emperor signed his abdication; however, the document on exhibit is only a copy. Minor apartments include those once occupied by Madame de Maintenon, the second wife of Louis XIV; those of Pope Pius VII, whom Napoléon kept a virtual prisoner; still another was Marie Antoinette's.

After a visit to the palace, wander through the gardens, paying special attention to the lovely, bucolic carp pond, and take caution while walking by some of the fearless swans. If you'd like to promenade in the forest, a detailed map of its paths is available from the **Office de Tourisme,** 4 rue Royale, near the palace (☎ **01-60-74-99-99;** www. tourisme-fontainebleau.com). You can also rent bikes nearby from **À la Petite Reine,** 32 rue des Sablons (☎ **01-60-74-57-57;** www. alapetitereine.com), for 5€ per hour or 15€ per day, with a credit card deposit. The **Tour Denencourt,** about 5km (3 miles) north of the palace, makes a nice ride and has a pretty view. Other mapped-out walking and bike tours of the city and environs can be downloaded from the Tourist Office Web site or you can get a map once you're there.

The **Palais de Fontainebleau (☎ 01-60-71-50-70)** is open October through March Wednesday through Monday from 9:30 a.m. to 5 p.m., April through September Wednesday through Monday from 9 a.m. to 6 p.m. It's closed on January 1, May 1, and December 25.

Dining options

If you're arriving by train and plan to visit only Fontainebleau, consider bringing a picnic from Paris. In fine weather, the château's gardens and nearby forest beckon. If you have a car, however, save your appetite for Barbizon (see below).

On the western edge of France's finest forest lies the village of **Barbizon,** home to a number of noted landscape artists — Corot, Millet, Rousseau, and Daumier. The colorful town has a lively mix of good restaurants, boutiques, and antiques shops — the perfect place to while away an afternoon. For lunch, try the **Relais de Barbizon,** 2 av. Charles de Gaulle (☎ **01-60-66-40-28).** They have a *prix fixe* menu at 30€, which features typical home-style dishes such as *confit de canard* and *baba au rhum* for dessert. The restaurant is open Thursday through Monday noon to

2:30 p.m. and 8 to 10 p.m., Tuesday noon to 2:30 p.m. Reservations are required on weekends.

If you stay in Fontainebleau for lunch, try **Le Table des Maréchaux** in the Hôtel Napoléon, 9 rue Grande (☎ **01-60-39-50-50;** www.naposite. com). Its 40€ three-course *ménu* may include a filet of sea bream with in a crunchy hazelnut shell, served with a green-tea-flavored stock. Finish up with a pear tart sprinkled with powdered sugar. In warm weather, diners can eat on the outdoor terrace.

The Cathedral at Chartres

The French sculptor Rodin dubbed this building "The Acropolis of France." Upon laying eyes on this greatest of High Gothic cathedrals, Napoléon declared, "Chartres is no place for an atheist." Perhaps the would-be emperor had been moved by the ethereal world of colored light that fills the cathedral (still the fourth-largest church in the world) on a sunny day, streaming through an awe-inspiring more than 2,500 sq. m (27,000 sq. ft.) of 12th- and 13th-century stained glass, turning the church walls into quasi-mystical portals to heaven.

It survived the French Revolution, even though it was scheduled for demolition. It withstood two world wars, when volunteers took down all its 12th- and 13th-century stained glass piece by piece. But for a majority of its visitors, the Cathédrale de Notre-Dame de Chartres (☎ **02-37-21-75-02;** www.diocesechartres.com; see the nearby "Notre-Dame de Chartres" map), one of the world's greatest Gothic cathedrals and one of the finest creations of the Middle Ages, comes second in importance to a small scrap of material housed inside. Known as the *Sancta Camisia,* it is said that it was worn by the Virgin Mary when she gave birth to Jesus. This sacred scarf was supposedly a gift from the Empress Irene of Byzantium to Charlemagne, and it has been resting in the cathedral of Chartres since A.D. 876 (**Note:** This refers to a different or earlier construction of the Chartres cathedral than we know today).

Getting there

You can see all this for around a 27€ round-trip train ticket from Paris's Gare Montparnasse, less than an hour's ride away. The **tourism office** (☎ **02-37-18-26-26;** www.chartres-tourisme.com) is right on the place de la Cathédrale.

If you'd like to drive to Chartres, take the A10/A11 highway from Porte d'Orléans and follow the signs to Le Mans and Chartres. The drive takes about 75 minutes.

Exploring the cathedral

Take one of Malcolm Miller's excellent 75-minute guided tours of Chartres Cathedral. Miller, an Englishman who has made the study of the cathedral his life's work, has published such books as *Chartres Cathedral* (Riverside Books Co.) and *Chartres Stained Glass* (Jarrold Publishing) and has been giving fascinating tours of the cathedral for more than 50 years. No need to reserve; meet inside the cathedral at the gift shop. Miller also gives private tours for groups starting at 125€ for up to 15 people. Call ☎ 02-37-28-15-58 or e-mail millerchartres@ aol.com for more information. Tours are Monday through Saturday at noon and 2:45 p.m. from Easter through November (although he is sometimes available in winter, too).

If you can't get in touch with Malcolm Miller, call the cathedral Welcome Center at ☎ 02-37-21-75-02. Guided Crypt visits are available, but in French only. They meet outside the cathedral at La Crypte store from April through October at 11 a.m. (excluding Sundays and holidays), 2:15 p.m., 3:30 p.m., and 4:30 p.m.; from June 22 through September 21, there is an additional tour at 5:15 p.m. From November through March, the tours leaves from the cafe gift shop in the north tower, at 11 a.m. and 4:15 p.m. (excluding Sundays and holidays). Crypt visits, which last 30 minutes, cost 2.70€ for adults, 2.10€ for seniors and children 7 to 18; it's free for kids 6 and under. Climb the tower for gargoyle close-ups Monday through Saturday from 9:30 a.m. to noon and 2:30 p.m. to 5 p.m. Admission is 7€ adults 26 and over, 4.50€ ages 18 to 25, free for children 17 and under. Note that the stone stairs are steep and winding and the climb isn't for everyone.

Sunday afternoons are a terrific time to visit, when free organ concerts (4:45–5:45 p.m.) and the filtered light coming in from the western windows make the church come wonderfully alive.

The cathedral that you see today dates principally from the 13th century, when it was built with the combined efforts and contributions of kings, princes, church officials, and pilgrims from across Europe. This Notre-Dame was among the first to use flying buttresses.

On your tour, begin at the very beginning — with the **entryway.** People say that Rodin sat for hours on the edge of the sidewalk, contemplating the portal, spellbound by its sculptured bodies draped in long, flowing robes with amazingly lifelike faces. Before entering, walk around to both the north and south portals, which date from the 13th century. The bays depict such biblical scenes as the expulsion of Adam and Eve from the Garden of Eden, and episodes from the life of the Virgin.

Next, just inside, are the **Clocher Vieux (Old Tower)** with its 105m (350-ft.) steeple dating from the 12th century, and the **Clocher Neuf (New Tower).** Originally built in 1134, the Clocher Neuf's elaborate ornamental tower was added between 1507 and 1513 following one of the many fires that swept through the cathedral.

You can climb to the top of the Clocher Neuf, but make sure your shoes aren't slippery — parts of the tower are without a railing and are quite steep and narrow.

Notre-Dame de Chartres

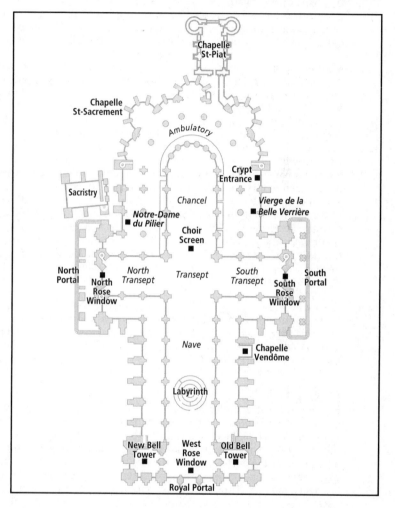

The cathedral is also known for its celebrated **choir screen.** Don't let the simple term fool you; this is a carved wood structure that took nearly 200 years to complete. The niches, 40 in all, contain statues illustrating scenes from the life of Mary. The screen is in the middle of the cathedral toward the altar.

Few of the rushed visitors ever notice the screen; they're transfixed by the stained-glass windows. Bring a pair of binoculars to better focus on the panes, which cover more than 2,508 sq. m (26,996 sq. ft.). The glass is unequaled anywhere in the world and is truly mystical. It was spared in both world wars, because in both wars, the glass was removed piece by piece. Currently, the Association Chartres, Sanctuaire du Monde has undertaken the considerable task of raising the millions of euro necessary for the restoration of the windows, which have suffered on both sides from smoke from the cathedral's candles as well as from pollution.

Most of the stained glass dates from the 12th and 13th centuries. Many visitors find it difficult to single out one panel or window of particular merit; however, the oldest is the 12th-century **Notre Dame de la Belle Verrière** (Our Lady of the Beautiful Window, sometimes called the Blue Virgin) on the south side. The colors from the glass are such a vibrant, startling blue that many find it hard to believe that the window is 1,000 years old. In the **nave** (the widest in France), have a look down at the 13th-century labyrinth. It was designed for pilgrims to navigate on their hands and knees as a form of penance, all 300m (1,000 ft.) of it. These days, much of it is covered with folding chairs for Mass. The wooden **Virgin of the Pillar,** to the left of the choir, dates from the 14th century. The **crypt** was built over a period of 200 years, beginning in the ninth century. Enshrined is **Our Lady of the Crypt,** a Madonna made in 1976 that replaced one destroyed during the Revolution. The *Sancta Camisia,* the holy relic that some people believe Mary wore during the birth of Jesus, is behind the choir screen in a chapel to the left of the church's treasury.

The cathedral is open April through September daily from 8 a.m. to 8 p.m., October through March daily from 7:30 a.m. to 7 p.m. Ask at the Chartres tourist office (☎ 02-37-18-26-26) outside the cathedral for information about tours in English and a schedule of Masses open to the public.

Dining options

Restaurants, cafes, and snack bars abound around town, but just a stone's throw from the cathedral is **Le Café Serpente,** 2 Cloître Notre-Dame (☎ 02-37-21-68-81). Facing the south side of the cathedral with outside tables, this restaurant serves traditional French fare at reasonable prices between 14€ and 22€ for two courses. House specialties are pigs' feet and veal kidneys, but typical bistro food, like confit de canard, are also available. If you're just there for a snack or light meal, the *salade composée* (large meal salads) and tasty omelets are available. The restaurant is open daily for lunch, and Monday through Saturday for dinner.

On the other side of the cathedral you can find **Le Cloître Gourmand,** 21 Cloître Notre-Dame (☎ 02-37-21-27-02), a charming and inexpensive restaurant that feels like you're eating in someone's kitchen. Here you can get simple entrees such as a potato leek soup for 6€; for a main course, they have a great pan-fried salmon with perfumed rice. The restaurant faces a shady side of the cathedral, allowing a view of medieval sculpture as you sip your *café.* The restaurant is open Monday through Saturday noon to 2 p.m.; it opens again around 7 p.m. for dinner.

For more upscale dining, take the time to wander through town where you'll discover **Le Moulin de Ponceau,** 21–23 rue de la Tannerie (☎ 02-37-35-30-05; www.moulindeponceau.fr). This chic restaurant can be on the expensive side, but it's worth it from the fresh market menu to the gorgeous scenery. Beautifully situated on the banks of the Eure River, this restaurant's terrace overlooks a stunning panorama of ancient houses, stone bridges, and weeping willows leaning into the gently flowing water. You might start with an appetizer of duck pâté served with foie gras and a red-wine jelly, moving on to a filet of marlin cooked in coconut milk served with homemade tagliatelles and crunchy vegetables. Menus are at 28€ and 38€ for three courses. To find rue de la Tannerie, head through old town, on rue au Lait, for example, in the direction of the Eure. The streets are very twisted, and there is no perfect route. Once you end up at the bank, cross the nearest bridge — rue de la Tannerie follows along its east bank. The restaurant is open Tuesday through Saturday noon to 2 p.m. and 7:30 to 9:30 p.m., Sunday noon to 2 p.m. If you have extra time, spend it exploring the medieval cobbled streets of the **Old Town.** At the foot of the cathedral are lanes with gabled and turreted houses and humped bridges spanning the Eure River. The turreted Norman house (it's the oldest-looking one there) on rue Chantault dates back nine centuries.

Stop in at the **Musée de Beaux-Arts de Chartres,** 29 Cloître Notre-Dame (☎ 02-37-90-45-80), to see paintings by old masters such as Watteau, Brosamer, and Zurbarán, and admire the museum's architecture, some of which dates back to the 15th century. The museum is open Wednesday through Monday 10 a.m. to noon and 2 to 5 p.m., Sunday 2 to 5 p.m. (to 6 p.m. daily May–Nov). It's closed on November 1 and 11 and December 25. Admission is 3.10€ for adults, 1.60€ for seniors and kids 12 and under, free for students.

Disneyland Paris

Disneyland Paris, known locally as **Le Parc Disneyland** (☎ 407-934-7639 in the United States, 01-60-30-60-53 in Paris; www.disneyland paris.com), is France's number-one attraction, with more than 50 million visitors a year. It celebrated its 15th anniversary in 2007. When it opened in 1992, the French were dead set against it; now 40 percent of its visitors are French, and half of those are Parisian. Set on a 2,000-hectare (5,000-acre) site (about one-fifth the size of Paris) in the suburb of Marne-la-Vallée, the park incorporates the elements of its Disney predecessors but gives them a European flair. Allow at least a full day to see Disneyland Paris.

Information about hotels and packages is constantly changing, so your best bet for staying up to date is to obtain the Disneyland Resort Paris brochure from the Web site a few months in advance.

Getting there

To get there, take the RER Line A from such central Paris RER/Métro stops as Châtelet-les-Halles or Nation or Gare de Lyon to Marne-la-Vallée/Chessy, within walking distance of the park. The RER station is in Zone 5 of the public-transport system, so the cheapest way there (and back again) is to buy a single-day Mobilis pass good through Zone 5, which costs 14€. Admission to the park varies depending on the season. From April through November, admission is 74€ adults, 63€ children 3 to 11. From December to March, admission is 68€ adults, 61€ children 3 to 11. The parks are free for children 2 and under.

Avoid lines at the resort by buying Disneyland passes at all RER A stations, except Marne-la-Vallée, and Métro stations including Charles de Gaulle–Étoile, Franklin D. Roosevelt, Gare de Lyon, Porte Maillot, Esplanade de la Défense, Anvers, Père-Lachaise, Place de Clichy, Gallieni, Havre-Caumartin, Villiers, Alésia, Barbès-Rochechouart, Châtelet, Denfert-Rochereau, and Gare de l'Est. The pass is good for either Disneyland Park or Walt Disney Studios but not both.

Within the park, a free shuttle bus connects the various hotels with the theme park, stopping every 6 to 15 minutes, depending on the time of year. Service begins an hour before the park opens and stops an hour after closing.

If you prefer to drive to Disneyland Paris, take the A4 highway east and exit at Park Euro Disney. Guest parking at any of the thousands of spaces costs 8€. A series of moving sidewalks speeds up pedestrian transit from the parking areas to the theme park entrance.

Exploring the park

The Disneyland Paris resort consists of two theme parks. The first, **Disneyland Park,** clusters together five "lands" of entertainment (Main Street, U.S.A.; Frontierland; Adventureland; Fantasyland; and Discoveryland) and is where most of the massive and well-designed hotels, a nightlife center (Le Festival Disney), swimming pools, tennis courts, dozens of restaurants, shows, an aquarium, and the Manchester United Soccer School are located. If your kids are younger than 7, they'll be best suited for Main Street, U.S.A., Fantasyland, Sleeping Beauty's Castle, and the afternoon parade. Children ages 7 through 12 will most likely enjoy Frontierland, the Phantom Manor ghost house, the Big Thunder Mountain roller coaster, Adventureland, Indiana Jones and the Temple of Doom roller coaster, and the Pirates of the Caribbean ride. Discoveryland, the Space Mountain roller coaster, and the Star Tours simulated spacecraft ride should please your teens.

Walt Disney Studios Park is the newer of the two parks and is set up as a movie studio come to life, where children participate in the movie-making process. The entrance is called the Front Lot and resembles the Hollywood Disney studios — water tower, gates, and all. En Coulisse restaurant is located here, serving the kind of food kids like and Americans are known for — hamburgers, pizza, salads, and ice cream. In a film studio resembling a street, kids can become a part of the filming of impromptu comedy sketches as they walk around the park; later in the day, they get to see themselves on-screen. In the Animation Courtyard, cartoon characters come to life via black light and mirrors, and children can play at being animators at interactive displays. The French Disney Channel has its studios here, in the Production Courtyard; kids get to see how a TV studio really works and may be asked to serve as extras. An international buffet, Rendez-Vous des Stars, is located here. The Back Lot features the Backlot Express Restaurant, serving sandwiches and other quick fare, and the Rock-n-Roller Coaster, a very fast and very loud ride (120 speakers playing Aerosmith) that whips you through an Aerosmith rock video. Calm down afterward by watching the stunt-show spectacular, which is highlighted by a high-speed car chase. Food kiosks sell popcorn, ice cream, hot dogs, and so on throughout the park.

A guide for visitors in wheelchairs gives important information about access to rides and other attractions all around the park. You can pick up a copy at City Hall in the Disneyland Park or call to have a copy sent to you (☎ **01-60-30-60-30**).

The hours of Disneyland Paris vary with the weather and season, so call before setting out. In general, however, the park is open daily from 9 a.m. to 8 p.m. It sometimes opens an hour later in mid-May, mid-June, and September and October. From September through December, the scheduling hours become erratic during certain weekends due to various school holidays, and they also vary with the weather. Definitely call or check online before you go at the Web site and phone number listed in the first paragraph of this section.

Avoid waiting in long lines with the free **FASTPASS.** After presenting the pass at the ride you want, you're given a time frame for when to come back and board the ride first upon your return. Ask for it at the ticket booth or City Hall.

Staying at Disneyland

If you want to stay at Disneyland overnight or for a few days, you need to book well in advance. Plenty of hotels are available at different price levels, and you can explore the options and book accommodations on the park's Web site at www.disneylandparis.com.

Monet's Gardens at Giverny

Monet moved to Giverny (☎ **02-32-51-28-21**; www.fondation-monet. com for Fondation Claude Monet, which runs the museum) in 1883, and the water lilies beneath the Japanese bridge in the garden and the flower garden became his regular subjects until his death in 1926. In 1966, the Monet family donated Giverny to the Académie des Beaux-Arts in Paris, perhaps the most prestigious fine-arts school in France, which subsequently opened the site to the public. Giverny has since become one of the most popular attractions in France, inspiring millions with its landscape and Provençal-themed house, but even the crowds can't completely overwhelm the magic.

Getting there

Catch an SNCF train at the Gare Saint-Lazare in Paris approximately every hour for the 45-minute trip to Vernon, the town nearest the Monet gardens. The round-trip fare is about 26€. From the station, bus no. 241 makes the 5km (3-mile) trip to the museum for 2.20€; a taxi ride costs 7€ to 10€. You could also rent a bike in Vernon or even go on foot — the route along the Seine makes for a nice walk.

If you're driving to Giverny, take the A13 highway from the Porte d'Auteuil to Bonnières, then D201 to Giverny. The whole trip takes about an hour.

Traveling to Giverny by tour bus is another option. **Cityrama,** 4 place des Pyramides, 1er (☎ **01-44-55-61-00**; www.cityrama.fr), has two trips to Giverny: a five-hour trip on Tuesday, Thursday, or Saturday for 70€ adults, 35€ children 4 to 11 (kids 3 and under ride free); and an all-day Giverny–Auvers-sur-Oise trip on Sunday or Wednesday for 166€ for adults, 115€ for children. Call or check online for specific dates.

Exploring the gardens

Even before you arrive at Giverny, you probably have some idea of what you're going to see — but nothing prepares you for the spectacular beauty of seeing the gardens up close. The gardens are usually at their best in May, June, and July. Should you yearn to have them almost to yourself, plan to be at the gates when the gardens open, or go on a rainy day (June is probably the busiest month, although they'll all be busy). You'll probably spend at least a half-day at Giverny, longer if you plan to eat lunch and visit the American Museum.

The gardens are open from April through November Tuesday through Sunday from 9:30 a.m. to 6 p.m., as well as Easter Monday and Whit Monday (51 days after Easter). Admission to the house and gardens is 6€ for adults, 4.50€ for students, 3.50€ for ages 7 to 12, and free for children 6 and under; reservations are required.

Some say Monet's influence was responsible for the influx of American artists into the village of Giverny in the late 1880s. Others say that Monet had little contact with the Americans, and it was Giverny's beauty that captured the hearts of painters such as John Singer Sargent and William Metcalf, who began spending their summers there. In any case, at one point, more than 50 American artists lived in Giverny with their families. You can see much of their work at the **Musée des Impressionnismes Giverny,** formerly le Musée d'Art Américain Giverny (☎ **02-32-51-94-65**; www.museedesimpressionnismesgiverny.com), just 91m (300 ft.) from Monet's house and gardens.

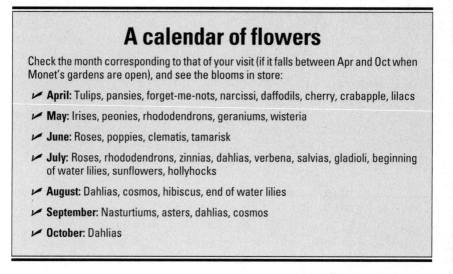

A calendar of flowers

Check the month corresponding to that of your visit (if it falls between Apr and Oct when Monet's gardens are open), and see the blooms in store:

- ✓ **April:** Tulips, pansies, forget-me-nots, narcissi, daffodils, cherry, crabapple, lilacs
- ✓ **May:** Irises, peonies, rhododendrons, geraniums, wisteria
- ✓ **June:** Roses, poppies, clematis, tamarisk
- ✓ **July:** Roses, rhododendrons, zinnias, dahlias, verbena, salvias, gladioli, beginning of water lilies, sunflowers, hollyhocks
- ✓ **August:** Dahlias, cosmos, hibiscus, end of water lilies
- ✓ **September:** Nasturtiums, asters, dahlias, cosmos
- ✓ **October:** Dahlias

The museum is open April through October Tuesday through Sunday from 10 a.m. to 6 p.m., as well as Easter Monday and Whit Monday (51 days after Easter). Admission is 6.50€ for adults; 4.50€ for seniors, students, and ages 13 to 18; 3€ for ages 7 to 12; and free for children 6 and under. Admission is free for all on the first Sunday of every month.

Dining options

Your entry ticket is no longer valid once you leave Monet's home, so think ahead about whether you want to eat lunch before or after your visit. It may be smart to arrive in the early afternoon to have a better chance of avoiding the crowds in the morning.

There are many little cafes and *crêperies* in the square directly across from Monet's house and on the adjacent street. A good restaurant in town is **Le Relais Normand** (☎ 02-32-21-16-12) in the Hôtel d'Evreux, an old Norman manor house with a fireplace and terrace. It serves such delicious dishes as roasted Normandy oysters with a nut and mushroom filling, pan-fried scallops served with a country-style carrot fondue, and roasted duck breast stuffed with girolle mushrooms. The three *prix fixe* menus cost 21€ and 30€. The restaurant is open for lunch Tuesday through Sunday from noon to 3 p.m.

Part V
Living It Up After Dark: Paris Nightlife

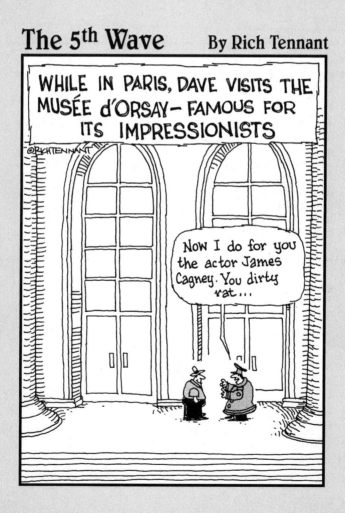

In this part . . .

Paris may not be a city that never sleeps, but it's just as fabulous after the sun sets as it is during the day. There is so much to do! Take your pick of French-language, English-language, or avant-garde theater; ballet; opera; symphony; and even cabaret spectacles like Moulin Rouge. But beware! Events may sell out quickly. Chapter 15 gives you the low-down on Paris's vibrant theater scene and previews the symphony, opera, and ballet. Chapter 16 hits the bars and clubs, jumping jazz spots, live-music venues, classy cocktail joints, and those naughty cabarets.

Chapter 15

Applauding the Cultural Scene

. . . .

In This Chapter

▶ Getting the inside scoop on the performing-arts scene
▶ Finding out what's playing and how to get tickets
▶ Taking in plays, symphony, opera, and dance in Paris

. . . .

*W*hatever your choice of the classic arts, you can be guaranteed to find it in excellent form in Paris. This is the city that gave the world playwrights Molière, Victor Hugo, Pierre Corneille, and Jean Racine, and produced actors Sarah Bernhardt and Antonin Artaud. Fortunately for visitors, you don't need to understand French to take in an evening of culture here. Paris has a world-class orchestra, opera, ballet companies — and brilliant venues that house them. There's a flourishing English-language theater scene, and cutting-edge theater productions with scope and visuals that make language secondary!

This chapter helps you find out what's going on and then gets you there.

Getting the Inside Scoop

Paris is one of *the* places in the world to see top-tier ballet and listen to world-renowned symphonies. Unlike New York City, where theaters are located in the area around Broadway and 42nd streets, and serious music and ballet happen at Carnegie Hall and Lincoln Center, in Paris cultural offerings are scattered around the city, from the **Opéra Bastille** in the 12th *arrondissement* to **Théâtre National de la Colline** in the 20th. Since late 2009 the director of the Opéra Nationale de Paris (which includes both the Opéra Bastille and the beautiful **Palais Garnier**) has been **Nicolas Joel,** a Paris native with international directing credits, including a celebrated 1996 production of *Andrea Chénier* at the Metropolitan Opera in New York, in which Luciano Pavarotti played the title character. Highlights of the 2011 Paris opera program include Puccini's *Madame Butterfly,* with international star Micaela Carosi in the title role, and Verdi's *Luisa Miller,* with musical direction by Israeli conductor Daniel Oren. In 2011, the Opéra Garnier will present its recurring production of another Puccini classic, *Tosca,* while the French national ballet company will perform Prokofiev's *Romeo and Juliet,* with the original 1984 choreography of Russian superstar Rudolf Nureyev. Another treat on the program is the guest ballet company, Russia's world-renowned Bolshoi Theater, performing the French Revolution–themed *Flames of Paris.*

Paris is home to an *early music* scene (music of the Middle Ages, Renaissance, baroque, rococo, and the early classical eras), led by the early music group **Les Arts Florissants** (www.arts-florissants.com), which was founded in 1979 and has performed baroque operas in Paris's biggest venues. Check out their Web site for a concert schedule and a links to buy tickets. You can also check out the Paris Convention and Visitors Bureau Web site (http://en.parisinfo.com) for venues and pricing.

The French just love American musicals! *West Side Story* celebrated its 50th anniversary in Paris to rave reviews, while *Cabaret, The Lion King,* and even *Zorro* had huge success, bringing in over 1.5 million spectators between the three. Parisians waited with bated breath for the French-language production of *Mamma Mia!,* which debuted in October 2010. Songs from musicals are especially popular and mainstream in France, sometimes selling albums before the show even opens. If you see a show, don't be surprised to hear some of its music on the radio.

On any given day, close to a hundred theatrical productions may be going on in Paris and the surrounding area. Because Paris is just a 3½-hour Eurostar ride from London, some of that city's finest actors have found their way across the channel and into the city's English-language theater community, where they joined up with American, Australian, and even some bilingual French *confrères* (colleagues). Productions in English may not be plentiful, but quality is high and a wide range of styles is offered.

Arrive early to performances. On the reverse side of some Paris theater tickets may be written: *Les spectateurs retardaires ne peuvent à être placés que lors d'une interruption du spectacle et en fonction de l'accessibilité.* In other words, late arrivals cannot be seated until there is an interruption (intermission) in the play, if they're seated at all. Others may say: *Pour bien garantir votre place, nous vous remercions en avance d'arriver un quart d'heure avant l'ouverture de la spectacle.* This means if you show up to the theater exactly at curtain-opening (instead of 15 minutes in advance), your seat may have been already given away, depending on the popularity of the show. Opera tickets say: *Les spectateurs retardaires ne peuvent à être placés qu'à la fin du premier tableau, du premier acte de l'ouvrage ou à l'entracte,* meaning that late arrivals can't be seated until the end of the first scene, the first act, or between acts. Some theaters won't even seat those who arrive after the curtain rises (in many cases, because the plays being performed are short with no intermission). You want to arrive at the theater or opera early anyway; the bars in these locations are generally very good and are relaxing places to unwind before the shows.

Dinner and a show

Because performances tend to start around 8 p.m. and French restaurants tend to open at 7 p.m., with dining lasting anywhere from 1½ to 3 hours or more, what's a hungry showgoer to do? Have a snack before the show, and feast afterward at one of the many cafes or brasseries open late. Some of the following are listed in Chapter 10, and plenty more can be found around the city.

✔ **Au Pied de Cochon** (1er) is open 24 hours.

✔ **Bofinger** (4e) is open until 1 a.m.

✔ The Latin Quarter's infamous **Brasserie Balzar** (5e) stays open until midnight.

✔ **Brasserie île Saint-Louis** (4e), on the tip of île Saint-Louis right across from Notre-Dame, is open until midnight.

✔ **Café Marly** (1er) in the Louvre's courtyard, is open until 1 a.m.

✔ You can order food at showy **Fouquet's** (8e), on the Champs-Elysées, until 2 a.m.

✔ **La Coupole** (14e), on boulevard du Montparnasse, is open until 1:30 a.m. on weekends.

A *placeuse* (an usher, usually female) wearing a small purse around her neck will show you to your seats. Yes, that purse is for tips, which are expected — generally 1€ or 2€ per person.

Paris audiences tend to dress up for performances, in nice jewelry and dressy pants or skirts for the women, jackets for the men. Generally, the nicer the venue, the dressier the look. Thus, for men a tie and jacket are recommended at the Palais Garnier, whereas an open collar under a stylish jacket would be the look for a performance at Bouffes du Nord.

Finding Out What's Playing and Getting Tickets

Several local publications provide up-to-the-minute listings of performances and other evening entertainment. *Pariscope* (www.pariscope.fr) is a weekly guide with thorough listings of movies, plays, ballet, art exhibits, clubs, and more. It can be found at any newsstand. *L'Officiel des Spectacles* (www.offi.fr) is another weekly guide in French. The *Paris Free Voice* is a former monthly publication, now online only, that spotlights events of interest to English speakers, including poetry readings, plays, and literary evenings at English-language bookstores and libraries. You can find it at cybercafes and English-language bookstores or at www.parisvoice.com.

Saving money on tickets

For half-price theater tickets for national theaters and other venues, go to **Le Kiosque Théâtre** (☎ **01-42-65-35-64**; www.kiosquetheatre.com), a kiosk with red signs at the northwest corner of the Madeleine Church (directly across from 15 place de la Madeleine; Métro: Madeleine), at place des Ternes (on the island median in the middle; Métro: Ternes), and on the promenade by the Tour Montparnasse (between the tower and the entrance to the train station, Métro: Montparnasse-Bienvenüe) to buy tickets for same-day performances. The panels all around the kiosk indicate sold-out shows with a little red man; a little green man tells you that tickets are still available. The kiosks are open Tuesday through Saturday from 12:30 to 8 p.m., Sunday from 12:30 to 4 p.m. Try to arrive no later than noon, because lines are usually long. Additionally, you can try the Web sites www.ticketac.com and www.webguichet.com for reduced-price tickets and last-minute deals, although these sites are in French only.

You can also get information online from the **Paris Convention and Visitors Bureau** (http://en.parisinfo.com) and **France Guide** (www.franceguide.com), which is the official site of the French Government Tourist Office. Likewise, try **Culture Kiosque** (www.culturekiosque.com) for excellent magazine-style sites about opera and dance in Europe, including schedules, reviews, and phone numbers for ordering tickets.

Ticket prices in this chapter are approximate; costs vary, depending on who is performing what on which day of the week. Call the theaters for information, or consult *Pariscope* and other entertainment listings. Many concert, theater, and dance tickets are sold through **Fnac** department stores and at the box office. You can find a dozen or so Fnac outlets throughout Paris; the most prominent is 74 av. des Champs-Elysées, 8e (Métro: George V). You can also reserve online at Fnac (www.fnac spectacles.com). Also try **Ticketnet** (www.ticketnet.fr), which allows you to buy tickets to cultural events online.

Raising the Curtain on the Performing Arts

The theaters listed here are national theaters supported by the government, but many private ones also exist. For full listings, consult *Pariscope* and *L'Officiel des Spectacles* (see above).

Attending the theater

A good mix of modern and classic tragedies and comedies comes alive in breathtaking performances in the **Salle Richelieu** of **Le Comédie-Française,** 2 rue de Richelieu, 1er (☎ **08-25-10-16-80** or 01-44-58-15-15 from abroad; www.comedie-francaise.fr; Métro: Palais Royal–Musée du Louvre). Performances are in French. Tickets cost 12€ to 39€.

Last-minute seats are on sale one hour before the start of the performance; people 28 and older can purchase a Section C ticket for 50 percent off, sometimes costing as low as 5€. For those who want to buy tickets at the theater, the ticket window is open daily 11 a.m. to 6 p.m. Or purchase full-price tickets online; the Web site is in French with some English, but it's fairly easy to navigate.

Also a part of Le Comédie-Française, the **Théâtre du Vieux Colombier,** 21 rue Vieux Colombier, 6e (☎ 01-44-39-87-00-01; Métro: Saint-Sulpice), is an intimate 300-seat venue where mostly modern works are performed. Tickets cost 8€ to 29€ for adults, 6€ to 12€ for those 26 and under. Buy nondiscounted tickets online at www.comedie-francaise. fr. Those purchasing tickets at a reduced rate from abroad can call ☎ 33-1-44-58-15-15 daily 11 a.m. to 6:30 p.m. (Remember to factor in the time difference.)

Le Comédie-Française also has a workshop in the **Carrousel du Louvre Studio-Théâtre** (☎ 01-44-58-98-58), where actors perform one-hour plays and readings. Video projections of plays and films are also shown here. Tickets are sold online at www.comedie-francaise.fr or at the ticket window one hour before the performance and cost 8€ to 18€ for adults, 6€ to 14€ for seniors, and 6€ to 9€ for people 27 and under.

Directly across the Seine from the Eiffel Tower in the Art Deco Palais de Chaillot, is the **Théâtre National de Chaillot,** 1 place du Trocadéro, 16e (☎ 01-53-65-30-00; www.theatre-chaillot.fr; Métro: Trocadéro), the space for contemporary popular plays, dance, and other performances. A highlight of the 2011 season is Le Ballet Biarritz performing suites from Tchaikovsky's *Sleeping Beauty, Swan Lake,* and *The Nutcracker.* The bar has a good view of the Eiffel Tower. Tickets are about 24€ to 32€ for adults, 11€ to 13€ for people 26 and under. Reservations can be made in person or by telephone Monday through Saturday 11 a.m. to 7 p.m. or through the theater's website.

The **Théâtre National de la Colline,** 15 rue Malte-Brun, 20e (☎ 01-44-62-52-52; www.colline.fr; Métro: Gambetta), has modern drama from around the world, and the **Petit Théâtre,** located upstairs, has short plays and offerings from international theater's less famous but up-and-coming playwrights. Arrive early to have a glass of wine and admire the view from the Café de la Colline in the lobby. Highlights of the 2011 season include Eugene O'Neill's Pulitzer Prize–winning play *Long Day's Journey into Night.* Tickets cost 27€ to 35€ for adults, 22€ for seniors, and 13€ for people 29 and under; on Tuesdays, adults and seniors pay 19€ for certain spectacles. To purchase tickets, visit the box office Monday through Saturday from 11 a.m. to 6:30 p.m. or buy online. This was the first theater in France where Shakespeare was performed in English.

Shows at **Odéon Théâtre de l'Europe,** 6 place de l'Odéon, 6e (☎ 01-44-85-40-00; www.theatre-odeon.fr; Métro: Odéon), vary from eclectic to classic; Lou Reed once read his poems at the Odéon. More recently the company put on a trilogy of plays by the godfather of Greek tragedy,

Aeschylus; in the same season, godmother of punk Patti Smith read passages from her autobiography *Just Kids.* Tickets in the Berthier theaters are 32€ for adults, 16€ for seniors and ages 29 and under. On Thursdays, adults pay only 24€. At Theatre de l'Odéon, tickets range from 10€ to 32€ for adults, 6€ to 16€ for students and seniors. To purchase tickets by phone, call ☎ 01-44-85-40-40 Monday through Saturday 11 a.m. to 6:30 p.m. Tickets also go on sale at the box office at each of the theaters 90 minutes before the show, or you can purchase online.

Seeking English-language theater

Summer is a good time to catch English-language theater in Paris. Start by checking out www.parisvoice.com for listings of plays in English. **Le Théâtre de Nesle,** 8 rue de Nesle, 6e (☎ 01-46-34-61-04; www.galerie denesle.com; Métro: Saint-Michel), and **Les Déchargeurs,** 3 rue des Déchargeurs, 1er (☎ 01-42-36-00-02 or 08-92-70-12-28 for reservations; www.lesdechargeurs.fr; Métro: Châtelet), sometimes stage English-language plays. For comedy in English, try **Laughing & Music Matters,** in the salsa club La Java, 105 rue Faubourg du Temple, 10e (☎ 01-53-19-98-88; www.anythingmatters.com; Métro: Goncourt–Hôpital Saint-Louis). This company is thriving, and the lineups are always terrific, featuring award-winning comics from the United States, the United Kingdom, Ireland, and Australia. Doors usually open at 8:30 p.m.; admission varies, but count on paying 15€ to 25€ at the door. The intimate **Théâtre de la Main d'Or,** 15 passage de la Main d'Or, 11e (☎ 01-43-38-06-99; Métro: Ledru-Rollin) sometimes has one-man acts or plays in English; in 2010, comedian Olivier Giraud began an extended run of his *How to Become Parisian in One Hour,* a comical introductory lesson for fitting in with the rudest of Parisians. Tickets cost anywhere from 10€ to 20€.

Other English-language theaters include the **International Players** (www.internationalplayers.co.uk), a nonprofessional but still high-quality Anglophone theater company that performs musicals and plays in its space just outside of the city limits in Saint-Germain-en-Laye (RER: Saint-Germain-en-Laye). Past productions include *The Lady in the Van; The Secret Diary of Adrian Mole, Aged 13¾;* and *April in Paris.* Actors in the international drama company **Drama Ties** (☎ 01-75-50-16-91; www.drama-ties.fr), started in 1901, put on their own original plays in English and use various theaters in and around Paris. **The Théâtre en Anglais** (☎ 01-55-02-37-87; http://theatre.anglais.free.fr), outside the city in Asnières-sur-Seine, performs classic plays in English with an excellent troupe. The 2010 season included *One Flew Over the Cuckoo's Nest* and *The Strange Case of Dr. Jekyll and Mr. Hyde.*

Then again, some theater isn't meant to be understood. In fact, sometimes *not* understanding the language can actually be a bonus. Several well-known avant-garde theater companies are located in Paris, including **Theatre des Bouffes du Nord,** at 37 bis bd. Chapelle, 10e (☎ 01-46-07-34-50; www.bouffesdunord.com), run by the legendary Peter Brook with Micheline Rozan, and **Le Théâtre du Soleil,** in the bois de

Vincennes, 12e (☎ **01-43-74-24-08;** www.theatre-du-soleil.fr), known for its stunning adaptations of both classic and original works. Even though the performances are usually in French, the scope of these productions is so large and the visuals are so profound, you may not even notice that you haven't understood a single word.

Listening to classical music and the symphony

Classical music concerts occur throughout the year, and many of them are quite affordable. Look for flyers at churches announcing schedule times, prices, and locations.

More than a dozen Parisian churches regularly schedule relatively inexpensive organ recitals and concerts. The most glorious, where the music is nearly outdone by the gorgeous stained-glass windows, is **Sainte-Chapelle,** 4 bd. du Palais, 1er (☎ **01-44-07-12-38;** Métro: Cité). Concerts take place every day between March and November at 7 and 8:30 p.m. You can also hear music at **Saint-Eustache,** 1 rue Montmartre, 1er (☎ **01-42-36-31-05;** Métro: Les Halles); **Saint-Sulpice,** place Saint-Sulpice, 6e (☎ **01-42-34-59-60;** Métro: Saint-Sulpice), which has wonderfully resonant eight-columned pipe-organ concerts on most Sundays at 4 p.m.; **Saint-Germain-des-Prés,** place Saint-Germain-des-Prés, 6e (☎ **01-55-42-81-33;** Métro: Saint-Germain-des-Prés); the **Madeleine,** place de la Madeleine, 8e (☎ **01-44-51-69-00;** Métro: Madeleine); and **Saint-Louis en l'île,** 19 rue Saint-Louis-en-l'île, 4e (☎ **01-46-34-11-60;** Métro: Pont-Marie). It may be a less magnificent setting, but the friendliness of the people attending Sunday concerts at the **American Church,** 65 quai d'Orsay, 7e (☎ **01-40-62-05-00;** www.acparis.org; Métro: Invalides or Alma-Marceau), makes up for the décor. Their Atelier concert series takes place at 5 p.m. Sundays. Check the Web site for other musical events.

Free concerts are staged occasionally in the parks and gardens (see Chapter 3 for a calendar). **Maison de Radio France,** 116 av. du President Kennedy, 16e (☎ **01-56-40-12-12;** www.radiofrance.fr; Métro: Kennedy–Radio France), offers free tickets to recordings of some concerts. Tickets are available on the spot an hour before the recording starts. The **Conservatoire National Supérieur de Musique** at the Cité de la Musique, 209 av. Jean Jaurès, 19e (☎ **01-40-40-45-45;** www.cite-musique.fr; Métro: Porte de Pantin), stages free concerts and ballets performed by students at the conservatory, while the **Concert Hall** here (☎ **01-44-84-44-84**) plays host to all types of performances, from jazz to world music.

The **Salle Pleyel,** 252 rue du Faubourg-Saint-Honoré, 8e (☎ **01-42-56-13-13;** www.sallepleyel.fr), is home to the Orchestre de Paris and gives 50 concerts a year. The Radio France Philharmonic also plays about 20 concerts a year here, and the lucky traveler may catch a performance of the London Symphony Orchestra, which often visits several times a season. This magnificent concert hall has been acoustically fine-tuned and refurnished with more comfortable seating and delivers some grand musical experiences. Reservations are best made by phone Monday through Saturday noon to 7 p.m. Senior citizens and those 26 and under take note: An hour before the show, any available last-minute tickets are offered at just 10€, a significant savings over tickets that normally can range from 15€ to 190€. There's a 15 percent discount on tickets for those with disabilities.

Enjoying opera and ballet

Whatever your choice of the classic arts — opera, ballet, concerts, recitals — you'll find it performed in Paris by local and international performers of the highest caliber in some of the most wonderful venues imaginable. Inaugurated in 1874, the **Châtelet, Théâtre Musical de Paris,** 1 place du Châtelet, 1er (☎ **01-40-28-28-40;** www.chatelet-theatre. com; Métro: Châtelet), is one of the top places to take in culture in Paris. *Edward Scissorhands,* the ballet, made its debut here in fall 2008, while a production of the musical *Show Boat* ran in 2010. Upcoming highlights include their annual summer dance festival *Les Etés de la Danse de Paris,* Rossini's celebrated opera *The Barber of Seville,* a performance of Handel's *Messiah,* and the creepy Sondheim classic *Sweeny Todd.* Tickets range from 10€ to 100€. The box office, open daily from 11 a.m. to 7 p.m., offers last-minute tickets at reduced prices to those 28 and under and to seniors 65 and over around 15 minutes before shows begin. There is a 2.50€ surcharge for Internet and phone reservations.

You can see dazzling performances by the national opera and ballet troupes at both the radiant **Palais Garnier,** place de l'Opéra, 9e (☎ **01-72-29-35-35** from abroad or 08-92-89-90-90 for reservations, 0.35€ per minute; www.opera-de-paris.fr; Métro: Opéra; RER: Auber), and the ultramodern **Opéra Bastille** (see below). The Palais Garnier conducts more ballet performances, and the Opéra Bastille puts on more opera. Tickets are priced from 5€ for seats that have little or no visibility (you can buy these only at the box office an hour before the performance) to 180€ for the first row of the balcony. Reserve by phone up to four weeks in advance and buy at the ticket windows for performances up to 14 days in advance (including same-day tickets). Making reservations online or by phone adds a 3€ surcharge. The box office, located in the building between the rue Scribe and rue Auber, is open Monday through Friday 9 a.m. to 6 p.m., Saturday 9 a.m. to 1 p.m.

The **Opéra Bastille,** place de la Bastille, 12e (☎ **08-92-89-90-90** for reservations, 0.35€ per minute; www.opera-de-paris.fr; Métro: Bastille), offers first-class comfort and magnificent acoustics at each level of the auditorium, although Parisians tend to think the building is a badly designed eyesore. The opera house is located at the place de la Bastille; at night, kids crowd the steps, showing off their skateboarding moves, talking on cellphones, and flirting. Tickets are priced between 5€ for reduced- and no-visibility seats to 172€ for the front rows of orchestra and balcony seating. Reserve by phone up to four weeks in advance or buy at the ticket windows for performances up to 14 days in advance (including same-day tickets). The cheapest seats are on sale only at the box office. Making reservations online or by phone incurs a 3€ surcharge; to make a reservation by phone, call Monday through Friday 9 a.m. to 6 p.m., Saturday 9 a.m. to 1 p.m. The box office, located at 130 rue de Lyon (the side of the opera house facing the Bastille monument), is open Monday through Friday 10:30 a.m. to 6:30 p.m.

The other major venue for opera is the stunning Belle Epoque **Opéra Comique,** 5 rue Favart, 2e (☎ **08-25-01-01-23** for reservations; www. opera-comique.com; Métro: Richelieu-Drouot), which offers wonderful musical theater in the Salle Favart, a more intimate venue than its opera hall counterparts (the auditorium is so small, you can hear people whispering onstage). Highlights for the 2011 season are Prokofiev's *Betrothal in a Monastery* and Offenbach's *Les Brigands*. Tickets are priced from 6€ to 115€ depending on the performance. The box office at place Boieldieu, 2e (at the front of the theater), is open Monday through Saturday 11 a.m. to 7 p.m., Sunday 11 a.m. to 1 p.m.

Chapter 16

Hitting the Clubs and Bars

In This Chapter

▶ Getting the lowdown on the latest hot spots
▶ Searching out your kind of music and dancing
▶ Unwinding over cocktails

*P*aris affords plenty of opportunities to paint the town *rouge* all night long. Bars usually close around 2 a.m., but most clubs don't open until 11 p.m., and the music doesn't stop pumping until dawn. Check the listings (in French) in **Night Life, Nova,** or **Pariscope** magazines, or look at the recently minted www.parisnightlife.fr.

Hot Spots for Cool Jazz

If there's one thing you can count on in Paris, it's that the stalwart **Caveau de la Hûchette,** 5 rue de la Hûchette, 5e (☎ **01-43-26-65-05;** www.caveaudelahuchette.fr; Métro or RER: Saint-Michel), will still be around. It's a legendary club in a cozy, cave-like space that has been welcoming jazz bands for more than 60 years. Locals, students, and tourists of all ages converge here for jitterbugging with a noisy, friendly crowd. Cover is 12€ Monday through Thursday, 14€ Friday through Sunday and holidays from 9:30 p.m. to 2:30 a.m. Students 25 and under pay 10€ all nights. Music starts at 10:15 p.m.

New Orleans jazz is on the menu at **Le Petit Journal Saint-Michel,** 71 bd. Saint-Michel, 5e (☎ **01-43-26-28-59;** http://claude.philips.pagesperso-orange.fr; Métro: Cluny–La Sorbonne). You can hit the club for the 48€ dinner, which includes a two-course meal, a drink, and music, or pay a 17€ or 20€ cover for entry with a drink included (the cheaper price is for nonalcoholic drinks). It's open Monday through Saturday at 7 p.m., with concerts starting around 9:15 p.m. If you're looking for old-school R&B, blues, and more contemporary jazz, check out its sister club, **Le Petit Journal Montparnasse,** 13 rue du Commandant-Mouchotte, 14e (☎ **01-43-21-56-70;** www.petitjournalmontparnasse.com. Métro: Gaîté or Gare Montparnasse). At **Aux Trois Mailletz,** 56 rue Galande, 6e (☎ **01-43-25-96-86** or 01-43-54-00-79; www.lestrois mailletz.fr; Métro: Saint-Michel) — a piano bar, restaurant, and cabaret — jazz pianists and singers put on evening shows for diners (not the best food, but you can just have their fairly expensive cocktails instead), and the cabaret is host to all kinds of music and dance, from jazz, swing, and funk to world music — sometimes running until 5 a.m.

Near Les Halles pedestrian district, the rue des Lombards is a terrific place to hear some of France's most interesting jazz; the clubs on this street formed the "Paris Jazz Club." Originally just a neighborhood venture, this group has member clubs all over the city and even the nearby suburbs; go to www.parisjazzclub.net for more information. Clubs on rue des Lombards include the granddaddy of Paris Jazz Club, **Duc des Lombards,** 42 rue des Lombards, 1er (☎ **01-42-33-22-88;** www. ducdeslombards.com; Métro: Châtelet–Les Halles), which is often crowded with casually dressed enthusiasts. A ticket to a show starts at 23€ and is usually no more expensive than 30€ (you can also reserve online). **Le Sunset** and **Le Sunside,** both at no. 60 (☎ **01-40-26-46-60** and ☎ **01-40-26-21-25,** respectively; www.sunset-sunside.com), are temples to eclectic (Le Sunset) and more traditional (Le Sunside) jazz that can be heard in the venue's basement and street-level bars. Ticketed concerts are priced around 25€; some shows are free (check the Web site for listings and discounted prices). World music fans go to **Le Baiser Salé** at no. 56 (☎ **01-42-33-37-71;** www.lebaisersale.com; Métro: Châtelet), an intimate venue that gets crowded with fans who love fusion jazz, funk, Brazilian, Afro-Caribbean, funk, and meringue. The tickets starts around 15€ and can be purchased at the door or on the Web through the Baiser Salé Web site or at www.fnacspectacles.com. The club is open daily from 7 p.m. to dawn, with concerts usually starting around 9 p.m.

It's often standing room only at **New Morning,** 7–9 rue des Petites-Ecuries, 10e (☎ **01-45-23-51-41;** www.newmorning.com; Métro: Château-d'Eau), where the best jazz musicians from around the world perform to an audience that knows their jazz. It's one of Paris's best jazz clubs, and past performers include Stan Getz, Dizzy Gillespie, Miles Davis, and Wynton Marsalis. The venue opens at 8 p.m. and concerts start at 9 p.m. Cover starts at around 15€, depending on the act, and advance tickets are available at www.fnacspectacles.com.

Jazz lovers who visit Paris on June and July weekends can laze among the flowers of the Bois de Vincennes's beautiful Parc Floral (Métro: Château de Vincennes) and hear world-renowned acts during the Paris Jazz Festival. For more information, go to www.parisjazzfestival.fr/en.

Rockin' Out to Live Music

If you're looking to go shake your goods on *la piste* (the dance floor), Paris will not disappoint. A wide array of venues is available, and they range in character from fancy and fashionable to dressed down and rocked out. Many smaller venues with dance floors showcase live music and talented DJs, and most are devoted to a particular music scene. In this section, I list some of the best venues for new and upcoming music of varying genres — rock, indie-rock, pop, electro, funk, and everything in-between. Because the scene is always evolving, check out *Pariscope* (www.pariscope.fr) and the recently created **Paris Nightlife** (www.parisnightlife.fr).

L'Alimentation Générale, 64 rue Jean-Pierre Timbaud, 11e (☎ 01-43-55-42-50; www.alimentation-generale.net; Métro: Parmentier), is a favorite venue of the indie-music crowd. Rock shows, electro, and all kinds of funky live music get played here. The club is open every day from 6 p.m. to 2 a.m.; the crowd is artsy, young, and hip. Cover is around 5€.

In a similar vein to Alimentation Générale (and within a five-minute walk) are **l'International,** 5–7 rue Moret (☎ 01-49-29-76-45; www.linter national.fr), which hosts eclectic rock concerts for the hipster set, and, just around the corner, **Le Nouveau Casino,** 109 rue Oberkampf, 11e (☎ 01-43-57-57-40; www.nouveaucasino.net), which also hosts live shows in the early evenings (think indie-rock, dance hall, dub, disco, and anything edgy), moving onto club nights from midnight until dawn. Cover is usually around 12€.

La Flèche d'Or, 102 bis rue de Bagnolet, 20e (☎ 01-44-64-01-02; www.flechedor.fr; Métro: Alexandre-Dumas), is reputed to host some of the best DJs in Paris. Denizens of all kinds of music flock to this former Charonne train station, where you can still see the tracks beneath a glass atrium. The club's weeknight openings vary, but count on its being in full-swing Thursday through Saturday from 8 p.m. until at least 2 a.m. Cover ranges from free to 15€, depending on the act, usually with a free drink included.

It doesn't matter that **La Bellevilloise,** 19–21 rue Boyer, 20e (☎ 01-46-36-07-07; www.labellevilloise.com; Métro: Ménilmontant), is a little off the beaten path, because it houses a great fusion restaurant (La Halle aux Oliviers), a two-level club, and even an art gallery in the daytime. DJs and live shows (rock, reggae, and every indie scene in between) take over the basement-level dance floor (crowd-surfing has been known to occur there), while the upstairs is an unpretentious lounge area with a great outdoor terrace for smokers. It's open Monday through Thursday 7:30 p.m. to 1 a.m., Friday and Saturday 7:30 p.m. to 4 a.m. Cover varies from 10€ to 15€, depending on the program.

Perched near the eastern edge of the Parc des Buttes Chaumont is **Rosa Bonheur** (enter the park by rue Botzaris and follow the footpath along the perimeter of avenue de la Cascade; ☎ 01-42-00-00-045; www.rosa bonheur.fr; Métro: Botzaris), a popular venue where you can buy *tapas*-style dinner to eat on the terrace picnic benches, and then return inside to dance until midnight. Best of all, there is never a cover. The crowd is as eclectic and diverse as the music, which ranges from disco and pop to hip-hop and indie rock. Sunday nights are a popular gay night, but the place is generally mixed.

If it's after midnight and you're in the center of the city, rock bar **Le Truskel,** 12 rue Feydeau, 2e (☎ 01-40-26-59-27; Métro: Bourse, Grands Boulevards), is a sort of Irish pub with a basement "microclub" that has been drawing in crowds of 20-somethings since it opened in 2002. Visiting big-name luminaries include indie groups Jarvis Cocker and Bloc Party, as well as U.K. bad boy Pete Doherty. It's open Tuesday 8 p.m. to 3 a.m., Wednesday through Saturday 8 p.m. to 5 a.m.

Toward the north of the city in the Pigalle red-light district, **Le Divan du Monde,** 75 rue des Martyrs, 18e (☎ 01-42-52-02-46; www.divandu monde.com; Métro: Pigalle), is a fantastic venue that hosts concerts and club nights with lots of dancing. Dress code is laid back, and you can hear anything from rock, pop, and world music to electro and deep funk. Concerts start Monday through Saturday anytime from 7 to 10 p.m., Sunday at 5 p.m. Cover varies according to the act but can start at 8€ for a DJ to 35€ for a concert. Nearby, the former lesbian cabaret **Chez Moune,** 54 rue Jean-Baptiste Pigalle, 9e (☎ 01-45-26-64-64; www.chez moune.fr; Métro: Pigalle), has been reinvented as a hip club for lovers of house, electro, and neo-disco beats. The mixed crowd is young and decidedly hip.

La Scène Bastille, 2 bis rue des Taillandiers, 11e (☎ 01-48-06-50-70; www.la-scene.com; Métro: Ledru-Rollin), is a trendy and upscale joint that has a cozy lounge with caramel-colored padded walls and room to dance to whatever music is playing. Nights without live bands are clubbing nights, led by a DJ. Concerts usually start at 10 p.m. and cost 10€ to 20€; nights with a DJ (check the Web site for calendar) usually cost 10€ or 15€.

Glam and Glitz in the Club and Lounge Scene

Paris clubs change their programming from night to night, with house music de rigueur at many places. Check *Pariscope* for concert schedules. Salsa, the hottest trend a few years back, is still going strong, as are techno, house, world, classic rock, and indie rock.

A word of advice: The fancier clubs have strict door policies and turn away those wearing sneakers, sweat suits, baseball caps, and shorts. Many nightclubs accept reservations, so if you're worried about getting past the bouncers, give your club of choice a call (or ask the concierge of your hotel to do it). To club on a budget, go out during the week when cover charges may be (officially or unofficially) waived. Yes, it's sexist, but women often get in free, especially if they're dressed in something slinky, low-cut, or short (or all three).

A recently developing nightlife scene can be found at **Jardin de Bagatelle,** 42 route de Sèvres à Neuilly, 16e (☎ 01-40-67-98-29; www. bagatellerestaurant.com), an outdoor restaurant in the Bois de Bologne with a chic and well-dressed clientele. At night the restaurant transforms to a swanky party with an outdoor dance floor, with DJs spinning electro, house, and light clubbing music. Drinks are expensive, but entry is free (if you get in before the lines form — my suggestion is to eat dinner at the restaurant, which is lovely, and then stay for the after-party). Getting there and back by taxi is your best bet as there are no nearby Métro stops; however, if you're planning to spend 15€ per drink at this BCBG affair, then the cost of a taxi ride is no object! Check Web site for organized club nights, from 11 p.m. to 4 a.m.

Barrio Latino, 46–48 rue du Faubourg Saint-Antoine, 11e (☎ 01-55-78-84-75; Métro: Bastille), is a restaurant/bar/club in a gorgeous building designed by Gustave Eiffel that delivers a terrific time — if you can get in. Often packed to capacity, it has three bars on four levels, private areas where you can see (but not be seen), a lounge, a winter garden, a second-floor restaurant serving Latino food, and energetic salsa and bossa nova music that sets everyone to dancing (and sweating!). It's open during the week from 11 p.m. to 2 a.m.; weekend club nights run until 5 a.m.

The high fashion, "beautiful people" crowd has consistently populated **Le Baron,** 6 av. Marceau, 8e (☎ 01-47-20-04-01; www.clublebaron.com), a lounge and club in a former upper-class brothel. This is definitely a scene to be seen in, so approach the door with confidence and wear your best designer shoes. Cover ranges from free to 15€ for entry, depending on the night, but the drinks are wildly expensive.

All kinds of electronic music plays on the lightship **Batofar,** across from 11 quai François Mauriac, 13e (☎ 01-53-60-17-30; www.batofar.org; Métro: Bibliothèque François Mitterrand or Quai de la Gare). It's a hot, sweaty, and ultimately fun time. Music can be anything from drum-and-bass to dirty electro pop, and the party continues until 6 a.m. There are also concerts that take place in the early evenings. Cover ranges from free to 15€, depending on the band or DJ for the night.

Cab (formerly Cabaret), 2 place du Palais Royal, 1er (☎ 01-58-62-56-25; www.cabaret.fr; Métro: Palais Royal–Musée du Louvre), has lost some of its luster in recent years, but a wealthy international crowd still enjoys fancy cocktails at premium prices. There is a restaurant that serves meals until 11 p.m.; afterward, you can rub shoulders with models, professionals, and some BCBG children of rich and old-name families. White banquets and shiny bar tops are matched with deep red velvet seating in some areas. Music leans toward house and electro-lounge beats. Cover runs 20€ to 30€. It's open Wednesday and Friday through Sunday from midnight to 5 a.m.

Elysée Montmartre, 72 bd. de Rochechouart, 18e (☎ 01-42-92-45-36; www.elyseemontmartre.com; Métro: Anvers), a club that serves the dual function of disco and major concert hall, celebrated its bicentennial in 2007. The birthplace of the cancan, now it's home to soirées that pull in more than 1,000 clubgoers. Moby, Björk, U2, and the Red Hot Chili Peppers are just some big musical acts that have headlined here. Check *Pariscope* for events and prices. Dances are usually held 11 p.m. to 5 a.m. Cover charges range from 15€ to more than 35€ depending on the event.

Formerly la Locomotive, then la Loco, **La Machine du Moulin Rouge,** 90 bd. de Clichy, 18e (☎ 01-53-41-88-89; www.lamachinedu moulinrouge.com; Métro: Blanche), is still a huge, tri-level club and concert venue, but now it's owned by the folks at the Moulin Rouge, right next door. With guest DJs from all over the world and eclectic concerts, the new direction brought a greater degree of sophistication than its previous, long-lasting incarnation. Open Thursday through Saturday, concerts generally begin around 8 p.m., with club nights running Thursday 11 p.m. to 2 a.m., Friday and Saturday 11 p.m. to 5 a.m. Cover varies but is usually around 12€.

Queen, 102 av. des Champs-Elysées, 8e (☎ 01-53-89-08-90; www.queen.fr; Métro: George V), a former gay megaclub has only one real queer night a week (Sun), but it's still one of the biggest clubs in town (internationally recognized DJs such as Bob Sinclar and Paul van Dyk make regular appearances here), with nightly crowds so thick, you may find it difficult to get a drink (if you manage to get in — the bouncers can be particular and occasionally anti-Anglophone). A walk-up balcony lets you watch the crowd from up high. Cover (including one drink, with or without alcohol) ranges from 15€ to 20€. It's open daily from midnight to 6 a.m.

Literally under a bridge (the Pont Alexandre III, to be exact) is **Showcase,** Port des Champs-Elysées under the Pont Alexandre III (☎ 01-45-61-25-43; www.showcase.fr; Métro: Invalides), is an almost unbelievable setting for dance parties and live bands, with gorgeous lighting along the very long bar and an up-close-and-personal view of the Seine. The scene is definitely BCBG, with lots of bottles, designer labels, and impossibly high heels. The music generally leans toward electro, house, and disco beats. It's open Friday and Saturday 11 p.m. until 7 a.m. Cover varies from free to 15€.

Nightlife in Gay Paree

Paris has been a destination for gay parties since before the Code Napoléon decriminalized homosexual relations back in the 19th century. Although some of these delightful dens are mainstays that maintain clientele for years (like Queen; see the preceding section), others appear and disappear as quickly as quirky clothing trends.

The local weekly or biweekly rags devoted to the nightlife, which include *2x* and *Illico,* do their best to keep up with the hottest destinations. You can pick them up in most gay bars or bookstores in and around le Marais. The pickings for lesbian locations are less profound, as usual; check out *Lesbia* magazine for club and bar listings. Other reading material includes *Têtu* and *PREF Mag,* which have special nightlife inserts and cover most of the country's gay bars and clubs. Also check out www.paris-gay.com for a complete list of gay bars, associations, and activities and a continually updated calendar of LGBT cultural events.

Possibly the friendliest gay venue in town, **Le Boîte à Frissons** (although still known by its former name, Tango), 13 rue au Maire, 4e (☎ 01-42-72-17-78; www.boite-a-frissons.fr; Métro: Arts et Métiers), has music ranging from accordion (the thrill box) to disco, with an emphasis on couples dancing. (No techno gets played here!) Singles dances are held often; consult the Web site for more information. Tea dances start late afternoon Sundays. It's open Thursdays and Fridays from 10:30 p.m. to 5 a.m. and 6 p.m. to 11 p.m. Sundays.

Le Central, 33 rue Vieille du Temple, 4e (☎ 01-48-87-99-33; www.hotelcentralmarais.com; Métro: Hôtel de Ville), is said to be the original gay bar of the Marais. It's also the downstairs of the Hôtel Central, which is the city's only gay-oriented hotel. The happy hour is usually populated with friendly tourists. It's open daily until 2 a.m.

One of Paris's oldest lesbian bars, **La Champmeslé,** 4 rue Chabanais, 2e (☎ 01-42-96-85-20; Métro: Pyramides), is a few blocks east of the avenue de l'Opéra, and features an older, sophisticated crowd. This comfortable bar for women has cabaret singing every Thursday night and on Tuesdays there are tarot card readings. Also featured are art exhibitions, literary readings, and other themed nights. It's open Monday through Thursday 3 p.m. to 3 a.m., Friday and Saturday 3 p.m. to 7 a.m.

Le Cox, 15 rue des Archives, 4e (☎ 01-42-72-08-00; www.cox.fr; Métro: Hôtel de Ville), is an especially popular bar, crowded with muscular guys in tight tank tops and short, cropped hair. If you're feeling this scene, it's a great place to start the evening.

Le CUD, 12 rue des Haudriettes, 3e (☎ 01-42-77-44-12; www.cud-paris.com), which stands for, curiously, "Le Classique Up and Down," is a two-level club with multiple rooms and a dance floor on the basement level. Open daily at 11 p.m., this place stays open until 7 a.m. on weekends and 6 a.m. on weekdays. The crowd here is young and diverse.

If you prefer a calm, more artsy crowd, then **Le Duplex,** 25 rue Michel Le Comte, 3e (☎ 01-42-72-80-86; www.duplex-bar.com; Métro: Rambuteau), is your cup of tea. Usually piping in jazz and lighter fare, actual conversation can take place without shouting over overcharged speakers. The work of local artists is often on display and the mood is light and convivial.

Le 3w Kafé, 8 rue des Ecouffes, 4e (☎ 01-48-87-39-26; Métro: Saint-Paul), sets a relaxed tone for a diverse mix of women, with styles running from pink-haired punk to denim and flannel. It features speed dating some weeknights. This place is simply jammed on weekends, and the crowd spills out onto the sidewalk. It's open daily 5 p.m. to 2 a.m.

Eager patrons often wait in a line outside to gain entry to **Open Café,** 17 rue des Archives, 4e (☎ 01-42-72-26-18; www.opencafe.fr; Métro: Hôtel de Ville). This is *the* classic gay watering hole of Paris, in business for years and still a favorite among locals and tourists. Basic cafe fare is served all day. It's open Sunday through Thursday 11 a.m. to 2 a.m., Friday and Saturday 11 a.m. to around 4 a.m.

Hipster Paris

With the 21st-century spread of youthful "hipster" culture (which defies definition but ultimately challenges the status quo) in areas of big cities like parts of Brooklyn in New York, Shoreditch in London, and Silver Lake in Los Angeles, the east of Paris around the Oberkampf neighborhood has venues that are decidedly welcoming with mixed gay and straight clientele. The places listed in this sidebar are great destinations not only for gay travelers, but also for anyone seeking culture over classification.

Rosa Bonheur (see "Rockin' Out to Live Music," earlier in this chapter) was opened by a venerable lesbian scenester several years ago and quickly became a popular hangout for queer women. However, its conviviality (and playlists) attracted such attention that soon every soirée they threw brought a mixed crowd, including folks of varying backgrounds and orientations.

The many bars and concert venues along **rue Oberkampf** and **rue Jean-Pierre Timbaud** are a testament to the scene of like-minded, artistic youths of all orientations. Because it's more of a neighborhood scene than anything else, in any of the numerous locations between République and boulevard de Belleville you can find bars and small clubs with mixed clientele.

The **Bataclan**, 50 bd. Voltaire, 11e (☎ 01-49-23-96-33; Métro: Oberkampf), is a performance hall and dance-club venue with a colorful exterior inspired by Chinese architecture. Aside from hosting concerts of eclectic and particular rock groups like Morcheeba, MGMT, and Yeasayer, they also host the monthly gay-themed (but mixed) parties Follivores and Crazyvores. Ultimately, no party or concert here is exclusively anything but hip and youthful.

In the artsy and eclectic 10e *arrondissement* is an establishment that defies definition, a reminder of why Paris remains a world cultural center. **Le Point Éphémère,** 200 quai de Valmy, 10e (☎ 01-40-34-02-48; www.pointephemere.org; Métro: Jaurès or Louis Blanc), is many things: a cafe and restaurant, but also a concert hall, art gallery, dance studio, and more. An urban commune of art and culture, it's no surprise that le Point Éphémère attracts like-minded folks of all orientations.

For those who enjoy thumping music and large crowds, **Raidd,** 23 rue du Temple, 4e (☎ 01-42-77-04-88; www.raiddbar.com; Métro: Hôtel de Ville), is the place for you. Dance, Top 40, and house music abound. Some nights have go-go dancers taking showers behind a glass wall. It's open Sunday through Thursday until 4 a.m., Friday and Saturday until 5 a.m.

Le Rive Gauche, 1 rue du Sabot, 6e (☎ 01-40-20-43-23; www.lerivegauche.com; Métro: Saint-Germain-des-Prés), hosts a regular lesbian party on Saturday nights for a young and stylish crowd. Men are welcome as long as women accompany them.

Kicking Back with Classy Cocktails

Whether you're looking for a bar to go to before clubbing or a quiet, romantic place to unwind with a drink, these locations are highly recommended. Most bars and lounges in Paris open daily at 9 p.m., but no one arrives until after midnight; they generally close around 4 a.m.

Andy Whaloo, 69 rue des Gravilliers, 3e (☎ 01-42-71-20-38; Métro: Arts-et-Métiers), is a hip spot to sip pricey drinks. Looking something like your grandparents' Moroccan-themed basement with old bottles displayed in the windows and Moroccan grocery sundries making up the décor, hip Parisian denizens pretend not to check each other out from low seats around the small room.

At **Alcazar,** 62 rue Mazarine, 6e (☎ 01-53-10-19-99; www.alcazar.fr; Métro: Odéon), elements of traditional brasserie style, such as banquettes and mirrors, are slicked up with modern flair and mixed with innovations, such as a mezzanine with indigo walls and heavenly overstuffed chairs. This place is ultra-sophisticated and its patrons quite chic.

Opened in 2007, **Experimental Cocktail Club,** 37 rue Saint-Sauveur, 2e (☎ 01-45-08-88-09; www.experimentalcocktailclub.com; Métro: Sentier), is one of the few places in Paris where you can get perfectly mixed, precision cocktails in the style of old speakeasies. The club is a fashionable place for celebrities and models (folks spotted here include star architect Philippe Starck and actor Adrien Grenier); the waitresses are purported to be the most beautiful women in Paris.

Harry's New York Bar, 5 rue Daunou, 2e (☎ 01-42-61-71-14; www.harrys-bar.fr; Métro: Opéra or Pyramides), has been one of Europe's most famous bars, as popular today as it was in the time of that notorious Lost Generation of writers who really knew how to ring up a bar tab. It is said that the Bloody Mary was invented here, and the selection of whiskey is amazing. The 1930s Piano Bar resembles the inside of a cozy yacht. Thirty-something French locals and tourists make up the crowd. Open every day from 10:30 a.m. to 4 a.m.

La Magnifique, 25 rue de Richelieu, 1er (☎ 01-42-60-70-80; www.lemagnifique.fr; Métro: Palais Royal–Musée du Louvre), is a whimsical restaurant, bar, and lounge decorated in elegant leather couches, with wood-paneled walls and understated print fabric wallpaper. Cocktails, though expensive, are top notch, and the lounge-music DJs set a light-hearted and chic atmosphere.

Le Bar, in the Hotel Plaza-Athénée, 25 av. Montaigne, 8e (☎ 01-53-67-66-65; Métro: Alma-Marceau), is one of the in spots in Paris, where a crowd with champagne taste sips drinks that cost more than some bottles of wine. Unless you're somebody (or on the arm of somebody), there's no guarantee you'll get in, and when you do, be prepared to withstand the once-over you'll receive from the other fabulously dressed people. Service is reportedly slow at times. Drinks start at around 20€.

The **Lizard Lounge,** 18 rue du Bourg-Tibourg, 4e (☎ 01-42-72-81-34; Métro: Hôtel-de-Ville), is small and stylish, a pleasant place to hang out with an arty, international crowd — if you can hear them. The music is louder the later into the night you get, and the heavy-gauge steel balcony overlooking the main bar doesn't offer much of a chance for quieter conversation. Still, this is a great venue on three levels with a menu of good beers and drinks. Live bands play or a DJ spins dance music in the refurbished basement weeknights and all weekend.

Sit outside for fantastic people-watching, or choose from three floors of funky-art-covered walls and sit in one of the antique chairs at **Les Etages,** 5 rue de Buci, 6e (☎ 01-46-34-26-26). Popular among young professionals, the cocktail list here is extensive and complete: Try all sorts of champagne-mixed fruit cocktails, or trust the bartenders to mix you something stronger but with just as much flavor. You can eat as many of the fantastic honey-roasted peanuts as you want, but after two refills, they'll definitely give a judgmental glare. It's open daily from 11 a.m. to 2 a.m.

Spending an Evening at a French Cabaret

Forget everything you think Parisian cabaret is like. Today's "cancan girls" are often overshadowed by light shows, special effects, and tinny recorded music, though if you're expecting to see lots of flesh in today's Parisian revues, you won't be disappointed. The shows are highly overrated and very expensive but continue to be a huge attraction for tourists. The infamous Folies Bergère no longer exists as a cabaret; it's now a concert hall.

When seeing a Parisian cabaret show, have dinner somewhere else and save yourself some cash. For the money you'd spend at the cabaret, you can have an absolutely fabulous meal at one of the pricier suggestions in Chapter 10. Some of the cabarets admit children, though not kids 3 or under. Be aware that every other member of the audience may be from another country — these are some of the least Parisian experiences you can have while still being in Paris.

The **Crazy Horse Paris,** 12 av. George V, 8e (☎ 01-47-23-32-32; www. lecrazyhorseparis.com; Métro: George V), looks like a strip club with the red silhouette of a naked woman on its glass doors. You can see *Désirs,* a striptease show that highlights each dancer (all of whom have drag-queen-like names such as Zula Zazou, Psykko Tico, and Nooka Karamel). Depending on your seats, cover and two drinks range from 80€ at the bar to 120€ in the orchestra with a half-bottle of champagne. Special dinner-show packages with restaurants De Vez, Chez Francis, and Fouquet's start at 150€. Sunday through Thursday shows are at 8:15 and 10:45 p.m.; Friday and Saturday shows are at 7, 9:30, and 11:45 p.m.

Artishow Paris, 3 cité Souzy, 11e (☎ 01-43-48-56-04; www.artishow live.com; Métro: Charonne), is by no means in the same vein as the other tourist-traps listed here. At this eclectic venue in the far corner of the 11e *arrondissement* is the best cross-dressing performance art you can see on this side of the pond. Clever, queer, and wildly entertaining, Artishow's performances have seen much praise by *Le Figaro,* along with other national media outlets. Dinner and a show cost between 95€ and 110€, depending on the season. Artishow even has a 12:30 p.m. lunch show (60€), if you had evening picnic plans.

The **Lido,** 116 av. des Champs-Élysées, 8e (☎ **01-40-76-56-10;** www. lido.fr; Métro: George V), features the revue *Bonheur,* which pays tribute to the sensuality of women. Spanning Paris and India and including movie and cabaret classics, it's supposedly the most expensive spectacle in Europe. The show with dinner and a half-bottle of champagne costs 140€ to 280€; with just drinks, the show starts at 80€ for the 9:30 p.m. show and 70€ for the 11:30 p.m. show. Check the Web site for such promotions as a combined evening at the Lido and Seine river cruise.

Frank Sinatra once performed here, at probably the most famous of the cabarets, the **Moulin Rouge,** place Blanche, Montmartre, 18e (☎ **01-53-09-82-82;** www.moulinrouge.fr; Métro: Place Blanche). It's been packing in crowds since 1889, and its signature cancan dancers, made famous in paintings by Toulouse-Lautrec, still bare breasts in the show's finale. Édith Piaf, Yves Montand, and Charles Aznavour made their reputations at the Moulin Rouge, though its show *Féerie* is nothing like an evening of French *chanson.* Instead, expect comedy, animal, and magic acts with scantily clad women bumping and grinding around the stage. Table seats have better views than seats at the bar. A bar seat with no drinks cost 90€ for the 9 p.m. show, 80€ for the 11 p.m. show. Dinner followed by the 9 p.m. show costs 150€ to 180€; you must arrive for dinner by 7 p.m.

The **Paradis Latin,** 28 rue Cardinal-Lemoine, 5e (☎ **01-43-25-28-28;** www. paradislatin.fr; Métro: Cardinal-Lemoine), bills itself as the most Parisian of the French cafes, and its building has quite the pedigree; it was designed by Gustave Eiffel. A genial master encourages audience participation during a show that's less gimmick-filled with more song and dance routines than the others. To save money, forgo dinner for the lower-priced Champagne Revue, which includes a half-bottle of bubbly and costs 85€; dinner (at 8 p.m.) plus show packages range from 123€ to 179€. Performances are Wednesday through Monday, with a 9:30 p.m. showtime.

Part VI
The Part of Tens

The 5th Wave   By Rich Tennant

"It serves you right for requesting a lap-dance from someone doing the can-can."

In this part . . .

Okay, these little extras won't make or break your trip, but they may just make it a little more fun. In Chapter 17, I give you the inside scoop on hidden corners of the city you (and even some native Parisians) may not have noticed. In Chapter 18, I tell you where to make like Manet and have a *déjeuner sur l'herbe* (luncheon on the grass) — in other words, the best places to go for a fabulous picnic.

Chapter 17

Ten (or So) Hidden Corners of Paris

. . . .

In This Chapter

▶ Finding quirks and oddities that make Paris unique

▶ Discovering hidden corners that even some Parisians don't know about

. . . .

*Y*ou could wander around the streets of Paris for years, literally, and never discover all the wonderful oddities that make this a great city. Although they may not be the biggest cultural discoveries of the century, before you are a list of nine quirky permanent parts of the City of Light that make us scratch our chins and go "hmm."

Beauty in an Ugly Place

There's no two ways about it: The neighborhood around Place Pigalle is kind of an eyesore. Full of sex shops, bars of ill repute where prostitutes hawk their wares, and the general seediness of a red-light district, the neighborhood doesn't have much beauty to look at. Except, of course, the very present surprise of avenue Frochot (Métro: Pigalle). At the southern end of rue Frochot, there's a small plaza flanked by a beautiful wrought-iron gate and a wall on the left side. The gate closes off a very picturesque cobbled street of avenue Frochot, which is one of the few areas of Paris with individual houses, some of which have exposed beams built into the exterior walls (unusual for Paris, it's said that this *maisonette* by the gate belongs to the caretaker). Famous residents of the street have included Toulouse-Lautrec, Django Reinhardt, Alexandre Dumas, and Pierre-Auguste Renoir. However, just as lovely as the avenue is the beautiful art deco stained-glass window directly next to it, depicting an ocean wave. Stunningly beautiful, it appeared briefly in the 2006 film *Paris, Je T'Aime* in the chapter starring Bob Hoskins and Fanny Ardant.

Jardin de la Vallée Suisse

Tucked away at the corner of avenue Franklin Delano Roosevelt and Vallée Suisse behind the Palais de la Découverte (Métro: Champs-Elysées–Clemenceau), this garden hidden by a series of tall hedges is a gem of Paris that is unusually quiet and intimate given its central location. Stone steps lead through an archway, and the interior garden boasts a canopy of trees, bamboo groves, a waterfall, and a reproduction of Greek columns surrounding a stone sculpture. Truly an escape from the bustle of an already beautiful city, this usually empty garden is worth stopping by during your stomping through the noisy 8e *arrondissement.*

La Maison Normande

For those with an interest in unusual architecture in Paris, this celebrated building in the eighth *arrondissement* is well known to residents but rarely receives the appreciation of an outsider. At the back of a courtyard at 8 rue Alfred de Vigny, 8e (Métro: Courcelles), there is a beautiful and unusual house in the traditional Romanesque Norman style. Especially lovely are the alternating red-and-cream tiling and the exposed wood exterior beams. The two-story column of bay windows, including the ornamental point on top, is especially charming.

La Pagode

Although local legend would have it that this historic movie theater was moved piece by piece from Japan, it was actually built in the 19th century as a reproduction of Japanese architectural style. A beautiful specimen of original architecture unusual for Paris, it was supposedly built by the manager of the nearby Bon Marché as a ballroom for his wife, who soon after divorced him. In the 1930s, it became a 400-seat movie theater. After years of use and then disregard, the La Pagode, 57 bis rue de Babylone, 7e (Métro: Duroc), was landmarked in the 1990s and must always be operated as a cinema according to French preservation law. Nowadays, after major restorations to its interior, it plays art films for the residents of the ritzy 7e *arrondissement.*

Le Jardin Alpin

Although it's no secret, most people are unaware of this miniature garden in the Jardin des Plantes (Métro: Place Monge), home to over 2,000 species of mountain plants. It's a miniature valley built like a rock garden, with even a tiny waterfall and a stream running through this wonder of ecological know-how. Referred to as a "microclimate," there's something really lovely about this hidden nook, which has plenty of benches for people to rest upon while taking in the nature.

Les Arènes de Lutèce

Although not exactly a secret, most tourists seem to miss the simple delight of the Arènes de Lutèce, a Gallo-Roman ruin from the first century A.D. that was discovered during an excavation during the mid-19th century. Formerly an amphitheater with room for 15,000 spectators, it was the site of many a deadly gladiator battle during the time when Paris was a Celtic city known in Latin as Lutetia. Author Victor Hugo was part of a movement to preserve the important architectural discovery, and nowadays the area, not far from the Jardin des Plantes, is a leisurely park, at 51 rue Monge, 5e (Métro: Cardinale Lemoine), with areas to lie down.

Les Villas du Danube

Although not the official name of this small area of the 19e *arrondissement,* several streets emanating from La Place du Rhin et Danube (tucked between le Parc de la Butte Rouge and le Parc des Buttes Chaumont; Métro: Botzaris or Danube), is full of steep, narrow lanes flanked by small, ivy-covered houses. All the streets in the vicinity begin with the name *villa* — thus, villa Danube, villa Amália, and so on. This rarity in Paris gives you the impression of not being in this city at all, but in a small town somewhere in the south of France.

Odd Sculpture at the Place Marcel-Aymé

When you take your requisite hike up to see the view from Sacré-Coeur, pop over to rue Norvins (Métro: Abbesses) and look for the allée des Brouillards (whimsically translated as the "alley of noisy people"). You should see one of the most bizarre sculptures around, not including, of course, the headless Saint-Denis (see below). There you will find a man's head, torso, and leg emerging from the wall — or at least the three pieces were mounted to look that way. That sculpture is a depiction of the French writer Marcel Aymé, who lived close by during his time and is interred in a small cemetery not far away.

Saint-Denis Holds His Head

Part of Parisian lore is the story of Saint-Denis, the first bishop of Paris. Legend has it that Roman soldiers tortured and decapitated him in the village of Montmartre, but that didn't stop him; Saint-Denis promptly picked up his severed head and walked nearly 4 miles north to the present-day site of the Basilique de Saint-Denis. However, when you're at Notre-Dame (Métro: Cité), taking in the sights, look at the left portal for an odd sculpture of a saint holding his head at chest level.

Chapter 18

Ten Great Places for a Picnic

In This Chapter

▶ Finding that special place to enjoy a meal in *plein air* (fresh air)

▶ Enjoying Paris like a Parisian

*P*ick up some delicious meats, sweets, and wines (see Chapter 12 for recommendations) from one of Paris's open-air markets, *traiteurs* (gourmet food shops), or grocery stores, and enjoy an open-air feast without the worry of tipping or dressing to dine. Best of all, you can lie down for a snooze right after you eat.

A word of advice: Such parks as the Luxembourg Gardens or the Tuileries jealously guard their lawns; you may have to walk a bit before you find a spot where you can spread out on the grass. But chairs are everywhere — some even have reclining backs! — and you can pull a few right up to a fountain and eat amidst the spray from the water. If this seems too public, your best bet is to try the vast Bois de Vincennes or Bois de Boulogne where you can picnic nearly anywhere. Don't forget to clean up afterward.

Bois de Boulogne

A former royal forest and hunting ground, this vast reserve of more than 880 hectares (2,200 acres) has jogging paths, horseback-riding paths, cycling (rentals are available), and boating on two lakes (Métro: Porte Maillot, Porte Dauphine, or Porte Auteuil). Picnic areas are abundant here. The **Longchamp** and **Auteuil racecourses** are located here, as is the **Jardin Shakespeare** in the Pré Catelan, a garden containing many of the plants and herbs mentioned in Shakespeare's plays.

Bois de Vincennes

Rent canoes or bikes or visit the **Parc Zoologique** (zoo) and petting zoo after you picnic on the extensive grounds at the Bois de Vincennes

(Métro: Porte Dorée or Chateau de Vincennes), which also has a Buddhist center, complete with a temple. The Chateau de Vincennes, where early monarchs such as Charles V and Henri III sought refuge from wars, is also the place where Mata Hari met her demise. The **Parc Floral de Paris** (☎ 01-43-43-92-95) is here with its spectacular amphitheater (and jazz concerts on summer Saturdays), a butterfly garden, a library, and miniature golf.

Jardin du Luxembourg

You can sit on metal chairs near the boat pond or spread out on grass open to picnickers directly across from the Palais de Luxembourg, on the park's south edge. Not far from the Sorbonne and just south of the Latin Quarter, the large park (Métro: Odéon; RER: Luxembourg) is popular with students and children, so it isn't the quietest of places. Besides pools, fountains, and statues of queens and poets, tennis and *boules* (lawn bowling) courts are available. See whether you can find the miniature Statue of Liberty.

Les Champs de Mars

Unlike other parks, which forbid using the grass for any personal activities, the Champs de Mars (Métro: La Motte-Picquet–Grenelle or École Militaire) is open for all forms of sunbathing, lounging, and, yes, picnicking. Located next to Paris's Ecole Militaire, the name (translated as "the field of Mars," the Roman god of war) is a reference to the Campus Martius in Rome, and the fields were once used for drilling and training the French army. A dinner picnic is best here (yes, you can bring wine) when flocks of Parisians come during the warm months to gaze at the Eiffel Tower. You can count the hours passing by, watching the blinking lights go on and off on the Eiffel Tower (until 1 a.m.). Listen for cheers and "awwwws" as people admire the Parisian symbol.

Parc de Belleville

Though the Parc de Belleville is out of the way, it's still a wonderful place to visit with children, watch the sun set across western Paris, or nosh on a baguette with *saucisson sec* (cured sliced sausage, a bit like French salami). The park has fountains, a children's play area, an open-air theater with concerts during the summer, rock formations, and grottoes that evoke the long-ago days when the hill was a strategic point to fight enemies like Attila the Hun. Nowadays, people dip their feet into the cool fountains to cool off during the summer heat waves. Beds of roses and other seasonal flowers line the walks, and views of the city's Left Bank become more pronounced the higher up the terraced pathways you go.

Take the Métro to Pyrénées; then walk down rue de Belleville and turn left onto rue Piat, where you see arched iron gates leading into the park (spelling out the words *Villa Ottoz*). A curved path leads you to tree-lined promenades (more than 500 trees are here), with the first of the magnificent Left Bank views peeping through the spaces between pretty houses. You can also take the Métro to Couronnes, cross boulevard de Belleville, and turn left onto rue Julien Lacroix where another entrance is located.

Parc de la Villette

Picnic at Parc de la Villette in the summer while watching an outdoor movie or listening to a concert. Afterward, you and your kids can visit the enormous children's museum complex, the **Cité des Sciences et de l'Industrie (Museum of Science and Industry),** and the **Musée de la Musique (Music Museum),** located on the grounds. This modern park has a series of theme gardens and includes an exotic bamboo garden and a garden featuring steam and water jets. Scattered throughout the park are playgrounds and other attractions (see Chapter 11). The most fun way to get here is to take a canal trip from Pont de l'Arsenal or the Musée d'Orsay (see Chapter 11). You can also take the Métro to Porte de la Villette.

Parc des Buttes-Chaumont

Parc des Buttes-Chaumont (Métro: Buttes-Chaumont or Danube) is one of the four man-made parks that Napoléon III commissioned to resemble the English gardens he grew to love during his exile in England. Built on the site of a former gypsum quarry and a centuries-old dump, it features cliffs, waterfalls, a lake, and a cave topped by a temple. One of Paris's best unsung parks, the careful landscaping and gentle suggestion of nature are truly relaxing and pleasant. You have plenty of places to lay out your picnic spread here. For a pleasurable walk to further whet your appetite, exit at Métro Danube. Walk east along rue David d'Angers until you find villa du Danube, a sloping road. Follow this through to villa de la Renaissance, and you'll discover rue de Mouzaïa: Along this walk and around here you can wander beautiful cobblestoned streets (all called "villa" something) with houses that look nothing like the rest of Paris, sporting ivied balconies and Provençal-style roofs.

Parc Monceau

Marcel Proust's favorite park, Monceau (Métro: Ternes) allegedly contains Paris's largest tree — an Oriental plane tree with a circumference of almost 7m (23 ft.). The painter Carmontelle designed several structures for Parc Monceau, including a Dutch windmill, a Roman temple, a covered bridge, a waterfall, a farm, medieval ruins, and a pagoda.

Garnerin, the world's first parachutist, landed here. In the mid-19th century, the park was redesigned in the English style. There is a small shop near the entrance where you can buy sweets and drinks, but I suggest visiting a local *boulangerie* instead. Very close by are the fantastic market streets rue Poncelet and rue des Levis.

Pont des Arts

Believe it or not, loads of people crowd onto this footbridge near the Louvre to set up dinner picnics during the nicer seasons. During the day, few people will be having meals on the bridge, but it gets crowded by 8 p.m., so it's best to arrive before then with your blankets spread out. Chances are, you'll meet some young Parisians — in these more intimate environments, you're more likely to be able to chat with friendly strangers. If the bridge gets too crowded, you can always move down to the quai de Conti below the bridge. If you don't mind walking with a load of food, you can grab your sundries from **La Grand Épicerie,** 38 rue de Sèvres, 7e (☎ **01-44-39-81-00**). The closest Métro to Pont des Arts is Saint-Germain-des-Prés.

Square du Vert Galant

This spot (Métro: Cité) is one of the most romantic in Paris, but it may be crowded with others depending on the time of day and year you visit — I guarantee you'll have it all to yourself in January. Descend the stairs near the middle of Pont Neuf (near the Pont Neuf tour boats) to this beautiful spot commemorating Paris's favorite king, Henri IV. You're at the very tip of île de la Cité, in the middle of the Seine. You can spread out on a bench under the trees and enjoy the stunning views of both banks and the river stretching out ahead. The square is 7m (23 ft.) lower than the rest of the island; this was the original level of Paris during the Gallo-Roman period. At sunset, this is a popular spot for romantics.

Quick Concierge

● ●

*H*ow do you use the telephones? Where can you find your embassy or consulate? This Quick Concierge offers answers to a variety of "Where do I . . . ?" and "How do I . . . ?" questions.

Fast Facts

American Express

The full-service office, 11 rue Scribe (☎ 01-53-30-99-00), is open Monday through Friday 9 a.m. to 6:30 p.m. (until 7:30 p.m. May–Sept). The bank is also open Saturday from 9 a.m. to 5:30 p.m., but the mail-pickup window is closed.

ATM Locations

As in big cities everywhere, ATMs are easy to find in Paris. Most bank branches have at least one outdoor machine, and there are ATMs in major department stores and in train stations. If you want a list of ATMs that accept MasterCard or Visa before you leave home, ask your bank or print out lists from www.mastercard.com or www.visa.com.

Baby Sitters

Visit the American Church's basement bulletin board where English-speaking (often American) students post notices offering baby-sitting services. The church is located at 65 quai d'Orsay, 7e (☎ 01-45-62-05-00; Métro: Invalides). Or try Allô Maman Dépannage (☎ 01-34-05-00-47; http://allo.maman.depannage.free.fr), which employs some English-speaking baby sitters. Specify when calling that you need a sitter who speaks English.

Business Hours

The *grands magasins* (department stores) are generally open Monday through Saturday from 9:30 a.m. to 7 p.m.; smaller shops close for lunch and reopen around 2 p.m., but this practice is rarer than it used to be. Many stores stay open until 7 p.m. in summer; others are closed Monday, especially in the morning. Large offices remain open all day, but some close for lunch. Banks are normally open weekdays from 9 a.m. to noon and from 1 or 1:30 p.m. to 4:30 p.m. Some banks also open on Saturday morning. Some currency-exchange booths are open very long hours; see "Currency Exchange," later in this section.

Camera Repair

Photo Suffren, 45 av. Suffren, 7e (☎ 01-44-67-24-25; www.photosuffren.com), repairs camera equipment on-site at this location not far from the Eiffel Tower.

Credit Cards

Call ☎ 0-800-90-11-79 if you've lost or had your Visa card stolen. **American Express** card and traveler's check holders in France can call collect ☎ 336-393-1111 for money and lost card emergencies. For **MasterCard**, call ☎ 0-800-90-13-87.

Currency Exchange

Using your ATM card to get cash in Paris is so much easier than exchanging currency — you usually get a better rate of exchange than you do at *bureaux de change* (exchange offices), hotels, restaurants, and shops. Most banks in Paris have stopped cashing traveler's checks and now steer tourists to *bureaux de change*. If you must use traveler's checks, for good rates, without fees or commissions, and quick service, try the **Comptoir Change Opera,** 9 rue Scribe, 9e (☎ 01-47-42-20-96; www.ccopera.com; Métro: Opéra; RER: Auber). It's open weekdays from 9 a.m. to 5:30 p.m., Saturday from 9:30 a.m. to 4 p.m. The *bureaux de change* at all train stations (except Gare de Montparnasse) are open daily; those at 63 av. des Champs-Elysées, 8e (Métro: Franklin D. Roosevelt), and 140 av. des Champs-Elysées, 8e (Métro: Charles de Gaulle–Étoile), keep long hours.

Despite disadvantageous exchange rates and long lines, many people prefer to exchange their money at American Express (see the "American Express" listing earlier in this appendix).

Customs

Non-EU nationals can bring into France duty-free 200 cigarettes or 100 cigarillos or 50 cigars or 250 grams of smoking tobacco; 2 liters of wine and 1 liter of alcohol over 38.8 proof; 50 grams of perfume, 0.25 liter of toilet water; 500 grams of coffee, and 100 grams of tea. Travelers can also bring in 175€ in other goods; EU citizens may bring any amount of goods into France as long as it's for their personal use and not for resale.

Returning U.S. citizens who have been away for 48 hours or more are allowed to bring back to the United States, once every 30 days, $800 worth of merchandise duty free. You'll be charged a flat rate of 10 percent duty on the next $1,000 worth of purchases; on gifts, the duty-free limit is $100. You can't bring fresh food into the United States; canned foods, however, are allowed.

Returning U.K. citizens have no limit on what can be brought back from an EU country as long as the items are for personal use (including gifts) and the necessary duty and tax have been paid. Guidance levels are set at: 3,200 cigarettes, 200 cigars, 3kg of smoking tobacco, 10 liters of spirits, 90 liters of wine, and 110 liters of beer.

Canada allows its citizens a once-a-year C$750 exemption after seven days, and you're allowed to bring back duty-free 200 cigarettes, 1½ gallons of wine or 1.14 liters of liquor, and 50 cigars. In addition, you may mail gifts to Canada from abroad at the rate of C$60 a day, provided they're unsolicited and don't contain alcohol, tobacco, or advertising matter. Write on the package "Unsolicited Gift, under $60 Value." All valuables need to be declared on Form Y-38 before departure from Canada, including serial numbers of valuables you already own, such as expensive foreign cameras.

The duty-free allowance in Australia is A$900 or, for those younger than 18, A$450. Upon returning to Australia, citizens can bring in 250 cigarettes or 250 grams of loose tobacco, and 2.25 liters of alcohol. If you're returning with valuable goods you already own, such as foreign-made cameras, you need to file Form B263.

The duty-free allowance for New Zealand is NZ$700. Citizens 18 and over can bring in 200 cigarettes or 50 cigars or 250 grams of tobacco (or a mixture of all three if their combined weight doesn't exceed 250 grams), plus 4.5 liters of wine or beer or up to three bottles containing 1.125 liters of liquor.

Dentists

Call your consulate (see "Embassies and Consulates," later in this section, for numbers) and ask the duty officer to recommend a dentist. For dental emergencies, call **SOS Urgences Stomatologiques Dentaire** (☎ 01-43-37-51-00 or 01-42-61-12-00) daily from 9 a.m. to midnight. Most dentists speak some English.

Doctors

Call your consulate (see "Embassies and Consulates," later in this section, for numbers) and ask the duty officer to recommend a doctor, or call **SOS Médecins** (☎ 01-43-07-77-77), a 24-hour service. Most doctors and dentists speak some English. You can also call for an appointment at the **Centre Médical Europe**, 44 rue d'Amsterdam (☎ 01-42-81-93-33; www.centre-medical-europe.com); consultations cost about 20€, and specialists are available.

Drugstores

Pharmacies are marked with a green cross and are often upscale, selling toiletries and cosmetics in addition to prescription drugs and over-the-counter remedies. If you're shopping for products other than drugs, buying them elsewhere, such as a *supermarché* (supermarket), is almost always cheaper.

A 24-hour pharmacy, **Pharmacie Les Champs**, is conveniently located at 84 av. des Champs-Elysées, 8e (☎ 01-45-62-02-41; Métro: George V).

Electricity

The French electrical system runs on 220 volts. You need adapters to convert the voltage and fit sockets. Adapters are cheaper at home than they are in Paris. Many hotels have two-pin (in some cases, three-pin) sockets for electric razors. Asking your hotel whether you need an adapter is a good idea before plugging in any electrical appliance.

Embassies and Consulates

If you have a passport, immigration, legal, or other problem, contact your consulate. Call before you go: They often keep strange hours and observe both French and home-country holidays. Here's where to find them: **Australia**, 4 rue Jean-Rey, 15e (☎ 01-40-59-33-00; Métro: Bir-Hakeim; **Canada**, 35 av. Montaigne, 8e (☎ 01-44-43-29-00; Métro: Franklin D. Roosevelt or Alma Marceau); **New Zealand**, 7 ter rue Léonard-de-Vinci, 16e (☎ 01-45-01-43-43; Métro: Victor-Hugo); **Consulate of Great Britain**, 18 bis rue d'Anjou, 8e (☎ 01-44-51-31-02; Métro: Madeleine); **Embassy of Ireland**, 4 rue Rude, 16e (☎ 01-44-17-67-00). The **embassy of the United States**, 2 av. Gabriel, 8e (☎ 01-43-12-22-22; http://france.usembassy.gov; Métro: Concorde), is open Monday through Friday from 9 a.m. to 6 p.m. Passports are issued at its consulate at 4 av. Gabriel, 1er (☎ 01-43-12-22-22), Monday through Friday 9 a.m. to noon. The consulate is open Monday through Friday 9 a.m. to 12:30 p.m. and 1 to 3 p.m.; it's closed on all French and U.S. holidays.

Emergencies

Dial ☎ 17 for the *gendarmerie* (police). To report a fire or if you need an ambulance, call ☎ 18 (Sapeurs-Pompiers) or ☎ 15 for Service d'Aide Médicale d'Urgence (SAMU), a private ambulance company.

Hospitals

Two hospitals with English-speaking staff are the **American Hospital of Paris**, 63 bd. Victor-Hugo, Neuilly-sur-Seine (☎ 01-46-41-25-25; Métro: Les Sablons or Levallois-Perret), just west of Paris proper, and the **Hôpital Franco-Britannique**, 3 rue Barbès Levallois-Perret (☎ 01-46-39-22-22; Métro: Anatole-France), just north of Neuilly, across the city line northwest of Paris. Note that the American Hospital charges about $600 per day for a room, not including doctor's fees. The emergency department charges more than $60 for a visit, not including tests or X-rays.

Information

Before you go, contact the **French Government Tourist Office,** Maison de la France, 825 Third Ave., 29th floor, New York, NY 10022 (France-on-call Hotline: ☎ 514-288-1904; http:// us.franceguide.com). The city's tourist-information office, **L'Office du Tourisme et des Congrès de Paris** (http://en.parisinfo.com), maintains two full-service welcome centers. Both offer basic information about attractions in the city, help with last-minute hotel reservations, make booking for day trips, and sell transportation and museum passes — but for a small fee. The central office, located at 25 rue des Pyramids, 1e (Métro: Pyramides), is open daily 9 a.m. to 7 p.m. Another at Gare du Nord (Métro: Gare du Nord), beneath a glass roof, is open daily 8 a.m. to 6 p.m.

Several auxiliary offices, or welcome centers, are scattered throughout the city. The Gare de Lyon (Métro: Gare de Lyon) is open Monday through Saturday 8 a.m. to 6 p.m. The office at Gare de l'Est (Métro: Gare de l'Est) is open Monday through Saturday 8 a.m. to 7 p.m. Paris's convention center, Paris Expo (Métro: Porte de Versailles), has an information desk open from 11 a.m. to 7 p.m. during trade fairs. To reserve tickets for shows, exhibitions, or theme parks, visit www.ticketnet.fr or call ☎ 0892-390-100.

Internet Access

There is no single chain of Internet cafes in Paris, so the best way to find one is to wander around the streets in the Latin Quarter, home to the Sorbonne and other colleges, which is the best thing to do while in Paris anyway. Rates start at around 1.50€ for the first ten minutes. Most hotels now have wireless Internet (Wi-Fi)

or free or low-cost computer access in the salon or lobby area.

Language

In the tourist areas of Paris, English is widely understood. As you move into more residential sections of the city, however, you'll probably meet people who don't speak English. I suggest carrying a pocket-size phrasebook such as *Berlitz Phrase Book: French,* available at all bookstores (or use the glossary in Appendix B).

Laundry and Dry Cleaning

The more expensive your hotel, the more it costs to have your laundry or dry cleaning done there. Instead, find a laundry near you by consulting the Yellow Pages under *Laveries pour particuliers.* Take as many coins as you can. Washing and drying 6kg (13 lb.) usually costs 8€. Dry cleaning is *nettoyage à sec;* look for shop signs with the word *pressing* on them, and don't expect to have your clothes back within an hour; you may be able to get them back the next day if you ask nicely. The dry-cleaning chain 5 à Sec has stores across Paris.

Liquor Laws

Supermarkets, grocery stores, and cafes sell alcoholic beverages. The legal drinking age is 16. Kids 15 and under can be served an alcoholic drink in a bar or restaurant when accompanied by a parent or legal guardian. Wine and liquor are sold every day of the year. *Be warned:* The authorities are very strict about drunk-driving laws. If convicted, you face a stiff fine and a possible prison term of two months to two years.

Lost Property

Paris's Prefecture of Police runs the central **Lost and Found,** Objets Trouvés, 36 rue des Morillons, 15e (☎ 08-21-00-25-25; Métro: Convention), at the corner of rue de Dantzig. The office is open Monday through Thursday 8:30 a.m. to 5 p.m. and

Friday 8:30 a.m. to 4:30 p.m. For Lost and Found on the Métro, call Gare d'Austerlitz (☎ 01-53-60-71-98), Gare de l'Est (☎ 01-40-18-88-73), Gare de Lyon (☎ 01-53-33-67-22), Gare du Nord (☎ 01-55-31-58-40), Gare Montparnasse (☎ 01-40-48-14-24), or Gare Saint-Lazare (☎ 01-53-42-05-57).

Luggage Storage

Most hotels will store luggage for you for free, and that's your best bet, especially when you plan to return to Paris after a tour of the provinces.

Maps

Maps printed by the department stores are usually available free at hotels, and they're good for those visiting Paris for only a few days and hitting only the major attractions. But if you plan to really explore all the nooks and crannies of the city, the best maps are those of the *Plan de Paris par Arrondissement,* pocket-size books with maps and a street index, available at most bookstores. They're extremely practical, and prices start at around 5€. You can find them in Paris bookstores; at the Target-like chain store, Monoprix (there is one in nearly every Paris *arrondissement*); bookstores; and *presse* stores (large versions of newsstands). Most Parisians carry a copy because they too get lost at times.

Newspapers and Magazines

Paris has a terrific events/nightlife/sightseeing weekly, called *Pariscope* (www.pariscope.fr), sold at every newsstand for 0.40€. A competitor is *L'Officiel des Spectacles,* costing a mere 0.35€. You also may want to check out the free English-language *Paris Voice* (www.parisvoice.com).

Pharmacies

See "Drugstores," earlier.

Police

Dial ☎ 17 in emergencies; otherwise, call ☎ 01-53-71-53-71.

Post Office

Large post offices are normally open weekdays 9 a.m. to 7 p.m., Saturday 9 a.m. to noon; small post offices may have shorter hours. Many post offices (look for the bright yellow signs) are scattered around the city; ask anybody for the nearest one. Airmail letters and postcards to the United States, Australia, or New Zealand cost 0.85€; within Europe, 0.75€.

The city's main post office is at 52 rue du Louvre, 1er (☎ 01-40-28-76-00; Métro: Louvre-Rivoli). It's open 24 hours a day for urgent mail, telegrams, and telephone calls.

Restrooms

Public restrooms are plentiful, but you usually have to pay for them. Every cafe has a restroom, but it's supposed to be for customers only. The best plan is to ask to use the telephone; it's usually next to the *toilette.* Street-side toilets, which are automatically flushed out and cleaned after every use, were converted to free in 2006.

Safety

Paris is a relatively safe city; your biggest risks are pickpockets and purse snatchers, so be particularly attentive in museum lines, popular shopping areas, around tourist attractions, on the Métro, and on crowded buses (especially in the confusion of getting on and off). Popular pickpocket tactics include someone asking you for directions or bumping into you while an accomplice takes your wallet, and bands of children surrounding and distracting you and then making off with purchases and/or your wallet.

Women need to be on guard in crowded tourist areas and on the Métro against overly friendly men who seem to have made a specialty out of bothering unsuspecting female tourists. Tricks include asking your name and nationality and then taking advantage of your politeness by sticking like a burr to you for the rest of the day. They're usually more harassing than harmful, but if you're too nice, you may be stuck spending time with someone with whom you prefer not to. A simple *laissez-moi tranquille* (*lay*-say mwa tran-*keel*; leave me alone) usually works.

Smoking

Paris restaurants and cafes are smoke-free, with smoking sections often set up outside.

Taxes

Watch out: You can get burned. As a member of the European Community, France routinely imposes a standard 19.6 percent value-added tax (VAT) on many goods and services. The tax on merchandise applies to clothing, appliances, liquor, leather goods, shoes, furs, jewelry, perfume, cameras, and even caviar. You can get a rebate — usually 12 percent — on certain goods and merchandise, but not on services. The minimum purchase, depending on the store, is 180€ in the same store for nationals or residents of countries outside the European Union. Chapter 12 has more on the VAT and how to deal with it.

Taxis

Because cabs in Paris are scarce, picking up one at a stand may be easier than hailing one on the street. Be careful to check the meter when you board to be sure you're not also paying the previous passenger's fare; if your taxi lacks a meter, make sure to settle the cost of the trip before setting out. Calling a cab to pick you up is more expensive because the meter starts running when the cab receives the call, but if you need to do it, call **Alpha Taxis** (☎ 01-53-60-63-50).

The initial fare for up to three passengers is 2.20€ and rises 0.90€ for each kilometer (⅗ mile) between 10 a.m. and 5 p.m. Between 5 p.m. and 10 a.m., the standing charge remains the same, but the per-kilometer charge rises to 1.15€. An additional fee of 1€ is imposed for luggage weighing more than 5kg (11 lb.) or for an extra bag. A fourth passenger incurs a 2.95€ charge.

Telephone/Telex/Fax

Public phone booths in Paris seem to be going the way of the dinosaur since the advent of cellphones. You may find a coin-operated phone in a cafe or restaurant, but most public phone booths are equipped to take *cartes à puces* (European credit cards or other cards with a microchip that are inserted directly into the phone) or *cartes à code* (which have a code you enter into the phone before dialing a number). Those without a cellphone find *cartes à code* the most convenient because you can use the card on the phone in your hotel. *Cartes à code* start at 7.50€ for about an hour's worth of phone access and increase in price. You can buy them at any *tabac* (tobacconist). For directory assistance, dial ☎ **12**. To make international calls, dial ☎ **00** to access international lines.

To charge your call to a calling card or call collect, dial **AT&T** at ☎ **0-800-99-0011** or **MCI** at ☎ **0-800-99-0019**. To call the United States direct from Paris, dial 00, wait for the dial tone, and then dial 1 followed by the area code and number.

For placing international calls from France, dial 00 and then the country code (for the United States and Canada, 1; for Britain, 44; for Ireland, 353; for Australia, 61; for New Zealand, 64), then the area or city code, and then the local number. For example, to call New York, dial 00 + 1 + the area code and number. To place a collect call to North America, dial ☎ 00-33-11, and an English-speaking operator will assist you.

For calling from Paris to anywhere else in France (the provinces, in other words, or *province*), the country is divided into five zones with prefixes beginning 01, 02, 03, 04, and 05; check a phone directory for the code of the city you're calling.

If you're calling France from the United States, the number you dial probably looks something like this: 011-33-(0)1-00-00-00-00. You must first dial the international prefix, 011; and then the country code for France (33), followed by the city code and the rest of the number. When dialing from outside France, leave off the 0, which is often indicated in parentheses, in the city code.

Avoid making phone calls from your hotel room; many hotels charge at least 0.75€ for local calls, and the markup on international calls can be staggering.

You can send telex and fax messages at the main post office in each *arrondissement* of Paris, but asking at your hotel or going to a neighborhood printer or copy shop is often cheaper.

Time Zone

Paris is six hours ahead of eastern standard time; noon in New York is 6 p.m. in Paris.

Tipping

The custom is to tip the bellhop about 1€ per bag, more in expensive hotels. If you have a lot of luggage, tip a bit more. Don't tip housekeepers unless you do something that requires extra work. Tip a few euro if a reception staff member performs extra services.

Although your *addition* (restaurant bill) or *fiche* (cafe check) bears the words *service compris* (service charge included), always leave a small tip. Generally, 5 percent is considered acceptable.

Taxi drivers appreciate a tip of 0.50€ to 1€ or whatever it costs to round up the fare to the next euro. On longer journeys, when

the fare exceeds 20€, a 5 percent to 10 percent tip is appropriate. At the theater and cinema, tip 1€ if an usher shows you to your seat. In public toilets, a fee for using the facilities often is posted; if not, the maintenance person will expect a tip of 1€ (put it in the basket or on the plate at the entrance). Porters and cloakroom attendants are usually governed by set prices, which are displayed; if not, give a porter 1€ per suitcase and a cloakroom attendant 0.50€ per coat.

Transit Info

When taking a train on the national train system, you must validate your train ticket in the orange ticket *composteur* on the platform or pay a fine. For information in English about Paris subways and buses (RATP), call ☎ 08-92-68-41-14.

Water

Tap water in Paris is perfectly safe, but if you're prone to stomach problems, you may prefer to drink mineral water.

Weather

From May through September you can expect clear, sunny days and temperatures in the 70s to high 80s Fahrenheit (21°C–31°C) at the height of summer. But be prepared for rainy or searingly hot summers, too. From late October through April, the weather is often gray and misty with a dampness that gets into your bones. Always bring an umbrella. Temperatures average about 45°F (7°C) in winter, and the low 60s Fahrenheit (17°C) in spring and autumn. ***Note:*** Ignore the song "April in Paris," and pack layers for your early spring trip to the City of Light. It's often quite chilly.

For current weather information, go to `http://europe.cnn.com/weather` or `www.weather.com`.

Toll-Free Numbers and Web Sites

Major airlines

Air Canada
☎ 888-247-2262
www.aircanada.com

Air France
☎ 800-237-2747
www.airfrance.com

Air Tahiti Nui
☎ 877-824-4846
www.airtahitinui.com

American Airlines
☎ 800-433-7300
www.aa.com

British Airways
☎ 800-247-9297
www.britishairways.com

Continental Airlines
☎ 800-523-3273
www.continental.com

Delta Air Lines
☎ 800-221-1212
www.delta.com

Icelandair
☎ 800-223-5500
www.icelandair.com

United Airlines
☎ 800-864-8331
www.united.com

US Airways
☎ 800-428-4322
www.usairways.com

Major car-rental agencies in Paris

Avis
Gare d'Austerlitz, 13e
☎ 08-20-61-16-29
www.avis.com

Europcar
60 bd. Diderot, 12e
☎ 08-25-82-54-63
www.europcar.fr

Hertz
Gare de l'Est, 10e
☎ 01-42-05-50-43
www.hertz.com

National
Gare de Lyon, 12e
☎ 01-40-04-90-04
www.nationalcar.com

Where to Get More Information

The information sources listed here are the best of the bunch; dig in before you go, and you'll be well prepared for your trip.

Tourist offices

For general information about France, contact an office of the **French Government Tourist Office** at one of the following addresses:

✔ **In the United States: The French Government Tourist Office,** 825 Third Ave., 29th floor, New York, NY 10022 France-on-call Hotline: ☎ 514 288-1904, ☎ 312-751-7800 in Chicago, or ☎ 310-271-6665 in Los Angeles; http:// us.franceguide.com

✔ **In Canada: Maison de la France/French Government Tourist Office,** 1800 McGill College, #1010, Montreal (QC) H3A 3J6 ☎ 514-876-9881 or ☎ 866-313-7262 (http://ca.franceguide.com)

✔ **In the United Kingdom: Maison de la France/French Government Tourist Office,** Lincoln House, 300 High Holborn, WC1V 7JH ☎ 09068-244-123 at a charge of 60p per minute; http://uk.franceguide.com

✔ **In Australia and New Zealand: Maison de la France Australia & New Zealand,** Level 13, 25 Bligh St. 2000 NSW, Sydney Australia ☎ 61-(0)2-9231-5244; http://au.franceguide.com

Surfing the Web

You can find plenty of excellent information about Paris on the Internet — the latest news, restaurant reviews, concert schedules, subway maps, and more.

✔ **Aéroports de Paris** (www.adp.fr): Click the British flag on this site's home page for an English version that provides transfer information into Paris and lists terminals, maps, airlines, boutiques, hotels, restaurants, and accessibility information for travelers with disabilities.

✔ **Bonjour Paris** (www.bonjourparis.com): This site should be one of the first you browse before your trip; it's full of useful information about Paris. You can find everything from cultural differences to shopping to restaurant reviews, all written from an American expatriate's point of view.

✔ **Café de la Soul** (www.cafedelasoul.com): A sleekly designed Web site for African-American travelers in Paris. The site features articles, travelogues, and links to resources in the City of Light.

✔ **French Government Tourist Office** (www.franceguide.com): Here you can find information on planning your trip to France, including practical tips, family activities, events, and accommodations.

✔ **Google Maps** (http://maps.google.com): On Google Maps, typing in a Paris address will bring up a detailed map of the surrounding area, including Métro stops and any relevant information that Google can find on the business, including phone numbers, official Web pages, and business hours.

✔ **Paris Convention and Visitors Bureau** (http://en.parisinfo.com): This site provides information on the year's events, museums, accommodations, nightlife, and restaurants.

✔ **Paris Digest** (www.parisdigest.com): Paris Digest selects "the best sights in Paris" and provides photos and links to them (as well as to restaurants with views and good décor), and information about shopping, hotels, and things to do.

✔ **Parisfranceguide.com:** This site has plenty of useful information about Paris, with current nightlife, restaurant, music, theater, and events listings. It's brought to you by the publishers of the *Living in France, Study in France,* and *What's on in France* guides.

✔ **Paris-Gay.com:** A comprehensive guide to LGBT culture, events, and places in Paris, this Web site is constantly updated and continually translated into English.

✔ **Paris.org:** So much information is on this site that you won't know where to begin. Lodging reviews are organized by area and the monuments standing nearby, and you can find photo tours, shop listings, and a map of attractions with details. Some of the information may be out of date.

✔ **Parler Paris** (www.parlerparis.com): This site should be among the first you browse before your trip, or sign up for the biweekly newsletter. Editor Adrian Leeds really knows Paris, and Parler Paris is a true insider's guide to visiting and living in Paris. Her insightful commentary covers everything from visits to hidden Paris places to delicious budget dining.

✔ **RATP** (www.ratp.fr): RATP is Paris's urban transit. Here, you can find subway and bus maps; timetables and information; and routes and times for Noctambus, Paris's night buses that run after the Métro closes. Click on the word "English" for the English-language version.

✔ **SNCF (French Rail;** www.sncf.fr): The official Web site of the French railway system, this site sells seats online for trips through France. You can also find timetables and prices here. Click on the Union Jack on the upper-left corner of the screen for English.

Appendix B

A Glossary of French Words and Phrases

Why *La Tour Eiffel* but *Le Tour de France?* Why *un* cabinet but *une* cabine? Simply put, in French and other Romance languages, nouns are assigned a gender. The article preceding the noun, such as *le* and *la* (which mean "the") and *un* and *une* (which mean "a" or "one"), corresponds to that gender. *La* and *une* are feminine; *le* and *un* are masculine. Plural nouns are preceded by *les*. An extra letter is added to the noun itself to signify feminine gender. So Brian Williams is *un journalist,* but Katie Couric is *une journaliste.* French schoolchildren spend years memorizing the gender of nouns; fortunately, no one expects you to do the same!

Basic Vocabulary

English	French	Pronunciation
Yes/no	*Oui/non*	wee/nohn
Okay	*D'accord*	dah-*core*
Please	*S'il vous plaît*	see-voo-*play*
Thank you	*Merci*	mare-*see*
You're welcome	*De rien*	duh ree-*ehn*
Hello (during daylight hours)	*Bonjour*	bohn-*jhoor*
Good evening (after 6 p.m.)	*Bonsoir*	bohn-*swahr*
Goodbye	*Au revoir*	o ruh-*vwahr*
Police	*La police*	lah po-*leese*
What's your name?	*Comment vous appellez-vous?*	ko-mahn vooz ah-pel-ay-*voo*

English	French	Pronunciation
My name is . . .	*Je m'appelle . . .*	jhe ma-*pell*
Happy to meet you	*Enchanté(e)*	ohn-shahn-*tay*
Miss	*Mademoiselle*	mad mwa-*zel*
Mr.	*Monsieur*	muh-*syuh*
Mrs.	*Madame*	ma-*dam*
How are you?	*Comment allez-vous?*	kuh-mahnt ahl-ay-*voo*
Fine, thank you, and you?	*Très bien, merci, et vous?*	tray bee-ehn, mare-see, ay *voo*
Very well, thank you	*Très bien, merci*	tray bee-ehn, mare-*see*
So-so	*Comme ci, comme ça*	kum-*see*, kum-*sah*
I'm sorry/excuse me	*Pardon*	pahr-*dohn*
I'm sorry	*Désolé(e)*	day-zoh-*lay*
Do you speak English?	*Parlez-vous anglais?*	Par-lay voo ahn-*glay*
I don't speak French	*Je ne parle pas français*	jhe ne parl pah frahn-*say*
I don't understand	*Je ne comprends pas*	jhe ne kohm-*prahn* pah
Could you speak more slowly?	*Pouvez-vous parler un peu plus lentement?*	poo-*vay*-voo par-*lay* uh puh ploo lan-te-*ment*
Could you repeat that?	*Répetez, s'il vous plaît*	ray-peh-*tay*, see voo *play*
What is it?	*Qu'est-ce que c'est?*	kess kuh *say*
What time is it?	*Quelle heure est-il?*	kel uhr eh-*teel*
What?	*Quoi?*	kwah
Pardon?	*Pardon?*	par-*dohn*
Help!	*Aidez-moi!*	*ay*-day moi!
How? What did you say?	*Comment?*	ko-*mahn*
When?	*Quand?*	cohn
Where is . . . ?	*Où est . . . ?*	ooh ay
Where are the toilets?	*Où sont les toilettes?*	ooh-sohn lay twah-*lets*
Who?	*Qui?*	kee
Why?	*Pourquoi?*	poor-*kwah*

(continued)

Basic Vocabulary *(continued)*

English	French	Pronunciation
Here/there	*Ici/là-bas*	ee-*see*/lah-bah
Left/right	*à gauche/à droite*	ah gohsh/ah drwaht
Straight ahead	*Tout droit*	too drwah
I'm American/Canadian/ British	*Je suis américain(e)/ canadien(e)/anglais(e)*	jhe swee a-may-ree-*cah (kehn)*/canah-dee-*ahn (en)*/ahn-*glay (glaise)*
I'm going to . . .	*Je vais à . . .*	jhe vay ah
I want to get off at . . .	*Je voudrais descendre à . . .*	jhe voo-*dray* day-son-drah ah

Health Terms

English	French	Pronunciation
I'm sick	*Je suis malade*	jhe swee mal-*ahd*
I have a headache	*J'ai mal à la tête*	jhay mal ah la tet
I have a stomachache	*J'ai mal au ventre*	jhay mal oh *vahn*-truh
I would like to buy some aspirin	*Je voudrais acheter des aspirines*	jhe *voo*-dray *ash*-tay days as-peh-*reen*
Hospital	*l'hôpital*	low-pee-*tahl*
Insurance	*les assurances*	lez ah-sur-*ahns*

Travel Terms

English	French	Pronunciation
Airport	*l'aéroport*	lair-o-*por*
Bank	*la banque*	lah bahnk
Bridge	*pont*	pohn
Bus station	*la gare routière*	lah gar roo-tee-*air*
Bus stop	*l'arrêt de bus*	lah-*ray* duh boohss

English	French	Pronunciation
By bicycle (travel)	*en vélo/par bicyclette*	ahn *vay*-low/par bee-see-*clet*
By car (travel)	*en voiture*	ahn vwa-*toor*
Cashier	*la caisse*	lah *kess*
Driver's license	*permis de conduire*	per-*mee* duh con-*dweer*
Elevator	*l'ascenseur*	lah-sahn-*seuhr*
Entrance (to a building or a city)	*la porte*	lah port
Exit (from a building or a freeway)	*une sortie*	oon sor-*tee*
Ground floor	*Rez-de-chaussée*	ray-duh-show-*say*
Highway to . . .	*la route pour . . .*	lah root por
Luggage storage	*consigne*	kohn-*seen*-yuh
A map of the city	*un plan de la ville*	uh plahn de la *veel*
Museum	*le musée*	luh mew-*zay*
No entry	*sens interdit*	sehns ahn-ter-*dee*
No smoking	*défense de fumer*	day-*fahns* duh fu-may
On foot	*à pied*	ah pee-*ay*
One-day pass	*ticket journalier*	tee-kay jhoor-nall-ee-*ay*
One-way ticket	*aller simple*	ah-*lay sam*-pluh
A phone card	*une carte téléphonique*	oon cart tay-lay-fone-*eek*
A postcard	*une carte postale*	oon cart pos-*tahl*
Round-trip ticket	*aller-retour*	ah-*lay* re-*toor*
Second floor	*premier étage*	prem-ee-*ay* ay-ta*j*
Slow down	*ralentissez*	rah-lahn-tis-*ay*
Store	*le magasin*	luh ma-ga-*zehn*
Street	*la rue*	la roo
Suburb	*la banlieue*	lah bahn-*lyuh*
Subway	*le Métro*	luh may-tro

(continued)

Travel Terms *(continued)*

English	French	Pronunciation
Telephone	*le téléphone*	luh tay-lay-*phun*
Ticket	*un billet*	uh *bee*-yay
Ticket office	*vente de billets*	vahnt duh bee-*yay*
Toilets	*les toilettes*	lay twa-*lets*
I'd like . . .	*Je voudrais . . .*	jhe voo-*dray*
A room	*une chambre*	oon *shahm*-bruh
The key	*la clé (la clef)*	lah clay

Shopping Terms

English	French	Pronunciation
How much does it cost?	*C'est combien?/Ça coûte combien?*	say comb-bee-*ehn?*/sah coot comb-bee-*ehn*
That's expensive	*C'est cher/chère*	say share
That's inexpensive	*C'est raisonnable/C'est bon marché*	say ray-son-*ahb*-bluh/ say bohn mar-*shay*
Do you take credit cards?	*Est-ce que vous acceptez les cartes bancaires?*	es-kuh vooz ak-sep-*tay* lay kart bahn-care?
I'd like to buy . . .	*Je voudrais acheter . . .*	jhe voo-dray ahsh-*tay*
Aspirin	*des aspirines*	deyz ahs-peer-*eens*
Cigarettes	*des cigarettes*	day see-ga-*ret*
Condoms	*des préservatifs*	day pray-ser-va-*teefs*
Contraceptive suppositories	*des ovules contraceptives*	days oh-*vyules* kahn-trah-cep-*teef*
A dictionary	*un dictionnaire*	uh deek-see-oh-*nare*
A gift (for someone)	*un cadeau*	uh kah-*doe*
A handbag	*un sac à main*	uh sahk ah mahn
A magazine	*un magazine*	uh mah-gah-zeen

English	French	Pronunciation
Matches	*des allumettes*	dayz a-loo-*met*
Lighter	*un briquet*	uh *bree*-kay
A newspaper	*un journal*	uh zhoor-*nahl*
A road map	*une carte routière*	oon cart roo-tee-*air*
Shoes	*des chaussures*	day show-*suhr*
Soap	*du savon*	dew sah-*vohn*
Socks	*des chaussettes*	day show-*set*
A stamp	*un timbre*	uh *tam*-bruh
Writing paper	*du papier à lettres*	dew pap-pee-*ay* a *let*-ruh

Elements of Time

English	French	Pronunciation
Sunday	*dimanche*	dee-*mahnsh*
Monday	*lundi*	luhn-*dee*
Tuesday	*mardi*	mahr-*dee*
Wednesday	*mercredi*	mair-kruh-*dee*
Thursday	*jeudi*	jheu-*dee*
Friday	*vendredi*	vawn-druh-*dee*
Saturday	*samedi*	sahm-*dee*
Yesterday	*hier*	ee-*air*
Today	*aujourd'hui*	o-jhord-*dwee*
This morning	*ce matin*	suh ma-*tan*
This afternoon	*cet après-midi*	set ah-preh-mee-*dee*
Tonight	*ce soir*	suh *swahr*
Tomorrow	*demain*	de-*man*
Now	*maintenant*	mant-*naw*

Index

See also separate Accommodations and Restaurant indexes at the end of this index.

General Index

• A •

A Bout de Souffle (Breathless) (film), 30
A La Cloche des Halles wine bar, 177
A La Mère de Famille (store), 272–273
A Priori Thé tea salon, 176
AARP, 62
Access America, 72
Access-Able Travel Source, 64
Accessible Journeys, 64
accommodations. *See also* Accommodations Index
  best picks, 12
  best room and rate, finding, 103–106
  breakfasts, 107, 110
  budget planning, 43
  cost-cutting tips, 45–46
  maps, 108–109, 112–113
  neighborhood index, 131–132
  online deals, 105–106
  options, 102–103
  price index, 132–133
  rates, 104–105
  reservations, 106–107
Aer Lingus, 51
Aeroports de Paris (Web site), 346
agnès b (store), 263
Air Canada, 51, 345
Air France airline, 51, 52, 58, 345
air show, 37
Air Tahiti Nui, 51, 345
Air Tickets Direct, 53
air travel
  airports, 51, 79–86
  best deal, finding, 53
  booking online, 54
  major airlines, 51–52, 345
  security measures, 75–76
Alcazar, 326
Alessi (store), 277
Alice à Paris (store), 268
AllHotels, 106
Allo Maman Dépannage babysitting services, 61
Alpha Taxis, 97
American Airlines, 52, 58, 345
American Church, 61, 315
American Express, 49, 50, 57, 338
American Foundation for the Blind, 64
Amorino ice cream, 179
Ancient Rome architectural period, 21
andouillette, 26
Andy Whaloo lounge, 326
Angelina tea salon, 176
Ann Tuil (store), 271
Annexe des Créateurs (astore), 258
Antik Batik (store), 260
antiques shopping, 265
Antoine et Lili (store), 264, 270
aparthotel, 103
Apartment Living in Paris, 102
apartment swaps, 102–103
apéritif, 139
Aquaboulevard, 219
Aquarium Tropical de la Porte Dorée, 216
Arc de Triomphe, 13, 192–193
arcade, 262–263
architecture, 20–23. *See also specific structures*
Armistice Day, 40
arrondissements, 87. *See also* neighborhoods
art attractions, 225–231
Art Nouveau architectural period, 22
Artishow Paris, 327–328

ATMs, 338
attractions. *See also specific*
    attractions
  art lovers, 225–231
  bridges, 240
  budget planning, 44
  cost-cutting tips, 47–48, 192
  family options, 213, 216–220
  historical, 220–224
  literary, 231–233
  maps, 190–191, 214–215
  nature lovers, 234–237
  religious, 237–239
Au Bistro de La Place cafe, 172
Au Nain Bleu (store), 278
Au Négociant wine bar, 177
Au Pied de Cochon, 311
Autour du Monde, 260
Aux Trois Mailletz jazz club, 318–319
Avenue Montaigne, 259–260
average temperature, 32
Avis car rental, 70, 345

• *B* •

baby bistros, 23
baby sitter, 61, 338
Baccarat (store), 267
bakery, 170–171
Balabus, 242
ballet, 316–317
Barbara Bui (store), 261
Barbizon (Fontainebleau), 296
Barlow, Julie (author)
    Sixty Million Frenchmen Can't Be
    Wrong, 30
Barrio Latino, 322
bars. *See* nightlife
Bastille Day, 38
Bataclan, 325
Bateaux les Vedettes du Pont
    Neuf, 203
Bateaux-Mouches, 203
Bateaux-Parisiens, 203
Batobus, 203
Batofar, 322
BE bakery, 170
Beaujolais Nouveau festival, 40

Beauty Monop (store), 264
Before Sunset (film), 30
Belle de Jour (store), 275
Berko, 171
Berthillon, 179
BHV (store), 15, 253, 277
Biennale des Antiquaires, 39
Bijoux Burma (store), 275
Bike About Tours, 245
bike travel, 99, 244–245
bistro, 136–138
blanquette de veau, 27
boat tours, 203, 242–243
boeuf bourguignon, 27
Bofinger, 311
bohemian fashion, 264
Boingo, 75
Bois de Boulogne, 234, 334
Bois de Vincennes, 234, 334–335
Bonjour Paris (Web site), 103, 346
books
  disabled travelers, 64
  family travel, 60
  French references, 29–30
  gay and lesbian travelers, 66
  senior travelers, 62
  stores, 265–267
boudin, 27
bouillabaisse, 27
boulangerie, 141, 157
Boulangerie Kayser bakery, 170
brandade, 27
brasserie, 137
Brasserie Balzar, 311
Brasserie de l'Ile Saint-Louis, 231
Brasserie Ile St-Louis, 311
Brasserie Lipp and Café les Deux
    Magots, 231
bridges, 240
British Airways, 52, 345
bucket shops, 53
budget
  average costs, 45
  cost-cutting tips, 45–48
  dining, 46–47, 140–141
  handling money, 48–49
  lost/stolen wallet, 49–50
  overview, 43–45

bus travel
  disabled travelers, 63
  Fontainebleau day trip, 294
  Giverny day trip, 304
  to hotel, 84–85, 86
  overview, 55, 96–97
  tours, 241–242
  Versailles day trip, 289
business hours, 338
Butte-aux-Cailles, 91

• **C** •

Cab dance club, 322
cabaret, 327–328
Cacharel (store), 271
Café Charbon, 172
Café Coton (store), 269
Café de Flore, 172, 232
Café de la Place, 173
Café de la Soul (Web site), 346
Café de l'Industrie, 173
Café les Deux Magots, 173
Café Marly, 173, 311
cafes, 136–138, 172–176
calendar of events, 34–40
camera repair, 338
Camper (store), 261
Canauxrama, 243
car travel
  Cathedral at Chartres day trip, 297
  Disneyland Paris day trip, 302
  driving regulations, 69
  Giverny day trip, 304
  overview, 98–99
  rental cars, 69–70, 345
  tours, 243
  Versailles day trip, 289–290
carnivals, 14, 36
Carrousel du Louvre Studio-Théâtre,
    313
Carte Orange pass, 95
cassoulet, 27
Catacombs, 219–220
Cathedral at Chartres, 297–301
Cathédrale Notre-Dame de Paris, 13,
    193–194, 195
Caveau de la Hûchette jazz club, 318
Céline (store), 260, 261

Celio (store), 269
cellphones, 73–74
Centers for Disease Control and
    Prevention, 73
Centre des Objets trouvé de la
    Prefecture de Police de Paris, 50
Centre Gai et Lesbien, 37
Centre Georges Pompidou, 194–195
Centre LGBT, 65
Centre Médicale Europe, 73
ceramics, 267
cervelles, 27
*C'est La Vie: An American Conquers
    the City of Light, Begins a New
    Life, and Becomes-Zut Alors-
    Almost French* (Gershman), 29
Champs-Elysées, 87, 89, 132, 181, 196
Chanel, 260
Channel Tunnel (Chunnel), 55
Chantelivre (store), 265
Charles de Gaulle Airport, 51, 79–85
Chartres, day trip to, 297–301
Château de Versailles, 287–294
Châtelet, Théâtre Musical de Paris,
    16, 316
Cheapflights.com, 54
CheapTickets.com, 54
cheval, 27
Chevignon (store), 257, 269
Chez Moune club, 321
Chiffon et Basile (store), 264
china, 267
Chinatown, 91
Chinese New Year Festival, 35
Chloé (store), 260
Chloé's, 171
choucroute, 27
Christian Dior (store), 260, 261
Christmas, 40
churches, 237–239. *See also specific
    churches*
Cité des Sciences et de l'Industrie,
    216–217
Citroën 2CV tours, 243
Cityrama, 241
Clarke, Stephen (author)
  *Talk to the Snail: Ten Commandments
    for Understanding the French*, 30
  A Year in the Merde, 30

classical music, 315–316
Classicism architectural period, 22
clothing
  bohemia fashions, 264
  children's stores, 268–269, 270
  dress codes, 136
  men's stores, 269–270
  size conversions, 247, 250
  women's stores, 271–272
Clown Bar, 177
clubs. *See* nightlife
cochonnet, 14
cocktail lounges, 326–327
coffee, 138
Colette (store), 271
collect calls, 343
Comédie-Française, 16
Comme des Garçons (store), 260
communication, 73–75, 343
Comptoir des Cotonniers (store), 261, 271
Comtesse du Barry (store), 273
Concert Hall, 315
Conciergerie, 221–222
confit de canard, 27
Conforama (store), 277
Conservatoire National Superieur de Musique, 315
consolidators, 53
Constantine, Helen (translator)
  Paris Tales, 29
Continental Airlines, 52, 58, 345
Cop-Copine (store), 270
coq au vin, 27
couscouseries, 23
crafts, 272
Crazy Horse, Paris, 327
credit cards, 49, 338
crêpes, 140
cruises, 203
Crypte Archeologique, 222
crystal, 267
cuisine
  common dishes, 26–28
  gourmet food shops, 169
  overview, 23–26
  restaurant index, 181–183
  street food, 168
cuisses des grenouilles, 27

culture, 16, 309–311
Culture Kiosque, 312
Cupcake & Co, 171
currency exchange rate, 339
customs, 79–80, 252, 339
cybercafes, 74–75
cycling. *See* bike travel

• *D* •

Damron guides, 66
dance clubs, 319–321
Darjeeling, 257
day trips
  Cathedral at Chartres, 297–301
  Château de Versailles, 287–294
  Disneyland Paris, 301–303
  map, 289
  Monet's Gardens at Giverny, 303–305
  Palais de Fontainebleau, 294–297
de Balzac, Honoré (writer), 232
Dehillerin (store), 277
Delta Air Lines, 52, 58, 345
dentists, 340
department stores, 253–256
dessert, 139
digestif, 139
dining. *See* restaurants; Restaurant Index
disabled travelers, 62–64
Disneyland Paris, 301–303
Diwali (store), 275
doctors, 340
Dolce & Gabbana (store), 260
Drama Ties, 314
dress codes, 136
drugstores, 340
dry cleaning, 341
Du Pareil au Même (store), 268
Duc des Lombards jazz club, 319

• *E* •

Easter, 35
easyJet, 52
Eiffel Tower, 13, 196–198
electricity, 340

Elysée Montmartre dance club, 16, 322

E-Mail, 73–74

Emanuel Ungaro (store), 260

embassies and consulates, 340

emergencies, 340

Emmanuelle Zysman (store), 264

English-language theater, 314–315

escalope, 27

escargots, 27

escorted tours. *See* guided tours

Espace Dali, 225

Espace Kiliwatch (store), 263

Etam (store), 271

euro, 48–49

Eurolines, 55

Europcar car rental, 70, 345

Eurotunnel, 55–56

Eveil & Jeux (store), 278

events calendar, 34–40

Evolutif, 257

Expedia Web site, 54

Experimental Cocktail Club, 326

• F •

falafel, 140–141

fall season, 33–34

family travel
  attractions, 213, 216–220
  baby sitters, 61, 338
  children's clothing, 268–269, 270
  overview, 59–61

Family Travel Files, 60

Family Travel Forum, 60

Family Travel Network, 60

fashion shows, 35, 39

fast facts, 338–344

Fauchon (store), 169, 273

faxes, 343–344

ferry service, 55

Ferrybooker.com Web site, 55

Festival Chopin à Paris, 37

Festival d'Automne, 39

Fête de la Musique, 37

Fête de l'Assomption, 38–39

Fête des Rois, 35

Fêtes de Nuit de Versailles, 36

Fêtes des Vendanges à Montmartre, 39

films, 30–31

five-day itinerary, 282

The Flâneur (White), 29

flea markets, 256–257

Flights.com, 53

flower, blooming, 305

Flying Wheels Travel, 64

foie, 27

Foire de Paris, 36

Foire du Trône, 36

Foire Internationale d'Art Contemporain, 39–40

Fontainebleau, 294–297

food shopping, 272–275

forfait, 105

Forum des Halles, 253

Fouquet's, 174

4 Roues Sous 1 Parapluie, 243

France Guide, 312

France Hotels Online, 106

Franck et Fils, 253–254

French Cabaret, 327–328

French Experience, 57

French Fashion Week, 35

French Government Tourist Office, 346

French Links tours, 243–244

French Open, 37

French Rail (SNCF) Web site, 347

French Revolution, 18

Frommer's Gay & Lesbian Europe (Frommer), 66

• G •

Galerie Colbert arcade, 262

Galerie de Jeu de Paume, 225–226

Galerie Ubu (store), 276

Galerie Vivienne arcade, 262

Galeries Lafayette, 89, 251, 254

gardens
  best picks, 14–15
  Giverny day trip, 303–305
  Versailles day trip, 287–294

Gare du Nord/Gare de l'Est (10e), 89

gay and lesbian travelers, 34–40, 65–66, 323–325

Gay Pride celebration, 37

Gelati (store), 272

Gelati d'Alberto, 179
Georges Rech (store), 260
Gershman, Suzy (author)
   *C'est La Vie: An American Conquers
      the City of Light, Begins a New
      Life, and Becomes-Zut Alors-
      Almost French,* 29
gesiers, 27
Gibert Joseph (store), 265
gift shopping, 275–277
Gigi (film), 30
Giorgio Armani (store), 260, 261
Givenchy (store), 260
Giverny day trip, 303–305
glass, 267
Global Blue, 250
Global Change, 49
Google Maps (Web site), 346
Gopnik, Adam (author)
   Paris to the Moon, 29
Gothic architectural period, 21
gourmet food shop, 169
Grandes Eaux Musicales, 36
gratuity, 138
Grom, 179
Groupement pour l'Insertion des
   Personnes Handicapées
   Physiques, 64
Gucci (store), 260
guided tours. *See also specific
   locations*
   bike, 244–245
   boat, 242–243
   bus, 241–242
   Citroën 2CV, 243
   disabled travelers, 64
   gay and lesbian travelers, 66
   overview, 56–57
   senior travelers, 62
   walking, 243–244

• *H* •

H&M, 253
Harry's New York Bar, 232, 326
health, 72–73, 350
Hédiard (store), 169, 273
Heilman, Joan Rattner (author)
*Unbelievably Good Deals and
   Great Adventures That You
   Absolutely Can't Get Unless
   You're Over 50,* 62
Hemingway, Ernest (author)
   A Moveable Feast, 29
Hertz car rental, 70, 345
"hipster," 325
history, 17–20, 220–224
Home Base Holidays, 103
Home Xchange Vacation, 103
Horne, Alistair (author)
   Seven Ages of Paris, 30
hospitals, 340–341
Hostelworld, 106
Hôtel des Invalides (Napoléon's
   Tomb), 198–199
Hotel Discounts, 106
house wares, 277–278
hovercrafts, 55
Hugo, Victor (writer), 283, 333
hydrofoils, 55

• *I* •

ice cream, 179–180
Icelandair, 52, 345
IGLTA (International Gay and Lesbian
   Travel Association), 66
IKKS (store), 261, 270
Ile de la Cité, 87–88
illness, 72–73
Institut du Monde Arabe, 222–223
insurance, 70–71
International Association for Medical
   Assistance to Travelers, 73
International Gay and Lesbian Travel
   Association (IGLTA), 66
International Players, 314
Internet access, 74–75, 341
iPass, 75
itineraries, 280–286

• *J* •

Jacadi (store), 257, 268
Jacenko (store), 269
Jardin de Bagatelle club, 321–322

Jardin de la Vallée Suisse, 332
Jardin de l'Acclimatation Bois de
     Boulogne, 217
Jardin des Enfants des Halles, 213
Jardin des Plantes, 199
Jardin des Tuileries, 14, 200
Jardin du Luxembourg, 14, 335
Jardin du Palais-Royal, 200
Jardin et Palais du Luxembourg, 201
jazz, 318–319
Jean Pierre Cohier bakery, 170
Jean-Claude Monderer (store), 261
Jean-Paul Gaultier (store), 263
Jérémie Barthod (store), 264
jewelry, 275–277
JSFP Traiteur (store), 273–274
Jules et Jim (film), 30

• *K* •

Kayak, 54
Kid Services, 61
Kokon To Zai (store), 263
Kookaï Le Stock (store), 263
The Kooples (store), 261

• *L* •

La Bellevilloise club, 320
La Bourse, 88
La Butte Glacée, 179
La Cave des Martyrs (store), 279
La Chaise Longue (store), 276
La Champmeslé, 324
La City (store), 272
La Clef des Marques discount
     store, 258
La Closerie de Lilas, 232
La Contrescarpe cafe, 174
La Coupole cafe, 174, 311
La Fée Verte cafe, 174
La Flèche d'Or, 320
La Flotille (Versailles), 294
La Fourmi Ailée tea salon, 176
La Générale de Pharmacie, 257
La Grande Epicerie de Paris (store),
     169, 274
La Grande Parade de Montmartre, 34

La Machine du Moulin Rouge club,
     323
La Madeleine, 237
La Magnifique, 326
La Maison du Chocolat (store), 274
La Maison Ivre (store), 267
La Maison Normande, 332
La Mosquée de Paris, 237
La Nuit des Musées, 36
La Pagode, 332
La Passion à Ménilmontant, 35
La Samaritaine department store, 226
La Scène Bastille, 321
La Tartine wine bar, 177–178
La Tour Eiffel, 13, 196–198
La Vaissellerie (store), 278
La Vie en Rose (film), 31
Ladurée tea salon, 176
Lafayette Gourmet, 15, 169, 274
L'Alimentation Générale club, 16, 320
Lancement des Illuminations des
     Champs-Elysées, 40
language, 26–29, 341, 348–353
Lanvin (store), 260
lapin à la moutarde, 28
L'Association des Paralysés de
     France, 63
Latin Quarter, 90
Laughing & Music Matters, 314
laundry, 341
Le 3w Kafé, 324
Le Bac à Glaces, 179
Le Baiser Salé jazz club, 319
Le Bar, 326
Le Baron club, 322
Le Bistrot du Peintre wine bar, 178
Le Boîte à Frissons, 324
Le Bon Marché department store,
     15, 254
Le Brebant cafe, 174–175
Le Café Serpente (Chartre), 300
Le Central, 324
Le Chemin de la Croix, 36
Le Cloître Gourmand (Chartre), 300
Le Cox, 324
Le CUD, 324
Le Depôt-Vente de Buc Bourbon
     discount store, 258
Le Divan du Monde club, 321

Le Drugstore department store, 255
Le Duplex, 324
Le Fabuleux Destin d'Amélie Poulain (film), 30
Le Flore en l'Ile, 179
Le Grand Tasting, 40
Le Grenier à Pain bakery, 171
Le Griffonnier wine bar, 178
Le Jardin Alpin, 332
Le Kiosque Théâtre, 312
Le Louvre des Antiquaires (store), 265
Le Marais, 88
Le Moulin de Ponceau (Chartre), 301
Le Mouton à Cinq Pattes discount store, 257, 258
Le Nouveau Casino, 320
Le Petit Journal Montparnasse jazz club, 318
Le Petit Journal Saint-Michel jazz club, 318
Le Point Éphémère, 325
Le Progrès cafe, 175
Le Relais Normand (Giverny), 305
Le Rive Gauche, 325
Le Sancerre cafe, 175
Le Sancerre wine bar, 178
Le Sunset jazz club, 319
Le Sunside jazz club, 319
Le Table des Maréchaux (Fontainebleau), 297
Le Théâtre de Nesle, 314
Le Théâtre du Soleil, 314
Le Tournon wine bar, 178
Le Truskel dance club, 16, 321
Le Village Saint-Paul (store), 265
Left Bank
    accommodations map, 112–113
    neighborhoods, 90–91
    restaurant map, 146–147, 166–167
Legrand Filles et Fils (store), 279
L'Epicerie de Bruno (store), 274
Les Arènes de Lutèce, 333
Les Arts Florissants, 310
Les Catacombes, 219–220
Les Caves Augé (store), 279
Les Champs de Mars, 335
Les Cinq Jours Extraordinaire, 36
Les Compagnons du Voyage, 64

Les Déchargeurs, 314
Les Égouts, 220
Les Etages, 327
Les Journées de Patrimoine, 39
Les Mots à la Bouche, 65
Les Philosophes cafe, 175
Les Villas du Danube, 333
lesbian and gay travelers. *See* gay and lesbian travelers
L'Eté en pente Douce cafe, 175
L'Habilleur discount store, 258–259
Liberty Travel, 58
Librarie Eyrolles (store), 265–266
Librarie La Hune (store), 266
Lido, 328
lièvre, 28
L'International club, 320
liquor laws, 341
Lire et Partir, 244
literary landmarks, 231–233
live music, 315–316, 319–321
Lizard Lounge, 327
local cuisine, 26–28
lodging. *See* accommodations
Lodgis, 103
lost property, 341–342
lost-luggage insurance, 71–72
lost/stolen wallet, 49–50
Louis Vuitton (store), 261
Louvre, 204–206
low season, 45, 46
LowestFare.com, 53
luggage, 342

• M •

Madelios (store), 270
magret de canard, 27
Maison de Balzac, 232–233
Maison de Radio France, 315
Maison de Victor Hugo, 233
Maison des Femmes de Paris, 65
Maison des Trois Thés tea salon, 176
Maison Européenne de la Photographie, 226
Maje (store), 264
Make My D (store), 264
Mango (store), 270

maps
  accommodations, 108–109, 112–113
  attractions, 190–191, 214–215
  Cathédral de Notre-Dame
    de Paris, 195
  day trips, 289
  Fontainebleau, 295
  Louvre, 205
  neighborhoods, 82–83
  Notre-Dame de Chartres, 299
  Paris, 10–11
  Père-Lachaise Cemetery, 210–211
  purchasing, 342
  restaurants, 142–143, 146–147,
    164–165, 166–167
  shopping locations, 248–249
  Versailles, 291
Marais, 282–284
marathons, 36
Marché aux Puces de la Porte de
  St-Ouen flea market, 256
Marché Bastille street market, 169
Marché Biologique street market,
  169–170
Marché des Enfants Rouge street
  market, 170
Marché Saint-Germain, 261
Mariage Frères tea salon, 176
markets, 169–170
Marrionaud, 257
MasterCard, 50
May Day celebrations, 35
MEDEX Assistance, 71
medical emergencies, 340
medical insurance, 71
MedicAlert identification tag, 73
men's clothing, 269–270
Métro subway, 81, 84, 92–96
Missoni, 260
Mobility International USA, 64
Mois de la Photo, 40
Mona Lisait (store), 266
Monet, Claude (artist), 303–305
money
  credit cards, 49, 338
  currency exchange, 339
  euro, 48–49

  handling, 48–49
  lost/stolen wallet, 49–50
  traveler's checks, 49
Monic (store), 276
Monoprix department store, 255
Montmartre, 201–202, 284–286
Montparnasse, 91
MossRehab, 64
Moulin de la Vierge bakery, 171
Moulin Rouge, 328
A Moveable Feast (Hemingway), 29
Musée Carnavalet, 223–224
Musée Cognacq-Jay, 226
Musée d'Art Américain Giverny, 304
Musée d'Art et d'Histoire du
  Judaïsme, 224
Musée d'Art Moderne de Paris,
  230–231
Musée de Beaux-Arts de Chartres, 301
Musée de Cluny, 14, 221
Musée de la Curiosité et de la Magie,
  217–218
Musée de la Sculpture en Plein Air,
  227
Musée de l'Orangerie des Tuileries,
  227–228
Musée des Impressionnismes
  Giverny, 304
Musée d'Orsay, 14, 202
Musée du Louvre, 204–206
Musée du Quai Branly, 228
Musée Grevin, 218
Musée Gustave Moreau, 228–229
Musée Jacquemart André, 227
Musée Maillol, 229
Musée Marmottan Monet, 229–230
Musée Picasso, 206
Musée Rodin, 14, 207
Musée Zadkine, 230
Museum of Natural History, 199
museums. *See specific museums*
music
  classical, 315–316
  jazz clubs, 318–319
  live, 315–316, 319–321
  ticket information, 311–312
Muskhane (store), 276

• N •

Nadeau, Jean-Benoit (author)
Sixty Million Frenchmen Can't Be Wrong, 30
Nafnaf, 257
Napoléon's Tomb (Hôtel des Invalides), 198–199
Natalys (store), 268
National car rental, 70, 345
National Passport Information Center, 67
nature lover attractions, 234–237
neighborhoods
accommodations index, 131–132
arrondissement, 87
Left Bank, 90–91
map, 82–83
overview, 86–87
restaurant index, 180–181
Right Bank, 87–90
shopping areas, 259–261, 263–264
New Morning jazz club, 319
New York Habitat, 103
newspapers and magazines, 342
Nicolas wine bar, 279
nightlife. *See also specific venues*
best picks, 16
budget planning, 44
clubs and lounges, 321–323
cocktail lounges, 326–327
cost-cutting tips, 47–48
dance clubs, 319–321
French Cabaret, 327–328
gay clubs, 323–325
"hipster," 325
jazz, 318–319
live music, 315–316, 319–321
Nina Ricci (store), 260
Nineteenth century architectural period, 22
Niou (store), 278
Nip' Shop discount store, 259
Noir Kennedy (store), 260–261
Now, Voyager, 66
Nuit Blanche, 39

• O •

Odéon Théâtre de l'Europe, 313–314
off season, 46, 104, 107, 197
Office de Tourisme et des Congrès de Paris, 91
101 Tips (magazine), 62
OneTravel.com, 53
opaque fare service, 54
Open Café, 324
opera, 316–317
Opéra Bastille, 16, 316–317
Opéra Garnier, 89
Opéra-Comique, 317
Opodo, 54
Orbitz Web site, 54
organ recitals, 16
Orly Airport, 85–86
Out Traveler (Web site), 66

• P •

package tours, 57–58
Pain d'Epis bakery, 171
Palais de Fontainebleau, 294–297
Palais de la Découverte, 218–219
Palais de Tokyo, 230–231
Palais Garnier, 16, 316
panini, 168
Panthéon, 207–208
Paradis Latin, 328
Parc de Belleville, 235, 335–336
Parc de la Bagatelle, 235
Parc de la Villette, 15, 216–217, 235–236, 336
Parc des Buttes Chaumont, 15, 236, 336
Parc Floral de Paris, 236
Parc Monceau, 236, 336–337
Paris (film), 31
Paris, Je T'Aime (film), 31
Paris, Quartier d'Été, 38
Paris Air Show, 37
Paris Canal tours, 242
Paris Convention and Visitors Bureau, 34, 63, 106, 312, 346
Paris Digest (Web site), 347

Paris Gay Village, 65
Paris International Photo Fair, 40
Paris Jazz Festival, 37
Paris L'Open Tour, 241
Paris Museum Pass, 47, 192
Paris Nightlife (Web site), 320
Paris Plage, 38
Paris Préfecture of Police, 81
Paris Respire, 244
Paris Tales (Constantine), 29
Paris to the Moon (Gopnik), 29
Paris Urban Transit (RATP) Web site, 347
Paris Visite Pass, 46, 224
Paris Walks tours, 243
pariscope (Web site), 320
Parisfranceguide.com (Web site), 347
Paris-Gay.com (Web site), 347
PariShuttle, 81
Parisian Village walking tour, 284–286
paris.org (Web site), 347
parking, 69–70
parks, 14–15. *See also specific parks*
Parler Paris (Web site), 347
Passage Choiseul arcade, 262
Passage des Panoramas arcade, 262
Passage du Grand Cerf arcade, 262
Passage Jouffroy arcade, 262
Passage Verdeau arcade, 262
Passport (magazine), 66
passports, 67–69, 79–80
Paule Ka (store), 260
Pause Café, 176
Père-Lachaise Cemetery, 208–211
performing-arts, 16, 311–312. *See also specific types*
Petit Bateau (store), 268
Petit Pont, 240
Petit Théâtre, 313
pharmacies, 340
pickpockets, 97, 197
picnics, 168, 334–337
pieds de cochon, 28
Pierre Cardin (store), 260
Pierre Hermé (store), 275
Pigalle, 89, 331
Place de la Bastille, 224
Place des Vosges, 209
Place du Tertre, 90, 211–212

Place Marcel-Aymé, 333
Place Monge street market, 170
PlacesToStay, 106
plateau de fruits de mer, 28
Platt, Polly (author)
    Savoir Flair, 30
Poilâne bakery, 171
police, 342
Pont des Arts, 240, 337
Pont Neuf, 240
Pont St-Michel, 240
Porte de Vanves market, 256–257
post office, 342
pot-au-feu, 28
Prada, 260
Premier Tax Free, 250
Priceline, 54
Printemps department store, 255–256
prix-fixe meal, 140
Promenade Plantée, 236–237
Pylones (store), 277

• *Q* •

Qantas, 52
Queen club, 323

• *R* •

Raidd, 325
Raimo Glacier, 180
ratatouille, 28
Ratatouille (film), 31
RATP (Paris Urban Transit) Web site, 64, 347
Ready-to-Wear Fashion Shows, 35, 39
Réciproque discount store, 259
The Red Wheelbarrow (store), 266
Relais de Barbizon (Fontainebleau), 296–297
religious attractions, 237–239
Renaissance architectural period, 21–22
rental cars, 69–70, 345
Rentals in Paris, 103
research, 29–31, 346–347
reservations, 106–107, 135–136

restaurants. *See also* Restaurant
   Index
   bakeries, 170–171
   best picks, 12–13
   budget planning, 44
   cafe compared with bistro, 133–138
   cost-cutting tips, 46–47, 140–141
   courses, 139–140
   cuisine index, 181–183
   dress, 136
   gourmet food shops, 169
   ice cream, 179–180
   local cuisine, 26–28
   maps, 142–143, 146–147, 164–167
   meal order, 139–140
   neighborhood index, 180–181
   overview, 136–137
   picnics, 168, 334–337
   price index, 183–185
   quick meals, 163–180
   reservations, 135–138
   snacking, 134–135
   street food, 168
   street markets, 169–170, 256–257
   tipping, 138
restrooms, 342
Right Bank
   accommodations map, 108–109
   neighborhoods, 87–90
   restaurant maps, 146–147, 164–165
ris de veau, 28
Rock en Seine, 38
Rodier (store), 257, 272
rognons, 28
Romanesque architectural period, 21
Rosa Bonheur club, 320, 325
RoyalCheese (store), 263
Rue Cler street market, 170
Rue d'Alésia, 257
Rue de Buci street market, 170
Rue des Francs-Bourgeois, 260, 283
Rue des Rosiers, 260, 284
Rue du Faubourg du Temple, 257
Rue Montorgueil street market, 170
Rue Poncelet street market, 170
Rue St-Placide, 257

• S •

Sacré Coeur, 209, 212
safety, 49–50, 75–76, 342–343
Saint-Denis, 333
Sainte-Chapelle, 16, 212–213, 315
Saint-Etienne du Mont, 237–238
Saint-Eustache, 238, 315
Saint-Germain-des-Prés, 238, 315
Saint-Julien le Pauvre, 238
Saint-Roch, 239
Saint-Séverin, 239
Saint-Sulpice, 239, 315
Salle Pleyel, 315
Salle Richelieu, 16, 312
Salon de Thé de la Mosquée de Paris
   tea salon, 176
Salon International de l'Agriculture, 35
Salvatore Ferragamo (store), 260
Samarina et Louis Mod, 257
SATH (Society for Accessible Travel
   and Hospitality), 64
Savoir Flair (Platt), 30
Scoop, 180
S.D. Spontini (store), 261
seasons, 32–40, 305
security, air travel, 75–76
Seine, 203
senior travelers, 62
Seven Ages of Paris (Horne), 30
Shakespeare and Company (store),
   233, 266–267
shopping
   antiques, 265
   arcades, 262–263
   bargains, 257–259
   best picks, 15
   books, 265–267
   budget planning, 44
   ceramics, 267
   children's stores, 268–269, 270
   china, 267
   clothing sizes, 247, 250
   cost-cutting tips, 47–48
   crafts, 272
   customs, 252
   department stores, 253–256

food stores, 272–275
gifts, 275–277
glassware, 267
house wares, 277–278
jewelry, 275–277
map, 248–249
men's clothing, 269–270
neighborhood specialties, 259–261, 263–264
overview, 246–247
soldes, 247
street markets, 169–170, 256–257
tax, 247, 250–252
teen stores, 270
terms, 352–353
toys, 278
wine, 279
women's stores, 271–272
Showcase club, 323
shuttle service, 81
SideStep Web site, 54
sightseeing, 13–14. *See also* attractions
Singapore Airlines, 52
Sixty Million Frenchmen Can't Be Wrong (Nadeau & Barlow), 30
size conversions, 247, 250
Smarter Travel Web site, 54
smoking, 343
snacking, 134–135
SNCF (French Rail) Web site, 347
Society for Accessible Travel and Hospitality (SATH), 64
Solidays, 37
Sonia Rykiel (store), 257, 260
SOS Medecins, 73
SOS Urgences stomatologiques et Dentaires, 73
soufflé, 28
Spartacus International Gay Guide, 66
sports. *See specific sports*
Spree (store), 264
spring, 33
Square du Vert Galant, 337
STA Travel, 53
Stefanel (store), 261
stolen wallet, 49–50
street food, 168
street markets, 169–170, 256–257

StudentUniverse.com, 53
summer, 33
symphony, 315–316
Synie's, 171

• *T* •

Talk to the Snail: Ten Commandments for Understanding the French (Clarke), 30
Tara Jarmon (store), 261
Tartine et Chocolat (store), 269
Taschen (store), 267
Tati department store, 256
Taverne Henri IV wine bar, 179
taxes, 247, 343
taxis, 80–81, 85–86, 97–98, 343
Taxis G7, 97
tea salons, 176
The Tea Caddy tea salon, 176
Techno Parade, 39
teenagers, 219–222, 270
telephones, 73–74, 343–344
temperature, average, 32
tennis, 37
tête de veau, 28
theater, 311–315
Théâtre de la Main d'Or, 314
Théâtre des Bouffes du Nord, 314
Théâtre du Vieux Colombier, 313
Théâtre National de Chaillot, 16, 313
Théâtre National de la Colline, 313
The Théâtre en Anglais, 314
three-day itinerary, 280–282
TicketNet, 312
time terms, 353
time zone, 344
tipping, 138, 344
T-Mobile Hotspot, 73, 75
Tour de France, 38
Tour Montparnasse, 87, 312
tourist information, 91–92, 341, 345–346
tours. *See also* guided tours
escorted, 56–57
package, 57–58
Tout Compte Fait, 257
toys, 278

train travel
    Cathedral at Chartres day trip, 297
    disabled travelers, 63
    Disneyland Paris, 302
    family travel, 60–61
    Fontainebleau day trip, 294
    Giverny day trip, 304
    to hotels, 86
    to Paris, 54, 55
    senior discounts, 62
    Versailles day trip, 288–289
traiteur, 141, 169
Travel 50 & Beyond (magazine), 62
Travel Assistance International, 71
travel insurance, 71–72
Travel Insured International, 72
travel terms, 350–352
traveler's checks, 49
Travelex, 49, 72
Travelocity Web site, 54
TravelWithYourKids, 60
trearooms, 138
trip-cancellation insurance, 71
Trocadéro (16e), 89–90

• U •

*Unbelievably Good Deals and Great
    Adventures That You Absolutely
    Can't Get Unless You're Over 50*
    (Heilman), 62
United Airlines, 52, 58, 345
US Airways, 52, 345

• V •

Valentino (store), 260
value-added tax (VAT), 247, 250–252
Velib', 99, 245
Versace (store), 260
Versailles, 287–294
Via Veneto, 257
Viaduc des Arts (store), 272
Village Voice (store), 267
Visa, 50
vocabulary, basic, 348–350

• W •

walking, 99–100, 243–244, 282–286
Walt Disney Studios Park, 302–303
water parks, 344
weather, 32–34, 344
wheelchairs, 62–63
White, Edmund (author)
    The Flâneur, 29
Willi's Wine Bar, 179
wine
    bars, 138, 177–179
    restaurant courses, 139–140
    shopping, 279
winter, 34
women's clothing, 271–272
World Shuttle, 81

• X •

XOOS (store), 261

• Y •

A Year in the Merde (Clarke), 30
Yves St-Laurent (store), 260

• Z •

Zadig et Voltaire (store), 261
Zazie Dans le Metro (film), 31

Accommodations Index

Castex Hôtel, 110
Citadines Louvre Paris, 110
Citadines Paris Opéra-Grands
    Boulevards, 110–111
Familia Hôtel, 111
Four Seasons Hotel George V Paris,
    111, 114
Grand Hôtel des Balcons, 114
Grand Hôtel Lévêque, 114–115

Hôtel Agora, 115
Hôtel Alison, 115
Hôtel Amélie, 115–116
Hôtel Balzac, 116
Hôtel Bonne Nouvelle, 116–117
Hôtel Claude-Bernard, 117
Hôtel de Fleurie, 117
Hotel de la Place des Vosges, 118
Hôtel de l'Abbaye, 118
Hotel de Seine, 119
Hotel de Suez, 119–120
Hôtel des Deux-Iles, 118–119
Hôtel du Jeu de Paume, 12, 120
Hotel du Lys, 120
Hôtel du Petit Moulin, 120–121
Hotel du Quai Voltaire, 121
Hôtel Esmeralda, 12, 121–122
Hôtel Henri IV, 122
Hôtel Jeanne d'Arc, 122–123
Hotel Jules, 123
Hôtel le Tourville, 123–124
Hôtel Lindbergh, 124
Hotel Louvre Forum, 124–125
Hotel Marignan, 125
Hôtel Montpensier, 125–126
Hôtel Saint-Jacques, 126
Hôtel Saint-Merry, 126–127
Hôtel Saints-Pères, 127
Hôtel Tiquetonne, 127
Hôtel Verneuil (7e), 128
Hôtel Vivienne, 128
L'Hôtel, 12, 129
Lord Byron Hôtel Residence, 129
Minerve Hotel, 130
9 Hôtel, 130
Pavillon de la Reine, 131

Restaurant Index

A La Petite Chaise, 144
A l'Affiche, 160
A.O.C., 144–145
Au Bascou, 13, 145
Au Bon Accueil, 145, 148
Au Pied de Cochon, 148
Auberge Le Pot de Terre, 145
Bofinger, 148–149
Brasserie Balzar, 149

Breakfast in America, 149
Café Marly, 173
ChantAirelle, 150
Chateaubriand, 150, 160
Chez Casimir, 150–151
Chez Marie, 86
Chez Michel, 151
Chez Omar, 151–152
Class'Croute, 157
Cococook, 157
Cojean, 157
Cuizines, 157
Fish La Boissonnerie, 152
Frenchie, 152–153, 160
Jour, 157
La Bastide Odéon, 153
La Cigale Récamier, 153
La Fidélité, 154, 160
La Poule au Pot, 155
L'Ambroisie, 154
L'Ami Jean, 160
L'Aréa, 155
L'As du Falafel, 157
L'Atelier de Joël Robuchon, 156
Le Bar à Soupes, 157
Le Café Serpente, 300
Le Cinq, 13, 157–158
Le Cloître Gourmand, 300
Le Comptoir du Relais Saint-Germain,
    156, 160
Le Hide, 160
Le Kokolion, 158–159
Le Moulin de Ponceau, 301
Le Père Claude, 159
Le Potager du Marais, 160–161
Le Relais Normand, 305
Le Repaire de Cartouche, 160
Le Square, 160
Le 404, 158
L'Epi Dupin, 159
Les Bouquinistes, 13, 161
Maison Chardenoux, 161–162
Qualité & Co, 157
Restaurant du Palais-Royal, 162
Restaurant Plaza Athénée, 162
Thomieux, 163
Ze Kitchen Galerie, 163